THE VAULT GUIDE
TO THE TOP 25 CONSULTING FIRMS
2009 European Edition

is made possible through the generous support of the following sponsors:

booz&co.

Roland Berger
Strategy Consultants

ESADE
Business School
Ramon Llull University

Teach First
LEARNING TO LEAD

OC&C
Strategy Consultants

TOWERS
PERRIN

OLIVER WYMAN

VAULT career library

BOOZ & COMPANY

7 Savoy Court, Strand
London WC2R 0JP
United Kingdom
Phone: +44 (0)207 393 3333
Fax: +44 (0)207 393 0025

Lenbachplatz 3
Munich 80333
Germany
Phone: +49 (0)89 5452 50
Fax: +49 (0)89 5452 5500
www.booz.com

The Stats

Employer Type: Private Company
CEO: Shumeet Banerji
Chairman: Joe Saddi
2008 Employees: 3,300+
2008 Sales: $4.8 billion
  (includes former combined operations
  with Booz Allen Hamilton)
No. of Offices: 57

Employment Contact

www.booz.com/global/home/join_us

Practice Areas

Corporate Finance
Information Technology
Mergers & Restructuring
Operations & Logistics
Organization & Change
Product & Service Innovation
Public Sector Mission Effectiveness
  (outside the US only)
Sales & Marketing
Strategy & Leadership

European Locations

Amsterdam • Berlin • Copenhagen •
Dublin • Düsseldorf • Frankfurt •
Helsinki • London • Madrid • Milan •
Moscow • Munich • Oslo • Paris •
Rome • Stockholm • Stuttgart • Vienna •
Warsaw • Zurich

See the Vault profile on Page 66

booz&co.

Accelerate your learning curve

OC&C
STRATEGY CONSULTANTS

Interesting Fact :

❝ 40 of OC&C's staff are Guinness World Records holders. ❞

6 New Street Square
London EC4A 3AT
United Kingdom
Phone: +44 (0)207 010 8000
www.occstrategy.com

European Locations

Brussels • Düsseldorf • Hamburg •
London • Paris • Rotterdam

The Stats

Employer Type: Private Company
Worldwide Managing Partner:
    Michael Jary
2008 Employees: 450
2007 Employees: 350+
No. of Offices: 15

Employment Contact

www.occstrategy.com/recruiting

Practice Areas

Business Unit Strategy
Group Strategy
M&A & Transaction Support
Organisation & Change
Product/Market/Channel Strategy
Strategy Realisation

See the Vault profile on Page 128

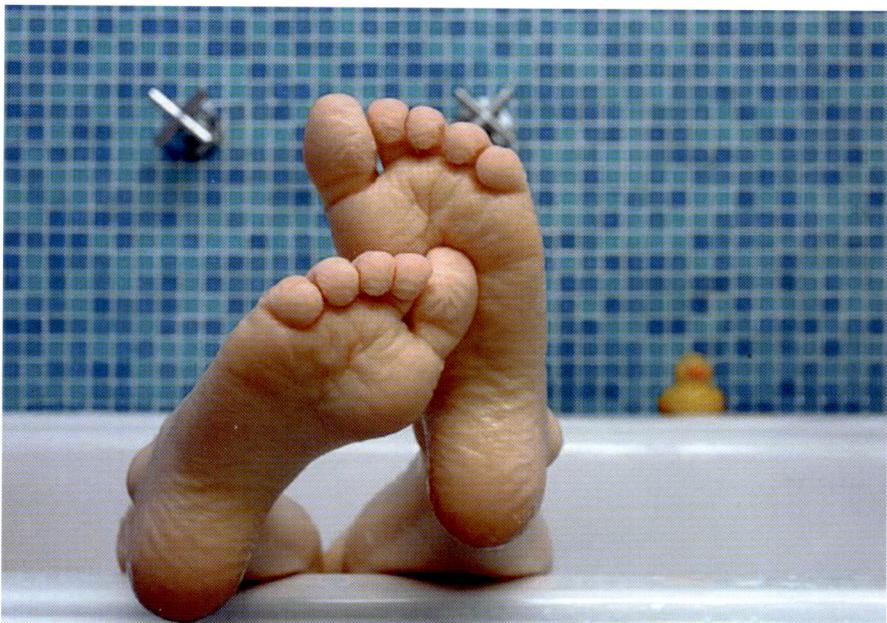

THINKING TIME

No matter where you happen to be thinking about your future, think OC&C

OC&C Strategy Consultants provide clear thinking on some of the most complex and exciting strategic problems in business today. From retail to media, industry to consumer goods, we solve the problems that keep the CEO awake at night.

To be part of our team, apply online at **www.occstrategy.com**

For more information about careers, internships and other opportunities visit www.occstrategy.com or email recruitment@occstrategy.com

OC&C
Strategy Consultants

TOWERS PERRIN

1 Stamford Plaza
263 Tresser Blvd.
Stamford, Connecticut 06901
United States
Phone: +1 (203) 326-5400
Fax: +1 (203) 326-5499
www.towersperrin.com

The Stats

Employer Type: Private Company
Chairman & CEO: Mark V. Mactas
2008 Employees: 6,000
2007 Employees: 5,400
2007 Sales: $1.57 billion
2006 Sales: $1.42 billion
No. of offices: 81

Employment Contact

www.careers.towers.com

Practice Areas

Actuarial Services
Change Management & Communication
Employee Benefits
Enterprise Risk & Capital Management
Executive Compensation
Financial Modeling Solutions
Health & Welfare Consulting
HR Function & Effectiveness
Insurance & Financial Services
Mergers, Acquisitions & Restructuring
Organization & Employee Research
Reinsurance Services
Research Surveys
Retirement Consulting
Retirement Risk Solutions
Total Rewards Effectiveness
Workforce Effectiveness

European Locations

Stamford (World HQ)
Belgium • France • Germany • Ireland •
Italy • Netherlands • Poland • Spain •
Sweden • Switzerland • United
Kingdom

See the Vault profile on Page 392

ESADE BUSINESS SCHOOL

Interesting Fact :

66   On-campus diversity is a highly enriching element of The
ESADE MBA enabling our students to fine tune their
multicultural leadership competencies and global outlook. Of
the 150 candidates in our Class of 2009 Full Time MBA
programmes, 83% are international students representing over
40 countries across all geographic regions. 99

TEACH FIRST

London
14 Heron Quay,
Canary Wharf,
London
E14 4JB
Tel: 0844 880 1800
Fax: 020 7900 3304

Midlands
Sandwell Academy,
Halfords Lane,
West Bromwich,
West Midlands
B71 4LG
Tel: 0121 5000 760
Fax: 020 7900 3304

North West
40 Princess Street,
Manchester
M1 6DE
Tel: 0161 234 0073
Fax: 0161 234 0074

CEO & Founder: Brett Wigdortz

Locations

Teach First works with schools in the following Local Authorities

London
Barking and Dagenham • Barnet • Bexley • Brent • Bromley • Croydon • Ealing • Greenwich • Hackney • Hammersmith and Fulham • Haringey • Hillingdon • Hounslow • Islington • Kensington and Chelsea • Lambeth • Lewisham • Redbridge • Southwark • Tower Hamlets • Waltham Forest • Westminster

Midlands
Birmingham • Enfield • Nottingham • Sandwell • Solihull • Walsall

North West
Bolton • Manchester • Merton • Newham • Oldham • Rochdale • Salford • Tameside • Trafford

Employment Contact

http://graduates.teachfirst.org.uk/

ROLAND BERGER
STRATEGY CONSULTANTS

Interesting Fact :

" More than 75 per cent of our projects involve challenges in the international arena. "

Highlight Towers
Mies-van-der-Rohe-Str. 6
80807 Munich
Germany
Phone: +49 (0)89 923 00
Fax: +49 (0)89 923 082 02
www.rolandberger.com

The Stats

Employer Type: Private Company
CEO: Prof Dr Burkhard Schwenker
2008 Employees: 2,000
2007 Employees: 1,700
2007 Revenue: €600 million
2006 Revenue: €550 million
No. of Offices: 36

Practice Areas

Corporate Development
Information Management
Marketing & Sales
Operations Strategy
Restructuring & Corporate Finance

European Locations

Munich (HQ)
Amsterdam • Barcelona • Berlin •
Brussels • Bucharest • Budapest •
Düsseldorf • Frankfurt • Hamburg •
Istanbul • Kiev • Lisbon • London •
Madrid • Milan • Moscow • Paris •
Prague • Riga • Rome • Stuttgart •
Vienna • Warsaw • Zagreb • Zurich

Employment Contact

www.careers.rolandberger.com

See the Vault profile on Page 94

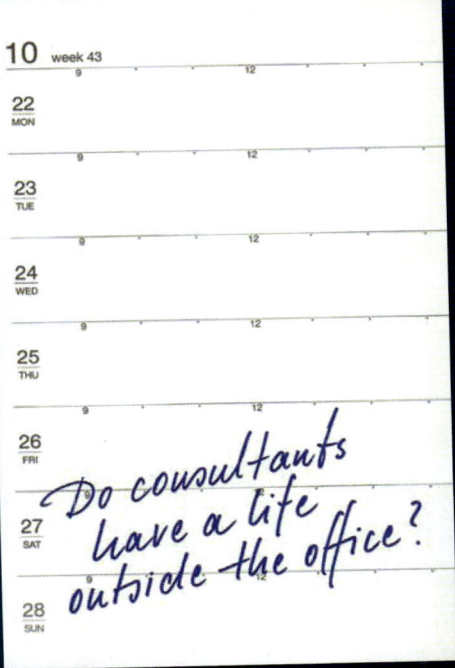

They say consultants work long and hard. That's true – but only half the story. You can be a good consultant only if you find the right balance of work and play. Each of us has a passion, whether it's sports, culture or social activities. → Our corporate culture supports our staff as they find the right work-life balance by promoting mutual respect and encouraging individual freedom. Make room in your life for the things that matter to you.

IT'S CHARACTER THAT CREATES IMPACT. WWW.CAREERS.ROLANDBERGER.COM

Roland Berger
Strategy Consultants

It's your life story.
It's your mission statement.
It's the key to the shiny new
penthouse of your future.
But until anyone actually sees it
it's just another sheet of A4.
Isn't it time to set your CV free?

guardianjobs.co.uk

THE MEDIA'S WATCHING VAULT! HERE'S A SAMPLING OF OUR COVERAGE:

"A rich resource of company information for prospective employees worldwide: Vault's content is credible, trustworthy and most of all, interesting."
- *The Guardian*

"[Vault tells] prospective joiners what they really want to know about the culture, the interview process, the salaries and the job prospects."
- *Financial Times*

"Thanks to Vault, the truth about work is just a tap of your keyboard away."
- *The Telegraph*

"The best place on the Web to prepare for a job search"
- *Money magazine*

"A killer app."
- *The New York Times*

"Vault has a wealth of information about major employers and job-seeking strategies as well as comments from workers about their experiences at specific companies."
- *The Washington Post*

Vault Guide to the

Top 25 Consulting Firms

· 2009 European Edition ·

ACKNOWLEDGEMENTS

We are extremely grateful to the Vault staff for their help in the editorial, production and marketing processes. Special thanks to Brandon Wilkerson, Melissa Newman and Phillip Stott for their insightful writing, and to Jesse Lee and Laurie Pasiuk for their editorial support.

To ensure that our research was thorough and accurate, we relied on a number of people within the consulting firms that we profiled. To the 1,875-plus consultants who took the time to be interviewed or to complete our survey, we could never thank you enough. Your insights about life inside the top consulting firms are invaluable, and your willingness to speak candidly will help job seekers and career changers for years to come. We also thank the consulting firms who were so helpful in the course of this project.

TABLE OF CONTENTS

The Best of the Rest

Appendix

A GUIDE TO THIS GUIDE

If you're wondering how our entries are organised, read on. We have created a glossary of terms to define the terminology and sections that we present in our profiles.

Firm Facts

European Locations: A listing of the firm's offices, with the city (or cities) of its headquarters bolded. We have only listed cities within Europe. If a company does not have a European headquarters, we list the American headquarters. For consultancies without an official headquarters, we list the European locations and include the address of the largest European office.

Practice Areas: Official departments and divisions that employ a significant portion of the firm's consultants. Practice areas are listed in alphabetical order, regardless of their size or prominence.

Employment Contact: The name of the department, correspondence address, contact telephone number and/or web site that the firm has identified as the best way for job seekers and applicants to submit their CV and/or answer any questions about the recruitment process and opportunities.

The Stats

Employer Type: The firm's classification as a publicly traded company, privately held company or subsidiary of a public or private company.

Ticker Symbol: The stock symbol for a public company, as well as the exchange(s) on which the stock is traded.

Chairman, CEO, etc.: The name and title of the leader(s) of the firm, or of the firm's consulting practice.

Employees: When disclosed, the total number of employees, including consultants and other staff, at a firm across all of its offices, unless otherwise specified. Figures from the two most recent consecutive years the information is available, if at all, are included.

Revenue: The net sales (in the relevant currency) that the firm generated in the specified fiscal year(s). Some firms do not disclose this information. Figures from the two most recent consecutive years the information is available, if at all, are included. Revenue refers to global operations, except where otherwise stated.

No. of Offices: The total number of a firm's offices world·wide, except where otherwise stated.

The Buzz

When conducting our prestige survey, we ask respondents to detail their views and observations about firms other than their own, and collect a sampling of these comments in The Buzz.

When selecting The Buzz, we include quotes most representative of the common perceptions of the firms held by other consultants, even if in our opinion the quotes do not accurately or completely describe the firm. Please keep in mind when reading The Buzz that it's often more fun for outsiders to criticise, rather than praise, a competing company. Nonetheless, The Buzz can be a valuable means of gauging a firm's reputation in the industry, or at least of detecting common misperceptions. We typically include four Buzz quotes. In some instances, we opt not to include The Buzz if we do not receive a diverse pool of comments.

Pluses and Minuses: Good points and, shall we say, less positive points, about working at the firm, as derived from consultant interviews and surveys. Pluses and minuses are consultants' perceptions and are not based on statistics.

The Profiles

The profiles broken down into three sections: The Scoop, Getting Hired and Our Survey Says.

The Scoop: The firm's history, clients, recent developments and other points of interest.

Getting Hired: Qualifications that the firm looks for in new associates, specific tips on getting hired as well as other notable aspects of the hiring process.

Our Survey Says: Actual quotes from surveys and interviews with current consultants at the firm on such topics as firm culture, hours, travel requirements, salaries, training and more. Profiles of some firms do not include an Our Survey Says section.

INTRODUCTION

Although it did not come without disruptions, 2007 marked another year of growth for Europe's consulting market. Consultancies came out of the gates strong early in the year, showing solid growth in most major sectors, especially management consulting and finance. However, the spectacular meltdown of the US subprime mortgage market sent ripples across the Atlantic, and the precarious economic conditions hampered both growth and revenue for the second half of the year. Not surprisingly, the trajectory of the industry has shifted, moving away from a focus on innovation and growth, to a more conservative approach that emphasises cost savings and efficiency. Nonetheless, ledgers remain in the black, and most consultancies have expanded their operations and are clamouring to hire new hands. Whatever changes lie ahead, the European consulting industry is meeting them with headlong optimism.

For this, our third edition of the *Vault Guide to the Top 25 Consulting Firms* (European edition), we cover both Europe-based consultancies and the European operations of international consulting companies. This year, we have profiled 51 consulting firms throughout Europe, and include rankings of the top-25 most prestigious consultancies—as determined by their peers—as well as rankings in a variety of quality of life areas.

The profiles in our guide are based on research and extensive feedback from over 1,875 consultants, addressing everything from company culture to compensation, and travel schedules to diversity. We cover both gigantic multinational firms and boutique consultancies with fewer than 100 employees, and everything in between.

Since 1996, Vault has been the leading career information publisher in North America. The *Vault Guide to the Top 50 Management and Strategy Consulting Firms* (North American edition) is now in its 11th edition. Graduates and young professionals have used our guides and our online resource to find employee surveys and insider information on more than 5,000 employers and 4,500 universities, including the world's top business schools and hundreds of industries and professions. In spring 2006, Vault Europe was launched, offering European graduates and young professionals relevant career information based on the successful model Vault has established in the US.

We are excited about this new edition of the *Vault Guide to the Top 25 Consulting Firms* (European edition), and we hope it will be of great value to current and future consultants in Europe.

Vault Editors
E-mail: editors@vault.com

PRESTIGE RANKINGS
for 2009

RANKING METHODOLOGY

For the 2008 Vault European Consulting survey, we selected a list of top consulting firms to include. These consulting firms were selected because of their prominence in the consulting industry and their interest to consulting job seekers. This year, over 1,875 consultants responded to our survey.

The Vault survey was distributed to the firms on Vault's list in spring 2008. In some cases, Vault contacted practising consultants directly. Survey respondents were asked to do several things. They were asked to rate each consulting firm on the survey on a scale of 1 to 10 based on prestige, with 10 being the most prestigious. Consultants were unable to rate their own firm, and they were asked to rate only those firms with which they were familiar.

Vault collected the survey results and averaged the score for each firm. The firms were then ranked, with the highest score being No. 1, down to No. 25.

We also asked survey respondents to give their perceptions of other consulting firms besides their own. A selection of those comments is featured on each firm profile as The Buzz.

Remember that Vault's top-25 European consulting firms are chosen by practising consultants at top consulting firms. Vault does not choose or influence the rankings. The rankings measure perceived prestige (as determined by consulting professionals) and not revenue, size or lifestyle.

THE VAULT 25 • 2009

Rank	Firm	Score	2008 Rank	HQ/Largest Office
1	McKinsey & Company	8.410	1	London
2	The Boston Consulting Group, Inc.	8.044	2	Boston
3	Bain & Company	7.530	3	Boston
4	Booz & Company	6.560	4	London
5	Mercer LLC	5.979	NR	London/New York
6	Oliver Wyman	5.927	5	New York
7	Roland Berger Strategy Consultants	5.873	7	Munich
8	Monitor Group	5.821	8	Cambridge, Mass.
9	A.T. Kearney	5.485	9	Chicago
10	OC&C Strategy Consultants	5.233	10	London
11	PricewaterhouseCoopers International Ltd.	5.207	NR	New York
12	Deloitte	5.049	13	New York
13	L.E.K. Consulting	5.041	11	London
14	Ernst & Young	4.864	NR	London
15	Accenture	4.820	15	London
16	Arthur D. Little	4.750	14	Paris
17	IBM Global Services	4.654	17	Madrid/Zurich/Armonk
18	Capgemini	4.509	16	Paris
19	Gartner, Inc.	4.413	21	Egham
20	Mars & Co	4.373	18	London/Paris
21	BearingPoint, Inc.*	4.275	23	McLean
22	AlixPartners, LLP	4.214	NR	Southfield
23	PA Consulting Group	4.213	19	London
24	NERA Economic Consulting	3.822	25	White Plains
25	Horváth & Partners Management Consultants	3.734	NR	Stuttgart

*BearingPoint, Inc. Management & Technology Consultants

PRACTICE AREA RANKING METHODOLOGY

Vault also asked consultants to rank the best firms in several areas of business focus. These areas are economic consulting, energy consulting, financial consulting, human resources consulting, operational consulting, and pharmaceutical and health care consulting. Consultants were allowed to vote for up to three firms as the best in each area.

The following charts indicate the rankings in each practice area, along with the total percentage of votes cast in favour of each firm. (As long as at least one consultant voted for more than one firm, no firm could get 100 per cent of the votes; if every consultant had voted for the same three firms, for example, the maximum score would be 33.3 percent.)

Economic Consulting

RANK	FIRM	VOTES %	2008 RANK
1	McKinsey & Company	20.09	1
2	NERA Economic Consulting	13.09	2
3	The Boston Consulting Group, Inc.	11.42	3
4	Bain & Company	9.28	4
5	PricewaterhouseCoopers International Ltd.	4.57	NR
6	Booz & Company	4.41	5
7	Deloitte	4.11	NR
8	Ernst & Young	3.96	NR
9	Oliver Wyman	3.20	NR
10	L.E.K. Consulting	2.74	NR

Energy Consulting

RANK	FIRM	VOTES %	2008 RANK
1	McKinsey & Company	28.67	1
2	The Boston Consulting Group, Inc.	17.41	2
3	Booz & Company	8.70	3
4	Bain & Company	8.19	4
5	Roland Berger Strategy Consultants	5.46	7
6	Accenture	4.61	6
7	A.T. Kearney	3.92	5
8	Arthur D. Little	3.41	8
9	Deloitte	2.56	NR
10	Atkins	1.37	10 (Tie)

Financial Consulting

RANK	FIRM	VOTES %	2008 RANK
1	McKinsey & Company	28.68	1
2	The Boston Consulting Group, Inc.	15.68	2
3	Oliver Wyman	11.00	3
4	Bain & Company	9.35	4
5	PricewaterhouseCoopers International Ltd.	5.16	NR
6	Deloitte	4.67	5
7	Ernst & Young	4.09	NR
8	Mercer LLC	2.04	NR
9	Accenture	1.95	NR
10	Booz & Company	1.85	NR

Human Resources Consulting

RANK	FIRM	VOTES %	2008 RANK
1	Mercer LLC	32.96	NR
2	Towers Perrin	11.80	2
3	Watson Wyatt Worldwide	7.30	3
4	Deloitte	4.68	4 (Tie)
5	Oliver Wyman	4.12	1
6	McKinsey & Company	3.93	4 (Tie)
7	PA Consulting Group	3.75	NR
8 (Tie)	Accenture	3.56	5
8 (Tie)	The Boston Consulting Group, Inc.	3.56	NR
9	PricewaterhouseCoopers International Ltd.	2.43	NR
10	Bain & Company	2.06	NR

Operational Consulting

RANK	FIRM	VOTES %	2008 RANK
1	Accenture	16.49	1
2	McKinsey & Company	10.62	3
3	A.T. Kearney	8.52	2
4	Deloitte	7.54	6
5	Booz & Company	6.98	5
6	IBM Global Services	6.79	4
7	Capgemini	5.31	8
8	Bain & Company	4.45	9
9	The Boston Consulting Group, Inc.	3.71	7
10	Roland Berger Strategy Consultants	2.96	10

The Vault Prestige Rankings

Pharmaceutical & Health Care Consulting

RANK	FIRM	VOTES %	2008 RANK
1	McKinsey & Company	26.03	1
2	The Boston Consulting Group, Inc.	21.09	2
3	ZS Associates	8.57	4
4	Bain & Company	7.25	3
5	Booz & Company	5.93	5
6	Monitor Group	2.97	NR
7	Deloitte	2.80	NR
8	A.T. Kearney	2.31	NR
9	PricewaterhouseCoopers LLC	2.14	NR
10 (Tie)	Accenture	1.98	NR
10 (Tie)	Roland Berger Strategy Consultants	1.98	NR

The Vault
QUALITY OF LIFE
Rankings
RANKING METHODOLOGY

In addition to ranking other firms in terms of prestige, survey respondents were asked to rate their own firms in a variety of categories. On a scale of 1 to 10, with 10 being the highest and 1 the lowest, respondents evaluated their firms in the following quality of life areas:

- Overall satisfaction
- Compensation
- Work/life balance
- Hours in the office
- Formal training

- Interaction with clients
- Relationships with supervisors
- Firm culture
- Travel requirements
- Offices

A firm's score in each category is simply the average of these rankings. In compiling our quality of life rankings, we only ranked firms from whose consultants we received five or more responses for a particular question. Only firms that distributed the Vault survey to their consultants were ranked. Consultancies that distributed the survey this year were:

- A.T. Kearney
- AAM Management Information Consulting Ltd.
- Abolon
- Alvarez & Marsal
- Bain & Company
- BearingPoint, Inc. Management & Technology Consultants

- Booz & Company
- Candesic Limited
- Celerant Consulting
- Commercial Advantage Consulting
- Corporate Value Associates
- Detica
- Diamond Management & Technology Consultants, Inc.

- Droege & Comp.
- Ernst & Young
- Infosys Consulting Inc.
- L.E.K Consulting
- Monitor Group
- Mott MacDonald Business & Technology Consulting Division
- NERA Economic Consulting
- OC&C Strategy Consultants

- Oliver Wyman
- PA Consulting Group
- PRTM
- Roland Berger Strategy Consultants
- Simon-Kucher & Partners
- Value Partners
- XLENT Consulting Group
- ZS Associates

The Vault Quality of Life Rankings

THE BEST 10 FIRMS TO WORK FOR

Which are the best firms to work for? For some, this is a far more important consideration than prestige. To determine our Best 10 firms, we analysed our initial list of 51 firms using a formula that weighted the most relevant categories for an overall quality of life ranking. Each firm's overall score was calculated using the following formula:

25 per cent overall satisfaction
15 per cent compensation
15 per cent work/life balance
10 per cent hours in the office
10 per cent travel requirements
5 per cent formal training
5 per cent interaction with clients
5 per cent relationships with supervisors
5 per cent firm culture
5 per cent overall diversity

Like our Top 25 ranking, our Best 10 is meant to reflect the subjective opinion of consultants. By its nature, the list is based on the perceptions of insiders—some of whom may be biased in favour of (or against) their firm.

RANK	FIRM	SCORE
1	Bain & Company	8.601
2	PRTM	8.117
3	Diamond Management & Technology Consultants, Inc.	8.091
4	OC&C Strategy Consultants	7.764
5	Monitor Group	7.678
6	Roland Berger Strategy Consultants	7.626
7	Oliver Wyman	7.587
8	L.E.K. Consulting	7.582
9	Booz & Company	7.503
10	Ernst & Young	7.375

Overall Satisfaction

On a scale of 1 to 10, where 1 means very poor and 10 means excellent, how would you rate your overall satisfaction with your firm?

RANK	FIRM	SCORE
1	Bain & Company	9.242
2	PRTM	8.810
3	XLENT Consulting Group	8.714
4	Monitor Group	8.600
5	Candesic Limited	8.571
6	OC&C Strategy Consultants	8.525
7	Roland Berger Strategy Consultants	8.462
8	Oliver Wyman	8.321
9	Alvarez & Marsal	8.313
10	Commercial Advantage Consulting	8.167

Compensation

On a scale of 1 to 10, where 1 is very poor and 10 is excellent, how would you rate your firm's compensation (including salary and bonus)?

RANK	FIRM	SCORE
1	Oliver Wyman	8.476
2	OC&C Strategy Consultants	8.360
3	PRTM	8.300
4	Bain & Company	8.203
5	L.E.K. Consulting	8.136
6	Roland Berger Strategy Consultants	8.077
7	XLENT Consulting Group	8.000
8	Booz & Company	7.727
9	A.T. Kearney	7.698
10	Diamond Management & Technology Consultants, Inc.	7.560

Work/Life Balance

On a scale of 1 to 10, where 1 is very poor and 10 is excellent, how would you rate your firm's efforts to promote a livable work/life balance?

RANK	FIRM	SCORE
1	XLENT Consulting Group	9.286
2	Diamond Management & Technology Consultants, Inc.	8.708
3	Candesic Limited	8.667
4	PRTM	8.348
5	Bain & Company	8.295
6	Detica	8.143
7	Commercial Advantage Consulting	7.667
8	Oliver Wyman	7.577
9	Ernst & Young	7.549
10	Booz & Company	7.328

Hours in the Office

On a scale of 1 to 10, where 1 means completely unsatisfied and 10 means extremely satisfied, please rank your satisfaction with the number of hours you spend in the office each week.

RANK	FIRM	SCORE
1	Candesic Limited	8.462
2	XLENT Consulting Group	8.286
3	Diamond Management & Technology Consultants, Inc.	8.120
4	Bain & Company	7.702
5	Commercial Advantage Consulting	7.667
6	PRTM	7.455
7	Alvarez & Marsal	7.400
8	Ernst & Young	7.292
9	Monitor Group	7.286
10	Corporate Value Associates	6.875

Formal Training

On a scale of 1 to 10, with 1 being very poor and 10 being excellent, how would you rate your satisfaction with the training offered by your firm?

RANK	FIRM	SCORE
1	Bain & Company	9.463
2	L.E.K. Consulting	8.273
3	Commercial Advantage Consulting	8.167
4	Roland Berger Strategy Consultants	8.000
5	OC&C Strategy Consultants	7.737
6	XLENT Consulting Group	7.714
7	Diamond Management & Technology Consultants, Inc.	7.667
8	PRTM	7.391
9	Booz & Company	7.373
10	Ernst & Young	7.352

Interaction with Clients

On a scale of 1 to 10, how satisfied are you with your opportunity to interact with your clients' top-level management?

RANK	FIRM	SCORE
1	ZS Associates	9.100
2	Monitor Group	9.088
3	Alvarez & Marsal	9.063
4	PRTM	9.046
5	Commercial Advantage Consulting	9.000
6	Bain & Company	8.957
7	Value Partners	8.762
8	Diamond Management & Technology Consultants, Inc.	8.739
9	Candesic Limited	8.714
10	Booz & Company	8.697

Relationships with Supervisors

On a scale of 1 to 10, where 1 means very poor and 10 means excellent, how would you rate your relationships with your superiors/supervisors?

RANK	FIRM	SCORE
1	Monitor Group	9.286
2	Bain & Company	9.126
3	Candesic Limited	8.923
4	PRTM	8.870
5	Detica	8.857
6	Alvarez & Marsal	8.750
7	ZS Associates	8.700
8	Commercial Advantage Consulting	8.667
9	Roland Berger Strategy Consultants	8.654
10	XLENT Consulting Group	8.571

Firm Culture

On a scale of 1 to 10, where 1 is not at all pleasant and 10 is extremely pleasant, assess your firm's culture.

RANK	FIRM	SCORE
1	Bain & Company	9.511
2	Monitor Group	9.200
3	Diamond Management & Technology Consultants, Inc.	9.040
4	Candesic Limited	8.933
5	Oliver Wyman	8.847
6	Commercial Advantage Consulting	8.833
7	Corporate Value Associates	8.813
8	OC&C Strategy Consultants	8.765
9	PRTM	8.739
10	Roland Berger Strategy Consultants	8.640

Travel Requirements

On a scale of 1 to 10, where 1 means excessive and 10 means minimal, how would you rate your firm's travel requirements?

RANK	FIRM	SCORE
1	L.E.K. Consulting	9.409
2	NERA Economic Consulting	8.188
3	Candesic Limited	8.083
4	Bain & Company	7.368
5	XLENT Consulting Group	7.286
6	Diamond Management & Technology Consultants, Inc.	7.280
7	ZS Associates	6.600
8	OC&C Strategy Consultants	6.555
9	BearingPoint, Inc. Management & Technology Consultants	6.357
10	Detica	6.333

Offices

On a scale of 1 to 10, with 1 being miserable and 10 being optimal, how would you rate your offices (your firm's offices, not your clients' offices)?

RANK	FIRM	SCORE
1	Corporate Value Associates	9.125
2	Diamond Management & Technology Consultants, Inc.	9.120
3	Monitor Group	9.059
4	Candesic Limited	8.929
5	L.E.K. Consulting	8.818
6	Bain & Company	8.755
7	Ernst & Young	8.563
8	Roland Berger Strategy Consultants	8.539
9 (Tie)	Detica	8.286
9 (Tie)	XLENT Consulting Group	8.286
10	Infosys Consulting Inc.	8.250

The Vault
DIVERSITY
Rankings

RANKING METHODOLOGY

Vault's survey also asked consultants to rate their firm's diversity with respect to women, with respect to minorities and with respect to gays, lesbians, bisexuals and transgender individuals. When asking consultants to assess their firm's diversity in these categories, we asked them to think about hiring, promoting, mentoring and other programmes.

The Best 10 Firms for Diversity

To determine an overall diversity score, we took the average of the scores firms received in each of the three diversity categories (women, minorities and GLBT).

RANK	FIRM	SCORE
1	Bain & Company	9.118
2	Diamond Management & Technology Consultants, Inc.	8.731
3	Booz & Company	8.673
4	Monitor Group	8.561
5	NERA Economic Consulting	8.218
6	Simon-Kucher & Partners	8.138
7	PRTM	8.090
8	Roland Berger Strategy Consultants	8.077
9	Ernst & Young	8.053
10	Mott MacDonald Business & Technology Consulting Division	7.837

Diversity for Women

On a scale of 1 to 10, where 1 means needs a lot of improvement and 10 means exemplary, how receptive is your firm to women in terms of hiring, promoting, mentoring and other programmes?

RANK	FIRM	SCORE
1	Candesic Limited	9.300
2	Bain & Company	8.800
3	XLENT Consulting Group	8.714
4	Booz & Company	8.587
5	Diamond Management & Technology Consultants, Inc.	8.333
6	Celerant Consulting	8.143
7	Value Partners	8.123
8	Monitor Group	8.000
9	Ernst & Young	7.937
10	Roland Berger Strategy Consultants	7.880

Diversity for Minorities

On a scale of 1 to 10, where 1 means needs a lot of improvement and 10 means exemplary, how receptive is your firm to minorities in terms of hiring, promoting, mentoring and other programmes?

RANK	FIRM	SCORE
1	Bain & Company	9.180
2	Booz & Company	8.946
3	Diamond Management & Technology Consultants, Inc.	8.917
4	Roland Berger Strategy Consultants	8.750
5	XLENT Consulting Group	8.571
6	Monitor Group	8.517
7	PRTM	8.353
8	Alvarez & Marsal	8.308
9	Celerant Consulting	8.286
10	NERA Economic Consulting	8.250

Diversity for GLBT

On a scale of 1 to 10, where 1 means very poor and 10 means excellent, how would you rate your firm's commitment to diversity with respect to gays, lesbians, bisexuals and transgender individuals?

RANK	FIRM	SCORE
1	Bain & Company	9.375
2	Monitor Group	9.167
3	PRTM	9.083
4	Diamond Management & Technology Consultants, Inc.	8.944
5	NERA Economic Consulting	8.778
6	Simon-Kucher & Partners	8.574
7	Corporate Value Associates	8.556
8	Booz & Company	8.487
9	Ernst & Young	8.085
10	Mott MacDonald Business & Technology Consulting Division	8.056

THE STATE OF EUROPEAN CONSULTING

The year 2007 was a year of sharp contrasts for the global consulting industry. For the first half of the year, at least, it was Big Business as usual: Booming markets and healthy profit lines encouraged companies to strengthen their operations by investing in advisory services. Within the UK and Ireland, Europe's largest consulting markets, the financial services, utilities and consumer goods industries propelled demand; across the continent, the solid performance of the energy, manufacturing, telecoms and utilities sectors also contributed to a proliferation of engagements. A 2007 report from the Management Consultancies Association (MCA) indicates that management consulting revenue among UK firms—which represents 27 per cent of the European market—climbed 10 per cent to £8.5 billion, a rate matched by the continent at large. Telecoms and transportation led the way in Germany, which accounts for about one-third of Europe's consulting industry. France's consulting market, Europe's third largest, brought in €10.6 billion in revenue in 2007, with demand from the public sector, as well as increased M&A activity, keeping consultants bustling. Globally, consulting growth rates are predicted to rise 5 to 10 per cent annually through 2010.

Stormy weather

Though business was strong throughout most of 2007, by the third fiscal quarter, it was obvious that a storm hovered—and it soon touched down. As years of dubious lending policies came to an abrupt and disastrous head, industries across the spectrum suffered and consequently reined in their strategy spending. Engagements dropped off swiftly. Recalling the 2001 economic downturn, a slump that took the consulting industry three years to recover from, analysts theorised that consultancies should hunker down for lean times.

> ❝ Growth in 2007 was largely spurred by the financial services industry. ❞

Despite uncertainty on the course of the economy, the European consulting industry nevertheless managed to close out 2007 in the black—though its revenue growth was a modest 6 per cent, significantly lower than in previous years. Profits accrued in the first half of 2007 went far in mitigating the dropoff in business at year's end. The global credit crisis, along with skyrocketing fuel prices and the falling American dollar, has put banks and other businesses in a precarious position. Doubts about the economy are also causing many consulting clients to adopt a cautious stance, and experts forecast that growth will slow even more. Fiona Czerniawska, director of the MCA Think Tank, noted that in 2008, there is "more caution among clients so far as spending on consultancy is concerned."

Similarly, consultancies report that engagements in 2008 are increasingly centred on trimming costs and improving efficiency, rather than spurring growth. And while analysts aren't yet predicting an all-out crisis, they are expecting tighter budgets and fewer engagements. Still, when life gives you credit calamities, make lemonade: In the short term, even the debt debacle is providing work, as financial services firms look to consultants for help with crisis management and recovery strategies.

Lessons learned

In the face of recession, one thing is certain: Consulting firms are better prepared than they were in 2001. After the dot-com trauma, clients became more sophisticated buyers, demanding better value, deeper expertise and more targeted solutions. Many now insist that their projects be staffed by senior-level consultants—industry experts who really know the sector—rather than fresh-out-of-school generalists, and consultancies have shifted their approach accordingly. There has been a conceptual shift as well—consultants now see themselves as partnering with a client over time to bring about long-term business improvements, rather than proposing a quick fix for a single problem. In addition, consultancies have tweaked their services to suit the market. For example, at a time when many clients are seeking to do business across geographic borders, firms have expanded their core service offerings to include globalisation strategies and offshoring advice.

Aim small, win big

With clients demanding targeted consulting services, more niche firms (many spun off from larger consultancies after the dot-com bust and its ensuing layoffs) have entered the landscape, jousting with the larger, well-established consulting shops for projects. Competition in the consulting world has no doubt gotten tougher, since small firms are often able to undercut the fees of blue-chip houses by keeping overhead low. Smaller consultancies may also get a foot in the door by accepting projects that aren't as "sexy", such as implementation or data migration, before taking on actual strategy work.

Further heating up competition are three of the Big Four accounting firms—PricewaterhouseCoopers, Ernst & Young and KPMG—that recently re-entered the consulting market (though KPMG's consulting presence in Europe is less pronounced than its Big Four cohorts). Between 2000 and 2001, these firms were compelled to spin off the consulting divisions from their audit and accounting practices after the US Securities and Exchange Commission clamped down on independence regulations to prevent conflicts of interest. Out of the Big Four, Deloitte is in a class of its own, having elected not to cast off its consulting wing. In 2007, the five-year noncompete agreements between the firms and their spin-offs came to an end, and PwC, Ernst & Young and KPMG have since been busy cranking up their business advisory services and financial and risk consulting divisions.

The hiatus did not diminish their brand value in clients' eyes: Consulting and advisory services were the fastest growing service lines for the firms, and all posted impressive financial results in 2007. European business lines proved particularly fruitful. Deloitte's European revenue grew 13 per cent, while PwC posted 22 per cent growth in Central and

> ❝ Engagements in 2008 are increasingly centered on trimming costs and improving efficiency. ❞

Eastern Europe and 9 per cent in Western Europe. Ernst & Young exhibited revenue growth of greater than 15 per cent in each of Northern, Central and Western Europe in fiscal 2007.

IT's coming up

Another marked change for the industry is consultancies' gradual merging of business consulting and IT and project management services. Many companies are wising up to the fact that technology plays an essential role in meeting strategic objectives and, as such, are increasingly turning to consulting firms that can offer both nontechnical solutions and IT systems. According to the 2008 MCA report, such engagements account for more than half of companies' consulting expenditure. Over the course of 2007, while income from strategy consulting diminished, IT consulting grew by 16 per cent. As business strategy and IT processes become increasingly interdependent, strategy and advisory firms have found it profitable to offer the kinds of tech services—such as database creation—that were previously performed by "pure tech" consultancies. For instance, Bain and McKinsey, traditionally strategy-oriented firms, are now exploring the benefits of integrating IT consulting into their service lines. And while niche firms do have their place in the technology industry, the biggest players have a leg up on winning clients, thanks to their ability to seamlessly weave customised IT solutions and software with business strategy.

The strength of financial services

The consulting industry's growth in 2007 was largely spurred by the financial services industry. In the UK alone, the sector accounted for more than £1.4 billion in revenue for the year. Demand was driven in part by the increase in M&A activity, which surged to unprecedented levels in the first six months of the year. By the second half of the year, however, deals dwindled as mortgage woes in the US reverberated through global credit markets. The resulting revaluation of credit spreads hampered European companies' ability to raise low-interest capital. The effect this will have on the consulting industry in the long term is yet to be seen, but there is likely to be intensified need among clients for credit risk analysis, refinancing assistance, and other credit- or finance-related services.

Despite the depressed conditions, the global M&A market reached a record $4.3 trillion in 2007, with Europe accounting for 39 per cent of that value. M&A deals typically provide a stream of work for consultants, who are called on to evaluate potential deals, find targets or conduct due diligence. Consultants are also brought in after deals to help handle postmerger issues. In response to the M&A boom of the last years, some firms have bolstered their M&A service lines. Companies focussed on M&A, including AlixPartners, LLP, Droege & Comp. and Alvarez & Marsal, are poised to cash in on the lucrative market.

Risk management and security are also driving the financial services industry's demand for consulting services. With a global market and increasing cross-border activity, businesses are more concerned with managing security issues. Regulatory consulting has also been a boost for consultancies, as banks fall in line with 2008 Basel II requirements. Research firm Kennedy Information reports that the financial services industry alone spent $60 billion on consulting services in 2007, a figure expected to rise more than 5 per cent annually through 2011.

The Eastern front

Eastern Europe is proving a viable new market for consulting activity. In fact, industry observers expect growth in Hungary, the Czech Republic and Poland to outstrip growth in more established Western European markets. Thanks to Eastern Europe's low-cost labour pools, outsourcing has so far driven the region's expansion. Though talent is not nearly as inexpensive as it is in India and China, workers in these countries have the advantage of geographic proximity and facility with European languages. In the future, however, consultancies expect the region's consulting needs to stretch far beyond outsourcing engagements. Following the deregulation of industries such as telecoms and utilities, Eastern European businesses are calling in consultants to help sharpen their profit focus. And now that Romania and Bulgaria have won inclusion to the European Union, companies in those nations are seeking out advisory services as they navigate EU compliance regulations.

Outsourcing excellence

Business process outsourcing activity in Europe continues to provide steady, lucrative work for consulting firms, and the EU now accounts for 51 per cent of global BPO contracts. According to a report from European import research firm CBI, the outsourcing market in Europe is set to grow from €11 billion in 2006 to €18.9 billion in 2011. The UK dominates Europe's BPO scene, though recently Belgium, the Netherlands and Luxembourg have been ramping up BPO activity.

India continues to be a prime area for growth, for both outsourcing and advisory service lines. Between 2005 and 2007, IBM doubled the number of its employees in India to over 53,000. In 2008, Deloitte announced plans to raise its India headcount from 7,500 to 12,000 by 2010. Accenture, too, considers India to be one of its largest developing markets. With a headcount of 35,000 in the country, it has more employees in India than in any other country. But as the labour market in India matures, salaries are inching upward at a rate of 15 per cent per year, making it more expensive for consultancies to hire local staff. At this rate, analysts say the country may soon price itself out of the offshoring competition. As such, companies have started looking beyond India, eyeing other emerging countries, such as Indonesia, Vietnam, the Philippines and Eastern European nations, for outsourcing opportunities.

While the BPO industry's overall outlook is positive, *Consulting Times* reports that 2007 was the first year that the total number of contracts declined, by 12 per cent. Part of the drop is due to the maturation of the market; businesses are increasingly using several specialist providers, and contracting each for just a single piece of the whole BPO project, rather than using just one outsourcing provider for all. As it stands, the human resources and financial services sectors are driving most BPO work.

A few good hires

Economic uncertainty aside, recruiting remains a top priority for many consultancies. The MCA reports that member firms employed over 33,000 consultants in 2007, a 9 per cent hike over 2006 levels. But the major consulting shops have been unable to keep up with current demand for talent, and have set ambitious hiring goals for 2008. Indeed, the steady drive for recruiting talent indicates that consulting firms are confident that the flow of engagements isn't likely to trickle off any time soon.

As clients continue to demand specialised expertise, consultancies are specifically seeking experienced candidates—lateral hires with a few years under their belt are preferable to newbie graduates. Specialist consultants also top recruiters' most wanted list, and MBAs with a background in the telecoms, high-tech, biotech or consumer products industries will likely have their pick of offers. In 2007, recruitment was heaviest for consultancies' outsourcing service lines, up 14 per cent over 2006, compared to 10 per cent for pure strategy consultants.

Some firms are also raising target hiring numbers to keep up with the slightly higher turnover that has resulted from industrywide poaching. According to the 2007 "Retention Report" by Top-consultant.com, attrition averaged 10 to 15 per cent throughout Continental Europe, with rates in the UK averaging 15 to 20 per cent. Recruiters estimate that they will need to bump up hiring by 25 per cent over 2008 to make up for staff losses. And since salaries in the industry rose only 4 per cent over 2007, consultancies also face the prospect of losing talent to higher-paying industries such as financial services. The most self-aware firms are acting quickly to keep their workforce challenged and interested by ensuring that compensation remains competitive, increasing the transparency of the promotion track and boosting resources for official training.

The green scene

Environmental awareness was also on the rise in 2007. Concerns about global warming led multiple early-adopter consultancies to initiate programmes aimed at reducing or even eliminating their carbon footprints. Some of the methods introduced to achieve these objectives include promoting the use of recycled and recyclable office materials, upgrading the air conditioning and computing systems to curb wasted energy, and minimising air travel to client sites. As a natural outgrowth of such initiatives, many environmentally conscious consultancies will also offer environmental advisory services to assist clients in their own conservation efforts, especially in light of tightening compliance standards. Among the major consulting firms to adopt green programmes in 2007 were L.E.K. Consulting, Capgemini and IBM Global Business Services. L.E.K., in particular, intends to eliminate all CO_2 emission, making it the first major management consultancy to become carbon neutral. ☐

PRACTICE AREAS

Operations and implementation

Operations consulting is the difference between strategy—making a plan—and putting that plan into action. Countries strong in production, such as Germany and the UK, are important markets for operations consulting.

For most of the century, operations consulting centred on cutting costs and increasing efficiency. In latter years, with clients more oriented toward growth, operations consulting adapted to tackle innovation and customer interaction engagements. Increasing caution in the market, however, has recently brought about a return to the earlier conventions. Operations consultants help clients rework processes to rapidly respond to competition or changes in the market. While strategy involves marking out clear goals, operations consulting focusses on the practical means of reaching these goals, ie, allocating resources, shifting value chain priorities, evaluating benefits of outsourcing, or examining customer service and distribution processes.

Examples of a typical operations and implementation engagement may include:

- Defining functions of a customer call centre for a credit card company
- Increasing the efficiency and shortening the cycle time of a supply chain
- Helping a large financial services company migrate to an offshore location

Human resources consulting

Even with fine-tuned strategies and streamlined operations, businesses can fail without the appropriate people in position to manage them. HR consulting addresses the issues of maximising the value of staff and placing the right employees in the right roles. HR consultancies are also hired for organisational restructuring, talent management, HR systems implementation, benefits planning and compensation.

An important subsection of HR consulting is HR outsourcing. Increasingly, clients are turning to HR consultancies to manage their internal HR systems. According to Kennedy Information, the combined global market for HR outsourcing and HR BPO reached $31 billion at the end of 2007.

Examples of typical human resources consulting engagements include:

- Recruiting and installing a senior management team for a company in transition
- Blending the culture and processes of an acquired company with its new parent
- Reviewing and updating employee benefits plans for a multinational corporation

Health care/pharmaceutical consulting

Health care and pharmaceutical consulting firms help clients evaluate opportunities in the market, cope with government regulations, manage costs and implement technology. According to a 2007 PricewaterhouseCoopers report, the global pharmaceutical market will more than double in value to $1.3 trillion by 2020. A niche with such promise is naturally overrun with companies all trying to get a piece of the pie. These consultancies will also see plenty of work from other fast growing life sciences sectors, such as biotech, diagnostics and medical devices.

Examples of typical health care/pharmaceutical engagements include:

• Assisting with billing and claims processing
• Facilitating market entry for a new drug or medical device
• Providing capacity optimisation services for hospitals

Economic consulting

In a global economy, no business is isolated from economic changes in other parts of the world. Clients are turning to think tank-like economic consultancies for guidance. Typically loaded with economics PhDs and MBAs, as well as industry experts, such firms investigate relevant economic factors to help clients resolve problems caused by competition, public policy and regulations. Quantitative analysis, statistical studies and modelling services are often a key part of economic consulting engagements. These firms are valued for their independence and ability to give candid counsel to clients affected by increasingly dynamic economic conditions.

Examples of typical economic consulting engagements include:

• Evaluation of fare policies for a public transportation service
• Modelling a company's tax burden region by region
• Weighting economic data to more precisely represent a target population

Financial consulting

Financial consultancies generally offer two types of services—either they work with financial services firms to enhance their strategies and performance, or they have a specific financial model they use with clients to enhance their performance. In both cases, the focus is typically on boosting shareholder value. The market has gained momentum as consultants are hired to help companies deal with global competition, develop offshore establishments, or seek new markets and customers. In the EU, demand is particularly strong in the compliance area, as financial institutions implement Basel II regulations. In the UK, for example, the market for financial consulting grew 20 per cent in 2007, to £1.4 billion. Other trends driving the expansion are a booming M&A market, divestitures, and growth in private equity and corporate strategy.

Examples of financial consulting engagements include:

• Performing due diligence prior to a major transaction
• Developing online strategies for a commercial bank
• Assessing total financial risk for a business portfolio

cKinsey & Company • The Bo
Company • Booz & Company
oland Berger Strategy Cons
earney • OC&C Strategy Co
rs LLP • Deloitte • L.E.K.
ccenture • Arthur D. Little •
Gartner, Inc. • Mars & Co •
echno logy Consultants • Al
roup • NERA Economic Cons
gement Consultants • McKins
ulting Group, Inc. • Bain &
ercer LLC • Oliver Wym
onsultants • Monitor Group •
eloitte • Pricewate rhouse

THE VAULT
25

MCKINSEY & COMPANY

No. 1 Jermyn Street
London SW1Y 4UH
United Kingdom
Phone: +44 (0)207 839 8040
Fax: +44 (0)207 339 5000
www.mckinsey.com

The Stats

Employer Type: Private Company
Chairman & CEO: Ian Davis
2008 Employees: 16,000+
2007 Employees: 14,000
No. of Offices: 90

European Locations

Amsterdam • Antwerp • Athens •
Barcelona • Berlin • Bratislava • Brussels •
Bucharest • Budapest • Cologne •
Copenhagen • Dublin • Düsseldorf •
Frankfurt • Geneva • Gothenberg •
Hamburg • Hanover • Helsinki • Istanbul •
Lisbon • London • Luxembourg • Lyon •
Madrid • Milan • Moscow • Munich • Oslo •
Paris • Prague • Rome • Sofia • Stockholm •
Stratford-Upon-Avon • Stuttgart • Verona •
Vienna • Warsaw • Zagreb • Zurich

Employment Contact

www.mckinsey.com/careers

Practice Areas

Functional Practice Areas
Business Technology Office • Corprate
Finance • Marketing & Sales •
Operations • Organization • Risk •
Strategy

Industry Practices
Automotive • Banking & Finance •
Consumer Goods • Energy & Materials •
Healthcare Payors & Providers •
Insurance • Media • Pharmaceuticals •
Private Equity • Public Sector • Retail •
Social Sector • Technology •
Telecommunications • Travel

Pluses

• The name itself
• "Continuous intellectual challenge and
  great camaraderie"

Minuses

• "We are overachievers: Nobody forces
  us, but we always end up killing ourselves
  for the extra impact"
• Weekend work is always a possibility

THE BUZZ
WHAT CONSULTANTS AT OTHER FIRMS ARE SAYING

• "Rolls-Royce of the industry"
• "Elite, arrogant, clones"
• "Top-notch, polished thinkers"
• "Standardised approaches,
  synchronised consultants"

THE SCOOP

McKinsey & Company

A s one of the oldest and most powerful consulting firms around, McKinsey stands out in terms of its established reputation and adherence to tradition. In 1926, James O. McKinsey, CPA and University of Chicago management professor, founded the business to give local companies financial and accounting advice. Before long, he realised that the companies' financial data could be interpreted to help make better management decisions. Thanks to this innovation, McKinsey is credited with the idea of using consultants, or "management engineers" for the first time. And although the firm is his namesake, it was one of his protégés, Marvin Bower, who is most remembered for shaping the direction of the firm. Bower took over leadership in 1950 after McKinsey's death in 1937. 100Known as one of the fathers of modern consulting, he is credited with helping management consultancy become a profession on par with medicine and law. Bower oversaw the firm's crucial growth period from 1950 through the late 1960s, when revenue jumped from $2 million to $20 million.

Tenets of tradition

Most notably, Bower is known for the way he moulded the McKinsey culture as we know it today. Back in the early days, Bower established rigorous standards for employees, such as a formal dress code and prescribed margins for all written reports and correspondence. More important was the five-part code of conduct, which remains in place today, outlining certain ideals consultants were to uphold. Among these values are putting client interests ahead of those of the firm, giving superior service and maintaining the highest ethical standards. Consultants are also instructed to be absolutely truthful with the client, regardless of whether the client disagrees. Perhaps the most notable tenet of the code is to protect the privacy of clients—to this day, McKinsey never publicises its big-name clients, nor does it tout successful engagements. Despite this, the firm doesn't lack for publicity, since the secrecy surrounding its work is itself often the focus of media attention. This lack of self-promotion is one reason the firm has been able to maintain its "mystique".

Today, McKinsey serves some of the world's largest companies, including two-thirds of the Fortune 1000 list. It divides its business into seven functional areas: business technology, corporate finance, marketing and sales, operations, organisation, risk and strategy. Its consultants cover industries including automotive, banking, high tech, pharmaceutical, the public sector and telecommunications. The firm also established a climate change special initiative in 2007, which focusses on the transitional challenges, across a number of sectors, associated with the move to a low-carbon economy. A significant portion of McKinsey's engagements come from large corporations—in fact, the firm advises 147 of the world's 200 largest corporations and 80 of the top-120 financial services firms. In addition, the consultancy works with a variety of social organisations, government agencies, institutions and nonprofits. McKinsey has a reputation as one of the most expensive firms in the business, though that doesn't seem to deter clients. According to media reports, most of McKinsey's big clients pay $10 million annually in fees.

Democratic structure

With over 16,000 staff, more than 1,000 of whom are directors and principals, McKinsey functions as a partnership, although it is set up as a private corporation. Every three years, the principals and directors (considered the firm's owners and managers) vote to select a managing director to lead the firm. Currently, the firm is led by Managing Director Ian Davis, a native of Kent, England. Davis is an Oxford grad who started with the firm in 1979. Having built his career in the London office, Davis is

> " McKinsey right now has a real hop in its step. "

the first managing director who never spent time working in the US offices. In 2003, Davis replaced Rajat Gupta, who led McKinsey for its maximum of three, three-year terms. Although Davis is characteristically described as a less public figure than his predecessor, he has earned a venerable reputation in the business world. In fact, *The Observer* has called him one of the 300 most powerful people in Britain.

Worldwide footprint

McKinsey has been rooted in the European market since 1959, when it established its first non-US office in London. Currently, the firm has extensive coverage in Europe, now maintaining 41 offices. McKinsey has no official headquarters and derives about 60 per cent of its revenue from clients outside the US. Though the firm has always had its share of international clientele, geographic growth had never been the main priority. It was under Gupta's leadership from 1994 to 2003 that McKinsey underwent aggressive global expansion, widening its reach from 58 to 84 locations and more than doubling its staff numbers. Revenue also soared under his direction—from $1.2 billion to $3.4 billion in 1993. In the past two decades, the firm has also entered less-developed hotspots like Eastern Europe, its most recent office in the region was opened in 2003 in Zagreb, Croatia.

McKinsey has also made strides in the Asian market, now with 16 offices spanning 13 countries. The firm's clients there are mainly financial institutions, high tech and telecommunications companies, and governments. The firm also owns a strategic alliance with two Southeast Asian venture capital firms, created to investigate telecoms investment opportunities in India, Singapore, Hong Kong and Indonesia. In 2004, the firm established Asia House, an outpost in Frankfurt dedicated to serving clients in Asia, the Pacific Rim and the Middle East. Asia House was created to help link up clients in Europe with Asian businesses, many of whom have an outpost in Frankfurt. McKinsey is also active in China from its four offices, the newest in Shanghai, established in 2003.

McKinsey also has an established presence in the Middle East and Africa, with offices in Dubai, Bahrain and Johannesburg.

Keeping a low high-profile

Although the firm is notoriously private, occasionally word gets out about one of its engagements. In the past, McKinsey has been called on by blue-chip firms such as Royal Dutch Shell, Hewlett-Packard, IBM, SwissAir and Pepsi. A number of educational institutions, nonprofit organisations and governments, have also sought McKinsey's guidance. Among them are the Bank of England, the Roman Catholic Church and the African Comprehensive HIV/AIDS Partnerships.

In 2007, British media company Emap hired McKinsey to carry out a review of its business, after it suffered from profit woes as customers have increasingly favoured the Internet and other new media sources over television. The consultancy advised the group on how to integrate its existing business with digital services. That same year, the Abu Dhabi National Energy Company PJSC hired the firm to advise on an overhaul of design and internal management processes. In 2006, McKinsey was called on by Swedish utility company Vattenfall to evaluate the economic impact of reducing global greenhouse gases. The results showed that it would cost less than half of 1 per cent of the global domestic product to reduce greenhouse gases. The study picked up quite a bit of coverage in the international media, and a handful of American corporations hired McKinsey to conduct a similar study focussed specifically on the US economy.

McKinsey has suffered some criticism for a few of its more public engagements involving failed corporations. The firm was a longtime strategy adviser to the now-defunct US firm Enron, which was led by ex-CEO and convicted felon Jeff Skilling, a former McKinsey consultant. Though McKinsey's name was tossed around during part of the 2006 trial, there was no evidence that its consultants would have had knowledge of Enron's financial cover-ups.

Alumni with influence

McKinsey also maintains a heady profile through its alumni who now occupy CEO posts at top companies all over the world. The list includes Michael L. Ainslie, former CEO and president of Sotheby's Holdings; Louis Gerstner, former CEO of the food giant RJR Nabisco and of IBM; Stephen Green, CEO of HSBC; Adair Turner, former director general of the Confederation of British Industry; and Don Cruickshank, former chairman of the London Stock Exchange. The firm's past and present talent also includes a number of notable names in politics. Within the UK government, former McKinsey consultants who were appointed to advisory positions were often referred to in the media as "brothers that sit at Blair's right hand" and "Tony's back room boys". That group included David Bennett, a former partner, whom Blair appointed to lead Downing Street's policy unit; Matthew Elson, who served as Blair's transport adviser in the policy unit for three years; and Nick Lovegrove, formerly an unpaid adviser to the Forward Strategy Unit.

Prime pick

McKinsey's tradition of secrecy and loyalty has no doubt made it more desirable in the eyes of top MBA grads. Coupled with the fact that the McKinsey name on a resume undoubtedly opens doors for its alumni, it's no surprise the firm gets to pick from the cream of the crop at the most prestigious grad schools. From the firm's inception, recruiting was a big priority for Bower, who predicted that the demand for talented management consultants would outpace the supply. As such, he pioneered the practice of snapping up candidates just out of graduate school, as well as seeking out employees with a few years of industry experience. Bower believed that new grads could best be moulded in the "McKinsey way" as generalist consultants exposed to a variety of industries. In 2008, McKinsey ranked No. 48 in *The Times'* Top 100 Graduate Employers survey, and has been listed among the top-50 employers for the past seven years running.

McKinsey's brightest minds

McKinsey Global Institute, founded in 1990, is where the minds of McKinsey convene to conduct economic research and business analysis. Today, the institute's studies and predictions are publicised throughout the media and serve to inform policy-makers worldwide. Recently, the institute put out its fourth annual "Mapping Global Capital Markets" report, highlighting the trends shaping markets today. The report found that Europe's financial markets are quickly catching up in scale to the US market. In 2006, Europe's financial markets reached $53.2 trillion, and showed stronger growth than those in the US—thanks to maturing equity and private debt markets. The report also noted that the euro is gaining on the dollar as the world's global reserve currency, a strong indicator of future growth.

And while McKinsey does not promote its business, it certainly promotes its consultants' research and white papers. *The McKinsey Quarterly* is the firm's widely read business publication that gives insight into its thinking on management and strategy. The March 2008 issue discussed how to run a successful M&A shop, and delved into the upcoming boom in infrastructure projects around the world and how to discover which ones would make the most profitable investments.

GETTING HIRED

Do you make the grade?

As one would expect for a firm of McKinsey's cachet, only those recruits with stellar marks from the top universities or business schools make the cut. Only recently did McKinsey's 12-year run as the No. 1 choice for new MBA graduates end, according to The Universum IDEAL™ Employer Survey 2007—for the first time, Google took the top spot. The firm is still the top choice among consulting firms, however, and candidates vying for a position will find that competition is fierce. Candidates who are up to the challenge of the rigorous weeding-out process can start by checking the web site for university recruiting events at their school, or to find out more about the opportunities available to experienced professionals. Across Europe, the firm draws recruits heavily from INSEAD, as well as from a few other top regional programmes.

For all things recruiting-related, head to the careers link on the McKinsey web site. Graduates who plan to attend campus recruiting events or those seeking a position should submit an application and CV online. Students are welcome to apply to more than one McKinsey office, and the firm states that it aims to place recruits in their office of choice. The bulk of interviews take place between October and January, though many offices accept applications and run interviews throughout the year.

The web site is also helpful in explaining how consulting with McKinsey differs from a job with a private equity firm or investment bank—for students who may be torn between the choices. Among other factors—like getting that "golden" name on your resume—the firm asserts that at McKinsey, new hires get a chance to develop a broader skill set, including analytical skills, organisation and operational improvement, rather than just focussing on the quantitative.

Fascinating cases

Insiders tell us that McKinsey's "very thorough", "very fair" and "transparent" hiring process typically consists of "one written test for analytical ability", as well as "two rounds" of multiple interviews. One recent hire recalls having "three interviews with associates/project leaders" in the first round, and "two interviews with partners" in the second round. A consultant in Milan expains, "It's a very structured and tough selection process. We start with a GMAT-like test (for young hires only), followed by typically five interviews. Interviews are based on business cases, and they are tough."

We're told that interviews will likely include a "fit question (eg, 'Describe a situation when you had to persuade someone')", a "motivation question ('Why you want to switch your current job for a business consultant?')" and a "discussion about your interests". In addition, some interviews follow a "standard case format", focussing on a "business case usually from the interviewer's practice". A senior business analyst reports that in his experience, "The case interview seemed more like a fascinating business discussion than an exam. However, you still have to be very structured and pragmatic (your hypotheses and solutions should be very clear and pragmatic, not theoretical)."

Words of advice

There's no need to wonder for long whether the interviews have gone well. Insiders say candidates can expect "detailed feedback immediately after each round", and one staffer remarks, "I received the offer the same evening I was interviewed."

A newbie in Moscow shares some "advice for others who are going to interview: Do not be afraid, take it as an interesting discussion of some business issue you could have with a friend. Do not be afraid to dispute and stand up for your own point of view. Do not be afraid to say something wrong, as you can admit you're mistaken rather than keeping silent. Do not be afraid if the interviewer's position differs from what you have said." The source adds, "I had a few strong disputes with the interviewers during the cases, as I disagreed with what they were saying (regarding business issues, not my performance), and they took it very adequately."

OUR SURVEY SAYS

Everyone gets along, mostly

Insiders at McKinsey report that their colleagues are diverse, "multinational" and young, with most "between 25 and 35 years old". An associate in London warns that, at times, his office seems to have a "highly political and clique-oriented culture around partners", but most staffers tells us that the "fun group of great people" they work with creates an atmosphere they describe as "inclusive", "nonhierarchical" and "caring". As one source in Milan states, McKinsey is an "incredibly values-driven, very strong culture. When I meet colleagues from the other side of the world, I'm surprised by how consistent our culture is around the globe, across borders, racial differences, religious differences and age differences." He adds, "People outside of McKinsey have no idea of how good the internal environment is. There's a very low competition level, lots of support and lots of people to learn from (and who are eager to teach)."

A number of respondents comment on the flat structure within the firm. As a partner in Istanbul states, "The continuously repeated phrase, 'there is no intellectual hierarchy' is actually true, not just a recruiting marketing spiel. But it also comes with a responsibility: You better work hard and be sure of what you will be saying."

On the move

We're also told that the environment is "demanding", and there's certainly "plenty of work" to be done. In London and Zurich, especially, sources say offices are characterised by "high intensity" and "long hours" (around 60 to 65 per week), with "lots of travel—three days away from home, on average", a consultant

> ❝ The continuously repeated phrase, 'There is no intellectual hierarchy,' is actually true. ❞

notes. But colleagues in Amsterdam, where there's an "emphasis on personal training", say their "hours are not bad," and tend to hover around "55 a week". And generally, respondents say that "the individual can influence requirements" when it comes to travel. Overall, one engagement manager insists, there's a "great degree of flexibility on when and where travel is required".

A partner agrees that there is flexibility afforded to consultants, but notes that that freedom is attainable only as you climb the ranks: "In the initial years, it was practically impossible for me to balance work/life—I always felt at the mercy of the engagement manager. But as I got experienced, I started to have relatively more control over my own schedule, ie, I could plan in advance my work if I had a social programme by working hard earlier, etc. When I was leading projects, I had increased my control (not hours, though) substantially." He adds, however, that although his control has increased, he is never able to predict when he will need to put in those hours. "What really bothers me is not the sheer amount of hours worked (typically 60 to 80 hours per week) but the unpredictability. I don't know whether I will need to work over the weekend or not until Friday evening or Saturday morning. That lack of control is bothersome."

"A real hop in its step"

Insiders across the map are happy with top-notch salaries, supplemented by as much as a "15 per cent bonus and 12 per cent pension", as well as health and life insurance.

A partner notes that there's a "long-term profit-sharing plan. Each year, a certain amount is deposited to a savings plan of your choosing. This money can only be accessed after you retire or you leave the firm." In addition, "in Europe, McKinsey typically provides a car and all gas expenses above associate level." Vacation days ranging between "20 days to six weeks" are an added benefit. The firm also gives back to the community through a "dedicated pro bono practice".

One business analyst happily remarks, "McKinsey right now has a real hop in its step, and I anticipate both excitement and growth in the future." And a colleague raves that the firm is "the best place in the world to begin a career". □

THE BOSTON CONSULTING GROUP, INC.

Exchange Place, 31st Floor
Boston, Massachusetts 02109
United States
Phone: +1 (617) 973-1200
Fax: +1 (617) 973-1339
www.bcg.com

The Stats

Employer Type: Private Company
Chairman: Carl Stern
CEO & President: Hans-Paul Bürkner
2008 Employees: 4,500
  (consulting staff only)
2007 Employees: 3,900
  (consulting staff only)
2007 Revenue: $2.3 billion
2006 Revenue: $1.8 billion
No. of Offices: 66

Practice Areas

Functional Practice Areas
  Corporate Development
  Global Advantage
  Information Technology
  Marketing & Sales/Branding
  Operations/Innovation
  Organization
  Strategy
Industry Practice Areas
  Consumer Goods & Retail
  Energy & Utilities
  Financial Institutions
  Health Care
  Industrial Goods
  Insurance
  Technology, Media &
    Telecommunications

European Locations

Boston (HQ)
Amsterdam • Athens • Barcelona •
Berlin • Brussels • Budapest • Cologne •
Copenhagen • Düsseldorf • Frankfurt •
Hamburg • Helsinki • Kiev • Lisbon •
London • Madrid • Milan • Moscow •
Munich • Oslo • Paris • Prague • Rome •
Stockholm • Stuttgart • Vienna •
Warsaw • Zurich

Pluses

• "Paternal environment"
• Down-to-earth mentality

Minuses

• Don't expect any downtime
• Strongly up or out

Employment Contact

www.bcg.com/careers

THE BUZZ
WHAT CONSULTANTS AT OTHER FIRMS ARE SAYING

• "The brains of the industry"
• "Snobby and formal"
• "More out-of-the-box than others"
• "Super-long working hours"

THE SCOOP

T he Boston Consulting Group (no prizes for guessing where it's based) is a firm on a mission—one that is simple to phrase, yet complicated to realise: "We seek to be agents of change—for our clients, our people, and society broadly." To do that, this preeminent global advisor on business strategy maintains 66 offices in 38 countries around the world, out of which 4,500 consultants advise clients that include several Fortune 500 companies, as well as nonprofit and government organisations. While those consultants cover every industry sector out there, the firm boasts particular expertise in business topics such as branding, globalisation, innovation, risk management and more.

Once upon a time in the Northeast

Back before there was such a thing as a consulting industry, there was a company based in a certain city in Massachusetts, known as The Boston Company. That company had a subsidiary, the Boston Safe Deposit and Trust Company, which, inspired by the example being set by consulting trailblazer Arthur D. Little (of which the firm was a client), tapped ADL consultant Bruce D. Henderson to start its

> ❝ There's an 'explicit CEO policy to reward and incentivise midcareer high performers'. ❞

own autonomous consulting wing. Henderson, a former bible salesman, had attended the nearby Harvard Business School, only to drop out 90 days before graduation to pursue an opportunity with Westinghouse Corporation—a decision that led to him becoming one of the youngest vice presidents in that company's history. Following on from there, Henderson moved to head up Arthur D. Little's management services unit, from whence he was poached in 1963 to set up the unit that would eventually become known as The Boston Consulting Group.

Handed over to its founder by its partners in 1975, BCG has remained private ever since, a fact that has allowed it to operate without worrying about short-term results and pleasing the whims of investors. Perhaps it is for that reason that the firm has kept changes at the top to a minimum, as it has followed the path of expansion from a single employee in a single office into the globe-spanning giant it is today. Since the firm's inception in 1963, it has had just five CEOs. The current holder of the title—and the president of the firm—is Hans-Paul Bürkner, who has been in the role since 2003, having joined the firm in 1981. Longevity isn't the only reason he's at the top of his game, however, as Bürkner boasts qualifications and distinctions that include a diploma from the University

The Boston Consulting Group, Inc

of Bochum, an MA from Yale (which must have made him popular in Boston), a Rhodes Scholarship and a DPhil from Oxford.

Picking up the mantle

So far, Bürkner is continuing along the path laid out for the firm by founder Bruce Henderson, who realised early in the game that the only element distinguishing one business from another was its strategy—a perspective that affected the burgeoning consulting industry every bit as much as it did his own firm. Under Henderson's leadership, business strategy advising grew to be one of the firm's core strengths. At the same time, providing business strategy became an industry in its own right, with the distinguishing factor between consulting firms being the particular strategy they offered. Even as Henderson passed on the reins to future generations, BCG's strategy seemed assured: global expansion, plus a policy of hiring the best and brightest graduates available from top schools around the US and, later, the world.

> ❝ The firm has a commitment to 'pushing the boundaries of thinking'. ❞

Eastern promise

In 2007—Bürkner's fifth year leading the consultancy—BCG opened five new offices. Two are situated in the US, increasing BCG's capabilities and reach in its home country to include the sizeable cities of Minneapolis and Philadelphia. The other three are all situated at the Eastern end of the ever-increasing zone known as Europe. The new office in Kiev marks the firm's first entry into Ukraine, and increases its ability to serve the emerging Commonwealth of Independent States market, as well as the Central and Eastern European area. The Kiev office will work in tandem with the firm's existing international facilities, addressing its specialties in industrial goods and heavy industry, consumer goods, retail, energy, financial services and telecommunications.

The other two new offices, meanwhile, are situated in Abu Dhabi and Dubai—the crossover point from the EU to the EMEA region. The two offices represent a twin-pronged foray into the Middle East. While the two offices will undoubtedly work together to serve the needs of clients in the area, each will house its own capabilities, tailored to the specific needs of their markets. Consultants in the boomtown of Dubai, for example, can expect to see much demand for expertise in real estate, as well as in tourism, multibusiness conglomerates, telecommunications and financial services. In addition, says the firm, "large Dubai businesses are increasingly rolling out their business models abroad and

The Boston Consulting Group, Inc

becoming global competitors." In Abu Dhabi, there is likely to be more of a focus on oil and gas exploration, basic materials, and heavy and light manufacturing, in addition to work with the financial service sector, the government and multibusiness conglomerates. Since Abu Dhabi and Dubai are amongst the fastest growing offices, BCG expects to bring on more consulting staff who will be complemented by experienced professionals culled from both regional and international markets.

In the news and in the trophy cabinet

As a firm whose consultants are regularly sought out for comment by leading news organisations, BCG is no stranger to publicity—and it has garnered much of that by establishing itself as a global employer of choice. Between September 2007 and April 2008, for example, the firm garnered at least four major accolades for its record on treating its employees. The run began in September with the 100 per cent score on the Human Rights Campaign's Corporate Equality Index that earned BCG a citation as a Best Place to Work for gay, lesbian, bisexual and transgender employees. Also that month, *Working Mother* magazine named the firm a Best Company for Working Mothers for the second straight year. Other major awards cropped up in January 2008, when *Fortune* named BCG to its 100 Best Companies to work for list, the third straight year it has been featured close to the top 10 (the firm placed 11th overall in 2008, and topped the best small company category). Most recently, in April 2008, the Great Place to Work Institute recognised the consultancy with a Great Place to Work award for its commitment to professional development.

Individuals at the firm have also received praise. *Consulting* magazine, in 2007, named Senior Partners Steve Gunby and Sharon Marcil to its top-25 consultants of the year, and additionally gave Marcil a special "women leaders" award for client service. Then, for 2008, the publication placed Antonella Mei-Pochtler, also a senior partner, on its annual top-25 list, and will honour retiring BCG Senior Partner Jeanie Duck with its second annual Lifetime Achievement Award.

Making the buzz

But what would a consulting firm be without its legions of consultants conducting surveys and research, and releasing their findings? BCG is no exception, regularly reporting on the fruits of its labours since the earliest days of its inception. Indeed, several BCG-developed tools have been responsible for changing the face of the management consulting industry, including concepts such as the "experience curve", "sustainable growth", "deconstruction of the value chain" and "web 2.0 networks". All of those theories (or buzzwords) have their roots in BCG research, and the firm is still hard at it today, ever seeking to not only define the challenges faced by business leaders, but to surmount them. Ongoing BCG research reflects current globalisation challenges for multinational companies and highlights a new era of "globality", marked by homegrown challenger companies from emerging markets, such as China, India, Brazil or Russia.

One example of the firm's research is the April 2008 global study with the World Association of Personnel Management Association. More than 4,700 executives from 83 countries shared their views on the most pressing human resources challenges, both today and in the future. Managing talent was found to be the most critical challenge worldwide. Managers also rated improving leadership development and managing work/life balance as urgent priorities. The report provides rankings and analyses of 17 HR challenges in seven major regions of the world and suggests specific actions to address those issues.

Institutional strategising

BCG's Strategy Institute is an organisation that looks to the world of academia and collects insights on strategy, which it in turn distils for the furthering of business strategy. In collaboration with the world's leading academic institutions, scientists and scholars, the institute claims to investigate the "modalities of strategic thought"—meaning, how people think about strategy, as opposed to what strategy is or how it's applied in any specific setting.

But the institute does provide examples, via its publications, of how each approach can advance our understanding of the world of strategy. A recent report in the spatial field, for example, is "Center and Periphery", by Bolko von Oetinger, published in June 2007. This piece cites examples that date back to the founding of Protestantism in 1517 to support a theory that those at the "centre" of life in any sphere (but particularly business) are always vulnerable to threats from "the periphery". Prime examples are the companies at the centre of the music industry, who became vulnerable when the iPod appeared and took over the centre, pushing others to the margins. Von Oetinger argues that "every business competes in a dialectical space between the centre and the periphery," and that "what they must realise is that centre and periphery are not theoretical concepts." In other words, successful firms must keep abreast or ahead of developments in their field in order to continue to occupy a position of power.

GETTING HIRED

Only the best

According to insiders, "finding a position with BCG is no joke." It is, however, eminently possible, if you happen to be a top grad, as the firm "makes offers to only the very best-quality people", even if that comes at the expense of the firm's growth. An insider in London points out that "we do not have quotas," which means that "our growth is limited by our ability to find the best people, rather than the commercial side of the business." Now there's some pressure for new hires.

The hiring process generally involves campus recruiting to find top students for entry-level positions. BCG's interview process includes case studies, examples of which can be found on the careers section of its web site. Among the tidbits of advice the firm doles out for dealing with the interview and case studies are to make sure to interact with the interviewers (rather than delivering a monologue on the case) and to take time to reach and deliver conclusions (rather than rushing in to try and impress anyone with the speed at which you can work). The typical case interview will involve the interviewee being asked to formulate a recommendation for a client using data provided by the firm. Typically, cases should take a little under an hour to work through, and interviewers are looking for evidence of sound reasoning that leads to logical, defensible recommendations for clients. Such is the way BCG consultants work in the real world, and evidence of such thinking is what will convince the firm to hire someone to join their ranks.

OUR SURVEY SAYS

Pushing boundaries, taking risks

Some of the things BCG staffers say about their firm are pretty much what you'd expect insiders at one of the biggest consultancies in the world to say. You'd expect, for example, to hear that the firm is "professional". Given that the firm positions itself as a thought leader, you might also expect consultants to praise the firm's commitment to "pushing the boundaries of thinking", and the fact that it "rewards taking risks". What might be less expected to crop up is a word like "forgiving"—evidence of the strength of BCG's commitment to innovation. Not only is successful risk taking rewarded, but failure is not automatically punished, despite claims of an up-or-out promotion mentality by some. Indeed, the consensus on the culture at the firm is perhaps best summed up by a Munich-based consultant, who depicts his workplace as a "supportive, cooperative meritocracy".

Not that it's all roses in the garden, however, as some complain of a "very strong and tangible CEO pressure to generate additional sales". How strong, exactly? Well, according to one source, "He would call individually to follow up."

On the road again

Travel-wise, the amount of miles logged by BCG consultants seems to depend on location—both that of their office and of their client. In Germany, for example "clients are very dispersed," a fact that leads one consultant to consult his air miles statement as he considered his answer. The source tells us he had logged "420,000 miles on Lufthansa within one year", a total gleaned from some "325 flights annually".

In the UK, a source reports that, although probably not up to German levels (mostly because of geographic differences), the need to travel is still a fact of life. "Projects are one-third London, one-third the rest of UK and one-third international," he says. In Germany, about 20 per cent of all projects are international. There is potential for regulating your time on the road, however, as the firm offers the "opportunity to state preferences for heavy or light travel", while those with a heavier schedule can also rest assured that most expenses "can be incurred to allow you what you need for personal reasons while working away", a source explains.

That last point is especially important on longer projects, some of which can last "up to nine months", although it is reportedly "rare for one consultant to be on a project for that long". That assertion is borne out by the average duration of a BCG project, which seems to be between six weeks and five months, according to respondents.

Looking forward to the weekend

In general, BCGers work four days a week in their client's company buildings and one day in their home office. Many staffers feel they are able to exercise some control over work/life balance, and respondents agree that it's "reasonable to expect weekends free"—which offers some comfort after long weeks on the road.

Plenty of beans to count

Fair reward seems to be high on the agenda at BCG, with a Munich-based consultant pointing out that "pay for midlevel consultants seems to be higher than at competitors." The flip side of that coin is that "partners and directors make less," but that's likely deliberate, as an insider tells of an "explicit CEO policy to reward and incentivise midcareer high performers".

There are even some benefits for those who leave the firm, as "BCG is highly supportive" when it comes to consultants "finding their next job". That goes for nonpartners as well, for despite the "strictly and permanently up-or-ou" "ulture, where "even partners have to leave after a nine-month grace period if th   t sell enough," a source in London claims that "'out' is a mutual decision" between the consultant and the firm, adding that "it is not stigmatised."

For those who are successful, the benefits are clear to see: a career with a heavy-hitter in the industry, clear progression prospects and, of course, buckets of cash. A source in Germany claims, quaintly, that "bonuses in 2007 were higher than 100 per cent of base salary." Meanwhile, in Sweden, a Stockholmer tells us the firm "supplements the government maximum level, so you actually get 80 per cent of your pay" as bonus.

Where in the world ...

Office spaces across the continent earn generally high praise, often along nationalistic lines. For example, a German respondent claims that "Munich and Berlin are the most favourite spots within BCG—so popular, that after May there are no more recruiting slots there," while a source in Sweden claims that the "BCG office in Stockholm is objectively a top-three BCG office, and a top office in Sweden." A consultant in London, however, voices some dissatisfaction with his surroundings, and even then with the roundabout admission that "moving to better offices and choice of workspace is high on partners' agenda, and there's company involvement in the decision."

Lending a helping hand

BCG is quite committed to the community and its surrounding environment. According to a London source, BCG provides "pro bono consulting for multinational and local organisations, national thought leaders and policy-makers, and has strong business-community links". The firm also works closely with the World Food Programme. □

BAIN & COMPANY

131 Dartmouth Street
Boston, Massachusetts 02116
United States
Phone: +1 (617) 572-2000
Fax: +1 (617) 572-2427
www.bain.com

The Stats

Employer Type: Private Company
Chairman: Orit Gadiesh
Managing Director: Steve Ellis
2008 Employees: 4,300
2007 Employees: 3,700
No. of Offices: 39

Practice Areas

Change Management
Corporate Renewal
Corporate Strategy
Cost & Supply Chain Management
Growth Strategy
IT
Mergers & Acquisitions
Organization
Performance Improvement
Private Equity

European Locations

Boston (HQ)
Amsterdam • Brussels • Copenhagen •
Düsseldorf • Frankfurt • Helsinki • Kiev •
London • Madrid • Milan • Moscow •
Munich • Paris • Rome • Stockholm •
Zurich

Pluses

- Learning curve remains steep
- "Focus on individual dvelopment"
- "Trainings are best-in-class"
- "Results-focussed, 'no BS' attitude"

Minuses

- "Flexibility sometimes fires back on you"
- "Partners can be a bit protective of clients"
- Conservative promotion process
- "Brand not as good as competitors' outside the US"

Employment Contact

www.joinbain.com

THE BUZZ
WHAT CONSULTANTS AT OTHER FIRMS ARE SAYING

- "Fun to work for"
- "Lacking sector expertise"
- "Fancy, sleek, money-driven"
- "Intellectual front-runners, social laggers"

THE SCOOP

B ain began as a small, home-based startup in 1973, launched by a group of former Boston Consulting Group consultants led by Bill Bain. From its inception, the firm took pride in doing things differently, such as getting new clients through word-of-mouth referrals and basing its fees on the financial results it achieved for the client. Today, the firm still claims to be focussed on the idea that consultants should deliver "results, not reports" to its clients. From its modest roots, Bain has grown to become one of the most prestigious strategy consultancies in the world. Today, it is headquartered in Boston and employs over 4,300 consultants in 26 different countries.

The largest portion of Bain's clients—about 50 per cent—are among the Global 2000 companies. Aside from major blue-chip firms, it also counts medium-sized businesses, private equity firms, governments and nonprofit organisations among its clients. Its expertise spans practically every industry sector, including consumer products, financial services, energy and utilities, health care, industrial products, media and technology. Bain's business is divided into 10 practice areas: change management, corporate renewal, corporate strategy, cost and supply chain management, growth strategy, IT, mergers and acquisitions, organisation, performance improvement and private equity.

European flavour

Bain's European network began with a single London office established in 1979. It has since built up a solid presence in the region, with a larger percentage of its business coming from the continent than from North America or Asia. In the UK, Bain counts almost half of the FTSE 100 companies as clients, while its clients elsewhere in Europe are a mix of multinational firms and global companies with local operations. The consultancy maintains offices in Amsterdam, Brussels, Copenhagen, Düsseldorf, Frankfurt, Helsinki, Kiev, London, Madrid, Milan, Moscow, Munich, Paris, Rome, Stockholm and Zurich.

Covering new ground

Though Bain has a thriving business in Europe and the Americas, it's not satisfied to leave the rest of the globe untapped. Like its consulting peers, Bain has been targeting booming areas like India and the Middle East for business. Unlike its competitors, however, the firm is specifically aiming for strategy work, rather than limiting its Indian offerings to outsourcing. Bain has a team of over 100 in New Delhi and Mumbai, established in 2006, but it has been involved in India for the past decade through its office in Singapore. The firm's clients span a variety of industries in the country, including private equity, industrial products and services, fast-moving consumer goods, telecoms and technology.

With an eye on the lucrative Middle Eastern market, Bain has established a client base of government bodies, private and public companies, investment companies and international groups. In 2005, it set up a location in Dubai, which became an official office in 2007. The Dubai outpost serves clients in Egypt and Gulf Cooperation Council countries.

Mastering mergers

Bain has also established itself as a leader in European private equity consulting. In 1994, it became the first consultancy to pioneer a private equity consulting practice, which is today four times larger than its next-closest competitor. Leveraging this size advantage, Bain has taken part in almost 50 per cent of Europe's private equity transactions over $200 million since 1997. More than 300 consultants currently work in the practice, from offices in North America, the Middle East, Asia, Europe and Australia. Private equity clients call on Bain for fund strategy, sector screening, deal generation, value creation, due diligence and exit planning.

Savvy investments

Bain boosted its own money-making capabilities in 1984, when it launched Bain Capital, a industry-leading spin-off created to invest in the firm's own clients. Bain Capital boasts over $78 billion in assets under management and has completed over 240 equity investments. The company and its affiliates—some geographic, such as Bain Capital Asia and Bain Capital Europe, and some specialised, such as Bain Capital Ventures (venture capital) and Sankaty Advisors (credit obligations)—now operate in select cities in Europe, the US and Asia, and are completely separate from Bain & Company.

Notable names

It's not unusual for Bain alumni to hold prime positions at top global corporations. In the US, former Bainies include Meg Whitman, former CEO of auction giant eBay and Ken Chenault, chairman and CEO of American Express. In Europe, Bain was once home to AVIS Europe CEO Murray Hennessy, Mike White, chairman and CEO of PepsiCo International, Prudential Assurance CEO Nick Prettejohn, CEO of FT Group Rona Fairhead, Cinven Director Hugh Langmuir, Ducati President Federico Minoli, Innocent co-founder John Wright, and CEO of TA Triumph-Adler AG, Dietmar Scheiter. And in July 2007, Senior Partner Robin Buchanan stepped up to the plate as the new dean of London Business School.

Bain also counts a few notable leaders among its own ranks. Orit Gadiesh, the firm's chairman since 1993, has been named to *Forbes'* annual list of The 100 Most Powerful Women each year from 2004 to 2007. Gadiesh, a Harvard grad and former Israeli soldier, is considered a management and strategy expert who also serves on the board of several academic institutions and the World Economic Forum Foundation. *Consulting* magazine presented Gadiesh with a Lifetime Achievement Award in November 2007. Steve Ellis, managing director since 2005, is a Stanford MBA who co-founded a Silicon Valley consultancy called Focus, Inc., before joining Bain in 1993. Chris Zook, one of the firm's star partners, leads the global strategy practice and the Bain Growth Project from his base in Amsterdam. As a

> " There is always an element of fun in everyone's approach to work and life. "

recognised management guru, Zook has been ranked among the world's top-25 consultants by *Consulting* magazine, and is a best-selling author. His most popular titles are *Profit from the Core* and *Beyond the Core*, published in 2001 and 2004, respectively, and *Unstoppable: Finding Hidden Assets to Renew the Core and Fuel Profitable Growth*, published in 2007, which discusses ways companies can build sustainable growth by taking advantage of undervalued, unrecognised or underutilised assets. Gadiesh, Ellis and Zook all regularly contribute their insights in publications such as the *Financial Times*, *Harvard Business Review* and *Investor's Business Daily*.

Consultants' choice

Bain is apparently a likable place to work, judging by the number of awards it's been given for being a top employer. In 2008, the Great Place to Work Institute named Bain the No. 1 best workplace in Spain. One year earlier, the Paris office took the top spot among the Top 100 Best Workplaces in France in the Great Places to Work Institute survey, as published in the *Financial Times*. Its offices in the UK and Germany have also made the list of the 100 Best Workplaces in Europe in recent years. And in *Consulting* magazine's 2007 Best Firms to Work For survey, Bain claimed the top spot, making the list for the fourth year in a row. The firm ranked No. 1 in six categories—compensation, work/life balance, career development, job experience, firm leadership and firm culture.

Read and respected

Bain consultants keep the firm's name in the business news with loads of published articles, research papers and books. In 2008, Chairman Gadiesh and Hugh MacArthur, leader of the firm's global private equity practice, co-authored *Memo to the CEO: Lessons from Private Equity Any Company Can Use*. The book posits that the most successful private equity masters follow a basic set of disciplines any senior executive can use to achieve successful results in his company. Also in 2008, consultants Mark Gottfredson and Steve Shaubert wrote *Breakthrough Imperative*, which "cracks the code on how the best business leaders get outstanding results from their organisations".

Insiders also contribute to *Bain Briefs*, the firm's self-published newsletters that focus on economic trends and current issues in global business. A January 2008 newsletter discussed the key issues in India's pharmaceutical industry and its future offshoring potential, and another analysed the trend of sustainability as a platform for growth.

Socially conscious

The firm devotes significant resources to its surrounding communities. Typically, Bain consultants apply their skills to pro bono consulting projects. For example, the London office has done major projects with Business Action on Homelessness, Save the Children UK and the Private Equity Foundation, among others. Staffers in Germany have recently supported the World Heart Federation and the Schwab Foundation for Social Entrepreneurship, while Stockholm consultants work with the World Childhood Foundation. Bain also looks for ways to pair its consultants with charity executives and social entrepreneurs for one-on-one mentoring and advice, and some individuals elect to participate in an externship with a charity.

Bain offices also give generously of their time. Bain Paris works with primary schools in underprivileged areas, and in London, consultants regularly volunteer to read with and mentor children in schools. The German offices organise "action days", where volunteers participate in group projects that benefit their cities.

GETTING HIRED

Seeking bright Bainies

Bain looks to "top European and US schools" when seeking the next crop of candidates. Undergraduate recruits come from the top universities across Europe and the US, and have backgrounds ranging from history to philosophy to economics. The firm hosts recruiting events all over the continent: in the Netherlands at Erasmus University and the University of Amsterdam; in Belgium at Gent Management School; Instituto de Empresa in Spain; IMD in Switzerland; in France, INSEAD, École Polytechnique and École des Mines; Copenhagen Business School, and in the UK,

London School of Economics, London Business School, Oxford and Cambridge—to name a few. Bain's web site keeps an updated searchable list of recruiting events for every school on its schedule. However, the firm also welcomes applications from students at universities not on the usual target list. The firm notes that it also hires recruits from top PhD and law schools. An advanced degree isn't required to join Bain—it simply wants to hire the cream of the crop in their chosen field of study.

Straight-shooter interviews

Competition to get in the door is notoriously tough, so Bain can be quite choosy when it comes to granting an interview. Insiders describe the interview process as a "smooth but rather drawn-out" experience. It generally involves "two rounds of interviews", consisting of "two to three interviews each". Interviews are "mostly case-based", with "some more formal and some less heavy". The firm "almost always gives numerical cases", because it is "checking

> " Our firm has the opinion that it is important to have 'complete' consultants. "

math skills", and sources say there are "no tricky questions on personality". The rest of the interviews are essentially "informal testing of team skills, leadership and cultural fit". A meeting with a manager usually kicks off the process, then for the second round, a candidate meets with three senior managers or partners. Each interview is "around 40 minutes long" and breaks down thusly: "five minutes to cover CV questions, 25 to 30 minutes to go over a business situation and 5 to 10 minutes for Q&A". Candidates may also be asked to "explain why you chose consulting and why Bain," and to "provide your GMAT score." Often, candidates will "find out the same day" whether they are hired.

During the case portion of the interview, "people are really helpful." One insider notes, "They don't try to embarrass you or make you have a hard time. Rather, they try to help you out and even make some calculations with you." After the case, candidates "have time to ask a couple of questions" on whatever topic they choose. To get an idea of specific questions that might be asked, applicants should "go to www.joinbain.com, select the office where you want to apply and pay special attention to the process explained there." A consultant recalls an example: "The interviewer provided some materials detailing the costs and revenue of a car rental company. Picking through the materials and with additional inputs from the interviewer, I was asked to identify the key actions the company could take to boost profitability." Normally, cases do not involve "crazy, out-of-the-box questions or brainteasers". Instead, Bain presents "real cases, based on real problems at real companies", and interviewers typically "draw on their own experiences".

Real life starts now

An internship at Bain is an "opportunity to see the real life of a consultant". Interns are treated "as full case team members", and are "put in front of the client from day one". Sources report that this "extremely positive experience" is a "great opportunity to get to know the firm and its culture and people". It's also a useful way to "pressure test what it is like working as a consultant". A former intern recalls, "I was given real case work to do on an actual client, and I interfaced with the client quite a bit. I also met lots of people at the firm via social events." We're told that most participants leave Bain's internship programme "happy to accept a full-time offer".

OUR SURVEY SAYS

Playing on the same team

At Bain, "the frat house stereotype just doesn't hold up." A consultant explains, "There are abundant opportunities to socialise and get to know the people you work with, but never any pressure to participate beyond your own interest." The firm's culture is "incredibly welcoming and friendly", filled with "helpful people at all levels". Staffers "don't take themselves too seriously", and "there is always an element of fun in everyone's approach to work and life." Despite Bain's large global network, it has a "strong entrepreneurial undercurrent", with many alumni having left to set up their own businesses. Insiders feel that Bain's is a "culture based on respect and desire to make a real impact on the client". Among consultants, "the drive for success is absolutely phenomenal," and everyone "helps each other out"— there is "very much a one-firm attitude". In the firm's "very informal and enjoyable" environment, "you get to know everyone very well."

That hardworking environment is tempered by a fun-loving spirit, we're told. One insider notes, "Hardly a meeting goes by without a good laugh." There are "lots of out-of-office events" to boot, so there is "always someone meeting to play sports, go the cinema, or go out for a drink or dance". One of the firm's most revered events is the annual Bain Soccer World Cup, in which "each office submits teams to compete in a football tournament." The tournament is "competitive, and participants take it seriously". One consultant remarks, "Since this is a completely voluntary event, it shows how much people identify themselves with the company." And although Bainees might be competitive on the field, in the office, "teams are cooperative." The culture is "very supportive" and "based on meritocracy", but it's "not at all hierarchical", sources say, adding that it's a company of "very little office politics".

Keeping tabs on balance

Bain is reportedly "very good about giving you the flexibility to organise your time so that you can pursue other interests". It makes "big efforts to track hours each week" in order to "make the balance sustainable". To that end, Bain issues weekly "surveys to see if we are satisfied with our work/life balance". Weekend work is "highly unusual", we're told, and working from home is possible in certain cases. In a firm that places "no value on face time", there is "definitely no expectation to stay at the office any later than you need to". Colleagues are generally "very accommodating of arrangements that are in place, provided that you

> " The firm 'invests a huge amount in its people'. "

are open about them at the start of the case". Sources say that achieving work/life balance can be "more difficult on private equity projects", but more often than not, "you are given the opportunity to plan your work in advance so you can also do other things." A consultant explains, "Our firm has the opinion that it is important to have 'complete' consultants. That means having people who are motivated, professional and highly qualified, and who enjoy giving their best at work, but without missing out on the other things that life offers."

The number of hours worked per week varies by consultant, but most average somewhere in the range of 60 to 65. Hourly demands "could always be better, but relative to peers at other firms, Bain always comes out on top". According to one insider, "There have been concerted efforts to reduce working hours and keep them under control. And when people are 'on the beach', they are not expected to be in the office at all." A typical project runs somewhere between three and six months, with a "firm average of four months", and time that one is not assigned to a client is "generally used to do client development work".

Custom travel

Consultants appreciate that travel is "only on an as-needed basis". A contact says, "We go to the client whenever there is a need to, but never just for the sake of being there." The firm's "relatively low level of travel is a strong contributor to the great atmosphere". "People are around more, so colleagues get to know each other better," a source notes. Higher-ups in the London office believe that "consultants should be as office-based as possible," so staffing at home is a "priority, unless the consultant prefers to be abroad". According to one respondent, "If you like travelling, Bain is the best place to be." Some consultants "do travel quite a lot", but the firm "always tries to adapt the company or project requirements to personal situations or needs".

And, of course, travel demands depend upon the particular office. For those based in Munich, for example, "being at the client site most days of the week is part of the job." In Amsterdam, "travel is very manageable, because the Netherlands is a small country," and the Brussels office is "quite international, so there are a lot of cases abroad". But regardless of which office you work from, "the firm takes preferences into account," and Bainees "very seldom camp at the client site".

Location, location, location

As these consultants often find themselves based in their home office, they have much to say on their office space. Bain's London office is in a "great location in the West End", but "space is somewhat limited." The offices, although "perfectly functional", are beginning to feel "quite cramped" as the firm expands. A contact remarks, "We're outgrowing our current space rather quickly." And the office "could do with more meeting rooms for impromptu internal meetings". The "open-office plan encourages meeting new people", and there is "no hot-desking", so consultants "at all levels have their own desks".

Opinions of the facility in Madrid are high: "Our Madrid office is clearly top notch. It is located in one of the most famous office buildings in Madrid. Furniture and IT systems are brand new and excellent. Designers clearly devoted much attention to ergonomics and natural light. There's also a kitchen with plenty of free food." The Stockholm crew works from "one of the best spots in the city", on top of the "No. 1 department store in Stockholm". In Munich, "office locations are poor," but "equipment is state-of-the-art," and the offices themselves are "the best in town". Bain's Brussels office is in a "top location", and offers "great facilities, and free food and drink."

The perks just keep on coming

Bain "strives to always be competitive with other top-tier firms" when it comes to compensation and, in fact, most consultants report high levels of satisfaction with their pay cheques. They tell us that compensation is "competitive for consulting", but "below financial professions demanding a somewhat similar skill set". The good news is that "compensation rises very quickly as you are promoted through the ranks," and when you hit manager level, there are "opportunities to invest in private equity clients' funds". There is also profit sharing and 401(k) contributions, and, in some locations, consultants receive "office performance bonuses". Bain requires consultants to pay for their own pensions, but it does cover health insurance.

The firm also offers "great opportunities to transfer to other offices for six to 12 months". This is a much raved about and utilised perk, as "80 per cent of associate consultants transfer to another office within their first three years"—the programme "works really well", respondents say. A consultant explains, "There is no hassle where you have to get recommended or have to know someone at the office you're going to. You just sign up, list one or two places you would like to go, and nine times out of 10, you get your first choice." In other benefits, consultants in London are treated to "an annual three-day summer off-site in Southern Europe," often in an "exotic destination", and "a Christmas ball for employees and guests". In that office, there is "free beer on Fridays", in addition to "regular firmwide social events" and "case team and peer group dinners". Consultants there also have the luxury of an "in-house doctor", as well as "lifestyle services" such as "massage, beautician and personal training". In other locations, consultants get "attractive car deals" and "subsidised gym memberships". Bain offers "MBA sponsorship" and also "supports language lessons" for those who need them. For new parents, some offices grant "six months' maternity leave, with the option to take an additional six months of unpaid leave", and "two weeks' paternity leave".

High-level interaction

We're told that junior consultants "can easily interact with partners and managers", and that partners make a "strong effort to increase connections with junior staff". One consultant shares, "I am regularly asked to go for an individual coffee with the lead partner, simply to chat about life and work, not just the case." To encourage communication between the ranks, Bain has "separate associate consultant/consultant and manager clusters", which are "opportunities to communicate to the higher levels any topic regarding improvement, agreement, congratulations or problems". At Bain, "anything can be translated to the superior level and will be taken into consideration," a source comments. Supervisors "provide excellent guidance and give consultants the opportunity to run with tasks".

In addition, superiors "include junior [members] as much as possible in interactions with clients' top-level management, whenever it adds value to the case". Some junior consultants express a desire for more client interaction, though, feeling as though "partners and managers engage with top-level management, but there is less top-level interaction for lower levels." Others say partners "could occasionally be better at passing knowledge down to the team, rather than the team having to search for the knowledge afresh". But many consultants speak of "very good relationships with partners and managers", and claim they "regularly interact with C-level client executives, including CEOs".

Pack your bags, we're going training!

Training is "both informal and formal" at Bain. The firm has "very good programmes across all levels", and pays "great attention to global trainings".

These off-site events often take place in "exotic locations", we're told, such as Mexico and Thailand—"much better than [competitors], which train in places like the Czech Republic and Germany". These "unforgettable" trainings can be "quite intense", but always "leave room for a lot of fun with colleagues". Overall, insiders deem training "absolutely exceptional".

In addition to the off-site event, the firm offers everything from "ad hoc professional development chats with mentors and managers, to weeklong formal sessions for entire peer groups". One consultant remarks, "I can't say enough about how impressed I have been with the company's performance in this dimension." As employees advance through the ranks, "you keep having international trainings for each of the levels you reach." And there is "continuous unofficial training on a daily basis" for everyone. Almost unanimously, Bainees agree that their firm "invests a huge amount in its people".

Promotion is in your hands

We're told that Bain is "a true meritocracy". Consultants who are ready "will be promoted", because there is no minimum time period required" at each level. The average time from new consultant to manager is "probably about three years", but it "depends entirely and solely on individual performance"—some people "may take up to four years" before advancing. Promotion to partner is on a different time line, though, because "other skills are required." There is "no up-or-out policy", an insider explains, since Bain consultants are "measured against fixed standards, not our peers". As such, there is "no incentive for peer group competition". Consultants who are underperforming have a "six-month advice period". Those who do not reach expectations in that time "will be asked to leave". On the flip side, "when you are a top performer, you advance very quickly at Bain."

Staffers appreciate that the firm's "review process is transparent", and "expectations are clear at each stage"—feedback is "near constant". One source remarks, "Bain offers a clear career path. I can see exactly how I could get to partner if I wanted to."

Slowly but surely

The firm "has come a long way on women's diversity"—today, "over half of new starters are women." However, it "needs more of these women to rise to the top ranks", as "it is completely ludicrous how few female partners there are." Women are "very much respected" and Bain is "receptive", but insiders say the problem is that "too few women apply." For instance, the number of women in the Brussels office is "quite limited", at about 25 per cent. That said, "a lot of actions are being done to change this."

Bain has "an active women's group and global women's conference", as well as "efforts underway to recruit women". One consultant remarks, "Once every two years, there is a [global] women's meeting for a couple of days to discuss worries of women in the office." Bain also is "working on the issue" by "making an increasing effort to be flexible toward women in an already very flexible environment". According to one respondent, "There are a number of women who have returned to Bain, or joined Bain, after having children, and most are extremely successful." The firm is "paying special attention to this topic", insiders say, and many observe that the overall men-to-women ratio is "shifting slowly, and we will surely see more female representation throughout the firm".

Embracing all

Staffers report that the London office is "very ethnically diverse and becoming more so all the time". At times, it can even feel like the firm is "being too obsessed with minorities". Bain has "an active minorities group and global minorities conference", and is making "efforts to recruit more minorities". It "feels like there is no bias whatsoever", as there is a "very diverse range of nationalities in the London office". In Brussels, though, "minorities are not represented," but this is not reflective of the firm as a whole, which "tries to promote openness to all backgrounds" and believes there is "absolutely no difference between minorities and majorities". In fact, "ethnicity is not even considered in hiring."

Gays, lesbians, bisexuals and transgender individuals are "well accepted by the company", and there is "absolutely no difference in the way they are treated". The firm "actively supports" GLBTs through a "sophisticated programme that even non-GLBTs can join". In its European offices, Bain has "a number of people who are openly out".

Endless opportunities to help

The consultancy supports "a variety of community involvement programmes". It "has everything, from pro bono projects to local community work to office green drives". The Bain Cares initiative, "a large programme involving 100-plus people who regularly give their time to help the community", covers a "wide range of programmes". And twice a year, the firm holds a "community impact day", during which all employees participate in some form of community work. Bain supports Prince's Trust, Community Action Network, Supporting Social Entrepreneurs and Habitat for Humanity, to name a few. There's also the "opportunity for individuals to identify specific causes that they are passionate about and get Bain support to pursue them further". One consultant, for example, "helped design a series of modules on business awareness that are now being taught to 14- to 16-year-olds in London schools". Offices and individuals, we're told, have the freedom to "contribute to the community in their own way". □

BOOZ & COMPANY

7 Savoy Court, Strand
London WC2R 0JP
United Kingdom
Phone: +44 (0)207 393 3333
Fax: +44 (0)207 393 0025

Lenbachplatz 3
Munich 80333
Germany
Phone: +49 (0)89 5452 50
Fax: +49 (0)89 5452 5500
www.booz.com

The Stats

Employer Type: Private Company
CEO: Shumeet Banerji
Chairman: Joe Saddi
2008 Employees: 3,300+
2008 Sales: $4.8 billion
  (includes former combined operations
  with Booz Allen Hamilton)
No. of Offices: 57

Practice Areas

Corporate Finance • Information
Technology • Mergers & Restructuring •
Operations & Logistics • Organization &
Change • Product & Service Innovation •
Public Sector Mission Effectiveness
(outside the US only) • Sales &
Marketing • Strategy & Leadership

Employment Contact

www.booz.com/global/home/join_us

European Locations

Amsterdam • Berlin • Copenhagen •
Dublin • Düsseldorf • Frankfurt •
Helsinki • London • Madrid • Milan •
Moscow • Munich • Oslo • Paris •
Rome • Stockholm • Stuttgart • Vienna •
Warsaw • Zurich

Pluses

• "They went out of their way to show
  me that I could be successful and a
  mother too"
• Meritocratic culture
• "International exposure"
• Entrepreneurial and intellectual
  environment

Minuses

• Some confusion in the face of recent
  reorganisation
• "Some long-winded internal processes"
• Can be "disorganised at times"
• "Very little flexibility once you are into
  a project"

THE BUZZ
WHAT CONSULTANTS AT OTHER FIRMS ARE SAYING

• "Punch above their true weight"
• "Modern classic with moderate
  presence"
• "Diversity, family-oriented"
• "All things to all men, master of few"

THE SCOOP

B ooz & Company is both the oldest and the newest face on the management consulting block. Founded in 1914 in Chicago, the firm is the oldest management consultancy still practising today, but its present iteration was created as recently as May 2008, when the commercial wing of Booz Allen Hamilton (now known as Booz & Company) was split off from the US government wing, which will continue to trade under the Booz Allen Hamilton name. The split—which at the time of writing has still to meet with shareholder and regulatory approval in order to be made permanent—came about when private equity firm Carlyle Group bought out the US government wing of Booz Allen Hamilton's business. Until the deal is ratified (which is expected to occur in mid- to late 2008), Booz & Company will remain a subsidiary of Booz Allen Hamilton. Post-ratification, the firm will become an independent entity, although the nature of the business it conducts is unlikely to change; it will continue to specialise in management consulting for businesses, government ministries (outside the US) and other agencies.

A clean break

Compared to Booz Allen Hamilton prior to the split, the new concern certainly bears more of a resemblance to the original vision of the company created by Edwin Booz back in 1914, when he set out to find solutions to help businesses that were within easy reach of his native Chicago. Known then as The Business Research Service, Booz toiled away alone for a number of years, before picking up partners along the way— Allen and Hamilton—who would add their names to his, while creating one of the best-known consultancies in the world. As the years rolled on, the consultancy increased in capabilities as well as geographic scope, opening an office in Zurich, its first outside the US, in 1957. Others would soon follow, and by the end of the 20th century, the firm could boast of a presence on every inhabited continent on the planet.

As the firm grew, it developed a reputation as a leading provider of consulting services for government agencies, both inside and outside the US, and it was this side of the business that led to the decision to split the firm. According to a May 2008 *Washington Post* article, there was a "longstanding, and often tense, internal debate over the company's structure" because of the inability to integrate the government and commercial practices effectively. Part of that inability, the article suggests, stemmed from differences in how the two sides of the business operated (small teams and short assignments for corporate clients versus one manager for hundreds of consultants on US government contracts that could stretch on for months or years), as well as difficulties over gaining security clearance for government work. According to Booz Allen Hamilton CEO Ralph Shrader, splitting the businesses made sense as they "have really grown up under completely different models". As with most things business-related, however, the major catalyst for the split was cold, hard cash, coming only after the Carlyle Group paid $2.54 billion for the US government side of the firm.

The heart of the matter

The final word on what Booz & Company is today is perhaps best introduced by what it isn't. It isn't a provider of services to the US government (that's Booz Allen Hamilton). It isn't a firm with 21,000 consultants (that was the total staff prior to the split for both sides of the business). It is, however, a 3,300-person strong organisation, with 57 offices operating in more than 30 countries, and capabilities in corporate finance, IT, mergers and restructuring, operations and logistics, organisation and change, product and service innovation, sales and marketing, public-sector mission effectiveness (outside the US only), and strategy and leadership. All of that is directed at helping clients that range from the likes of Deutsche Post and Wolters Kluwer to government departments in (potentially) any country outside the US. How closely, if at all, the firm will work with Booz Allen Hamilton remains to be seen.

> “ Managers face 'high expectations to train juniors adequately'. ”

Heading up Booz & Company is former managing director of Booz Allen Hamilton's European business, Shumeet Banerji. A former faculty member at the University of Chicago Graduate School of Business, he joined Booz's Chicago office in 1992, and has worked in various capacities at the firm, serving both public- and private-sector clients during stints in the US, Asia and Europe. Banerji, who received his PhD from the Kellogg Graduate School of Management at Northwestern University, will be based in London in his role as CEO.

Flying high

Given that the two sides of the business were operating almost as separate entities prior to the split, it's not too difficult to put a finger on the kinds of projects the commercial side was working on, and is likely to continue to produce in future—especially outside the US. In 2006, for example, the firm provided research and support on a European Commission project known as Single European Sky—an attempt to boost European air traffic management by changing its focus from national boundaries to flight patterns. The ongoing project is aimed at reducing costs and increasing the efficiency with which blocks of airspace can be used. Currently, European airspace is divided by national border, but the project proposes to "knock down" those borders and create a more efficient, manageable system of dividing the space.

Streamlining the (legal) drug trade

The consultancy has also done work for pharmaceutical giant Pfizer. Pfizer approached Booz seeking a solution to a problem it was experiencing with drug distribution in Europe. With drug prices controlled at national levels throughout the continent, it was profitable for some wholesalers to purchase medications in one EU country, and then sell them in another EU country at a higher price. The problem with the system was that there was potential for the supply chain to be infiltrated with counterfeit medications, especially where pharmacies were purchasing from wholesalers and intermediaries, rather than direct from the manufacturers. Working together, Pfizer and Booz devised a distribution model that saw the firm provide a direct-to-pharmacy model—a move that cut the middleman out of ownership or possession of the pharmaceuticals, but still allowed those firms to act as paid-for-service intermediaries in the sale of the drugs. The model—which was rolled out in the UK early in 2007—allowed Pfizer to take great steps toward securing its supply chain, and also increased its direct relationships with pharmacies.

Settle back with some Booz for company

When they're not off reconfiguring the way the world works, Booz's staff find other ways to keep busy—like producing books and reports on the state of various industries. Recent publications include Partner Christopher Vollmer's book *Always On: Advertising, Marketing, and Media in an Era of Consumer Control*, which argues that new methods of marketing will be required to keep up with the ever-evolving digital age. That title was published in early 2008, along with a book by Booz Partners Kaj Grichnik and Conrad Winkler. Titled *Make or Break: How Manufacturers Can Leap from Decline to Revitalization*, the book is as close to the cutting edge as Vollmer's, investigating the strategies that are creating success for manufacturers in the modern manufacturing era.

Among the recent reports and white papers by the firm's consultants is March 2008's "The Bounty of Biofuels—Perception Versus Reality", by Senior Partners Bill Jackson and Eric Spiegel, Partner Leslie Moeller and Senior Associate Praneet Gupta. As the title suggests, the authors are concerned with clearing up common misconceptions over biofuels, while also discussing likely outcomes for the industry. Meanwhile, Booz also publishes a quarterly magazine called *strategy + business*. Billed as the bridge "between theory and practice in contemporary global business", the publication features journalists, academics, consultants and corporate strategists, who all weigh in on a variety of high-profile business topics and help the firm maintain its "thought leadership" role.

Bubbly for Booz

One of the most difficult decisions the new Booz & Company and Booz Allen Hamilton consultancies face is how to split the family silverware following the separation. Among the treasured mementoes to be squabbled over are the various trophies for good employment practices that adorn the sideboards in Booz Allen Hamilton's headquarters in McLean, Virginia. In January 2008, for example, the firm was recognised for the fourth consecutive year on *Fortune*'s 100 Best Companies to Work For; it also appeared on *BusinessWeek*'s Best Places to Launch a Career list in 2007. A final set of baubles to fight over, meanwhile, are the nine consecutive Employer of Choice Awards from *Working Mother* magazine, up to and including 2007's award, which cited the firm for its commitment to helping working mothers, including its child care programmes and availability of paid leave.

GETTING HIRED

Making an impact

Booz performs a "tough screening based on grades, letter and international experience". Those who make the initial cut have anywhere between "four and 10 interviews", insiders say. All rounds involve "case questions as well as personal suitability questions". During first-round interviews, a consultant explains, "candidates advance if at least two interviewers definitely agree." In the second and third rounds, which are normally conducted with partners and principals, "everyone needs to agree" in order for a candidate to advance. Normally, "you get contacted within a day or two with the result." A staffer remarks that during the course of the hiring process, interviewers demonstrate "uncomplicated and unpretentious personalities".

Sources tell us interviewers make decisions based on "performance on the case, as well as personal impact". In addition to cases, candidates should expect to field "general questions on experience" based on their CV, and interviewers may also want to hear about "your interest in the firm". Respondents report that most interviews are about an hour in length, "each consisting of two parts, so 30 minutes with one person and 30 minutes with another". According to one, "There is generally only one case study or market sizing question per 30-minute interview." Candidates may be asked to perform "a typical cost reduction/profitability analysis" or answer questions like, "How many cars do you need to operate the London Tube? What would you do to solve the UK's pension problem? What is the mobile penetration rate in Egypt?"

Where to find 'em

Insiders say Booz recruits "all over". Associate-level candidates come from "top MBA schools in the US and Europe", including INSEAD, London Business School, Harvard Business School and Kellogg. Consultant hires are pulled from top local universities—for instance, "mostly from Oxford and Cambridge" in the UK, but the firm does "accept applications from other [local] schools". Elsewhere on the continent, the firm looks to "all top German universities and business schools, in addition to multiple top schools in the Netherlands".

Find out what it's really all about

An internship at Booz is a "great international" experience through which interns "learn tons of stuff." Indeed, former interns insist it is a "fantastic way to sample consulting as a career". Interns, who are "treated like new joiners, get great exposure to real casework and real teams", and have a chance to make a "real impact". One source recalls, "I worked on two projects, and my preferences were taken into account. I wanted to work abroad, and did so on one project." Partners were "very welcoming" of new interns, and "flexible in accommodating their needs". According to a colleague, an internship at Booz is "absolutely mind-blowing". Impressed by the firm's "culture, content and colleagues," many former interns say they chose to stay on full time, "despite offers from other top-tier consulting firms, including McKinsey".

OUR SURVEY SAYS

On work and play

In describing the Booz culture, insiders describe their colleagues as "young and ambitious". There is an "atmosphere of friendship and real teamwork", which creates "enthusiasm and intellectual eagerness". In this reportedly "collegial" environment, "loners are doomed to fail." The vibe is "very open and personal", with "doors always open for employee concerns". Indeed, a consultant says, there is "no sign of any elbow culture". The combination of "very intelligent but diverse people" makes the culture "fun and friendly". As one effusive source puts it, Booz has "the greatest parties and the funniest partners".

And while staffers are sure to make time for fun and frivolity, they also "focus on delivering value to clients". The firm places value on striking a "balance between relationship skills and analytic prowess", we're told. Another feature of this hardworking environment is its entrepreneurial side; as a consultant explains, "Booz's culture is one that encourages you to be proactive in your career development. Taking your career in your own hands is the best way to achieve your goals."

Get out your time sheets

Not unlike its competitors, hours at Booz are "unpredictable and can be long". Most consultants work 50 to 65 hours a week, on average, but "there are projects that demand more hours and others less." Some nights end at 6:30pm, whereas others require staying until the "early hours of the morning". Project length also "varies a lot", with an average of about two to three months. One consultant remarks, "This is a tough industry, so we know we have to work hard. It is very manageable, though." And, a colleague explains, the long hours are "related to the strategic nature of the projects" Booz takes on. Some recent "high staff turnover" can make matters worse, several sources note. Fortunately, the firm places "emphasis on quality of work, not volume", so face time is limited.

That said, some respondents argue that the "excessive demands on time" can make it "difficult to achieve a healthy work/life balance". The firm does take some initiative in trying to minimise the effects of work on personal life, however. For instance, consultants expect "long hours on weekdays", but can normally count on weekends off, as "there is a keen focus on no weekend work." A staffer explains, "Satisfaction with work/life balance is monitored biweekly and an ombudsman team intervenes in critical cases." One insider says of Booz's work/life balance approach, "While some companies have similar policies on paper, Booz really lives it." Overall, though, achieving balance is "really dependent on the project, the client and, to a certain extent, the project manager". "I've had projects where I would spend my days working and sleeping when I could, whereas others have allowed me to have a good life outside of work," a consultant shares. In general, we're told, "senior staff encourage their juniors to limit their work."

Lots of face time with clients

Booz consultants "always work with the client from the client's site", which means "consultants need to travel a lot." Indeed, staffers tell us that travelling "Monday through Thursday is the norm." One insider offers more detail: "You fly out on Mondays and return on Thursdays. The usual 1-2-3-4-5 rule applies for consultants— one project at a time, two projects a year, three nights a week away from home, four days a week at the client site and five days of work per week." Booz has a "strong policy of Fridays in the office, and this expectation is communicated to the client". A UK-based source notes that some people manage to avoid extensive travel by "making clear their family commitments and getting staffed more frequently on

London-based jobs". However, candidates considering a position at Booz should expect "generally heavy travel requirements". Those who are especially gung-ho about seeing the world will be pleased to find that the recent split from Booz Allen Hamilton has opened up a new programme: "It is now possible to take advantage of inter-office exchanges for 12-plus months, which is a great way to build focussed international experience," explains a recent hire in London.

Checks and balances

Booz offers a "competitive management consulting salary" and provides "equity for partners". The firm also helps in "tax management, including offshore accounts setup, which reduces tax liabilities". Consultants get an "attractive pension plan", in addition to an "insurance package that includes health, disability and life". Other perks include "gym membership, art memberships, one-on-one coaching for specific needs, free Friday drinks in the office and budgets for socialising with mentees". The firm also covers "100 per cent of your mobile phone". Consultants receive laptops, and can help themselves to "fruit and Friday lunches". There's also a "day care allowance" and "a two-week bonus holiday" for new parents. Aiming to make life on the road as comfortable as possible, the consultancy offers a "flexible expense policy and business-class travel". It also "sponsors staff to do their MBA". A consultant remarks, "Tuition reimbursement is a great perk, which helps in mitigating the student loans outstanding."

London makeover

We're told that Booz's offices are "often located in the city centres". London staffers enjoy "clean and spacious offices in a great location". The space was refurbished in 2007, insiders say, resulting in "lots of space (eight floors), dedicated facilities for parking cycles, shower rooms, kitchens on every floor and dedicated client meeting rooms". Of the spruced-up location, some say it is a bit "cramped and impersonal" and could use more "team spaces", but it does provide "offices for all partners and senior staff". Some find the new layout "too open, with little space for storing personal matters". There's also a "slight lack of colour and warmth". Likewise, a consultant based in Amsterdam says his office has a "lack of private space for meetings and sensitive calls", but otherwise is a "very spacious and nice environment". The Zurich team works from a "fantastically central location", insiders say.

Partners get mixed reviews

Staffers give managers high marks overall, with some consultants reporting "very good relationships" with their supervisors. According to one source, "We have a very teamy company culture and 360-degree feedback, which ensures that juniors are well integrated and accepted on a team." In addition, the firm's "excellent apprenticeship model" allows for "steady opportunities to participate in top-level conversations". Small teams and a "1:7 partner to staff ratio" mean there is a "high level of contact with seniors". Of course, experiences vary, with some respondents describing their managers as "extremely open", whereas others are labeled as "arrogant". Certain sources complain of a "lack of process clarity".

And although some "partners like to keep most of the key relationships to themselves," many consultants enjoy "excellent client exposure, including CEOs". A source states, "We work very closely with client teams, which gives great exposure to line jobs and helps inform future decisions about where one would want to work outside of consulting."

Training from all angles

Booz has a "broad training programme that is well linked to career development processes". The firm offers a "mix of official and on-the-job training", consultants explain, with "good offerings for juniors", though training options are fewer for seniors. Insiders say training is "very much dependent on your ability to take time off from projects", so taking advantage of offerings is "up to you". Booz is reportedly "flexible" in its approach to training, with many optional courses, both "online and face-to-face, that are tailored to consultants' needs", a staffer tells us. Otherwise, a great deal of training is "done on the job", and there is also a "formal mentoring system in place". One consultant explains, "Each person has two mentors. Additionally, each cohort is supportive and we share best practices and problems, so everyone is able to help and learn from one another." Mentoring is not taken lightly, and managers are faced with "high requirements to train juniors adequately on the job".

Move up or jump ship

Booz's promotion policy is "strictly up or out", respondents agree. An insider explains, "Top performers move levels every two years, with potential of reaching partnership in six to seven years." Consultants advance "according to preset levels, but faster promotions are possible". To determine promotions, consultants are assessed annually through a "comprehensive process". One source reveals, "An appraiser, [usually] from another office, interviews a number of people who have worked with you. If you exceed the expectation of your job, you are promoted." Those who fail to exceed expectations after three years are "coached to seek employment elsewhere". A colleague notes that there is "some flexibility around timing, but for most, pressure to perform is felt very strongly".

Creating a faster path to the top ...

Still, any negative feelings about the climb to the top are eased by a general excitement over the recent split from Booz Allen Hamilton, which we're told is bringing with it an "accelerated career path to partner". A senior associate explains, "There has been a clear statement that we want to increase meritocracy, ie, allowing faster career tracks for outstanding people." And a colleague adds, "We've already seen the benefits of this over the last two months with more early promotes than I've ever seen before in the firm." "The internal path to partnership is probably clearer now," another agrees. "In the past, you had to discuss with the huge US government business how many people you can make partner. And now, being a pure strategy consulting player, it's easier because you just have one business model under your roof. So when you take off complexity, you also take off uncertainty, and I'm pretty sure the partner engine is working smoother now."

... while maintaining the status quo

Overall, an insider notes of the change in corporate structure, "I think that the split will help us to become more flexible. We have become smaller, which has the advantage of more entrepreneurship locally." A principal in Munich agrees, "Now, with over $1 billion in revenue (as a separate entity), we have more entrepreneurial freedom and lighter processes. We don't have to accommodate 21,000-plus people, we can just create processes for our smaller group. This will make us more efficient in terms of investing, expansion and moving from one office to another office."

Otherwise, respondents say that, overall, the split has had "no tangible effects so far" on life at the firm, and is "more of an internal thing than an external thing—just a new name and logo". "My job hasn't changed, the people I work with on a regular basis are still at the firm and the work we're doing remains as challenging and stimulating as ever," reports a London-based staffer. Still, he adds, "Intangibly, I feel a sense of excitement in London (and elsewhere—I work very globally) that I haven't sensed in a long time. There is a pervasive feeling that the split is a good thing and that we're very well placed for the future. I expect, going forward, that our brand and profile will improve (perhaps exponentially) and that our business will continue to grow at a healthy rate." Similarly, an associate agrees that "day-to-day business has remained exactly the same, working with clients on their most complex commercial issues. The brand, however, has driven a sense of excitement and reinvigorated pride in our heritage, but it really is business as usual."

Juggling motherhood

Consultants say Booz has "several diversity initiatives" in place and has "made great strides recently" in addressing the issue of women in the workplace. For example,

Booz & Company

the consultancy has a women's network that "addresses the recruitment, retention and promotion of women". Through the efforts of this group, the firm seeks a "50/50 gender split at the entry level". Although the ratio "decreases with seniority", it is normally due to "life choices, as evidence shows that the percentage of women who get promoted is no fewer than that for men". They say the firm is "great at attracting and hiring" women, but nonetheless, "retention is an issue." Although there is "no difference in the way women and men are treated", insiders say Booz is "poor at retaining women in top levels". In the London office, for example, there is "only one [female] partner".

As for balancing the demands of consulting with being a mother, Booz does offer a "special programme for female consultants to return to work after having children", but sources say consulting still is "hard to combine with normal family life". As one staffer notes, the firm is "still at the low side in terms of clear policies for pregnant women". There is "no provision of clarity on expectations after birth, in terms of options for less travelling or working from home". A contact suggests, "More extended child care options, like nanny services, would be a big plus."

Embracing diversity

When it comes to ethnic diversity, Booz is "among other top-tier consultancies", respondents claim; as one source puts it, the firm "has always been an ethnically diverse place to work". Booz's "very rigorous screening and recruiting approach offers equal opportunities to everyone", and the firm "wins prizes for diversity on a regular basis". In the London office, "local British people comprise less than 20 per cent of the office." According to one consultant, "It is perfectly normal to work on a team where every team member is of a different nationality. This is true at all levels of seniority."

Similarly, gays and lesbians are "visible, up to highest partner ranks", and the firm has an "extensive programme in place to facilitate retention" of this demographic. One insider says of the treatment of GLBTs, "It is not even a topic. Colleagues live very openly." Generally speaking, Booz is a "fairly open place, as long as you perform".

Booz for the cause

Booz participates in "large pro bono assignments, as well as locally organised charity projects". In addition to work for such big-name organisations as the Special Olympics, efforts are "driven by the people in each local office". One London-based consultant states, "There are regular fund-raising and pro bono consulting drives for the British Red Cross. Booz also supports the students of St. Aloysius College [a boy's high school] as a part of its 'Chance to Shine' programme, by providing tutoring, mentoring and pro bono consulting." Chance to Shine, the source continues, "began with cricket matches, followed by mentoring schemes where consultants would have regular meetings and chats with individual students about studies and jobs". More recently, the firm has been "organising business studies classes for them, with business simulations and group presentations". In support of the British Red Cross, staffers "run the marathon, complete the Three Peaks Challenge and hold annual concerts and regular competitions". Booz also does "lots of work for local schools with disabled children". ▢

Booz & Company

77

MERCER LLC

1 Tower Place West
Tower Place
London EC3R 5BU
United Kingdom
Phone: +44 (0)207 626 6000
Fax: +44 (0) (0)207 929 2705
www.mercer.com

The Stats

Employer Type: Subsidiary of Marsh &
   McLennan Companies, Inc., a Public
   Company
Ticker Symbol: MMC (NYSE)
CEO: M. Michele Burns
2007 Employees: 18,000+
2006 Employees: 16,500+
2007 Revenue: $3.2 billion
2006 Revenue: $3 billion
No. of Offices: Offices in 41 countries

Practice Areas

Communication Consulting
Health & Group Benefits Consulting
Human Capital Consulting
Investment Consulting
Investment Management
Mergers & Acquisitions
Outsourcing
Retirement Consulting
Surveys & Products

European Locations

London (European HQ)
New York (HQ)
Austria • Belgium • Czech Republic •
Denmark • Finland • France • Germany •
Holland • Hungary • Ireland • Italy •
Norway • Poland • Portugal • Spain •
Sweden • Switzerland • Turkey • United
Kingdom

Plus

• "The diversity of the team"

Minus

• Little work/life balance

Employment Contact

www.mercer.com/joiningmercer

THE BUZZ
WHAT CONSULTANTS AT OTHER FIRMS ARE SAYING

• "Specialised consulting firm with deep
  industry knowledge"
• "Hardworking"
• "Attractive company culture"
• "Soft, not analytical"

THE SCOOP

A division of Marsh & McLennan Companies (MMC), Mercer is one of the leading names in global human resources consulting. Operating in 41 countries, the firm has some 18,000 employees dedicated to providing solutions for company retirement plans, health and benefit provision, human capital strategy and outsourcing. In addition, Mercer also specialises in HR-related surveys and products, communication and the "people issues" involved in mergers and acquisitions. A subsidiary investment group, Mercer Investment Consulting, specialises in investment advisory, monitoring and management for businesses. Additionally, in 2007, Mercer launched an asset management business in Europe that provides outsourced multi-manager solutions.

Growing business, shrinking name

Parent company MMC, meanwhile, is an $11 billion concern headquartered in New York City. With a history that dates back as far as 1871, the firm actually created the division that would go on to become Mercer when it established its employee benefits division in 1937. The division became known as William M. Mercer in 1959, following MMC's acquisition of that firm the same year. The next half-century would see the firm change names twice more, updating to the more descriptive Mercer Human Resource Consulting in 2002, before settling on the single-word appeal of Mercer in September 2007. This last move was designed to provide continuity in the Mercer brand, while shifting the focus away from just the company's HR dealings and onto the wider range of services it now offers.

The latest rebrand also coincided with the creation of the Oliver Wyman brand by MMC—a move in which several consulting strands bearing the Mercer name were packaged as a separate, complementary concern that now operates as a sister company under the MMC umbrella. Among the units grouped together were Mercer Oliver Wyman, Mercer Management Consulting and Mercer Delta Organizational Consulting. In 2007, when MMC pulled in some $11.35 billion, its consulting arm contributed a total of $4.8 billion, of which Mercer was responsible for some $3.2 billion—up 7 per cent from 2006's figure. The remaining MMC revenue, incidentally, was generated by Mercer's three other sibling firms—Marsh, Kroll and Guy Carpenter—whose risk and insurance services are also available to Mercer and its clients.

A European shopping spree

Prior to the firm switching to its single-word identity, it had been on something of an acquisition spree across Europe, snapping up several firms in the space of a few years as it attempted to increase its holdings across the continent. Between 2001 and 2003, in fact, the firm purchased no less than seven European consulting concerns. First up was Germany's Constantia Neuberger Bednar & Partners in 2001, followed by Sweden's Delphi Insurance Brokers and Dutch firm Schnitker en Voortman in 2002. The following year was the busiest in terms of acquisitions, as the firm took advantage of the troubles being endured by the Big Four accounting firms, gaining control of KPMG's benefits consulting wing in Switzerland and its German retirement practice, as well as PricewaterhouseCoopers' actuarial opinions practice in Germany. Also in 2003, Mercer extended its Scandinavian footprint, acquiring Benefit Network ASA and Benefit Network Consulting AS in Norway and Sweden, respectively. Another significant purchase in Europe came in 2006, when the firm brought on Swiss-based Pendia Associates, an investment and retirement consultancy. Then, in late 2007, Mercer acquired German benefits consultancy Höfer Vorsorge, giving the firm a solid HR and benefits consulting presence in Germany.

Good news for English speakers—and "netizens"

With 20 offices in the UK, it would be fair to say that the bulk of Mercer's European holdings are located on British soil (France, by contrast, has just one, Germany has five, Italy two and Spain four). Indeed, the firm has a total of just 43 European offices outside the UK. As a result, one unsurprising statistic is that most of the firm's work in Europe concerns the UK—with particular focus recently on the hot-button issue of pensions and retirement. The firm made news in late 2007 when it was revealed that pension plan buyouts in the UK had increased significantly in the last three months of the year. Mercer, as a leading pensions consultancy, has played an advisory role in several pension plan buyouts in the past, and has every reason to expect to do so again in the future. A December 2007 article in *Pensions & Investments* magazine cited a survey by PricewaterhouseCoopers that found some 27 per cent of UK companies "are considering offloading some or all of their pension assets and liabilities". Further, around 11 per cent are seeking to do so within the next five years.

As if in anticipation of this eventuality, Mercer launched an online auction service in 2007 that helps find buyers for companies seeking to offload pension schemes. Quoted in the same *Pensions & Investments* article, Mercer's principal and senior actuary in London, Stuart Faloon, summed up the benefits Mercer could offer to clients. "Instead of spending three or four weeks chasing around all the insurance companies, we can collapse that negotiating time scale into an afternoon," he explained. And while it's limited to the UK at present, the strategy has global potential. "If this proves successful in the UK, and then Europe, there may well be some interest coming from the US," said Faloon.

That's not the only web-based tool the firm has brought onstream for employers of late, however. In April 2008, Mercer launched Holidayconnect, an online module that helps employers allocate and manage holiday entitlements for their staff. The system follows from Healthconnect, an earlier application that monitored and managed employee absence.

Not exactly clipboards on High Street

Mercer keeps its consultants busy producing reports, surveys and research on issues related to its areas of expertise. In March 2008, for example, the firm's UK wing released the results of a survey into global pay practices, which found that less than half of participating organisations classed as "multinational" had a global compensation programme in place. According to the survey, however, more than half of the firms had global programmes in place for management compensation (the figure rises to 84 per cent for executives), with US firms more likely to have them in place than European firms. Other recent research includes a survey of pension fund asset allocation in Europe (published in April 2008) and a survey analysing the increasing expatriate population in the Middle East and its effect on fueling growth in Western-style pay and benefits, also published in April.

Eastern investment

The majority of Mercer's expansion work of late has been taking place outside the European theatre, with a particular focus on the Asia Pacific region. In addition to naming a handful of top execs in the region in 2007 and 2008, the consultancy has announced an intention to invest some $50 million to increase its footprint in India. As part of that effort, Mercer launched an investment consulting business on the subcontinent in February 2008, complementing its existing global investment consulting operations. The new business will focus on researching asset and portfolio management service firms in the country.

GETTING HIRED

Chock full of info

Mercer's careers site is jam-packed with all the information a job seeker could desire. Not sure which location is right for you? Check out profiles of offices across Europe and the world for insight into the office social scene, local community involvement and nearby sights of interest. Want to know more about Mercer's business areas to see which one suits your interests? Scroll through descriptions of the firm's business areas, including client management, communication and retirement consulting. Curious about Mercer's employee backgrounds? Read up on a handful of staff bios. Still not convinced? Scope out the calendar of Mercer recruiting events to find one near you.

Interested applicants can create a personal profile online, and then search for jobs that match your information—or sign up to be alerted by e-mail when a suitable position avails itself. It's also possible to view all open positions or to search for specific openings by job type, location, keyword and/or line of business. Each job posting includes an extensive description of responsibilities and necessary qualifications.

Don't call us, we'll call you

Mercer explains that applicants "should receive an e-mail confirmation that we have received your application or profile. From there, your application will be reviewed and you will be contacted if you are selected for an interview." Following up with the firm is not encouraged; rather, Mercer insists, "If you have received the e-mail correspondence that your application was received, you can be assured that we will evaluate your qualifications and get back to you if we want to set up an interview."

For those who make the cut, insiders tell us that "normally, nongraduate applicants go through three case studies and two CV interviews," although the specific hiring process "depends on the level and the teams" to which they've applied.

OUR SURVEY SAYS

What to expect

Sources say new hires can look forward to a reasonably competitive "salary scheme with flexible contributions", "flexible benefits" and a "car allowance of 12 per cent of salary". Reported work hours range from 45 to 60 per week, but a principal warns that it can be tough to find a good work/life balance, since "meeting client expectations, especially when working for high-profile clients, is critical and is viewed as being a priority over personal life." Staffers note that "most of the clients are in London," so for those located reasonably nearby, "travel is not really an issue."

Another Mercer highlight, respondents say, is that it is "very diverse and increasingly so". That being said, with respect to gender diversity, the consultancy could use some improvements. One respondent remarks, "At the more junior end, my team is mostly female," although he notes, "This would be more the exception than the rule." And an executive reports, "There has been a recent spate of female promotions," though he admits that, to date, "there are very few women principals."

Dissecting the Mercer ladder

Overall, when it comes to promotion, the policy is "definitely up or out at the analyst level". And as "most training is on the job," it's likely important to soak up as much knowledge as you can and make a solid impression early on. At some point, though, the scenario changes: A higher-up remarks, "It is vague—it is not up or out after a certain level." For example, "Individuals can choose to be career senior associates, if needed." Then again, "advancement can be quite quick, depending on ability and commitment." Insiders note that "on a team level", Mercer's atmosphere is "very supportive", although it "can sometimes be hierarchical on a more corporate level". □

Mercer LLC

1166 Avenue of the Americas
New York, New York 10036
United States
Phone: +1 (212) 345-8000
www.oliverwyman.com

The Stats

Employer Type: Subsidiary of Marsh &
  McLennan Companies, Inc., a Public
  Company
Ticker Symbol: MMC (NYSE)
CEO: John P. Drzik
2008 Employees: 2,900+
2007 Employees: 2,500
2007 Revenue: $1.5 billion
2006 Revenue: $1.2 billion
No. of Offices: 40+

Practice Areas

Business Transformation
Delta Organization & Leadership
Finance & Risk
Marketing & Sales
Operations & Technology
Strategy

European Locations

New York (HQ)
Barcelona • Düsseldorf • Frankfurt •
Hamburg • Istanbul • Lisbon • London •
Madrid • Milan • Munich • Paris •
Stockholm • Zurich

Pluses

• "Young and relaxed culture"
• "Best firm for financial services
  consulting"
• "Great opportunities to go up the
  ladder"
• International staffing

Minuses

• "Difficulties adapting to its new size"
• Infrastructure can be slow
• "Not yet a world-beating brand"
• "Power concentrated in big hubs (New
  York, London) versus local offices"

Employment Contact

www.oliverwyman.com/careers

THE BUZZ
WHAT CONSULTANTS AT OTHER FIRMS ARE SAYING

• "On the up and up"
• "Rebranded—don't know what they
  stand for"
• "Nice atmosphere, happy people"
• "Dry work"

THE SCOOP

Oliver Wyman is part of the Marsh & McLennan Companies, a global professional services network with brands and affiliates in more than 100 countries. Oliver Wyman is the keystone of the Oliver Wyman Group, which also includes NERA Economic Consulting and Lippincott, a brand and identity consultancy. Oliver Wyman is the largest company in the group, counting more than 2,900 consultants who work out of 40 cities in 16 countries. In 2007, the Marsh McLennan companies combined brought in over $11.1 billion in revenue, with Oliver Wyman contributing about 13 per cent—over 26 per cent higher than the year prior.

Combined strengths

Oliver Wyman may have resulted from a fairly recent merger (between Mercer Management Consulting, Mercer Delta Organizational Consulting and Mercer Oliver Wyman in May 2007), but the companies that joined to make up the current organisation have been around for a while. Each of the three contributed their particular specialty to form one of Oliver Wyman's consulting practices. The former Mercer Oliver Wyman, a management consultancy specialising in financial services and launched in 1984, became the financial services and risk practice. The traditional management and strategy consulting business came from the Mercer Management Consulting brand, itself born of the 1992 merger of two Marsh & McLennan companies. Oliver Wyman's Delta Organization & Leadership practice began as Delta Consulting Group, which was established in 1980 by leadership guru David Nadler, and acquired by Mercer Inc. in 2000.

Oliver Wyman's consulting services cover the following industries: automotive, aviation, aerospace and defence, communications, media and technology, energy, financial services, industrial products and services, health and life sciences, retail and consumer products, and surface transportation sectors. Its clients include numerous Global 1000 companies, more than 80 per cent of the world's 100-largest financial institutions and heads of Fortune 1000 companies.

Continental roots

Though Oliver Wyman is based in New York, the firm has been entrenched in Europe since the establishment of the London office in the 1980s. In the 1990s, Oliver Wyman set up shop in Frankfurt and Madrid. Meanwhile, Mercer Management Consulting acquired firms in France and Germany to gain a European presence of its own. In 2002, Oliver Wyman set up a Milan outpost, as Mercer Management Consulting expanded its services in Switzerland, buying up St. Gallen Consulting Group, an insurance and retail financial services consulting firm.

Today, over 50 per cent of the firm's employees are European, while 23 per cent hail from the US and 10 per cent from other countries. Oliver Wyman's two largest European locations are London, which serves UK and Western European clients, and Frankfurt, which caters to financial firms in German-speaking Europe. Other European offices include Barcelona, Düsseldorf, Hamburg, Istanbul, Lisbon, Madrid, Milan, Munich, Paris, Stockholm and Zurich.

Up, up and away

Oliver Wyman Group has been growing at a compound rate of 22 per cent since 2003, expanding both in the industries it serves and geographically, particularly in the Middle East and Asia. Additionally, investments in its health care and life sciences offerings will help the firm take advantage of what should be one of the fastest growing management consulting markets over the next several years.

Still, while the majority of Oliver Wyman's growth is driven organically, the firm has also been broadening its reach through acquisitions. In April 2008, it acquired Acadamee, a provider of leadership learning solutions based in the UK. The purchase will expand the firm's Delta Executive Learning Center (ELC), which focusses on executive education for Global 1000 companies. One month prior, it snapped up Hemeria, a Paris-based management consultancy that works with industrial and service companies. Hemeria's 80-plus employees will expand Oliver Wyman's Paris practice and add clients in the automotive, manufacturing, aviation, aerospace, consumer goods and retail, defence, process and surface transportation industries. The financial services group was further augmented with the January 2008 acquisition of Celent, a consultancy focussed on the global financial services industry. Celent's operations in Boston, New York City, San Francisco, London, Paris, Milan, Tokyo and Beijing became a separate unit in Oliver Wyman's financial services practice. Also in January, Oliver Wyman acquired Harbour Consulting, an automotive industry consultancy based in the US.

Nonprofit focus

One of the components of Oliver Wyman's commitment to work/life balance includes a fellowship programme that benefits the nonprofit sector. Employees can choose to work for an organisation for six months, while the firm pays a stipend equivalent to 40 per cent of their salary. As an extension of that programme, the firm announced a new alliance with microlending organisation Kiva.org in May 2008. The formal externship programme will dedicate consulting staff to support Kiva's expansion. Oliver Wyman has been involved with the online person-to-person lending organisation since its inception in 2005, when consultants participating in the firm's nonprofit fellowship programme helped Kiva's site get off the ground.

Experts at research

Oliver Wyman's brainy consultants frequently publish reports on the state of the industries they serve. For example, the "State of Financial Services Industry" report, now in its 11th year, is the firm's annual study on the global financial industry. In February 2008, Oliver Wyman released its first annual "State of the Industry Report", which analyses the communications, media and technology industries in emerging economies. November 2007 saw the launch of the semiannual *Oliver Wyman Journal*, a management publication covering business strategy, operations and leadership; the first issue featured thought leadership in the area of strategic risk through a case study of a fashion retailer. And in March 2007, the consultancy published a study on the banking market in emerging European countries. The firm's consultants are also regularly quoted all over the map, in such publications as *Le Figaro*, *BusinessWeek*, *The Economist*, *Financial Times*, *Emirates Business* and *Handelsblatt*.

GETTING HIRED

Looking in lots of places

Oliver Wyman "actively" recruits at "all the top schools and high-ranked business schools" across the UK and Europe, including LSE and Oxbridge in the UK; Mannheim, WHU, Munchen and Bamberg in Germany; Bocconi, Luiss, Politecnico of Milan and Turin, Normale di Pisa in Italy; HEC, ESSEC, ESCP-EAP and Centrale in France; and Stockholm School of Economics and the Royal Institute of Technology in Sweden. Sources say the recruiting net is being cast "much wider" these days, extending beyond traditional target campuses.

Still, insiders believe Oliver Wyman's hiring process is "harder than most". A combination of CV and case interviews is involved, the better to assess a candidate's "ability with numbers and charts". Case questions are described by staffers as "quirky and creative", as well as "quite quantitative"—as a consultant explains, they're "not usually something that is easy to prep for, as we rarely use typical case questions".

Either way, candidates don't have to wait too long to find out how they did. Respondents praise the "exceptionally fast decisions after interviews", and say that's "something the firm does very well".

One-of-a-kind questions

Most candidates at Oliver Wyman will go through two rounds of interviews, for a total of five to 10 meetings. A numerical and critical reasoning test may be applied as a preliminary screen, then come multiple interviews and, in some cases, a group exercise. Depending on their location, candidates may be "required to travel for the second round". A Milan hire recalls a first round of "five interviews in my home country office, then five in another European hub". The structure of the rounds can vary between offices in Europe, but insiders agree that no matter where they're held, Oliver Wyman interviews are "very thorough, fun and challenging".

Those offbeat case questions may well include curveballs like, "Would the Bank of England's gold reserves fit in this room?" "What would be the implication if I invented a fabric that doesn't wear out? And how should you value this information?" "How much money do you think the city of Westminster collects through parking meters every year?" "Can you tell me if any two dogs in France have the same number of hairs?"

Social opportunities

Internships at the firm are "extremely good", former interns tell us. It's a "very well-organised programme, with one week of training to start, followed by nine weeks on a project," a source explains. While the training period is short, staffers agree it's "adequate". As the firm explains, its approach is to treat interns as actual consultants, versus giving them some kind of watered-down experience. Another former intern raves, "I was given significant responsibility on a live case from day one!" A London-based insider remembers being "staffed on an interesting case in Switzerland". The summer internship at Oliver Wyman "was much better organised than at other firms," a colleague notes. "The people seemed much more interested in me as an individual and spent much more effort on a highly personalised recruiting effort." Indeed, the internship provides experience and training—but it also offers "good opportunities for social bonding", staffers say.

OUR SURVEY SAYS

Geek friendly

"Fun" and "irreverent" are words many respondents use to describe the Oliver Wyman culture, saying their offices are "collegiate, friendly and nonhierarchical", as well as "informal, down-to-earth and unpretentious". "The firm has a small-firm culture, despite its rapidly growing size," a consultant in London explains. "People are genuinely nice and fun to hang out with," says another. "This is especially important if you're in a remote location for a longer project. You become good friends with your fellow consultants." It's "very casual, except with clients", a colleague adds.

At the same time, the fact that there's "a lot of intelligent and open-minded people" makes for an "intellectually stimulating"—even "academic"—workplace. It's "a little nerdy", one source admits, but that's because consultants are so "focussed on getting the right answer". Oliver Wyman is "clearly a class above in terms of work and people", boasts another.

The firm's "internationality" is a draw for some, who say "global staffing" allows "basically free choice of office" and the "opportunity for global assignments and high-profile work." Others praise the "specialisation model", which allows them to delve deeply into areas of interest.

Prime pay

Compensation at Oliver Wyman gets high marks from staffers. "For an entry-level consultant, it is the most competitive in the market," a source in Paris claims. A recent hire adds, "The base salary is the same as a top-tier, bulge-bracket investment bank." In addition, sign-on bonuses are described as "very attractive", and a partner explains that other bonuses and additional compensation are "highly linked to individual production". "It has happened that a part of the bonus has—voluntarily—been equity in clients," adds a consultant, and a senior staffer believes the "firmwide bonus policy for consultants creates a unified feel. Support professionals also participate in this bonus."

Perks include things such as a "company share plan, a pension fund, and travel and accident insurance", as well as "expensable 'buddy' lunches between colleagues", gym memberships, happy hours in the office and, as part of the firm's efforts to promote work/life balance, the opportunity to take sabbaticals and unpaid leave.

Well, the hotels are nice

Insiders tell us their weekly workloads fluctuate, as "there is no such thing as an average assignment." "I have done everything from 15-month projects to six- to eight-week projects," a senior associate reports. Downtime between projects also varies; some sources report several months without being assigned to a client, while for others the annual downtime is measured in a matter of weeks.

Although "consulting means long hours, and there will always be crunch periods," most people at Oliver Wyman "are extremely understanding and will listen if you say that you need more personal time", a consultant claims. "Getting a good work/life balance is perfectly possible here," a colleague adds. "You just have to be disciplined. There will be tough times, but you can make it work—it's largely up to you to do so." Consultants appreciate that, as often as possible, Fridays are "spent in your home office", and while late-night and weekend work is sometimes necessary, "it's not the norm."

As for being on the road, this depends on many factors, including "which languages you speak well. More languages, more travel." "The amount of work sold in the UK in recent years has meant less foreign travel for London consulting staff," adds a UK-based source. For others, the "interesting destinations" compensate for "increased stress, tiredness and demands on time". "I wouldn't work here if there weren't as many travel opportunities," declares one insider, adding, "I've worked in Bangkok, South Africa, all over Europe and the UK." Besides, the firm's expense policy for business away from home "is very reasonable, which helps make travel more attractive."

> ❝ The company has a small-firm culture, despite its rapidly growing size. ❞

Doors are open

Consultants describe training as a "mixture of formal and informal", with an emphasis on "on-the-job learning, as Oliver Wyman works on an apprenticeship model". An analyst points out that "colleagues are always willing to help with any questions and share tips; I've never been left stuck with a problem without offers of help." We're told that "major efforts" are being made in the realm of formal training, with "more time expended on it now than a year ago". As one respondent comments, the "standard of internal courses is really improving".

As for managers, they're said to be "very approachable", and insiders report a "very nonhierarchical relationship to supervisors". "It is a very flat, open-door company," a Paris-based consultant observes. "I met and chatted with the group CEO two weeks ago when he visited." "Our partner group, like the firm, is young and ambitious," adds another source. "I am frequently in dialogue with, and the primary advisor to, C-suite executives of the largest financial institutions in the world. I am 34." And while "interacting with the most senior level of management occurs after being with the firm for a number of years," most staffers are pleased with their exposure to clients. "I presented on my own to board members of one of the biggest UK companies in my second year," one insider shares.

Make progress

The promotion policy at Oliver Wyman is "not strictly up or out", and some say the path up the ladder is "a bit faster than usual, due to a faster degree of specialisation" for most consultants. Reaching partnership takes "six to nine years", and a London insider says "consultants advance as quickly as they are able to." "Individuals take their own time to develop, which varies quite a bit by their current role," adds another. That said, "people are expected to show progress and/or potential," a staffer notes.

Parlez-vous international?

Women, ethnic minorities and GLBT employees have "absolutely equal opportunities" within the consultancy, but some say there's work to be done in this area. "The firm is highly receptive to hiring more women, but we do have trouble in recruiting women," a source in London reports. Adds a partner, "We do struggle to retain talented women past the first four or five years." However, Oliver Wyman is "actively seeking to encourage more applications", and the firm's female employees "get together regularly to discuss experiences". In addition, GLBT employees, present in all levels of staff from partners to support professionals, "are generally very open" about their orientation, a respondent says, "and it's no problem at all. In fact, it's just not an issue."

The ethnic makeup of most Oliver Wyman offices is "very multicultural", insiders tell us, in keeping with the firm's global spirit. "There is a real blend of people," raves one source, which is "absolutely brilliant if you want to top up on your language skills!" A colleague illustrates the point: "I'm a French consultant, currently working in Helsinki four days a week. Yesterday, I had a team dinner in a French-Finnish restaurant with a Romanian partner who's based in New York but spending his time between Austria and Moscow, another English-Kenyan partner and an English-Israeli consultant. Did I mention I'm originally Lebanese?"

New digs, coming up

London sources are excited about their relocation "to what looks like an amazing new space in late 2008," and they say the move can't come a day too soon. "Given the growth rate, our office is now far too small," a consultant explains, and this problem is echoed by consultants in other locations. "We tend to outgrow our offices very fast," a Milan-based staffer says. In Frankfurt, "offices are not growing at the same speed as the company and employee numbers." One partner says Oliver Wyman takes an "anti-Lear jet approach" to its office space, creating work areas that are "functional and friendly but not luxurious".

In its local communities, Oliver Wyman has begun to do "pro bono work", as well as sponsoring a "charity of the year, with things like charity auctions to raise funds". Consultants praise the efforts of corporate good citizenship, but call it a "work in progress", and one source speaks for many when he says, "There are such efforts, but I am not very familiar with them." □

ROLAND BERGER
STRATEGY CONSULTANTS

Highlight Towers
Mies-van-der-Rohe-Str. 6
80807 Munich
Germany
Phone: +49 (0)89 923 00
Fax: +49 (0)89 923 082 02
www.rolandberger.com

The Stats

Employer Type: Private Company
CEO: Prof Dr Burkhard Schwenker
2008 Employees: 2,000
2007 Employees: 1,700
2007 Revenue: €600 million
2006 Revenue: €550 million
No. of Offices: 36

European Locations

Munich (HQ)
Amsterdam • Barcelona • Berlin •
Brussels • Bucharest • Budapest •
Düsseldorf • Frankfurt • Hamburg •
Istanbul • Kiev • Lisbon • London •
Madrid • Milan • Moscow • Paris •
Prague • Riga • Rome • Stuttgart •
Vienna • Warsaw • Zagreb • Zurich

Employment Contact

www.careers.rolandberger.com

Practice Areas

Corporate Development • Information
Management • Marketing & Sales •
Operations Strategy • Restructuring &
Corporate Finance

Pluses

- "Nonpolitical" culture
- "Potential to shape the culture of the company"
- Great opportunities for growth
- "You can focus on a certain industry—consumer goods, pharmaceuticals, automotive—right from the beginning of your career"

Minuses

- It's not unusual to travel five days a week
- "You work like hell"
- "If you don't know too many languages, international exposure is often limited to neighbouring countries"
- "Project staffing can sometimes be inflexible, as there are fewer options for partners staffing projects"

THE BUZZ
WHAT CONSULTANTS AT OTHER FIRMS ARE SAYING

- "Gaining position"
- "Tough German work environment"
- "Strong in the German market"
- "Bark bigger than bite"

THE SCOOP

Roland Berger hit two significant landmarks in 2007: The consultancy turned 40, while the man who founded and lent his name to it turned 70. Today, the firm is one of the biggest strategy consulting outfits in the world, and the largest that got its start in Europe. To this day, 26 of the firm's 36 worldwide offices are located within Europe, meaning it is very active on its home turf, but a committed international approach since its founding has seen its influence stretch across four continents and more than 25 industry sectors.

The firm constantly aims for "creative strategies that work", an approach that means not being afraid of doing the unorthodox, and not necessarily following the same quantitative methodologies as its rivals. As such, Roland Berger tends to hire consultants from a wide range of backgrounds and academic disciplines—anyone, in fact, that can help its clients "see their vision become reality", according to the firm, as "that is the yardstick by which our clients ultimately measure us."

One man, one vision

Roland Berger founded the firm as a one-man strategy operation in Munich in 1967, growing it into a major player in its field and employing 100 staff within a decade of its founding. The consultancy has passed many landmarks along its journey to its present state; in 1980, for example, it became the first European firm to gain acceptance into the US Association of Consulting Management Engineers (ACME). That acceptance was an early indicator of Berger's international reach, and especially impressive given that the firm didn't arrive in the US in a permanent way until 1995, when it established its New York office. A second followed in Detroit in 1998, while early 2008 saw the firm's total on the continent rise to three, with the establishment of a Chicago hub.

The major part of Berger's international vision to date, however, has been across Europe, where it boasts six German offices as well as 20 more in 18 countries outside its homeland. The most recent of these is the firm's office in Istanbul, its first in Turkey, despite the fact that it has been doing business there for some time. Opened for business in April 2008, the office represents a further commitment by the firm to expand business in not only Central and Eastern Europe, but in the Middle East to boot.

Roland Berger has also dedicated itself to community development in Central and Eastern Europe, with the 2005 establishment of the Counterparts initiative, in cooperation with the Goethe-Institut. In March and April 2008, the initiative sponsored the Festival for Contemporary German Choreography in Moscow. The high point of the festival was a ballet performance of *The Seagull*, staged by John Neumeier. Also a high point: Dr Uwe Kumm's (managing director of Roland Berger Russia) press conference on the theme of doing business in Russia. In the fall of 2008, Counterparts planned to open a Roland Berger Library in St. Petersburg. This would be the third such library, joining those already established in Dubrovnik, Croatia and Krakow. In 2006, the initiative helped the Polish National Opera stage *The Magic Flute*.

Principal principles

There are three core values that, according to the firm, inform almost everything that happens within its walls: excellence, entrepreneurship and partnership. The first of these refers to the firm's capabilities in executing all the usual consulting-type work—analysis, strategising and the like. The second, meanwhile, encapsulates its commitment to finding consultants capable of shouldering responsibility and treading new paths in their quest to bring improved performance and results to clients. The final value—partnership—focusses on the company's willingness to work alongside client firms to achieve results. Indeed, Roland Berger maintains that "we see our clients and consultants as a joint team."

> ❝ The firm's 'rewarding and open' culture supports 'nonbureaucratic ways of working'. ❞

A well-rounded approach

"Outstanding management consultants are more than just brilliant analysts and strategists," says CEO Prof Dr Burkhard Schwenker. "Above all, they are strong and creative personalities from a variety of backgrounds." That comment underscores the approach the firm takes in identifying less-than-typical consulting types. On average, the consultancy has fewer MBAs than its rivals, but a lot more PhDs and grads with nonbusiness-related degrees. To attract the type of grads and experience it's looking for, the firm regularly hosts employment events at universities all over Europe, and it has also begun hosting an event known as "Empower yourself, refine your skills." That event has so far taken place in Roland Berger's competence centres in Paris in 2006 and Amsterdam in 2007, and is aimed at giving potential employees a look at how a consultancy operates, as well as the chance to learn from Roland Berger consultants and clients in the field of energy and chemicals competence. In 2007, the event gave interested parties the opportunity to work on a case from the firm's files, and to demonstrate their ability to develop and present strategies and solutions.

Roland Berger's ability to identify top consultants doesn't stop at its own door, however. In February 2008, the consultancy presented its third annual Best of European Business Awards at the European Business Summit in Brussels. The firm started the awards as a means of rewarding the best-performing businesses in Europe, and encouraging companies to take their work to a higher level. At the 2008 ceremony, awards were given in two main categories—growth and cross-border mergers and acquisitions, and a special prize was also doled out to BASF for their commitment to green business practices.

Taking the rough ...

As company founder and the chair of its supervisory board, Roland Berger has long been acknowledged as one of the most well-connected and influential people in Germany—a fact that has occasionally led the firm into hot water. Back in the early years of the new millennium, his close ties with former German Chancellor Gerhard Schroeder, for example, led some to question whether the consultancy was being awarded contracts based on its connections rather than its competencies. The chorus making that call gained volume in 2004, after it was revealed that the firm's consultants overestimated the number of visitors expected at the World's Fair in Lower Saxony in 2000, an event many saw as a failure. As a result, the firm lost, according to Berger, up to 6 per cent of its revenue in 2004 as government agencies became skittish about being associated with the firm. Relations have since recovered, but Berger remains a well-connected figure in both European business and politics.

... with the smooth

Come March 2008, Roland Berger (the man) demonstrated a less controversial side to his public persona, with the unveiling of plans to create his own foundation to honour individuals and organisations that display an "outstanding commitment to human rights and dignity". The mooted foundation includes plans to award annual prizes of €1 million for suitably impressive behaviour. In addition, the foundation will provide scholarships for children from less privileged backgrounds to improve access to higher education. The foundation's goals are rooted in Berger's own childhood in Nazi Germany, where he witnessed firsthand the effects of breaches of human rights.

Although Berger may have other areas of focus in his life, his company continues to plough its furrow in the consulting field. In addition to the work it has been carrying out for clients, the firm also produces a highly regarded industry magazine, *think:act*, and consultants regularly churn out industry-specific reports. One recent report discussed the challenges faced in trying to encourage "green" behaviour among citizens (the secret is to financially incentivise the process, apparently). *think:act*, meanwhile, has won the best career publishing magazine title for three years running—2005 through 2007—and focusses on presenting new perspectives on top issues for CEOs.

GETTING HIRED

Standard procedure

Roland Berger's "classical" hiring process normally involves "six interviews, including presentations and cases". Typically, the first round involves "short cases with senior consultants". Second rounds consist of "one extensive case study presented to a project manager". And those who make it to the final stage will "interview with a managing partner". Some may also be asked to take a "general knowledge and mathematics test" at some point. Insiders describe Roland Berger's process as a "typical consultancy interview structure", but specific questions and cases can "depend on the interviewer". Some examples include: "How many gas stations do you expect to operate in Germany? What is the average profitability of a gas station? What is the weight of a fully loaded Boeing 747? What are important issues in a post merger integration?" Candidates should also expect to field "general questions about your CV". During this process, interviewers have their eye out for "leadership potential, maturity, self-consciousness, teamwork, analytical skills and problem solving." One insider offers a tip: "When presenting cases, the loudest voice doesn't mean a thing." Sources say that the firm's hiring process leaves candidates impressed by its "entrepreneurial humility and very high-quality standards."

The firm recruits from "all major top universities and business schools", including MIT, London Business School, INSEAD, Harvard, Oxford and Cambridge.

Real-world experience

Roland Berger internships are "challenging, but fun and interesting". The "hands-on" experience paints a "realistic picture of consulting", former interns report. Interns enjoy "direct involvement on projects, with real responsibilities and client exposure". A former intern based in Warsaw recalls, "I participated actively in three due diligence projects and had the chance to create a case study for students from the Warsaw School of Economics." The six-month-long internships make it possible "to be engaged in more than one project", and those who participate in these longer internships tend to get tougher assignments. One consultant comments, "The difficulty of tasks rises with the duration of the internship." Regardless of length, internships at Roland Berger provide an "opportunity to work with many different people on very interesting projects". It's not uncommon for interns to be "integrated from day one".

OUR SURVEY SAYS

Entrepreneurs working together

Roland Berger, insiders say, is an "entrepreneurial" firm, filled with "people with great knowledge and skills, as well as humour and positive energy". Consultants "always look for excellence without being arrogant". And the firm's "rewarding and open" culture supports "nonbureaucratic ways of working", as well as "open and direct feedback". Lest you think these consultants keep their heads to the grindstone, sources also tell us that this "fun crew knows how to work and party hard". One consultant says, "Working for Roland Berger is extremely fun. Besides working intensively together, we spend time playing sports, having team lunches and dinners, and playing foosball in our leisure room." A colleague boasts that Roland Berger is the "company with the best soccer team in our industry". Consultants also are proud of the fact that the firm's founder is still "very active" within the company and serves as "an inspirational figure within the organisation".

But the culture can differ country by country. According to one source, "Smaller country organisations such as in the Czech Republic and the UK seem a lot more familiar and entrepreneurial than the German home base." Insiders say the firm could "internationally work together more efficiently, as it sometimes feels a bit like the small countries against Germany". One London-based respondent says his placement "gives the opportunity to work in a smaller office setting, while also providing the support and benefits that come from being a part of a global strategic consultancy". At times, however, the smaller office size can result in "inflexible project staffing", which can lead to "project assignments that are less than ideal for the consultants involved". Regardless of office size or location, Roland Berger "promotes diversity" and "doesn't try and fit everyone within one strict company profile". Consultants appreciate that they are given "the freedom to act as entrepreneurs within the company".

Positively unpredictable

Hourly demands are "very dependent on the project", we're told, with consultants logging anywhere between "45 and 100 hrs per week". The average tends to be somewhere between 50 and 65 per week, with demands escalating "before final presentations". One source states, "On average, I work from 9am till 8:30pm, including only a short lunch break of about 30 minutes." Work hours can be "unpredictable", but fortunately, "the expectation is that you only stick around if you have work to do." A colleague agrees that "face time does not get valued that highly."

Average assignments last "between 10 and 12 weeks". Sources explain that due diligence cases tend to take "between three and six weeks, while more operational-oriented assignments can last up to six months". An insider remarks, "We try not to burn consultants on projects by keeping them a max of six months on the same job." We're also told that there can be "wasted hours because of bad planning or organisation", and Roland Berger puts "pressure on quality within short deadlines".

Maintaining balance

By strategy consulting standards, work/life balance for Roland Berger consultants is "quite reasonable". It can sometimes be "hard to create this balance while working on intense projects", but overall, "working hours are OK and weekends are usually free of any work commitments." One consultant remarks, "Roland Berger is really attentive to our work/life balance. They understand the power of a healthy family life." To help staffers make time for family, consultants are given "30 days of holiday per year", and the firm "organises some family events each year". Staffers say the Brussels office recently launched an initiative to improve the work/life balance of employees: The local management team hired a consultant "to give us tips on ergonomics, healthy food and sports". Since the initiative launched, "almost all employees got involved in sports, be it running or football or cycling, once a week during lunch time."

Roland Berger also offers new parents a "variety of possibilities, such as part-time models and sabbaticals". One consultant shares, "Since I am a mother with two young children, the balance between work and family life is essential. I am used to leaving the office quite early in the evening to take care of my children, and often work home at night." In general, "sabbaticals and vacation can be taken quite flexibly."

On the road again

Travel demands at Roland Berger "depend on the kind of project". For some, the travel is "not a major problem", although many consultants spend a lot of time away from home, with some "travelling five days most weeks". A contact says, "On average, I spend three to four nights a week in hotels, and take two to four flights per week." Others spend only "two days out of the office per week max". Although Roland Berger does not promote "useless travelling", it's not uncommon for consultants to collect "many, many frequent traveller miles", because "most projects have an international scope." A London-based consultant explains, "If staffed on a project run from Germany, you can expect to travel up to five days every week." Regardless of specifics, the bottom line is, "Travel is part of the job of a consultant." On the bright side, Roland Berger has a "weekend travel scheme that helps to bring friends and couples together when we're assigned to locations".

Wide variety of perks

The consultancy offers a "very attractive compensation package for juniors". In addition to "competitive salaries", it provides a "pension scheme and contributes the equivalent of 12.8 per cent on top of the savings you set aside". Part of bonuses is "related to company results, not only personal performance", and profit sharing is available at the partner level. The most popular perk is the company car, and we're told consultants can "get any kind you want". They also get "mobile phones for personal use", "elaborate health insurance", language courses and a "paid PhD programme". One source adds, "The London office offers a corporate gym membership in a nearby fitness site, free of charge." Staffers also enjoy "free dinner if working after 9pm" and a "free taxi home if working after 10pm". The firm holds "pub nights once a month" in some offices, and also pays for "office lunches once a month". Not to be overlooked is the annual office trip—last year to Iceland. New parents receive "special holidays" and are supported with "more flexibility to organise their private life"; they're also given "support in finding day care". And if there's any doubt left in your mind, an insider comments, "In general, we are pampered with all kinds of extras."

Rooms with a view

The quality of office spaces at Roland Berger differs by location, with "some that are excellent, like the Munich headquarters, and others less so". The office in Paris is "well furnished and well placed", and in Warsaw, there is "no assigned desk for consultants"—rather, "you take whatever place that's currently free." The crew in Brussels spend their time in "luxurious offices in a prestigious building in a residential and green area", while London-based cohorts are "located right near Green Park" and have a "top-floor view of Berkeley Square", putting them "within walking distance of many of London's best areas".

Side by side with top-level leaders

Consultants say they enjoy "close management and coaching". It's the kind of place where "good ideas get support, budget and are rewarded." One staffer remarks, "The quality of the project managers is amazing at Roland Berger. If I compare them with those at [my former employer], they are much more experienced at Roland Berger and I learn much more." In London, we're told, there is "unbelievable access to the office's partners". Supervisors "listen to what junior consultants say, and work closely with all levels". They also "take an interest in our lives outside of work".

Consultants appreciate that they are given "high involvement and responsibility with clients from early on", and get to work on "very interesting projects at top clients". One insider states, "We are given the opportunity to interact on a day-to-day basis with top-level management at our clients, most of the time in a real partner relationship." In short, Roland Berger isn't shy about granting its consultants "freedom in developing client solutions".

Training from many sources

Training at Roland Berger is "both official and unofficial". An insider explains, "Every level has an amount of obliged seminars to attend, which are typically organised in Germany and regroup people from all offices." Initial training is two weeks long, after which "everyone is assigned a mentor, who helps you out with more day-to-day issues and smooth integration within the office." Staffers say the firm's official training programmes are "strong for basic skills and client-specific skills". In addition to "numerous available seminars and courses", on-the-job training is a "vital part of every day".

On the up and up

Advancement at Roland Berger is "not strictly up-or-out", but "progression and commitment must be clearly noticed" in order to move up. Respondents tell us there have been "some cases of people being asked to leave", but it's more common that "low performers decide to leave voluntarily". Consultants "advance relatively fast", as "promotions are quite frequent"—and the timetable for advancement "increases as you become more senior within the firm". Evaluations take place "twice a year", and the normal time frame is "12 to 18 months to be promoted to the next position". One consultant clarifies, "This does not mean your wage can only be increased at these points in your career." All in all, insiders feel that the process is "very transparent".

Women still a minority

Although there are "women at all levels" within Roland Berger, the "female quota is still low"—the firm "knows this is an issue and continues to work on it". Some of the "strong improvements" that are being made include a "dedicated coaching and mentoring programme for women". The Brussels office is "about 35 per cent women", making it the office with the highest ratio of women. A contact says this "gives an extra positive effect on the atmosphere" in that location. Throughout the rest of company, the "few women present are well cared for, and promoted and mentored in an appropriate way". One consultant remarks, "There are no differences between men and women regarding hiring, promoting, mentoring and salary package."

Sources say ethnic diversity is "not an issue" at Roland Berger, as "recruiting is purely meritocratic." Minorities are "treated the same as any other consultants". And although there are "mostly Germans in the German offices", there is "no discrimination noted". A respondent in London reports, "The London office is very diverse in terms of nationalities and races represented." And in Brussels, there is a "wonderful mix", including people from Uzbekistan, Lebanon, the US, Algeria, Germany, India, France and the Congo.

Similarly, insiders say treatment of gays and lesbians is a "not an issue at all". A consultant says, "Sexual preferences are not discussed. I would say 99 per cent of our consultants are hetero, and if they are gay or lesbian, they do not talk about it."

Supporting culture and education

Roland Berger does a "small number of pro bono projects per year", in addition to participating in "social projects and government initiatives". The firm has a "strong corporate responsibility programme", and offers "several sponsorships", particularly in the areas of culture and education. It also offers financial support for orphanages, galleries and universities, and has even "sponsored a library in Krakow". A consultant adds, "We pay special attention to ecological factors by not printing unnecessarily and recycling."

Two Canal Park
Cambridge, Massachusetts 02141
United States
Phone: +1 (617) 252-2000
www.monitor.com
www.themonitorgroup.co.uk

The Stats

Employer Type: Private Company
Chairman: Mark Fuller
2008 Employees: 1,600
2007 Employees: 1,400
No. of Offices: 30

Practice Areas

Economic Development & Security
Innovation
Marketing & Pricing
Organization & Leadership
Strategy

European Locations

Cambridge, Mass. (Global HQ)
Amsterdam • Frankfurt • London •
Madrid • Moscow • Munich • Paris •
Zurich

Pluses

- "A global experience"
- Extremely flexible about personal time
- "Autonomy to shape one's career and everyday life"
- "A place for optimists to change the world"

Minuses

- Lack of brand recognition
- "The firm tends to reward people who never say no"
- "Needing to fight for resources for each case"
- "Occasionally under-resourced because we lack scale in key geographies"

Employment Contact

www.monitor.com/
cgi-bin/iowa/careers

THE BUZZ
WHAT CONSULTANTS AT OTHER FIRMS ARE SAYING

- "Open-minded, creative"
- "Losing steam in Europe"
- "Good people policies"
- "Chaotic"

THE SCOOP

U nsurprisingly for a firm founded by a group of Harvard academics, Monitor Group trades on intelligence—both the kind it brings to the table and the kind it gathers to aid its clients. Billing itself as an "integrated resource for growth" that partners with its clients, the Cambridge, Massachusetts-based firm has 30 offices in 19 countries from which it offers professional services to a client list that is largely confidential (but which is known to include members of the Fortune 500, as well as governments and nonprofit organisations).

Pick your platform

The firm offers its services across three platforms: strategy consulting services (by far the largest portion of its business), capability building and capital services. The last of these is the domain of Monitor's affiliated merchant banking umbrella firm, Monitor Capital, the most prominent arm of which is the private equity firm known as Monitor Clipper Partners. Monitor Capital also includes Monitor Ventures, an early-stage venture capital fund, as well as Angra Partners, a Brazilian private equity fund.

The advisory and capability-building services, meanwhile, serve clients in a fairly exhaustive list of industry sectors: aerospace and defence, automotive, consumer goods, energy and utilities, financial services, government, industrial products, IT and telecoms, media and advertising, nonprofit and the social sector, pharmaceuticals, life sciences and health care, private equity, professional services, retail, and tourism and travel.

Putting ideas into practice

The consultancy was founded in 1983 by a group of six former Harvard University students and professors, intent on finding practical applications for the theory then being taught in the business school (not to mention the added attraction of generating some dollars in the process). Within five years of founding the firm close to their alma mater, the group had expanded into Europe and Asia, opening an office in London as early as 1985. Global expansion has not dimmed the firm's Harvard connection any, however—current Chairman Mark Fuller is a former assistant professor at the venerable institution, while Monitor's "thought leaders" include at least seven further Harvard alumni and current or former professors.

Among those thought leaders is co-founder Michael Porter, who still serves as a Bishop William Lawrence University Professor at Harvard, and whose books

Competitive Advantage: Creating and Sustaining Superior Performance and *Competitive Strategy: Techniques for Analyzing Industries and Competitors* provided the backbone of ideas around which Monitor Group was formed. Accenture named Porter one of the top-50 business intellectuals of our time, and he has since written 14 more books and over 80 articles on business.

Growth counselors

In its mission to advise on all aspects of growth, Monitor has focussed on developing capabilities in key growth-related disciplines. Its historic roots are in corporate and competitive strategy. Moreover, marketing and pricing—housed in Monitor's m2c (market to customer) unit—form a second pillar of Monitor's growth advisory offerings. More recently, Monitor has invested heavily in building out its innovation (Monitor Innovation) and organisation and leadership (Lattice Partners) practice areas.

Rounding all this out, Monitor is making a name for itself by advising two other groups of clients: nonprofits and regional and national governments. Over the years, Monitor has developed a practice in advising national governments on economic competitiveness. Much of its work in this space is done by a group known simply as regional economic competitiveness. Meanwhile, the Monitor Institute focusses on advising nonprofit, philanthropic and social-sector institutions.

Retention principles

One of the core values at Monitor is retention of existing clients. The firm derives more than 85 per cent of its revenue from repeat customers—a statistic it has maintained since 1992. Those clients are a closely guarded secret at the firm, however. Rumour has it, in fact, that Monitor consultants even refer to clients by code names within the organisation to preserve their anonymity.

Road map for Libya

Such an instance occurred when the government of Libya, led by the controversial Colonel Muammar Qaddafi, revealed that it had been working with Monitor to develop a road map for the future of the nation. Seeking a way out of the economic turmoil created by his father's dictatorship, London School of Economics grad Saif al Islam Qaddafi called on the consultancy in 2005, after meeting and establishing a relationship with Michael Porter.

Since then, the company has been working in Libya and attempting to get past many of the problems holding the country back—not the least of which is a lack of potential leaders, a problem created by the authoritarian government. According to a *BusinessWeek* article in February 2007, the firm set up a three-month leadership programme—dubbed a "mini-MBA"—in the country to identify and hone some home-grown talent to aid the country in generating and sustaining more business. While the country still has much to see in the way of concrete results, there are signs that things are improving. Following years of government-led boycotts by American businesses, many are beginning to return to the country following Qaddafi's 2003 decision to stop pursuing the development of weapons of mass destruction. As a result of both this decision and Monitor's restructuring advice, Western banks and oil companies have since been linked with moves into the country.

Publish and be ... lauded

Monitor prides itself on its expertise and thought leadership in key disciplines that it believes are critical to helping its clients grow. Among other things, many of Monitor's experts, therefore, regularly produce works of business and consulting research or scholarship. All told, its employees have published more than 80 articles in the *Harvard Business Review* since the firm was

> ❝ A 'roll up your sleeves and hammer out a solution' kind of place. ❞

founded, not to mention having penned some of the most influential books on business strategy in the last quarter of a century. The firm also produces white papers and industry reports for its clients. One example is Jeffrey Rayport's "The Truth About Internet Business Models", which found that—gasp!—"there will be no magic bullet" for unlocking the key to web-based commerce. Rayport even goes as far as stating that business is more art than science, and that no business model will ever be fully adequate. That theory is at the heart of a lot of the consultancy's thinking and advice—treat each client's business as unique, and find a unique way to solve it. A more recent work is Joseph Fuller's "The Beneficent Dragon", published in the spring 2008 issue of the *MIT Sloan Management Review*. In it, Fuller questions, and ultimately rejects, the widespread notion that China's economic growth will harm the US economy.

Within Monitor's organisation and leadership group, a report by consultant Chris Argyris examines the paradoxes inherent in decisions taken by executives. The paper, titled "Organizational Dynamics: The Executive Mind and Double-Loop Learning", found that there were three key paradoxes in executive reasoning and, therefore, decision making. The first of these is that reasoning leads to both productive and counterproductive consequences. This then creates the second paradox for the executive—of not realising this because they become disconnected from the reasoning process in the very act of making a decision. The final paradox is that the same skills can lead to both success and failure—something that undermines the reasoning process. Having identified these, the article then seeks to answer the question of why each of these should be, and what effect they have on businesses and the decision-making process. Ahh, to operate at the point where business meets psychology!

Life in the Fast lane

Every year since 2003, Monitor has teamed up with the good people over at *Fast Company* magazine to produce the Social Capitalist Awards—an awards ceremony that highlights nonprofits that are working toward the greater good of society (the social part), using methods gleaned from the business world (the capitalist part). Newcomers to the list in 2008 included the Acumen Fund, an organisation that "identifies and supports enterprises that provide health, water, housing and energy to the poor", as well as The New Teacher Project, which seeks to raise teaching standards in low-performing schools.

Marking the fifth year of the awards, at the 2008 ceremony there was also recognition for organisations that had received recognition every year. These included human rights group Witness, as well as City Year, an organisation that sends young adults throughout the US and South Africa to perform a year of service. And the awards don't stop there; in addition to the top-45 nonprofits, recognition was also bestowed upon the top-10 profit-making social reformers—firms that included Better World Books, which collects used books and sells them to fund literacy programmes worldwide.

Monitor's meritocracy

Like many other firms in the consulting industry, Monitor emphasises its meritocratic approach to pay and promotions. However, the manner in which the firm practises this principle, especially on the subject of promotions, is unique. For starters, the firm doesn't categorise its consultants in terms of classes. Thus, there are no evaluation time frames during which staffers are considered for promotions to the next level of responsibility. In fact, the concept of promotions is rather misplaced at Monitor.

A Monitor career path can probably best be described as a series of transitions. Its consultants carry out specific roles on projects, and they are assigned these roles based on their performance on previous projects. For example, entry-level consultants may begin transitioning into module leader responsibilities as soon as they demonstrate their aptitude as case team members, regardless of whether this happens within their first few months or first few years at the firm. Beware, though—whereas Monitor is more flexible than most consultancies when it comes to upward mobility and rapid advancement, it has limited tolerance for underperformance and sluggish development.

GETTING HIRED

Brush up on cases

Monitor has a "rigorous interview process, involving two case study interviews in the first round, and a final round that includes a group exercise, a video exercise and a final discussion". The goal of the process, in addition to assessing "analytical skills" and "strategic thinking", is "to ensure that candidates understand how Monitor works". The firm places "very strong emphasis on data analysis and rigorous thinking". As such, interviewees are presented with a "significant amount of data and exhibits, and are asked to read them and answer questions". An example might be the following: "What is the total market size for such-and-such market in 2005 through 2009, using the data and exhibits provided?"

We're told that the typical hiring process is "two rounds", usually involving "two 30-minute interviews on written cases" in the first round, and a half-day set of interviews in the second round. Fortunately, a consultant explains, "candidates have time to read the written cases prior to a conversation with the interviewer, and you are allowed to use a calculator." They are normally "eight-to-10 page cases that replicate on-the-job problems and include details about an industry, exhibits and a few questions". Written cases are followed by "face-to-face" meetings to discuss findings. Some first rounds also include a fit interview, although some candidates do not experience that until the second round. Interviewers, especially during the second round, look "to test values and maturity". Second rounds "vary by office" and can sometimes involve "a feedback and role-play interview as well".

The best of the best

Overall, insiders say Monitor's interview process is "more thorough and long-term-focussed than competitors'". The goal, a source explains, is to "test presentation capabilities, teamwork and soft skills through group cases and role play." The firm is "looking for how candidates interact as a team tackling challenging case questions". Only candidates who showcase both "interpersonal skills and analytical ability" will be considered. And although the whole process may seem a bit over the top, respondents say that Monitor's interview process is often what sealed the deal when it came time to choose a firm. A source states, "I met some great people when interviewing, and I wanted to be part of a community of really smart and hardworking, but at the same time modest and fun, people."

Monitor hires from "elite undergraduate schools", including Cambridge, Oxford, London School of Economics, McGill and the Ivies. At the MBA level, the consultancy considers candidates from the "top programmes", such as London Business School, INSEAD, Harvard and Wharton. And although the firm has "several focus universities in major countries, applications are accepted from all schools".

A summer well spent

Anyone questioning whether to join Monitor would likely be easily swayed by one of the firm's former interns, who raves about the "superb" experience, which provides "ample opportunity to test the career and show your worth to the firm". A source recalls, "I was a history major who knew nothing about business, and they tutored me in Excel, PowerPoint and Access, and by the end of the summer I felt like I had come an amazingly long way." Some even gush that the Monitor internship "ranks among the best experiences of their lives".

The consultancy "invests a great deal in the summer interns", who have the opportunity to work on "real cases and have real client interaction". Opportunities to meet and learn from the most senior partners are "arranged regularly, and colleagues are generous with their time". The casework during internships is "highly interesting and motivating", and interns are given a "genuine chance to contribute to the intellectual agenda". The firm also plans "regular social activities to integrate interns into the community".

OUR SURVEY SAYS

Not a cookie-cutter environment

Consultants are proud to say that Monitor Group is not a place of "cookie-cutter solutions". The firm has "deep roots in strategy" and its consultants are "intellectually curious" with an "unwavering dedication to helping clients win". Within its "highly collaborative" culture, there is a "strong emphasis on feedback and open communication". Insiders describe the vibe as "informal and meritocratic", which creates opportunities for "fast advancement" for those who earn it. In addition, the firm provides consultants with the "autonomy to shape their own career". An insider remarks that the firm is "not too hierarchical, and the small size means there is opportunity to work on both client-facing and internal projects". "You can, to a large extent, influence what types of projects you want to do and which industries and geographies you are interested in," a colleague adds. And another agrees that "each individual consultant can really shape his experience, and no two experiences will be the same." However, this sometimes "poses some challenges in making sure that everyone is receiving the right level of developmental attention", and the unconventional environment "occasionally feels a bit unstructured". But for those who are motivated, "it allows consultants to start making important career choices the moment they start working."

Respondents also explain that Monitor's is a "no-elbow culture", in which people are "down-to-earth and noncompetitive". As one puts it, it's "a real 'roll up your sleeves and hammer out a solution' kind of place". The consultancy is a "global organisation that has kept a very entrepreneurial culture", which has helped it attract "people who don't follow the classical consulting career paths". In fact, we're told, "a number of Monitor's consultants have been

> ❝ Each individual consultant can really shape his experience. ❞

in the military and bring an extraordinary perspective." People at the firm do "interesting things outside of their professional life and bring that originality and perspective to our work". As evidence of Monitor's interesting crew, "many who leave the firm go on to nontraditional jobs, such as pastry chef, charter school founder, dogsled trainer, policewoman and filmmaker."

On your own clock

Hours as a Monitorite can be long, we're told, with most consultants clocking "at least 60 hours" at week. And they can also be unpredictable—a source says, "Even when you're working 60 hours a week, you usually don't know which 60." Work hours "vary significantly depending on case assignment". The good news is, "putting in face time is not a requirement at Monitor," and if things are slow, "taking personal time is fine." Overall, sources say the company is "extremely flexible, you work hard when you need to". Staffers "don't need to pretend to be working if it is not absolutely necessary". According to one insider, "People are really understanding here of how you work best. No one has ever complained about me rolling into the office at 10 or 10:30am!"

Pack your bags

Going to work for Monitor means "significant travel needs to be expected." Mostly because of the consultancy's "rapid expansion in emerging markets", consultants "travel extensively to other Monitor offices and to clients around the world". The firm "does not demand travelling beyond what is necessary", though, and "it's often your choice if you want to take a travel case or not." That said, insiders make it clear that "travel is a key component" to a gig at Monitor, so applicants should "expect to travel a lot." That said, the firm "is sensitive to travel burnout", and it's "not uncommon", sources tell us, to be granted a case close to home after a case requiring significant travel.

But for those who enjoy being on the road, and "if you're into more 'extreme' work travel, this is the place for you." A contact says, "Monitor has sent me to nearly every continent in the world!" And many report having hit "many different continents" within their first year on the job. Monitor sends consultants to such exotic places as Morocco, Algeria, Saudi Arabia and Siberia. Indeed, as one respondent comments, "travelling is part of Monitor's value proposition."

You gotta work to live

Those who don't value world travel as much say "travelling abroad is a crucial barrier to work/life balance." On the bright side, consultants "hardly ever work on weekends" and they have the freedom to "work from home to be closer to family". Although "there isn't much time for anything other than work from Monday through Friday, most weekends are free." Achieving balance can be "very challenging", though, and requires "being organised and communicating a lot with family". Insiders feel that, on the whole, Monitor is "very sensitive" about personal time, and "work/life balance is strongly encouraged." The consultancy "encourages people to take vacation and there is no value in face time". Still, insiders say work/life balance is something "you have to work at, as it's not something that the firm delivers to you on a plate".

High pay for high performers

Compensation at Monitor is "very much individualised". A consultant states that those who are performing well can "make more money than at any other consulting firm". However, "one will earn somewhat below the industry average if performing less strongly." Some feel this results in "disproportionate rewards for high performers". And whereas "Monitor has good starting salaries," pay packages "lose competitiveness over time". Overall, respondents feel that average compensation at Monitor is "lower than at other leading firms".

Adding another layer of disappointment is that the firm offers "very little clarity into how the bonus is calculated". Monitor applies a "total annual compensation system", which, according to one insider, "means that two people that performed equally will get the same total package at the end of the year, rather than simply the same bonus". In other words, "bonus is the difference between the total package you deserve and the salary you were paid throughout the year." Some feel this system is "much more fair than a straightforward bonus system", while others think "bonuses represent too high a share of total compensation."

In terms of additional benefits, consultants get "health, travel and life insurance", as well as "partially covered gym memberships, company cars and cell phones with unlimited calling". The firm also offers "flexible arrangements, including transfer opportunities and the ability to work from any office". There is a "pension scheme", and partnership shares become available "when you reach group leader". New parents enjoy "substantial parental leave and, in an informal way, the firm is highly constructive in helping new parents". Monitor helps out "by putting them on nontravelling allocations and easily granting leave". And for all employees, "Monitor is very flexible regarding holiday time." A contact says, "No one says anything if I tack a day or two onto a business trip to do a little exploring of my own."

Senior interaction galore

Monitor consultants tell us their supervisors and clients are "generally great people" who are "very approachable and down-to-earth". "Supervisors tend to be very open and accessible," and consultants are "empowered, respected and given the opportunity to engage with the firm's and clients' senior management". An insider says, "I have hardly ever seen any other company where top management is so close to the people, reaching out to feel the pulse." A colleague adds that Monitor's leaders are "great counsellors who care about employees' career paths".

Consultants also get "great exposure to senior clients" and are expected to take "maximum ownership of the client relationship". Client interaction for junior consultants can "depend on the case", but in general, "there is lots of opportunity for senior client access for those who are ready and willing to take it." Many respondents say they "work with senior clients daily and independently", while others claim they get "all the senior client interaction they want—and more!"

Training gets a face-lift

Historically, "most training at Monitor has been on the job." But recently, "training has been revamped and upgraded significantly." New programmes, designed "for junior and senior case team leaders, focus on leadership, project management and client development skills". The programmes are "global, bringing consultants together from around the world". Under the new model, "newbies receive boot camp training at a regional orientation." Then, during the first two years at the firm, "you are expected to participate in four training sessions, including operations research, finance, marketing and feedback." Project leaders receive a "one-week intensive training session at the headquarters in Cambridge, Massachusetts". Sources feel that the new training requirements are "just the right level—enough that junior people feel invested in it and not too much that they are out of the allocation pool for too long". However, others say the firm's unofficial training is still "where the magic happens". It is a "very strong part" of Monitor's culture, and people "really invest themselves in it". A contact says, "This is a job where you really need to learn by digging into a project."

Find your own path

Monitor's promotion policy is "not up or out", respondents say, as the firm has a "very individualised career development plan". The process, although "sometimes not very structured", is "ultimately meritocratic and relatively nonpolitical". A consultant explains that there is "clear intent to provide individual developmental paces", and "some people progress faster than others." For this reason, the consultancy "is a great place to progress faster than at other firms", but it is "an awful place to manage your expectations because there are no officially set markers for advancement".

As a general rule, "as long as the firm sees potential for further development, you will be given time to develop at your own individual speed." High performers can advance "extremely quickly, whereas low performers are dragged along for quite a while". Some respondents feel that a more "up-or-out attitude is emerging", but most cases are still "handled with the individual's story in mind". One way or the other, "constant growth is expected" of all staffers. A source explains that it "usually takes about 24 to 30 months" to be promoted from associate to consultant, and "top performers can be invited to partnership within five to six years."

Five-star offices

Monitor consultants work from "stunning buildings in good parts of town, with great working spaces". The firm has a "preference for private offices shared by two to three consultants", so there are "few open spaces, but still enough space for all to breathe". Paris wins the award for rave reviews. A source based there says, "Our office in Paris is beyond fantastic! The place should be a museum, but instead it's the best office and best address in Paris." The location has "tons of windows, nice furnishings and high ceilings". And as an added bonus, the facility has historical significance: It is "the former Hotel Particulier, where the composer Chopin died". The London-based crew is pleased with their lodgings as well. They work from "one of the most interesting historic buildings in London, with architecture and décor that is unusual and beautiful". To top things off, "there is a Michelin-starred restaurant and a wonderful café downstairs."

The Zurich office has "great support staff" and is located with "easy access to public transportation". Madrid also is located "quite centrally", and consultants there make use of "a huge terrace space in summertime". And overall, although they can be "time-intensive to reach from airports", Monitor's offices are "usually located in very nice, high street areas". Most agree that the firm has a knack for picking the "best spots in each city" to set up shop.

Retaining women is tough

"Monitor has a strong commitment to women," insiders insist. It is reportedly "very good at hiring women directly out of undergraduate programmes", and there are "no egregious examples of sexism". However, when it comes to retaining female consultants, the firm falls short. As a source points out, Monitor is "less effective at keeping women after their first three to four years". A colleague agrees that the consultancy is "not out in front in terms of structuring roles and opportunities to retain women at more senior levels". But there are "a few programmes designed

> 66 There is a 'strong emphasis on feedback and open communication'. 99

to provide support to women who are interested in making this a longer-term career choice", a respondent notes. There is an "informal women's network in each of the offices", but "little formal mentoring", a source comments, although Monitor did launch a "women's leadership initiative" in 2007, and others claim the firm is doing "all it can to retain women". According to a contact, "The career is hard on women who want to have a family; it has nothing to do necessarily with the firm." For those willing to make the sacrifices, "there is no reason why a woman can't succeed at Monitor."

Accepting environment

Sources say Monitor has a "very multicultural workplace and is very receptive to minorities". In some offices, "clubs have been set up for various minorities," and the firm has a "clear set of policies" on equal rights. Many consider the firm's "cosmopolitan, highly diverse pool" to be "one of its strengths", though others claim "diversity recruiting has been a challenge," adding that Monitor could use "more role models of different racial backgrounds".

In addition, Monitor is a "very open and accepting work environment" that has a "significant GLBT community in many offices"—with a "specific GLBT organisation and code of ethics" to boot. Consultants tell us that some of the firm's "very top staff is gay and out". Monitor has a "strong network within the company" and also "sponsors a number of gay-in-the-workplace conferences and attends GLBT hiring fairs".

Dedicated to many causes

The consultancy undertakes "lots of pro bono work" and, in fact, has a unit dedicated to it—Monitor Institute. The firm works for such causes as "the Bill & Melinda Gates Foundation in Botswana, Immigrants in Ireland, Teach for America and Business Against Crime, to name a few". Consultants also work "extensively" with New Profit Inc., a foundation that gives grants to nonprofits that are stable, strong enterprises. A contact says, "We provide them with an ongoing case team, with rotating team members, that allows NPI to invest in its portfolio companies with both money and consulting expertise." In addition, the firm is "highly involved in becoming carbon neutral, and is very environmentally conscious".

Furthermore, individual consultants are "usually supported" in their social endeavors. One insider says, "I'm teaching school kids once a year for a week on business topics, and the company pays me my full salary and any travel costs." Monitor "regularly organises charity drives and significantly encourages involvement" from its staff. A consultant explains that involvement is "not always reflected in compensation", but it is "expected and encouraged at the more junior levels to develop more well-rounded consultants". It's no wonder the firm was "recently awarded a prize for its efforts in the social sector". □

A.T. KEARNEY

Lansdowne House
Berkeley Square
London W1J 6ER
United Kingdom
Phone: +44 (0)207 468 8000
www.atkearney.com
www.atkearneyprocurement
   solutions.com

The Stats

Employer Type: Private Company
Managing Officer & Chairman of the
Board: Paul Laudicina
2008 Employees: 2,500
2007 Employees: 2,400
2007 Revenue: $785 million
2006 Revenue: $727 million
No. of Offices: 51

Practice Areas

Innovation • IT Strategy • Marketing &
Sales • Operations (Manufacturing,
Procurement, Supply Chain) •
Organization & Transformation •
Strategy (M&A, Organic Growth) •
Sustainability

Employment Contact

See the careers section of the firm's
web site

European Locations

Chicago (HQ)
Amsterdam • Berlin • Brussels •
Bucharest • Copenhagen • Düsseldorf •
Frankfurt • Helsinki • Lisbon • Ljubljana •
London • Madrid • Milan • Moscow •
Munich • Oslo • Paris • Prague • Rome
• Stockholm • Stuttgart • Vienna •
Warsaw • Zurich

Pluses

• Diversity of projects
• "International environment (even when
  working at your home office)"
• Immediate exposure to high-level clients
• "A.T. Kearney really is energetic about
  building and growing the firm
  nowadays"

Minuses

• "The assumption that you are available
  for the firm 24/7"
• Some internal processes are
  cumbersome
• "Longer tenure than competitors, no
  proper up or out"
• "Limited recognition and appreciation
  from directors and partners"

THE BUZZ
WHAT CONSULTANTS AT OTHER FIRMS ARE SAYING

• "Good name; traditional"
• "Still viewed as 'in crisis'"
• "Attracts very smart people"
• "Client first, firm second, individual last"

THE SCOOP

U S-based A.T. Kearney stands tall amongst the ranks of some of the oldest management consultancies, tracing its lineage back to McKinsey & Company. There, Andrew Thomas Kearney joined the Chicago-based firm in 1929 as one of its first partners, working alongside former University of Chicago accounting professor James Oscar McKinsey. In 1939, two years after McKinsey died, the company was divided into two arms: McKinsey and Kearney (which Kearney operated from Chicago), and McKinsey & Company (which New York office head Marvin Bower ran from Manhattan). Some seven years later, Bower bought from Kearney the exclusive rights to the name McKinsey & Company, at which time Kearney renamed his concern A.T. Kearney & Associates, working with clients primarily on operational and manufacturing efficiencies.

Sights set across the globe

Though it still maintains its corporate headquarters in Chicago, the global management consulting firm today has 51 offices worldwide, 24 of which are in Europe. A.T. Kearney opened its first non-US office in 1964, in Düsseldorf, and from there set its sights on the rest of the world, planting flags in major business centres across Europe, North America and Africa. In 1972, the company chose Tokyo as the city in which to establish its Asian presence, later branching out into Latin America in 1994.

> ❝ Travel is expected, but is often fun and rewarding. ❞

New parents spawn growth

In 1995, A.T. Kearney was acquired by Texas-based global technology services giant Electronic Data Systems. The pairing was mutually beneficial at the outset, providing A.T. Kearney with a straight line to many of EDS's top-shelf clients (and vice versa), while also affording EDS a much-needed boost in consulting service expertise.

But beneath this fair-weather sky brewed a storm. The EDS acquisition in 1995 essentially morphed A.T. Kearney's privately owned partnership model into that of a subsidiary of a publicly held company—which didn't sit particularly well with managing partners at A.T. Kearney, whose compensation levels commensurately morphed to reflect those of executives at a public concern. Along with cultural differences at the senior management level, the tech boom that had proven so pecuniarily beneficial in 1998 burst shortly thereafter, putting A.T. Kearney at a

A.T. Kearney

competitive disadvantage in recovery. While other consultancies were able to effectively absorb losses when the economy dipped, A.T. Kearney did not fare so well, as aggressive downsizing took its toll in brand equity. The company also continued to struggle to shore in monies for its parent, posting declining revenue year to year.

Back in black

In 2005, buzz abounded that EDS was looking to offload A.T. Kearney. Sure enough, the rumours proved to be true, as Monitor Group made an offer to buy. But when Monitor withdrew its offer that August, EDS decided to sell A.T. Kearney back to the consultancy's management team. A few short months later, in January 2006, the deal was done. Over 170 A.T. Kearney officers in 26 countries participated in the buyout, which did not include the consultancy's executive search unit and maintenance, repair and operations management group.

A.T. Kearney now operates once again as an independent, privately owned concern, and the buyout proved to be quite beneficial to the firm's bottom line. Revenue in 2007 was $785 million, up from $750 million in 2006. And, remarkably, the oftentimes strained relationship between management factions at EDS and A.T. Kearney today is friendly, with both companies engaged in a multiyear service and marketing agreement in which A.T. Kearney continues to provide consulting services to EDS and its clients.

Breadth of services and specialties

Today, the independent A.T. Kearney employs some 2,500 people worldwide, 65 per cent of whom are consultants. The company's service practices include merger, growth and IT strategies, along with enterprise services transformation, and innovation and complexity management. The consultancy also operates a procurement solutions arm devoted to sourcing and supply chain management.

Areas of industry specialty within A.T. Kearney include aerospace and defence, automotive, communications, consumer and retail, financial, government, technology, pharmaceutical and health care, process industries, transportation and travel, and utilities.

Captain on deck

At A.T. Kearney's helm today is Managing Officer and Chairman Paul Laudicina, who joined the firm in 1991 and was named chief in 2006. With over 25 years of global consulting and management experience, Laudicina is only the seventh person to lead the consultancy in its 80-year history. He is the author of the book *World Out of Balance*, and was named one of the Top 25 Most Influential Consultants by *Consulting* magazine in 2005 and 2007.

Council affords insight to global leaders

Mr. Laudicina is also founder and chairman of A.T. Kearney's Global Business Policy Council, which stands amongst the consulting industry's longest standing strategic services organisations for CEOs. Established in 1992, the GBPC was created specifically to provide business leaders with an early warning system about potential shifts in economics, politics, technology, demographics and culture that have the potential to disrupt global business.

Hosting annual summits for global CEOs, this group also produces numerous intellectual capital products and consulting services that help provide insight into important global trends. For instance, its Foreign Direct Investment (FDI) Confidence Index and regional FDI Confidence Audits analyse the drivers that influence foreign direct investment trends. On the services front, the council's global business diagnostic offering identifies and assesses new opportunities and vulnerabilities in globalisation strategies. Meanwhile, its market attractiveness profiling system serves to pinpoint promising markets for expansion, and its guided planning through scenarios system helps organisations prepare sound strategies for long-term growth.

A.T. Kearney also manages the European CPO Club, hosting a group of top European supply chain and procurement management thought leaders at two annual meetings.

GETTING HIRED

Better clear the bar

Sources say there's a "very high bar" set at A.T. Kearney, which results in a "very competitive" hiring process—in fact, as one consultant explains, "the number of candidates that makes it through the process can be quite small." "We just hire the best," a vice president confirms, so it's no surprise that the firm is willing to "spend a lot of time and energy" on recruiting and interviewing candidates.

The consultancy recruits at "many of the major universities in Europe", including INSEAD, LBS, SDA Bocconi, Polytechnique, Centrale, Mines, Ponts et Chaussées, Supelec, ENSAM, ESSEC, Oxford, Cambridge, Manchester and Ljubljana University and the Universitiy of Zagreb, to name just a few. "Nonbusiness-, technical-, law-

and natural sciences-focussed universities" are also potential targets, and in addition to campus recruiting, the firm will look for hires "on a referral basis".

Case-intensive

"Depending on the office, the recruiting process can differ," insiders tell us, and besides geographical variations, "there are different processes depending on rank." In general, candidates should expect at least "three rounds" after an "initial resume screen". The first round may consist "of two interviews with midlevel managers or associates", with some case study questions. A consultant notes that the second round is more intensive—"a full-day assessment centre with presentations, three interviews, group exercises and written evaluations". Interviews in this round will likely involve meeting with "one or two partners". Those who go on to a third and final round will meet "with a managing partner".

> ❝ You can have direct interaction with your client very early. ❞

"In all of the interviews, business cases have to be solved and brainteasers may appear," one insider warns, but an associate clarifies that they're genuine "case studies, rather than simple or trick questions". Interviewers may also ask "questions on the CV", as well as questions designed to gauge a candidate's awareness of market conditions, for example, "questions on current financial data, like exchange rates".

Sources recall a variety of case questions, like, "Define a market entry strategy for a car tire manufacturer." Other questions candidates have fielded include, "What is the market size, in terms of yearly production, of water glasses in the country?" "If the CEO of a big utility group asked you for advice in a cost-reduction project, how would you approach this task?" "Would you advise a foreign utility company to enter the electricity market of a given Central/Eastern European country?" "How will the energy landscape in the Middle East look in 20 years?"

On the team

A summer internship at A.T. Kearney "is barely different from being a business analyst at the company", a respondent notes. "It's more like your three-month trial with the company." The experience is "demanding", but former interns say they "learned a lot" and "had direct client interaction and responsibility". "I became, from my very first day, a regular project team member," says a source. Another agrees, "I worked as part of a team at a client site. I was immediately integrated and could develop and implement my own ideas."

During the internship, interns receive "additional support from experienced consultants", and find that there's "mentoring available through the whole programme". Working at A.T. Kearney for a summer "convinced me to sign" the full-time offer that followed, says a current consultant.

OUR SURVEY SAYS

They get results

Respondents describe the A.T. Kearney environment as "highly demanding and results-focussed", "more action- than intellect-driven". Staffers label themselves as "open and collaborative", "pragmatic and striving for excellence". There's a "democratic decision-making style", says one source, which "often results in no decisions, but also offers freedom and room for individuality". Inside an A.T. Kearney office—or at a client site—you'll find "a good mix of talented people with different backgrounds and a down-to-earth approach". Many employees come to the firm "with different skill sets and interests", and say "initiative and entrepreneurship are rewarded." "A.T. Kearney has an ambition to bring out the best in each consultant without streamlining everyone into a specific A.T. Kearney format," explains a recent hire.

At times, the demands of work means there's "less focus on socialising", and one senior manager believes the firm "is becoming more competitive and indifferent to the human resources". But, adds a source in Warsaw, the culture "really depends on the office. The developing market offices are still learning what A.T. Kearney values are."

Ready to go?

Travel requirements vary widely, "depending on the region you work in", and they may also "vary by practice" and by the specifics of each project. French sources, for example, say "a majority of clients are based in Paris, so Paris consultants don't need to travel a lot, except on international missions." A Copenhagen insider notes, "The offices in the Nordic region staff together, so this means that there is a bit of travelling between the Nordic offices if you are staffed on a project that is in another Nordic country, rather than your home country."

One problem with the firm's travel policy, says a source, "is that staffing does not look at your previous engagements to counterbalance international projects with local projects. Some people will spend a year abroad, while others stay in the office." Adds another, "Travel logistics take up a lot of time, which is typically widely underestimated by the supervisors."

For some, though, travel is manageable and is even considered a perk of the job. According to one consultant, "Travel is expected, but is often fun and rewarding, and there are also ways to reduce the burden of travel if you wish." "I managed to put limits and carve out my niche," a manager in Madrid says, "but most people sacrifice more time and family than I do. Fridays in the office should be given a higher priority and enforcement." And whereas one respondent says the demanding schedule can make it "difficult to sustain a relationship", others say their project managers "try to build in flexibility to be at home, unless it's absolutely necessary to be at the client." Either way, adds a manager, there's "less travel as you progress through the ranks".

Clients come first

Working hours are "long but manageable", insiders say, reporting that they often log 60 hours per week. The range stretches "from 50 to 80 hours" a week, one associate says, "depending on the project workload". The "art of managing long hours has to do with my own ability to set limits," explains a colleague, adding "the work/life balance has improved substantially over the eight years I have been with the firm. This may be a factor of the changing demographic of our consultants. Many have families, whereas in the past, most were single." "If you are able to prioritise well and work efficiently, you can really have 50-hour workweeks," agrees another.

As for project duration, it "varies between two weeks and two years", a managing director says, "but the average assignment is about 10 or 12 weeks." "Time off is usually planned after intensive and long projects," adds another source. Although work/life balance may be a function of your own time management skills, it also largely "depends on the engagement manager and on the nature of the projects". A Londoner advises, "The government practice is better. If the clients are commercial, the hours are much worse." On international assignments, the balance "is extremely difficult to maintain, but your project manager's personality" and ability to manage can make all the difference. And ultimately, the consultancy's commitment to results wins out. While employees believe the firm is making strides toward improving work/life balance, as one vice president puts it, "the client is the driver, not the company."

Travel in style

Compensation at A.T. Kearney is "higher than industry but lower than competitors", but respondents say they receive some solid perks, like profit sharing and health insurance, "a company BlackBerry", "nanny service", "skiing weekends", "good parties" and discounts "on travel, theatre, sports, etc." The firm also provides "flexible part-time models for consultants and flexible leave of absence programmes for mothers and fathers". As one new father explains, "Parental leaves are supported and arranged in a very fast and nonbureaucratic way." On the road, a manager says, "Expenses on projects are usually quite generous, which means we can have a good lifestyle when working." There's also a "very attractive company car policy starting at the senior business analyst level: You get free choice of car, and the company pays the leasing fee up to a fixed amount, and gas is included."

Two complaints arise, however, when it comes to compensation: bonus calculations are "always unclear", and the consultancy "does not provide extra compensation when you are staffed on projects abroad, not even in the Middle East, while some of our main competitors do".

Little time to train

"While we have an up-or-out" promotion policy, an insider says, "some degree of flexibility is applied." Moving up takes "two to four years per level, on average, but this changes depending on the market situation". And some complain about a "lack of transparency" regarding promotions; a manager says promotions "are very political, even at a lower rank".

The firm's training "is getting better", we're told, with "very strong coordination" between its European locations. "We have a half-dozen core training modules that are very valuable," an employee reports, but "we could do better on practice- or topic-specific training." Others believe the training offerings are sufficient, but admit that they don't always have room for them in their schedules. "It is quite difficult to have time to enroll in a training course," one harried consultant claims.

Juniors share the stage

There's a "strong emphasis on people development", and senior staff "are very accessible". "All my managers have spent substantial time developing my skills and making sure I am continuously challenged in my daily work," a London associate shares. Overall, insiders say, a "friendly and nonhierarchical" feeling prevails: "Arrogant attitudes are not welcome." "Teams are exactly that," a manager shrugs. "The only difference between team members is really just experience."

Even without much experience, sources say they get plenty of "highly visible" exposure to clients—a "really unique" feature of the firm. "The good thing with ATK is that you can have direct interaction with your client very early," a business analyst comments. "In my first project, I was working directly with the client." "The entire team, from analysts to partners, attends and eventually participates in client presentations," adds an associate. Concludes another, "As a business analyst, I've done two presentations in front of two CEOs of midsized and large companies. Not bad for a 25-year-old consultant!"

Room for improvement

There's also "not enough" charitable activity at A.T. Kearney, employees say. The firm does "rather limited" pro bono work, but many sources say they are unaware of any community activities in their offices. When there are, "it is usually driven by individuals' interests." "There will be a large drive on this front over 2008," a source claims. Others point to the firm's recent commitment to become "the first carbon neutral consultancy" by 2010, as evidence that it's paying more attention to doing good.

In Germany, however, insiders do participate in "about three to four pro bono projects a year" and lots of "pro bono coaching of students' social initiatives" via the Create A Difference programme.

International, but not always open for discussion

The firm gets mostly high marks on ethnic diversity: "We tend to have people from all over the place," a business analyst in Amsterdam says. Another notes, "There is full respect for people coming from different countries or different cultures." Adds a source, "Although I have not seen the stats, it seems that the firm has a higher-than-usual mix of nationalities, cultures and backgrounds—a very positive attribute." However, one London insider points out a lingering problem: "There is very little representation of minorities after manager level."

Being openly gay at A.T. Kearney can be tough, though, employees say. It's "a hidden subject," says one gay source, and a colleague notes that "there's no obvious or apparent programme or support group" to encourage awareness of GLBT issues. Instead, there's a tacit "don't ask, don't tell" policy. Things may be different across the pond, however; the firm notes that although it does maintain a global GLBT network, with a support group and a dedicated site on the company intranet, the network is stronger in the US than in Europe.

When it comes to gender diversity, the situation "has tremendously improved in the last years", one veteran believes. There's an "ongoing initiative to hire more women", but a source in Paris notes that there are still "no women above manager in this office". "Most of the women are part of the support staff, assistants or consultants in low positions," a senior business analyst observes. Concludes another source, "I believe the firm is doing a lot. It does not, however, succeed enough. Maybe some more scrutiny as to why this is the case would be necessary." □

A.T. Kearney

VAULT
10
PRESTIGE
RANKING

OC&C STRATEGY
CONSULTANTS

6 New Street Square
London EC4A 3AT
United Kingdom
Phone: +44 (0)207 010 8000
www.occstrategy.com

The Stats

Employer Type: Private Company
Worldwide Managing Partner:
   Michael Jary
2008 Employees: 450
2007 Employees: 350+
No. of Offices: 15

Practice Areas

Business Unit Strategy
Group Strategy
M&A & Transaction Support
Organisation & Change
Product/Market/Channel Strategy
Strategy Realisation

European Locations

Brussels
Düsseldorf
Hamburg
London
Paris
Rotterdam

Pluses

- Early exposure to clients
- "Exciting clients and projects"
- "You are always learning new things"

Minuses

- "Lack of diversity"
- "Having to explain where I'm working—our name recognition is still low"
- Limited resources

Employment Contact

www.occstrategy.com/recruiting

THE BUZZ
WHAT CONSULTANTS AT OTHER FIRMS ARE SAYING

- "Smaller, good reputation"
- "Due diligence shop"
- "Best paying"
- "Narrow scope"

THE SCOOP

O C&C Strategy Consultants is an international consulting firm with a three-pronged strategy for helping clients achieve their dreams. The first step is to create a corporate strategy that employs a creative vision of how the company can achieve its very best. Then the firm establishes a market strategy that helps the client remain competitive in its field. The last step is strategy realisation, where OC&C puts these plans into action and "makes it happen" for the client.

The consultancy was established in 1987 by Chris Outram, who served as chairman until February 2005. Outram is still active with OC&C, but today the firm is headed up by ex-Booz Allen Hamilton consultant Michael Jary. In the 20 years that OC&C has been in business, it has seen huge growth, with new offices popping up all over the globe. Today it has locations in Europe, North America, the Middle East and Asia, and its main areas of operation are group strategy, product and channel strategy, organisation and change, strategy transformation, and mergers and acquisitions support. OC&C covers a wide range of sectors, including retail, consumer goods, media, telecommunications, technology, travel, industrial, financial services and private equity.

Private equity experts

OC&C is a big name in the field of private equity consulting in Europe. It has worked with a whole roster of big-name private equity clients, including Apax, Blackstone Group, Cinven, CVC, Hg Capital, KKR, Permira and Texas Pacific Group, and its research often features private equity as a primary focus. Recent reports include a publication on the role of private equity in the consolidation of construction companies in Germany and another about how private equity principles apply to public companies.

Best place to work

OC&C Strategy Consultants is a popular employer name among Europeans. In May 2007, the Düsseldorf office was named one of the 100 Best Workplaces in Europe, after the Netherlands office received the award in both 2005 and 2006. The firm earned this distinction from the Great Place to Work Institute, a research organisation dedicated to recognising employee-friendly workplaces.

Middle East expansion

OC&C announced in August 2006 that it would partner with Middle East Strategy Advisors. MESA specialises in corporate restructuring, and boasts of over $2 billion worth of tangible adjustments in the past three years. Bringing in MESA as a member firm was a prime opportunity for OC&C to expand its reach in the Middle East.

Points for innovation

In addition to acting as a top European consulting firm, OC&C also serves as a cutting-edge source of research. In April 2008, the firm released an innovation index, a study that assesses the most innovative companies in the UK. The results in the category of food and beverage manufacturers was a bit surprising. OC&C found that the private equity-owned company Weetabix was the No. 1 most innovative company from 2004 through 2006. Weetabix, which has an estimated valuation of £225 million, bested bigger companies like PepsiCo, Cadbury Schweppes, General Mills and Muller, which occupied the No. 2 through No. 5 spots.

Though it may seem odd that a private equity-owned firm holds the top spot on the innovation index, OC&C's research reveals it to be perfectly natural. "PE ownership does not stifle innovation," the company said in its report. Instead, private equity is "particularly strong in the level of new product innovations they have introduced". There were two other private equity-owned firms on OC&C's index, Young's Bluecrest and Birds Eye, both frozen food companies.

Food for thought

OC&C's expertise in the food production industry came in handy in 2008 when it landed an account with Marks & Spencer, British retail giant. The firm will work with Marks & Spencer on reviewing its food supplier base, in an economy in which food production is getting more and more costly. With the price of commodities rising and more customers turning to locally grown foods, producers like Grampian and Premier Foods find themselves having to adjust their prices to compete with larger chains. Marks & Spencer's supplier base includes several hundred food producers, which OC&C will help to review.

GETTING HIRED

Cases come first

The hiring process at OC&C will generally start with "a numerical and logical reasoning test, followed by two rounds of interviews, each with case study-based interviews". "The first round consists of a numerical test, a presentation case and a normal case," an insider explains. "In the second round, you get three cases with three partners, or two partners and a senior project manager or principal." "Several of the case studies will involve some element of market sizing," a source explains.

For the most part, "interviewers will hone in on the cases, as opposed to, 'Why do you want to work for OC&C?'" The questions themselves may be "based on a project the interviewer has done", says a manager, adding, "We don't want candidates to prepare for a specific type of question, but we like them to be creative and to show their business sense and their ability to structure and analyse."

Interview rounds may include an "informal lunch with consultants and junior managers", and respondents say the "thorough" process moves quickly. "If we can, we try to do [both rounds] on consecutive days and get an offer the next day," an insider reports. "If we think you are good enough, we offer you a job—we don't try to fill quotas."

Busy, but recruiting

Current staffers recall a variety of case-based questions during their interviews. "I got this one: A retail company specialising in apparel asks you to help them understand why profit has been declining over the last three years," one consultant shares. Other challenges have included, "Estimate the market for

>   We take what we do seriously, but we don't take ourselves seriously.

energy drinks in Germany," "Assess whether a painter on £20K would make more money if she became self-employed, using reasonable assumptions about costs and earnings" and, "In a saturated market, what are your opportunities to further profitably grow your business?"

OC&C "welcomes applications from all schools", but actively recruits at Cambridge, Oxford, London, Edinburgh, Bristol, St. Andrews and Warwick, as well as Rotterdam, Delft, Amsterdam, Utrecht, Groningen and Eindhoven in Holland; HEC, ESSEC, ESCP, École Polytechnique, École des Mines, École Centrale and École des Ponts in France; WHU, HHL, EBS, Munich and Cologne in Germany; plus INSEAD and LBS for MBA hires. Candidates may hail from "public universities as well as several private business schools". OC&C is "open to all schools, looking for top talent wherever it comes from", but generally speaking, it aims for the "top 10 of every country where we have an office". If not every campus is on the firm's recruiting calendar, "it's a function of time, not discrimination," one consultant remarks. Some schools aren't visited "due to the difficulty of keeping consultants free to attend lots of career fairs; it doesn't mean there's a black mark beside candidates from other universities."

Reason to join

Remarking on the firm's summer internship scheme, a former participant calls the experience "great, and the reason why I signed up with OC&C". Agrees another, "It was a great experience—ample exposure to the client, very good team atmosphere. That's why I joined." Other ex-interns say they were "on the team from day one", getting a chance to experience "the work as a professional". "I was provided with far more opportunity than I expected," says a staffer who appreciated the chance "to truly understand the job". Yet another satisfied former intern says his time was spent "working on due diligence of a food retailer. I was given the same training as new joiners and was producing output for client presentations" from the get-go.

OUR SURVEY SAYS

Work hard, play hard

So who works at OC&C? "A fun group of clever people who know how to work hard but also how to switch off and relax", according to sources, who call the firm "entrepreneurial" as well as "honest" and "straight-up". "We take what we do seriously," one respondent says, "but we don't take ourselves seriously." That means the atmosphere is "intellectual and inclusive, but very focussed on delivery". Things can get "competitive, but not in a negative way", and "enthusiastic" co-workers are "always up for a game of table soccer", one of the firm's favourite sports. ("There does tend to be a laddish culture," says a London source.)

"Expectations are high, which makes OC&C a tough place to work, but at the same time a good place to learn," an insider explains. A "do whatever is necessary to get the job done" mentality prevails, "which can sometimes lead to stressed and overworked staff". "As a smaller firm, we tend to overdeliver, which sometimes takes a lot of energy and hours," agrees another. OC&C consultants are proud that their firm "is going places fast", but all that growth comes at a price: "overselling and a slight negligence of internal development and staff satisfaction". One source laments "having to turn down interesting work because we are always at capacity".

Passport optional

"With a little bit of time management and expectation management, you are able to have a well balanced work and social life" at OC&C, where the work/life balance is "a specific and measured objective at all levels of the firm". Of course, "as in all consulting, there are inevitable periods of imbalance toward work during project crunches." "Flexibility here goes both ways," a project manager says. "When there is a deadline, you might have to skip an evening appointment. When there isn't, it is no problem to go—a fact we discuss openly within our teams."

Officially, the firm is "committed to a 55-hour week, on average", and one associate consultant says long hours "are usually compensated" by a lighter workload another week. However, the need to keep up with business has some consultants feeling the strain. Says one insider, "There seems to be real emphasis on achieving a work/life balance, and the firm seems to be genuinely trying, but in practice this seems to be getting more and more difficult."

Assignment length "varies strongly", we're told, but "a typical project would be around two to three months." "Our projects are relatively short, so you are never stuck on a long and boring project," one source points out. As for travel, it's "an individual objective, rather than an indispensable requirement. Anybody willing to travel will be staffed abroad, and others can remain in their home country." Adds a UK consultant, "Some clients are based quite close to London, in which case we would normally commute there every morning and occasionally come back to the office in the afternoon." Those who do hit the road find that "we travel in a team, so travelling makes you get closer with your colleagues—you learn to value their strengths and tolerate their weaknesses."

Sweet wheels

Most respondents are reasonably content with their compensation, especially when it comes to "starting graduate salaries" and "the base salary" for all staffers, which they consider "top of the market". However, the bonus "is not much to shout about at the associate consultant level", and one insider says the end-of-year bonus for all consultants "will never compare to a top banker's". Another observes, "The pay is good, especially for consulting firms, but I don't think it is that favourable when you consider the work/life balance."

Firm perks, on the other hand, include "profit sharing and insurance", and "subsidised language courses and gym membership for any gym you want to attend". OC&C also runs "a cycle-to-work scheme where they pay for a bicycle for you to ride". "German consultants benefit from a very attractive car deal," and one auto-obsessed Düsseldorf source lauds the "lavish" options that include "Audi TT, Audi A4, BMW 320 Touring, VW Golf R32 and many others".

There's also "a set of incentive events" each year, ranging "from a good dinner with the team up to a great retreat with the whole company, including significant others".

Annual company events include destinations like "a weekend in Marbella and one at a castle in Germany, and a weekend in Mallorca". "We have a large Christmas party each year, where consultants can invite 10 of their friends, and every two years we go on a three-day ski trip," a Rotterdam insider reports. Sources also praise the firm's "Personal Development Bank, which funds activities unrelated to work", allowing employees to follow their passion out of the office, "may it be dance classes, wine tasting or mountain climbing".

Lads' land

Insiders bemoan the "lack of female role models and credibility of females" at OC&C, but some say gender diversity is improving. "A lot of our newcomers in the last two years have been women," a London source says, and a peer in Rotterdam agrees that "the proportion of women has increased significantly" in recent years. However, there's still "little cultural diversity and awareness of other cultures and experiences", and one staffer points out that "almost everyone has been a consultant all their life, so there's no diversity in the experience aspect, either."

"Though I want to stress that there are no barriers to minorities working at OC&C at all, in practise, the share of minorities in the office does not reflect the share of minorities in university laureates, which form the pool of prospective employees," admits an insider. Adds another, "This is not necessarily a criticism of the firm's management, simply that there exists a culture that has predominantly evolved around a white middle-class Oxbridge staff base. This is changing, but still predominant." And although there are "not very many openly gay" consultants around the office, at least one senior source states that "I am openly gay, and I have never encountered anything but welcoming and friendly attitudes."

> ❝ Supervisors and directors are very approachable and easy to talk with. ❞

Help you up (or out)

"On average, associate consultants are expected to advance to a consultant level within three years," but "in practise, this can be two to three-and-a-half years." An associate director explains that there's an up-or-out principle in place, but it's "applied flexibly to reflect individual development trajectories". What's more, those who do wind up heading out instead of up typically "get a lot of attention and support in order to find a suitable next career opportunity".

Within OC&C, "supervisors and directors are very approachable and easy to talk with," creating a "hierarchy-free environment". That's intentional, an associate director explains: The "close relationship" between associate consultants and directors makes it possible for juniors "to race down the learning curve quickly".

Record-setting training

Though some "would like to have more training opportunities" on the job, others say "the best way to learn is on a project." "A large fraction of the training is unofficial," a source explains. "You learn a lot while doing the job." Support from colleagues and supervisors makes it "fairly easy" for new hires to get up to speed, but most agree that "official training could and should be more efficient."

The exception is OC&C's popular "international training week", in which the entire firm heads off to a major city for networking and learning sessions. Insiders rave that it's "a great opportunity to interact with colleagues from other offices, and offers very good training courses".

Apparently, international training week brings out OC&C's creative side in all kinds of ways: Look for the firm's name in the *Guinness Book of World Records*, because it set three new records "as part of a team-building effort" at a recent gathering in Barcelona. (Those would be: "most people in a multi-legged race, least amount of time required to pop 1,000 balloons using 40 people and most people standing up simultaneously with arms crossed".)

Giving back

OC&C is "committed to doing at least six weeks of pro bono work per year", and "everyone has the opportunity to participate in pro bono projects," many of which are organised in conjunction with nonprofit partners. Consultants can also "dedicate some of their time to their own community and charity projects".

But when they're hard at work, staffers have good things to say about their office space. OC&C's base in London relocated in April 2008 to "outstanding" new offices "in the heart of the city", with "360-degree panoramic views over London". Sources in other locations say they're "on maximum capacity level" because of recent growth; nevertheless, OC&C earns high marks for convenient office locations, "large spaces", "ample parking", "large desks in spacious team rooms", as well as amenities like "soft drinks", "a kitchen" and, of course, "a table football room". □

PRICEWATERHOUSECOOPERS INTERNATIONAL LTD.

300 Madison Avenue, 24th Floor
New York, New York 10017
United States
Phone: +1 (646) 471-4000
Fax: +1 (813) 286-6000
www.pwc.com

The Stats

Employer Type: Private Company
Global CEO: Samuel A. DiPiazza Jr
2008 Employees: 146,000+
2007 Employees: 146,000+
2007 Revenue: $25.2 billion
2006 Revenue: $22 billion
No. of Offices: 766 offices in 150
   countries worldwide

European Locations

New York (HQ)
Network of member firms in:
Albania • Armenia • Austria • Belgium •
Bosnia & Herzegovina • Bulgaria •
Croatia • Cyprus • Czech Republic •
Denmark • Estonia • Finland • France •
Georgia • Germany • Gibraltar • Greece •
Greenland • Hungary • Iceland • Ireland •
Israel • Italy • Latvia • Liechtenstein •
Lithuania • Luxembourg • Macedonia •
Malta • Moldova • Monaco •
Montenegro • Netherlands • Norway •
Poland • Portugal • Romania • Russia •
Serbia • Slovak Republic • Slovenia •
Spain • Sweden • Switzerland • Ukraine •
United Kingdom

Practice Areas

Advisory
Assurance
Tax

Pluses

• "The fantastic quality of the partners
  and staff"
• Opportunity to be recognised based
  on individual performance

Minuses

• Assignments are sometimes repetitive
  in nature
• "Client volatility"

Employment Contact

Follow the Careers link at www.pwc.com

THE BUZZ
WHAT CONSUTANTS AT OTHER FIRMS ARE SAYING

• "Increasing reputation and presence"
• "Big and slow"
• "Great culture, great work/life balance"
• "Full of themselves and their brand"

THE SCOOP

B ig Four accounting firm PricewaterhouseCoopers has been steadily building its consulting practice in recent years, following the sale of its original consulting wing to IBM in 2002. These days, PwC's management consulting operations (or performance improvement, as the firm is calling it these days) focus on governance, risk and compliance, as well as financial and IT effectiveness. And it's not difficult to see why—the firm's advisory division (which includes its consulting operations) has increased its revenue from $3.4 billion in 2004, when business consulting was all but unheard of at the firm, to $5.7 billion in fiscal year 2007. That latter figure includes a 14.6 per cent increase in the division from 2006 to 2007 alone, a figure that was driven in no small measure by an increased focus on performance improvement. Overall revenue for the firm was $25.2 billion in 2007—a jump of some 10.5 per cent from 2006. Of that total, $11.4 billion was generated in Europe.

The making of the biggest name in the business

The history of the various entities that have merged over the years to form PwC stretch back as far as 1902, while other organisations acquired by the firm have a much longer life span even than that. The deal that created the longest name in the upper echelon of accounting firms, however, took place as recently as 1998, with the mega-merger of accounting giants Price Waterhouse and Coopers & Lybrand. The firm that exists today is structured as a network of member firms under the PwC umbrella. While each member firm operates independently within its own geographic locale, there is a considerable amount of cooperation and networking between them, ensuring that the company works as both a global entity and on a local scale. As evidence of that scale, consider that the firm operates in 150 countries, with a network of 766 offices and counting. Its employees number almost 147,000, with 41 per cent of those based in Europe.

Given its sheer size and country coverage, not to mention the independent setup of its member firms, it should come as little surprise that PwC services on offer vary slightly from place to place. Whatever the exact menu on offer in any one locale happens to be, however, the services will fall into one of three core PwC offerings: tax, advisory and assurance. The last of these was responsible for more than half of PwC's total revenue in 2007, pulling in over $13 billion. Tax is next in order of value, raking in $6.2 billion, closely followed by the $5.7 billion posted by the assurance group. The tax group is also the fastest growing at the firm, with revenue growth in excess of 15 per cent for 2007, compared to 14 per cent for advisory, and just 6.7 per cent for assurance. As for clients, meanwhile, the firm works with some of the biggest

PricewaterhouseCoopers International Ltd.

names in global business, including the likes of AXA, JPMorgan Chase and Lloyds TSB in finance; 3M, Honeywell, IBM, Sony and Walt Disney in technology, infocomm and entertainment; and Anheuser-Busch, Caterpillar, Ford, Johnson & Johnson and many more in consumer and industrial products and services.

Setting the record straight

PwC's previous consulting operation was an IT-heavy concern (hence its eventual sale to IBM), that also specialised in management consulting. Following the collapse of Enron and the revelation of then-Big Five firm Andersen's involvement, the decision was made to sell off PwC's consulting unit to avoid the sort of conflict of interest that had arisen with Andersen both auditing and advising Enron. Prior to the sale in 2002, PwC had toyed with the idea of spinning the division off as a separate entity, to be registered in Bermuda and known as Monday. In the wake of Enron and a number of other high-profile accounting-related business scandals, however, the prevailing climate did not favour anything that could be perceived as less than above board—including setting up a business in an offshore tax haven. In addition, then-newly enacted Sarbanes-Oxley legislation had established more stringent rules for public accounting firms that were still being digested. With this as a backdrop, IBM's $3.5 billion offer for the unit in mid-2002 seemed the perfect solution, and the deal went through in October of that year, officially ending PwC's involvement in the consulting world. That said, PwC did hold on to certain segments of the business, including its government advisory, which remained inactive for several years.

> ❝ PwC's culture is 'demanding but fair', and 'collegiate yet challenging'. ❞

The second coming

Come 2005, the firm began re-establishing its consulting credentials in the US, focussing on federal government units such as the IRS, Social Security and the Department of Defense, before casting out abroad for business advising government agencies around the world. That side of the business remains one of the key consulting areas for PwC, along with outsourcing, one of the firm's particular strengths. That outsourcing expertise comes through in regular publications, studies and white papers released by the firm. One major piece of recent research concerns the world of outsourcing, and its benefits and limitations for clients. Among the findings in PwC's 2007 Global Outsourcing Survey is the startling finding that some 91 per cent of survey respondents said they would outsource again, regardless of their present level of satisfaction with the process in their organisation. That fact

PricewaterhouseCoopers International Ltd.

alone gives the firm reason to be cheerful, given that it facilitates outsourcing for clients, and is committed to increasing satisfaction levels by raising the value gained from outsourcing for its clients. Or, as the report puts it, "At PwC we are not interested in driving down costs in an inappropriate manner. We are committed to helping clients and service provider partners achieve productive, sustainable outsourcing arrangements such that each achieves their specific business objectives."

Perhaps the reports that have made the biggest impact of late, however, concern the future of the global economy. In 2007, the firm released one study projecting that an E7 group of emerging economies—China, Brazil, India, Indonesia, Mexico, Russia and Turkey—will have overtaken the performance of the current G7—the US, Japan, Germany, France, the UK, Italy and Canada—by at least 25 per cent by the year 2050. In March 2008, meanwhile, a follow-up report predicted that China will have outstripped the US as the world's largest economy by 2025, but it also analysed 13 countries beyond the E7 BRICs (Brazil, Russia, India and China), identifying Vietnam as having the potential to be the fastest growing in the world between now and 2050.

And with a keen eye on the Far East, PwC has announced that it plans to invest between $50 and $100 million in China in the near future to hire new talent for advisory and tax services. As the first phase of this expansion, PricewaterhouseCoopers China appointed 57 new partners for its mainland China and Hong Kong practice in June 2007.

Local focus, international expansion

In addition to those global reports, the firm also produces studies on a more local level. In the UK, for example, recent region-specific research has focussed on issues such as the state of the country's junior mining industry. The Luxembourg branch, meanwhile, has a phenomenal output of reports on the lay of the local land, with titles including "Opportunities and Competitive Re-Positioning of Luxembourg Private Banking by 2012-2015" and "Cities of the Future—Luxembourg City Profile".

GETTING HIRED

An eye to the top

The best starting point for finding both graduate and experienced-hire employment opportunities with PwC is the careers section of the firm's web site. There, applicants will find links to PwC sites in more than 50 countries throughout Europe and the Middle East, each containing information on how to apply for a position locally. Although the recruitment process for graduates varies in detail from one country to the next, one consistent point is the firm's determination to recruit from the top universities in each region. A source in London tells us that his office "recruits at a range of top universities in the UK and Continental Europe", although "more diversity in terms of universities can be seen in recent intakes." A source in Lisbon, meanwhile, points to several institutions throughout Portugal at which PwC recruiters can be found, including Universidade Nova de Lisboa, Universidade Catslica de Sco Paulo, ISCTE, Faculdade de Economia do Porto, ISEG, ISCAL and ISCAP.

The hiring process is described as "long-winded sometimes, but fair", and consultants say it involves "normal capacity tests, group and individual exercises, and interviews". A staffer makes a point of noting that "there are two rounds for graduates." Of those, "the first consists of a case interview and a CV interview, and a numerical ability test. The second consists of the same elements (except the test) with senior staff, as well as a range of other exercises." In preparation, one consultant in the UK offers the following advice: "Be prepared, know why you want to work for PwC, why you want to work within the role you're applying for and have some awareness of business issues, with commercial awareness scoring very high marks in the selection process."

OUR SURVEY SAYS

Passive, aggressive

PwC insiders describe the culture at their firm as "demanding but fair", and "collegiate yet challenging". While most sources agree with those descriptions, it does seem to be the case—unsurprisingly—that offices in Europe come in all different flavours. In London, for example, one source says "the key element of corporate culture at PwC Strategy is its openness and friendliness. With the group being a relatively small practice, where one can know most people, one never feels bad asking questions even about basic things." Over in Madrid, however, the touchy-feely side is apparently less important. "The culture is highly aggressive for being a consulting firm. Furthermore, I would describe it as being meritocratic and fast-paced," a consultant remarks.

Breaking down the hours (and hours)

That fast-paced lifestyle can lead to consultants putting in some long hours. While one respondent claims that "50 to 60 hours per week should be a reasonable estimate of an average week across the project cycle," he's obviously not employed in Madrid. A staffer there tells us that hourly input can run to "90 to 110 on large complex deals, 70 to 80 on normal deals and 50 to 60 when staffed on internal/non-billable tasks". Another source, meanwhile, sums up the differences thusly: "Work/life balance varies significantly among different teams and people. The transaction-related nature of many projects PwC Strategy works on implies often short projects, hence a short cycle of pressure (with the first week of the project normally being relatively easy, and the last one very pressing). Everyone is expected to work hard when necessary, but arrangements to take some time off after a challenging deadline are not uncommon." This last point suggests that the key to achieving balance lies mainly with consultants requesting time off—a suggestion seconded by colleagues. "Those who don't achieve balance usually have only themselves to blame," says one insider. A cohort in London chimes in, noting that "[achieving balance] is very much up to the individual. Many of us are not good at doing this."

Life for associate consultants seems to be a more highly regulated affair, however, making work/life balance that much easier to manage. "Most work associate consultants and (to a slightly lesser extent) consultants do is office-based," an associate in London explains. In addition, "day or two-day trips to see the client facilities out of London are common in some projects, but not extensive site-based work." That's not to say that PwCers don't travel—the amount "can vary a lot", according to a source in Lisbon. Some of those who do clock major travel time express reservations about doing so. A primary reason for that is one of the firm's cost-cutting measures, which has a direct impact on consultants. According to a senior figure in London, PwC's "lousy economy-only policy in Europe makes flying a nightmare". Feel free to take a moment to dab away your tears.

Perking up

Despite the inconveniences of sitting in the back of the plane, PwC consultants have few complaints about the benefits and perks on offer. Aside from their competitive salaries, consultants wax lyrical about a "comprehensive benefits package" that includes such niceties as private health care, child care vouchers, "flash cars", flexible working days and even "charge codes for company events". All of which comes as icing on top of a "very individualised" training scheme that encompasses both formal and on-the-job elements, and that contains "great programmes and continual reminders to train and keep on top of the field". With that dedication to improving the skills and abilities of its consultants, it's little wonder that PwC is "not up or out" in its promotion scheme—far from it, in fact, with one consultant suggesting that "people tend to be promoted about a year after they've earned it." □

PricewaterhouseCoopers International Ltd.

1633 Broadway, 35th Floor
New York, New York 10019
United States
Phone: +1 (212) 489-1600
Fax: +1 (212) 489-1687
www.deloitte.com

The Stats

Employer Type: Member firm of Deloitte
 Touche Tohmatsu
Global CEO: James H. Quigley
Global Consulting Managing Partner:
 Ainar Aijala
2008 Employees: 150,000
2007 Employees: 146,600
 (25,000 in consulting)
2007 Revenue: $5.2 billion
 (consulting only)
2006 Revenue: $4.5 billion
 (consulting only)
No. of Offices: Over 600 in nearly
 150 countries

Practice Areas

Enterprise Applications
Human Capital
Operations
Strategy
Technology Integration

European Locations

New York (Global HQ)
Offices in more than 35 countries in
Europe, along with access to audit, tax,
consulting and financial advisory
professionals in nearly 150 countries
through the member firms of Deloitte
Touche Tohmatsu

Pluses

• "The opportunity to be connected with
 different types of businesses"
• Strong learning and training
 opportunities

Minuses

• "More work than staff at present"
• "Lack of benefits"

Employment Contact

www.careers.deloitte.com

THE BUZZ
WHAT CONSULTANTS AT OTHER FIRMS ARE SAYING

• "Thinkers and doers"
• "Formulaic approach to consulting"
• "Good people with powerful contacts"
• "Wouldn't know strategy if it took
 them out to tea"

THE SCOOP

Deloitte Touche Tohmatsu (DTT) is a collection of more than 70 firms with a global reach that encompasses nearly 150 countries and 150,000 employees, and offers services in four major areas: consulting, audit, tax and financial advisory. Organised as a Swiss Verein, DTT's member firms each have access to one another's areas of expertise (often working side-by-side on projects), while maintaining separate identities and legal standing. Member firms serve everyone from major global corporations (with whom, after reigning in $23 billion in revenue in 2007, DTT surely ranks) to government bodies, public institutions and local businesses.

Deloitte generated some 45 per cent of that $23 billion figure in fiscal 2007 through its consulting activities—not bad going for a firm that is primarily known as one of the Big Four accounting firms. Even more impressive is the fact that those figures squarely place the firm as the world's largest management consultancy outfit.

And then there were four

As accounting industry watchers will know, there was once a Big Five, until the fall of Arthur Andersen over the Enron scandal. That event caused the other big accounting shops (PricewaterhouseCoopers, KPMG and Ernst &Young) to divest their consulting businesses over concerns that auditors selling consulting services to auditees constituted a conflict of interest—exactly the sort of conflict that had led to the Enron affair in the first place. Of the Big Five, only Deloitte kept its consulting arm intact, a decision spurred mainly by the 2003 realisation that it would be more expensive to divest the concern than to keep it on. Accordingly, Deloitte held onto the division and

> 66 Deloitte 'has an open environment in which ideas can be floated by anyone'. 99

focussed on finding a consulting clientele that its accounting arm was not responsible for auditing. That approach has led the firm to where it is today—a position where the consulting practice generates almost as much revenue as its core accounting business. That heady fact puts the company in "a category of one"—an expression that often pops up in characterisations of Deloitte, both by analysts and in the firm's own literature.

Freedom to be independent

Deloitte's consulting units vary significantly from country to country, as each division is given the freedom to meet the differing needs of the clients it serves, wherever it may find them. In the US, for example (where it is known as Deloitte LLP), the company offers packages in customer relationship management (CRM), enterprise applications and supply chain management as part of its overall enterprise application offerings. In the UK, meanwhile, the enterprise application offerings are limited to CRM and enterprise resource planning.

Overall, however, although the terminology and methodology may differ, Deloitte essentially offers the same service to all clients the world over—the opportunity to tap into its expertise in management, strategic planning and decision making, and to utilise it for major projects such as rolling out new technologies or completing a merger.

Consultants—writing the future

Regardless of geographic sector, the research the company conducts is available to clients worldwide—in the form of books, articles and reports that consultants produce to share insights, strategy and business knowledge. Recent examples include Deloitte's February 2008 outsourcing survey, which found that many relationships between companies and their outsourcers are fraught with tension, to the point of being dysfunctional. Focussing on technology companies, the report included a state-of-the-industry analysis, and found that, among other things, outsourcing companies thought that more than 75 per cent of their clients hadn't planned their outsourcing needs properly—a problem caused by viewing outsourcing merely as a money-saving exercise. From insights such as these, Deloitte is able to aid clients in resolving the issues it identifies, and helps them prosper in the global marketplace.

In addition to research with a global focus, the firm conducts surveys and research with a more specialised, local sphere of concern. In the UK, for example, Deloitte recently released reports concerning the challenges facing UK life and pension providers, as well as analysis of "the emergence of pan-European retail banks through cross-border M&A". The latter report examines the fact that, in the last two years, "eight of the 12 big European M&A deals have been cross-border retail banking deals," and considers the future implications for the industry, drawing comparisons—and predictions—from the last decade of M&A activity in the American banking sector.

Indian expansion

Like many companies, Deloitte has been concentrating on emerging markets of late and, in February 2008, announced a planned expansion in India as part of that strategy. The company, which maintains two offshore centres in Hyderabad and Mumbai, stated its intention to increase headcount in the country to 12,000 by 2010, up from 8,750 at the time of the announcement. More than 50 per cent of those recruits planned are for the consultancy division, as the local market for consulting services is increasing across the strategy and operations, human capital and technology sectors. Deloitte's eventual aim is to have some 20,000 employees in India by 2014.

UK—unilateral kudos

Deloitte has been going from strength to strength across all sectors in the UK, posting record revenue of £1,802 million in 2007. Of this, some 24 per cent was generated by the consulting wing, which has become well known for its ability to help companies improve performance by restructuring debt and designing new business plans. It's a strategy that's paying off for the company on

> " Work is output-focussed, not input-focussed. "

the mantelpiece as well as on the balance sheets, as the firm was rewarded with wins in three out of nine categories at the inaugural Consultant of the Year awards in November 2007. The awards, sponsored by the Management Consultancies Association and *The Sunday Times*, saw Deloitte consultants take home awards in the human resources, information technology and best new consultant categories.

In February 2008, meanwhile, *The Sunday Times* further expressed its appreciation of Deloitte, naming the parent company No. 12 on its list of Best Big Companies to Work For. According to the paper's findings, "the accountancy firm last year extended fully paid paternity leave to two weeks, enhanced its pension benefit and increased its career break option from one to two years."

GETTING HIRED

Three's a charm

Qualified candidates for positions at Deloitte will most likely have "three levels of interviews" in the firm's "very well-structured and straightforward" hiring process. The first round, conducted by HR, focusses on "general tests, group interaction, logic tests" and the like. The second round is conducted by "senior consultants or managers", and generally consists of "complex business case studies". A recent hire in Lisbon gives an example: "What is the best method of auctioning, the Dutch model or the British model?" Finally, the third round is typically an "interview with a respective area partner", which, as one staffer quips, usually consists of "chit-chat".

Discovering talent

Insiders report that Deloitte recruits at "all top universities". Its recruiting efforts are widespread and comprehensive, and it holds self-named "discovery days" at traditional campus recruiting and career fairs. The firm's web site offers a country-specific search for all recruiting events taking place around the globe. With over 100 offices in Europe, recruiters seek out talent in almost every country. For example, in Germany, the firm recruits from the University of Mannheim, the University of Stuttgart and the University of Applied Sciences in Berlin; in Sweden, the University of Oregro; and in France at ESC.

The Careers Gateway section of the web site also gives plenty of information for new graduates and experienced hires about possible career paths at the firm. There's a job database searchable by region or practice area, and candidates are welcome to submit a CV directly online for any open positions.

OUR SURVEY SAYS

Straight up service

Deloitte staffers praise the firm's "performance-oriented, honourable, transparent and straightforward" culture, where people "think straight and talk straight", but there's also a "sense of fun". A longtimer reports that Deloitte has an "open environment in which ideas can be floated by anyone". And a London-based insider adds that despite an "edge of competitiveness, there's a reassurance that when the chips are down, people are there for you". The firm fosters "personal contribution and growth", we're told, and maintains a "real open-door policy" among supervisors. A partner notes that "there's a lot of emphasis on and encouragement for building long-term relationships," and at Deloitte, "people are at the centre of attention."

Celebrating diversity

Respondents also say the firm cultivates a "tolerant" environment and stresses "celebrating the power that diversity brings". One executive notes that his "current team of 48 is drawn from over 10 countries", and a colleague adds that the firm "commonly hires disabled employees". In addition, "there is an active GLBT network," although as one insider puts it, sexual orientation is as small a concern as "diversity of hair colour". He adds, "It is great to see a firm deal with this in such a 'nonissue' manner." Still, though, a few insiders do warn that it would be difficult "to be a mother and career woman" at Deloitte, and there's still "a long way to go at senior grades" when it comes to gender balance.

Output is what counts

Staffers of all backgrounds and persuasions generally report spending between 50 and 60 hours a week at the office. By and large, we're told these hours are acceptable and that "there are formal measures in place" to promote a livable work/life balance. For example, a staffer in Lisbon explains that "Deloitte in Portugal has a policy of not working during the weekends"— and a senior consultant

> 66 When the chips are down, people are there for you. 99

in Frankfurt says that consultants in his office "never work on the weekend", either. In addition, staffers have the "ability to work from home when needed". A partner in London happily reports, "I accommodate being a mother of children informally and flexibly, with the support and active encouragement of colleagues and peers." And even a partner who is no stranger to 90-hour weeks says emphatically that he is "absolutely" able to balance the job with his personal commitments.

Still, one senior source warns that the "work is output-focussed, not input-focussed," which means "I need to set my own boundaries." And a frustrated senior consultant in the Netherlands complains, "Usually you are not authorised to state the real time you spent at the assignment. Extra hours are forbidden." He claims that he is able to balance work and life at the firm, but qualifies that by adding, "Sometimes I force this to happen."

All over the map

Time spent travelling varies widely among staffers, with some setting out daily and others never leaving home. A partner in London who's on the road three days a week claims that "client-based travel is noticeably reducing though, partly because of our and their green agendas." Meanwhile, a consultant in Germany comments on his regular Monday through Thursday travel schedule: "That's OK, because most Fridays as well as weekends I am at home." Less satisfied, a frequent traveller in the Netherlands warns, "Projects are usually held only at the client site, which means you can be asked to travel all weeks during several months." Plus, he adds, "The time spent travelling doesn't count as billable hours. This impacts the time span you spend outside your home." On the plus side, many of those who travel say "it often means going to some of the best places in the world."

Frugal fringe benefits

Insiders largely do agree that salaries at Deloitte are above average for the industry, and some say they are markedly so. One source who does bemoan the size of his paycheque feels that the "consultancy firms pay less than other industries" in general.

We're told that partners receive equity in the firm, and other benefits include medical and dental coverage, "support for education programmes, eg, PhD, CFA, etc.", and "support for relocation". In addition, the firm puts money into keeping up its facilities—respondents say offices are "getting better all the time", with a particularly "massive investment" in the London campus, including a gym and a restaurant. Some consultants wish there were "more fringe benefits" (like a "car policy"), but at least, as one staffer raves, "the biannual parties with open bar are just mad!"

Making an impact

Deloitte gets consistently high marks for being "very active" in the community through "extensive volunteering and pro bono programmes", and for having "the biggest give-as-you-earn of any professional services firm", a partner insists. In addition, a senior consultant reports, "We have a global programme called Impact Day," and the firm has organised "two bespoke schemes for school leavers' employability skills and disability sport competitors."

Speed to supervisor

The solid "training opportunities" at Deloitte are a firm strong point as well, with the "large e-learning base" of particular interest. There's also plenty of learning on the job, as the "clients are fascinating" and, adds a partner, "they trust us to work on their most difficult projects."

In most countries, the firm has an up-or-out promotion policy, where consultants are "required to get to the next level after two years, on average". The positive side of the system is that promotions are "well defined" and there is a "very extensive feedback system". One senior consultant notes that "sometimes it is much too complex, but it works fine." So fine, in fact, that advancement is regarded as "fast". A respondent in Lisbon reports that in his office, the firm leans more toward an "up-or-out-or-flat" policy, since the country "has very strict laws protecting employees". But those who do climb the ladder there can generally expect to reach "manager level in five to seven years". ☐

40 Grosvenor Place
London SW1X 7JL
United Kingdom
Phone: +44 (0)207 389 7200
Fax: +44 (0)207 389 7440
www.lek.com

The Stats

Employer Type: Private Company
Global Chairman: Iain Evans
2008 Employees: 850+
2007 Employees: 750+
No. of Offices: 19

Practice Areas

Finance
Marketing & Sales
Operations
Organization
Strategy
Transaction Services

European Locations

London (Worldwide HQ)
Milan
Munich
Paris

Pluses

• "Very competitive" compensation
• "Increasingly comprehensive" training
  programme
• Minimal travel

Minuses

• "Not many women in senior
  management"
• Hours can be tough
• "Very limited client contact" for
  associates

Employment Contact

www.lek.com/careers

THE BUZZ
WHAT CONSULTANTS AT OTHER FIRMS ARE SAYING

• "Transaction experts"
• "Working, working, working"
• "Lots of talent"
• "Quantitative geeks"

THE SCOOP

Headquartered in London, L.E.K. Consulting employs over 850 business consultants in 19 offices worldwide, offering individual solutions to its clients' problems, rather than employing a cookie-cutter approach. The firm specialises in gathering, distilling and analysing data to increase the level of certainty with which its clients can approach the decision-making process.

L.E.K.'s clients include major organisations in both the private and public sectors. Between 2004 and 2007, for example, the firm provided services for more than 25 per cent of the FTSE 100. Those companies and their public-sector and international counterparts are leaders in a fairly exhaustive list of industries: aerospace and defence; agribusiness; air transport and airports; business services; building and construction; consumer products; destination and tourism; energy and environment; financial services; government; health care services; industrial products and services; life sciences, medical devices and biotech; media and entertainment; natural resources; private equity; retail; surface transport and logistics; and telecommunications.

Dot dot dot, no dash

The firm can trace its roots to 1983, when three former Bain partners, including current Chairman Iain Evans, founded LEK Partnership. Punctuation and "Consulting" were added to the company name (though the firm has always been in the consulting business) in 1993, following a merger with US firm Alcar Group that greatly expanded its global footprint.

The company that exists today offers services across four continents (Europe, North America, Asia and Australasia), and six major business consulting platforms: strategy, transaction services, operations, marketing and sales, finance and organisation. Within each of these service offerings, the firm follows a policy of "evidence, not opinion", relying on its core skills of analysing both qualitative and quantitative data to strategically advise its clients.

On the case

In its project work, L.E.K. aims to resolve strategic issues and reduce uncertainty in decision making by using detailed quantitative data analysis and qualitative assessment. But getting a feel for how that helps its clients is a slightly more complicated affair. On the corporate strategy side, a typical project for the firm involves review and financial analysis of potential strategic changes to a utilities company's portfolio—a move that led to the company's stock doubling in the space of three months, and again within a year. Within L.E.K.'s business unit strategy consulting wing, meanwhile, a recent costing analysis of all the operating units of a major US corporation led to the termination of several inefficient programmes and tens of millions of saved pounds.

To characterise the firm as a mere observer of the business world would be to resign it to the role of critic—a description that fails to take into account the development work its consultants carry out for clients. Within L.E.K.'s operations segment, for example, its new concept development team is tasked with assisting clients in coming up with systems and strategies to add value to their businesses. One such case involved L.E.K. building optimisation models to compare the current state of a global airline's business practices with several alternative strategies. Using the models— built after surveying 2,000 of the airline's customers—the firm was able to assess and project such factors as reactions from competitors and product life cycle, leading to the client increasing market share as a result of its findings.

Family-friendly, yet international

L.E.K. prides itself on its family-friendly working environment, offering part-time and flexible hours to consultants with family commitments, while at the same time offering the more footloose among them the opportunity to work abroad, should they so desire. The firm's international transfer system allows staff to gain experience in an L.E.K. office in a different part of the world. According to the firm, more than a third of its staff has taken advantage of that opportunity, working on cases that have involved an extensive stay abroad.

Taking a stand for environmentalism

In December 2007, the firm proved that the working environment isn't the only one it cares about. That month, L.E.K. announced its intention to become carbon neutral across its global network of offices as of January 1, 2008—quite a New Year's resolution. To do so, the firm employed its own expertise in evaluating the carbon emissions of each and every one of its offices—a figure that includes everything from computer monitors on standby to emissions from business travel—beginning in 2006. Commenting on the decision, Chairman Iain Evans touched not only on his firm's desire to mitigate its effect on the environment, but also of the opportunity that taking such actions offered his firm from a business standpoint. "Companies are recognising that sustainable business strategies can deliver real shareholder value and we are seeing an increasing number of clients who want to understand the commercial impact of their carbon footprint," he said. "As this service area grows and climate issues become more prominent, clients and employees alike expect us to show leadership through our own policies."

Putting shareholder scores on the doors

The year 2008 marked the firm's 25th year in business, as well as the 13th consecutive year it has partnered with *The Wall Street Journal* to publish its annual "Shareholder Scoreboard" report. Using market cap as a means for ranking the world's largest companies, the report analyses the returns those companies offer their shareholders. For non-US audiences, the firm also publishes Scoreboards in *The National Business Review*, *The Australian* and *The Bangkok Post*. In addition, L.E.K.'s consultants regularly publish their findings in books, journals and periodicals worldwide, as well as the firm's own industry-specific reports for executives and its Shareholder Value Insights publication.

From time to time, L.E.K. also benefits from ranking systems conducted by other organisations. That was certainly the case in February 2008, when the firm was selected as *M&A Magazine*'s M&A Specialist Due Diligence Provider of the Year. Commenting on the award, *M&A Magazine* Editor Patrizia Rossi described L.E.K. as "sophisticated, discreet and professional", and

>   66 Consultants tend to be 'intense and driven, though not internally competitive'. 99

went on to comment that the firm had "delivered good growth in the past year, supporting over 90 transactions with a combined value of £23 billion".

Back in April 2007, meanwhile, L.E.K. received the Queen's Award for Enterprise for International Trade. The award came as recognition for the fact that the firm had increased its international exports from the UK by 50 per cent between 2004 and 2007—an increase that saw the value of those exports rise to £56 million. The firm was the first strategic management company to win the award.

GETTING HIRED

Question time

Associate candidates at L.E.K. go through "two rounds of interviews and a numerical test". At the MBA level, there is "no additional testing", although MBAs will have up to "four interviews". The first round is with a manager and partner, and the final round is with partners. For associates, the first round of interviews is "usually with managers and associate consultants or consultants, and involves the usual mini-case study/market-sizing exercise, as well as a general chat about points of interest on your CV". During the final round, associate candidates can expect to meet with partners exclusively. The final round "covers similar topics", but the "case study is a bit trickier and the questions a little more probing". Case studies are "often taken from current casework".

Candidates may be asked questions similar to the following: "How many people are members of a commercial health club in the UK?" Or, "How big is the UK mobile phone market, excluding handset sales?" Other examples include, "What is the revenue of a London taxi driver? How many newspapers per year are sold in the UK? How would you develop a revenue projection for a new drug? How would you size the subprime credit card market in the UK? Should your client enter that market? Why?" In addition to case studies and market-sizing exercises, candidates may be asked about "personal motivation and drives".

Oxford and then some

L.E.K. recruits from "many top schools", including "all top UK and three European schools, plus top European MBA programs". Applications are "encouraged from any institution", but Oxford, Cambridge, LSE, Warwick, UCL, Imperial, ICADE (Madrid) and Stockholm School of Economics are "targeted specifically". Some say the "associate intake is very much Oxbridge-dominated." The London office generally recruits at the MBA level from London Business School and INSEAD, as well as from "US institutions".

Insiders say it's a good idea for candidates to "attend careers fairs and presentation evenings to get a feel for the firm." And another tip: "In the cover letter, try to demonstrate clear and logical flow, as well as proving you know something about the firm."

Might as well be full time

Internships are a worthwhile way to get a leg up on the incoming competition, as interns function "pretty much the same as an average associate or consultant". Participants in the programme get "lots of experience and responsibility, despite being unskilled". Interns spend eight to 10 weeks working with "several different case teams", and respondents who started out as interns tell us the experience provides "a lot of opportunity for both formal and informal mentoring." Many interns "receive full-time offers before the end of the summer".

Consultants are attracted to L.E.K. for its "better people, better pay" and "minimal travel", which causes them to select the firm over competitors. L.E.K.'s "reputation and training" are appealing, as is the "the nature of projects", which involve "much more strategy work" than the competition. Consultants appreciate the "friendliness of people" they encounter during interviews and are drawn to "the way in which L.E.K. tackles problems."

OUR SURVEY SAYS

A hardworking team

The atmosphere at L.E.K. is "analytical and challenging, but not unreasonable and arrogant". Consultants tend to be "intense and driven, though not internally competitive". In the London office, "partners are very involved in the casework, and the delivery of a project feels like a real team effort." The office has a "lively, though not playful, feel". A consultant reports, "L.E.K. always hires a great bunch of people who all get on and work hard at the same time." There is a "really young feel to the firm", and since there is "a large graduate intake of around 40 per year", there is always "the opportunity to make a new group of friends." Some complain that the firm's "external reputation is not as good as other leading firms'". But still, L.E.K's "strong team culture and very bright and dedicated colleagues" make it a "great place to start your career".

L.E.K. consultants enjoy covering "a large number of industries in the first couple of years", which is something "everyone is equally excited about". This makes for a "fun yet intellectually challenging" environment that's "focussed on results and performance"—and because everyone is so focussed, there is "very little banter during the day". But while L.E.K. is "numbers-focussed and fast-paced", it is "not a stressful environment".

We're in this together

In general, "people are very friendly and there are no big egos." At this "mutually supportive" firm, senior consultants are "very approachable if you have a problem with a piece of work". There is "no back-stabbing", and one insider points out, "If a problem is found when presenting work to partners, consultants and managers will cover for any discrepancies, as opposed to dropping an associate in it." There is "an aspirational nature around the office, which means that people are pushed, but not in a way that feels like they are not supported". In this "we, not I" culture, insiders tell us, "people are the greatest asset." It's not surprising, then, that many L.E.K.-ers go on to do great things. The firm counts Sean Williams, executive director of markets and projects at the Office of Fair Trading, and Damon Buffini, the current boss of private equity firm Permira, among its "high-profile alumni".

No need for a travel bag

Unlike many consulting firms, L.E.K. keeps "travel to an absolute minimum". First-year associates leave the office "very rarely", since L.E.K. is an "office-based firm, as opposed to client-based". The firm's focus on "high-level strategic questions enables employees to work, on average, four days out of five in the office". A consultant says, "I am doing my first six-week, off-site assignment after two years. Before this, I have travelled one day per week, max."

Because of the limited travel, "there is no Monday-to-Thursday culture." Some associates have spent time "working at the firm's Munich or Paris offices to assist with cases", but with "most clients being London-based", working at the client site is rare. As such, "travel has minimal impact on work or personal life" for L.E.K. consultants.

Short projects, demanding hours

Although travel is kept to a minimum, "especially for junior consultants", in-office hours at L.E.K. "can at times be demanding". Firm leaders, we're told, tend to be "absolutely reasonable, given the demands of the job", but consultants feel that they "do not have control of their time". The firm makes "every effort to make sure that work doesn't interfere with specific social plans, but occasionally plans have to be cancelled." Hours can be "unpredictable", but typically amount to about 55 to 60 per week. This can vary, sources say, with "some weeks when the hours are fine and some weeks when they are awful". Consultants say "the worst thing about the long hours" is having to work them with "no notice". The good news is", L.E.K. has a 'time off in lieu system', by which, if you work more than a certain number of hours a week … you automatically get a day off as soon as possible to make up for it."

The average project at L.E.K. is around six weeks—some can run as short as one to two weeks for private equity cases or as long as "two-to-four months for corporates". Some say, though, that "a weak management tier can lead to inefficient use of team time."

Save your plans for the weekends

Achieving work/life balance "can be a challenge" at L.E.K. Because of the "high unpredictability" of work hours, many consultants "avoid making personal commitments Monday through Thursday". To help stifle unpredictability, the firm has a "traffic light system to give advance warning of any late nights for the working week." For the most part, insiders say "the system works well," but "there can be the feeling that late nights—red-light notifications—are handed out too easily." The system is designed to "discourage very late or unscheduled late nights," but "special circumstances can demand extreme commitments." A source notes that while "some managers try to accommodate personal commitments," occasionally "you are left feeling guilty for having a life." This makes "regular weekday commitments tricky, given the lack of long-term foresight regarding workload". Insiders say senior positions within the firm can be "particularly demanding". There is, however, a "good effort by the firm's events committee to organise occasional bonding events." And fortunately, "weekends are almost always free."

Nicer on the inside

Lack of travel also allows consultants to work from a "modern" London office with "a fantastic design and a really comfortable working environment." The "beautiful office" is "light and bright", and is "well supported by transport links." The location offers "fantastic getaways for lunch", although some say it is "slightly lacking in bars and restaurants nearby". Due to a "lack of other professional firms nearby, the area does not have a city vibe." Still, consultants enjoy "very high-quality standards" inside the office, where "everybody is very accessible," as "only the partners have separate glass offices." Lately, though, consultants say the office has felt "a bit cramped" due to rapid growth of the firm, and it "lacks meeting space".

Generous pay packages

Compensation at L.E.K. is reportedly competitive, and "the profit share in 2007 was in line with expectations." Bonuses come in the form of a "global profit-sharing scheme", by which "every employee receives the same percentage of his individual total annual earnings." In recent years, the profit-share percentage has been "around 20 per cent" of base compensation. In addition, joiners receive "a signing bonus after undergrad and on return from business school." However, L.E.K. "does not have a pension scheme or make any pension contributions". In London, salaries are "reviewed every six months", which means that "it starts to increase, from an already high base, really quite quickly." And at the manager level, "pay is definitely in the top quartile." In other offices, pay increases come "every 12 months". As another boost, the firm offers "the opportunity to work in other offices for six months during your first three years". However, "if you are sent to another office, you have to pay your own accommodations and you only get local pay," which normally means "a pay cut from London pay". The firm notes, however, that this is in line with competitive regionalised salaries.

In addition to salary and bonus, L.E.K. consultants enjoy "many social events, including a weekend-long sailing trip, yearly trips abroad, ice skating and boat parties". There are also "case team dinners to top restaurants in London". The firm picks up the tab for "taxis if working after 9pm, and dinners if working after 8pm".

Consultants get subsidised gym memberships, private health insurance and "free worldwide personal travel insurance covering winter sports". They're also allowed "personal days, in addition to holiday, for funerals, weddings and moving house". Moreover, the firm recently launched a "family-friendly policy", which involves "market-leading maternity and paternity leave, and opportunities for flexi-time". L.E.K. hopes its new programme will be best in class since at this juncture, there are "next to no senior female staff", an insider reports.

Limited client contact

Due to L.E.K.'s office-based culture, opportunities to interact with clients are "very limited" at the first-year associate level, but things "get much better in the second and third years". The firm assures us, though, that consultants joining post MBA have regular client contact. Newbies also say that "more partner-associate interaction would be beneficial to the associates," but point out that there is "plenty of manager-associate interaction". Many "interact with the midlevel managers on a day-to-day basis", and some are asked to "sit in meetings with the most senior clients". For the most part, though, "partners and managers meet with clients."

Casework at the firm can be "quite hierarchical"—as a respondent notes, there are "times when partners don't adequately specify what they want at the start of a case, causing a junior consultant to start again from scratch in a very limited time frame." At times it can feel like there is a "limited focus on management skills and coaching in the partner group." But on the whole, senior personnel "are very driven and smart, but reasonable and not arrogant." That said, "senior staff are very approachable and social," sources tell us. A consultant states, "Socialising is not hierarchical. Ninety per cent of the time, even on hard cases, I have had a great time because the team atmosphere has been fantastic."

Taking training up a notch

L.E.K. has a "specific three-year training programme with regular morning training sessions", in addition to "mentoring and buddy systems". The programme "starts with a two-week orientation with other associates, covering the required computing skills and an introduction to business skills". This is supplemented with "regular personal development sessions every two to three weeks", which cover topics such as accounting, strategy and model building. In recent years, "training is getting much better and the firm seems to be taking it more seriously." A consultant says, "When I first started, you were not able to go to training if you had urgent casework, but now training is more of a priority." A great deal of training still takes place on the job, but the formal offering is becoming "increasingly comprehensive", albeit "still lagging a little bit". Since so much training takes place in the office, "it's really useful having the associate peer groups around you rather than away at clients."

Most move up or out

Promotions at L.E.K. are "purely merit-based", with "some people taking longer than others" to move up. There is "no strict up-or-out policy", but "most people who do not go up choose to go out sooner or later." In general, "standards are very high, and the competitive types of people we hire do not tend to hang around if they're not succeeding." In the beginning, associates "often progress with their peer group"— some say promotions are "virtually automatic in the first three years". But after that, "people tend to accelerate up the firm at different rates." Moving through the senior ranks "is meant to be on merit", however, "it seems more and more to be based on tenure—out or up rather than up or out." Staffers say the firm could be tougher about "weeding out the duds, as there are always a couple each year that get through". Promotion from associate to consultant "typically takes four years or so", and moving from consultant to partner is normally "five more years". Consultants agree that their firm has "very little room for slow progression". Generally, "consultants are promoted [to manager] within two years of joining, or they are offered help seeking other opportunities."

Room for improvement

Diversity at L.E.K. is "good at the associate and consultant level, but decreases in more senior people". Some say "procedures need to put in place" to rectify the fact that there are "not many women in senior management". Although the firm is "very receptive to women in the recruiting rounds", there are still "many more men than women". Insiders report that the lack of women has more to do with "the proportion of applicants", but a contact admits, "Maybe we could do more to encourage applications from women." L.E.K. recently implemented "a progressive family-friendly policy", designed to "improve our perception among potential female applicants and make it easier for exceptional females at the firm to balance the demands of work with their personal lives". Currently, there are "next to no senior female role models", but junior women say they "never feel disadvantaged". The consensus seems to be that the drop-off at the senior levels is "natural, given the work style".

With regard to ethnic diversity, we're told that the "London office is extremely diverse" and percentages of minorities are "pretty good" at junior levels. However, there is "no diversity in the partner group".

Tri-ing to promote community involvement

L.E.K. "hosts charity events throughout the year". The firm's "biggest contribution" is an annual charity triathlon for the Aplastic Anaemia Trust, of which L.E.K. has been a supporter "ever since the charity started in the early 1980s". The firm "encourages staff to do the triathlon", and in 2007, "25 people from L.E.K. participated and the firm raised over £26,000." L.E.K. is also "embarking on a programme to help sponsor and encourage children through university who otherwise might not decide to go". The programme, called Inspire, is a fully incorporated nonprofit organisation providing low- or no-cost consulting services to nonprofits focussed on education and youth development. A contact explains, "Volunteers devote time outside of their normal consulting jobs to provide strategic thinking and results-oriented analysis guiding organisational strategy, expansion opportunities, fund-raising models and impact assessments." L.E.K. does other "various pro bono work" and is proud to have been the first strategy consulting firm to go carbon neutral in January 2008. ☐

Becket House
1 Lambeth Palace Road
London SE1 7EU
United Kingdom
Phone: +44 (0)207 951 2000
Fax: +44 (0)207 928 1345
www.ey.com

The Stats

Employer Type: Private Company
CEO: James Turley
2008 Employees: 77,800*
2007 Revenue: $14.5 billion*
2006 Revenue: $12.18 billion*
No. of Offices: 700

* Assurance and advisory only

Practice Areas

Business Advisory Services
  Customer
  Finance
  People & Organization Change
  Performance Management
  Process Transformation
  Strategy
  Supply Chain & Operations
  Technology Enablement

European Locations

London (Global HQ)
Offices in 38 countries throughout
Europe

Pluses

• "Positive leadership"
• Prestige
• "Very strong sense of integrity and
  values"

Minuses

• "Hierarchical culture"
• Limited training opportunities for lower
  levels
• "Too focussed on internal politics"

Employment Contact

www.ey.com/global/content.nsf/
  International/Careers

THE BUZZ
WHAT CONSULTANTS AT OTHER FIRMS ARE SAYING

• "Down-to-earth"
• "Too big too quick"
• "Multi-skilled from a financial
  background"
• "Formulaic approach to consulting"

THE SCOOP

Having sold its consulting division to French giant Capgemini for some $11 billion in 2000, Ernst & Young has been steadily rebuilding its business advisory services ever since. The current consulting division, like those at fellow Big Four accounting firms, is part of the firm's assurance wing, and goes by the name—in EY's case—of business advisory. In addition to the assurance and advisory division, EY offers three more areas of core service: strategic growth markets, tax and transaction advisory services. Over 130,000 EY employees within those divisions serve a wide range of industries, including asset management, automotive, banking and capital markets, biotechnology, consumer products, insurance, media and entertainment, mining and metals, oil and gas, pharmaceutical, power and utilities, real estate, technology and telecommunications.

They don't *do* consulting ...

Within the firm's assurance and advisory division, meanwhile, there are a mere three subdivisions: assurance, risk advisory services and the aforementioned business advisory services. This entire division grew 16 per cent between 2006 and 2007, compared to the firm's overall growth rate of 15 per cent. EY shies away, however, from referring to any of its activities as "consulting", as Chairman and CEO James Turley explained in the firm's yearly review in 2007: "'Consulting' is a very broad and no longer particularly helpful term," because of the scale of what it covers—everything "from business strategy through to implementation and outsourcing".

... but they do consult

According to Turley, "some parts of consulting—such as providing advice on risk management, process enhancement or performance improvement—not only sit well with the EY brand but positively enhance our ability to deliver high quality service to all our clients." Accordingly, EY provides those services to complement its three core business areas. Turley also pointed out that other consulting services, "such as systems implementation of outsourcing", do not mesh with EY's strategy or business model. "That", he notes "was the consulting business we sold to Cap Gemini in 2000 and which we do not intend to re-enter." Got that? Advice but no implementation. Strategy but no outsourcing. Such is the Ernst & Young consulting model of today.

Not so young, but definitely earnest

Although headquartered in the UK today, the firm's lineage stretches back to Cleveland in 1903, when brothers A.C. and Theodore Ernst opened an accounting shop with the imaginative name Ernst & Ernst. Three years later, Scottish immigrant Arthur Young, together with his brother Stanley, opened another eponymous accounting shop—Arthur Young and Company—in the fair city of Chicago. Between them, the companies spent the next 85 years pushing the boundaries of the accounting business, more or less inventing management accounting (Ernst) and developing an expertise in training (Young).

The British connection was established in 1957, with a merger between Ernst & Ernst and UK firm Whinney Murray & Co. That movement, which created Ernst & Whinney, was the last significant development in the history of the firms until 1989, when a merger created Ernst & Young, which went on to become one of the original Big Eight audit firms. That number has since fallen to four, due to mergers and the Enron scandal—the latter event responsible for the tightening of Securities and Exchange Commission restrictions in the US. Tighter conflict-of-interest regulation led to EY's sale of its consulting wing in 2000, a deal that came with a five-year noncompete agreement with buyer Capgemini. Since that agreement ran its course, EY, as seen above, has been steadily rebuilding its capabilities, and currently employs nearly 70,000 staff in its worldwide assurance and advisory division. In the three years business advisory has been trading, accelerated growth has seen it reach the same size and value as when it was sold to Capgemini in 2000 (and within a much shorter time frame than it took the former management consulting services business to reach that same stature).

Global movers

In a significant shake-up of its operations, the firm announced in April 2007 that its global executive and global advisory council had approved the integration of practices of all 87 countries in which EY operates throughout Europe (Western and Eastern), the Middle East, India and Africa. The integration is not a sealed deal yet, and requires the approval of the 3,300 partners in the proposed EMEIA unit. Should they endorse the union, it would become a single, 60,000-employee-strong entity with a single executive team, and worth some $11.2 billion in revenue. The move is aimed at taking the firm to the next level in terms of globalisation, with current UK head Mark Otty nominated to lead the new division. Turley said that the move "reflect[s] the increasingly global nature of our borderless business environment, which is changing the expectations of both our clients and our people, and which requires nothing less than a truly global approach from our organisation".

Headline-grabbing clients

While a complete list of EY's clients would undoubtedly be a long and luminous affair, it's perhaps best to work instead with a representative sample. Clients basically fall into two camps—those where the firm attests to financial statements, and those where it doesn't. In the former camp are firms of the stature of Amazon, Coca-Cola, Intel, Renault and UBS, whereas the latter group includes AXA, Citigroup, eBay, Johnson & Johnson and Vivendi.

Inevitably with such a wide client base, there will be occasions where clients make headlines for the wrong reasons. One such example came in late 2007, when client Société Générale made news upon discovery of rogue trader Jerome Kerviel's actions. Although there is no suggestion that EY was in any way responsible, the firm's 2007 Global Review devoted a page to discussing the challenges involved in auditing SocGen's operations. Those challenges, presumably, are a lot stiffer since the discovery of Kerviel's impropriety—which, it should be noted, occurred long after the report was published. An unfortunate case, on EY's behalf, of retrospective mirth.

Getting it right

The firm received somewhat better news in April 2008, when its business advisory services team received the UK Management Consultancies Association Best Business Strategy Project award. The award recognised the team's work in creating a strategy and road map for the future of another luminous client—Sony Professional Solutions Europe. EY's strategy maps the way for Sony PSE to become a world-class service company and to more than double its revenue in three years. That same month, EY was recognised as one of the Top 50 Companies for Diversity by *DiversityInc* magazine. The publication lauded the firm's efforts to support career development, workforce planning, communication and leadership accountability for minority professionals, and to provide diversity programmes.

In February 2008, meanwhile, the firm was one of six inaugural members to be inducted into *Training Magazine*'s hall of fame, an exclusive honour that recognises outstanding achievement in workforce training and development. Additionally, the firm landed on *Fortune*'s 100 Best Companies to Work For list in January 2008, the 10th straight year it has made the list. The consultancy ranked 57th overall in terms of prestige, and No. 18 among large companies.

GETTING HIRED

Assessment goes both ways

Hiring at Ernst & Young is a "two-way process". "It's about a candidate finding out about the firm as much as the firm finding out about the candidate." Typically, the first round involves an "interview with a business case study review". This normally lasts "about 45 minutes", we're told. If successful, candidates "progress to an assessment day", which includes "a case study, group exercise, partner interview and a presentation". Case studies, insiders say, can be "detailed and several pages" in length. Experienced hires have "at least three interviews, one of which is with a partner". For people with "less than eight years of experience, only two interviews are needed".

Some respondents claim there has been a "history of too many interviews at EY", but say the current process is "correct and pointing in the right direction"— nowadays, interviews run "very smoothly". In most cases, recruiters and interviewers "have done their background work very thoroughly". Consultants report that the firm's interview style is "informal" and "more like a chat" than a structured meeting. Candidates should "expect a friendly but direct approach with pointed questioning". Overall, the process is "robust and challenging," as evidenced by the fact that "the quality of our new graduates entering the firm is exceptional."

For some, though, the process feels "a little disjointed", and it can "take time to receive feedback on performance and to progress though the various stages". Others, however, have received "a hired-or-not-hired decision on the same day". In fact, one consultant describes the process as "very fast", concluding with "an answer at the end of the assessment day". Once onboard, this source was "followed up by a good induction programme and a request for feedback on how to improve".

Swayed by the name

Candidates appreciate that at EY, you "do not get messed around by the recruitment process". During the interview process, "people seem friendlier and more open" than at some competitor firms. Candidates are attracted to the consultancy's "big-company backing", which creates "broader opportunities of consulting experience and more structured career progression". The "values-led company" draws people for its "flexible working conditions" and "admirable ethos". One consultant remarks, "They have demonstrable aspirations to be the best, which shows in the infrastructure investment and the hiring policy." Many view a gig at EY as an opportunity to be a part of a "new growing business within a professional services powerhouse".

OUR SURVEY SAYS

Up-and-coming culture

Ernst & Young is a "busy but sociable" place, sources report. The consulting business is "just two years old", so the culture is "still new and establishing itself". Insiders feel that because the group "does not yet have its own identity", it can sometimes feel as though there's a "tendency to simply copy other Big Four firms, rather than differentiate". But so far, the culture is being defined by "huge enthusiasm" exhibited by a "great bunch of people". It's a "growing business that everybody is passionate about", which means people have a "great work ethic" and a willingness to "take accountability". Insiders say team members are "focussed and professional", but "everyone from junior colleagues to senior partners gives their time willingly for work-related advice, or simply to get to know you better." Since the "structure is still in flux", however, some consultants "may feel a little unsettled by it". But those who respond to the firm's "ambitious and collaborative" atmosphere will find it a "very stimulating place to build a career".

Ernst & Young is "big on team chemistry and insight", which creates an "inclusive and supportive" culture. The environment can be "fast-paced and challenging", but people are generally "very flexible and accommodating of different needs". A consultant says of the firm's leadership, "They really value you as an individual and recognise that the reputation of the firm is just the sum of

> ❝ It's a 'growing business that everybody is passionate about'. ❞

our personal reputations." Consultants are "encouraged to embrace modern techniques and ideas, and to share knowledge with other members of the firm." They're given the opportunity to do that at the office and through a "high dosage of social events". Given EY's size, "you can't know everyone," and some say the association with the big-name accounting firm makes things feel "hierarchical and traditional".

Different travel stories

Travel requirements at EY differ for everyone. Some consultants "hardly ever travel", working mostly on "London-centric, office-based" projects. Some of these home-based consultants may "travel in the UK and Ireland, but have no obligations beyond that". For others, "travel is the worst part of the job." A source states, "I have no time for a social life, never know where I am going to be and I never work with the same people on projects, so I'm not familiar with who my colleagues are." When on the road, "work hours are excessive, in not always great conditions." Those who have more intense travel requirements, "need to have an understanding family", as "you are never at home with the children during the working week."

In an attempt to maintain work/life balance, "occasional push-back is required," as "engagements tend to be away from home for at least four days per week." The good news is, "these engagements tend to be limited to no more than four months per year." And according to a contact, "Family commitments are taken into consideration, and there is no possibility that staff with a young family would be pressured to take a role requiring significant overseas travel." Still, familial relationships aren't the only ones affected by travel: Working at the client site "makes it hard to maintain connections back at the office". Those who are on the road a lot "miss out on socialising and feeling like part of the team". Adding to the burden is the fact that travel demands are "sometimes made with too short notice".

It's reasonable to expect balance

Ernst & Young takes these concerns to heart, insiders say, and "takes work flexibility and work/life balance very seriously". Hours are reportedly "reasonable" and "remote working is possible under certain circumstances." As such, balance can "depend on what assignments you are on and where the clients are located". In addition, consultants are "encouraged to put family events ahead of work", and "holidays are respected." But for the most part, people "work hard during the week and keep the weekends for family". A contact tells us, "There is a strong emphasis on making this work for people, and it goes beyond the rhetoric everybody has." For some, "the unpredictability of working days often precludes involvement in sports or social clubs." But more often than not, consultants find that EY is "very supportive in trying to ensure that work/life balance is achieved", and "looks at ways to flex this for the individual". In short, insiders say, those with "effective time management" skills are "able to pursue a number of interests" outside the office.

Project length can vary "anywhere from four weeks to six months". The number of hours worked per week "depends mostly on the individual", with the average consultant logging around 50 hours. That can range "between 40 and 65 hours," however, depending on the project. Sometimes "hours can get excessive," but according to one source, "People who work long hours choose to do so because of personality type or a misguided expectation that this will help them succeed." A colleague agrees, noting that EY consultants "do not have to stay on for the sake of appearances". Consultants "generally work from 8am to 7pm most days". Junior consultants are "assessed on their chargeability", but client billable time "decreases with seniority, when more time is expected to be spent selling work and developing new business".

Bonus? What bonus?

"EY does not do bonuses." This puts the firm "out of kilter with direct competitors". An insider comments, "Not having a bonus at manager level is a drawback. It's balanced out with the rest of what EY has to offer, but it does make you think twice about joining when otherwise it should be a very straightforward decision." But there are upsides: The compensation package covers health insurance and a "tax-efficient pension" that includes matching, and there is also "profit sharing for partners". The firm's "very flexible benefits package" includes "something for everyone, irrespective of their stage of life or family status". In addition, EY's referral scheme is "very good—£10,000 for a partner and £5,000 for a manager". There is also an "award scheme by which managers and above can grant any number of immediate £100 prizes to individuals who demonstrate the firm's values". Still, "the company could improve incentives and rewards for top performers."

Other benefits include car allowances, expense accounts and "unlimited client meals and entertaining". Consultants are given the "opportunity to buy extra holidays", and the firm offers "a number of green benefits, such a discounts on push bikes" and carbon offsetting. New parents are offered the "ability to work part time", and there is a parent support group "to help address issues with becoming a new parent". Staffers are pleased that the firm offers "better-than-average maternity benefits". Additionally, consultants can take advantage of an "Apple store discount", which presumably helps make up for the fact that on site there are "poor IT facilities".

Hot-desking in hot offices

London-based consultants work from a "stunning building right on the Thames overlooking Tower Bridge". The location is "superb", sources say, with a "smart interior" that's "a pleasure to work in". The "first-class" offices have "great light and good furniture", as well as "unique artwork on the walls." One insider remarks, "I have never worked in such good offices. However, space is becoming limited as the firm grows." In the open-plan office , there are "hot desks only, and limited desks at that". This is "frustrating" and "can be a pain at times". A contact says, "Hot-desking, while a good use of resources for the firm, is not a great way for individuals to work." Moreover, "it's often difficult to find meeting room" because overcrowding has caused "break-out areas to be used for working space". And unlike the "fabulous-looking" London office, "the regional office in Bristol is in need of modernisation."

Mixed reviews on management

Many EY consultants get "great exposure to top-level client staff". Respondents are grateful that senior colleagues "do not try and block you from being in front of a client". According to one source, "I previously spent 10 years with Accenture. I have found that at EY, I am working with C-level clients on a daily basis, which was never the case at Accenture."

That said, some feel that the firm's "very hierarchical structure" can make it "difficult to interact with seniors and clients' top-level management". But many find that partners are "extremely supportive" and inspire "mature, open dialogue". "Partners not only accept direct and open communication, they expect it and encourage it," a staffer asserts. As for relations between the higher-ups themselves, we're told there can be "some jockeying for position at the director level, as directors position themselves for partnership", and "some leaders in the firm are afraid to make tough decisions."

Official about training

EY puts "a lot of effort on developing people, on integrating them and understanding where they want to go in their careers". The firm has made "significant investments in methodology and training, and really seems committed to growing its people". As for its format, training is "mainly official at lower grades and informal at higher grades", and offers "excellent range and opportunity". In addition, consultants are presented with "plenty of choice and guidance on what they should be taking". Courses are "high quality, especially the '101' courses, which are excellent and represent a real investment in staff". In addition, mentoring and guidance is "taken very seriously and is actively promoted" at EY. A number of respondents say that although some of the best learning happens on the job, there is "very little unofficial training due to work commitments of the senior team."

Setting expectations

Ernst & Young's promotions policy is known as "grow or go"—the "expectation is that you will progress". Generally, staffers spend "at least two to three years" at each level, and the estimated timeline for progressing from consultant to partner is "roughly 12 years". A consultant explains, "As long as you are making a better contribution year on year, there is a home for you. If you stagnate, then it's time to leave." Because EY's consulting team is new, "there has not been the opportunity for people to sit at grade for years." In short, in this "high-performance culture, rapid progression is possible for talented consultants".

Some say there is a "lack of clarity on how promotion happens", and claim that it's a "relatively opaque process in which objective measures carry limited weight". Sometimes it "seems like we are working it out as we go along", a respondent pipes in. Other sources note that "promotion can be slow" and can be "dependent on who you know rather than what you know".

Working to improve diversity

Ernst & Young takes diversity "very seriously. The firm has a 50/50 male-to-female ratio," and there is "lots of work happening to devise new ways of creating and maintaining diversity"—for example, a "senior women's development programme" that runs seminars for women. However, sources say there are still "limited women in partner roles, and they are not particularly visible on a day-to-day basis". Despite "real and evident commitments to inclusiveness," there is "still a lot of work to be done with respect to women and taking them seriously". EY "would like to see many more applications from senior women", and is "trying really hard" to encourage them, insiders report.

Similarly, the firm is "very receptive" to ethnic minorities, but there are "not many minority executives". The effort to improve minority presence is "taken very seriously, with numerous campaign activities". We're told that sexual orientation is "not relevant" in the firm's personnel moves, and there is "no negativity toward the GLBT community"—there is even a "firmwide gay and lesbian group". Regarding diversity on the whole, Ernst & Young is "very open and supportive", and "all staff are treated how they would like to be treated." According to one senior-level source, "Minority status is irrelevant. I don't care about my staff being male or female, gay or straight, or white or black. All I care about is that they are good at their job."

Big believer in the cause

Ernst & Young supports community involvement "in a big way", respondents report. The firm backs a "wide breadth of initiatives, from the arts through to business", and all employees are granted "two paid days per year to participate in a community activity". The firm's "significant investment" in community work includes "lots of charitable work, pro bono, interaction with the local community and clothing drives". Some efforts are "team-based", such as "working at a school for underprivileged children", but there are also "plenty of opportunities for individuals to choose something of their own". EY sends "corporate responsibility e-mails to promote charitable activities taking place", and "matches sponsorship for any charitable endeavour you undertake". □

60 Queen Victoria Street
London EC4N 4TW
United Kingdom
Phone: +44 (0)207 844 4000
Fax: +44 (0)207 844 4444
www.accenture.com

The Stats

Employer Type: Public Company
Ticker Symbol: ACN (NYSE)
CEO: William D. Green
2008 Employees: 178,000
2007 Employees: 170,000
2007 Revenue: $19.7 billion
2006 Revenue: $16.65 billion
No. of Offices: Offices in over 150 cities
in 49 countries

Pluses

• "Ability to align to an industry or skill"
• "A great starting job for young people"
• Excellent training opportunities
• "Breadth of opportunity"

Minuses

• Some projects can be very long
• Easy to get lost in such a large firm
• "Poor performance rating process"
• "Working away from home"

Employment Contact

careers.accenture.com

European Locations

Austria • Belgium • Czech Republic •
Denmark • Finland • France • Germany •
Greece • Hungary • Ireland • Italy • Latvia
• Luxembourg • Netherlands • Norway •
Poland • Portugal • Romania • Russia •
Slovak Republic • Spain • Sweden •
Switzerland • Turkey • United Kingdom

Practice Areas

Management Consulting: Customer
Relationship Management • Finance &
Performance Management • Strategy •
Supply Chain Management • Talent &
Organization Performance
Outsourcing: Application Outsourcing •
Business Process Outsourcing •
Infrastructure Outsourcing
Systems Integration & Technology:
Complex Solution Architecture •
Enterprise Architecture • Enterprise
Solutions • Information Management
Services • Infrastructure Consulting
Services • Integration • IT Strategy &
Transformation • Microsoft Solutions •
Mobile Solutions • Research &
Development • Service-Oriented
Architecture
Operating Groups: Communications & High
Tech • Financial Services • Products •
Public Service • Resources

THE BUZZ
WHAT CONSULTANTS AT OTHER FIRMS ARE SAYING

• "Diverse, family-friendly"
• "Line production—too large"
• "Great people"
• "Old fashioned, inflexible"

THE SCOOP

A ccenture got its start in 1989, when a small group of partners from Arthur Andersen firms around the world joined together to form a consulting business. Andersen Consulting, as it was named, set out to be a technology consultancy and integrator, implementing systems and devising IT strategy for businesses. After a long negotiating process that began in 1998, the consulting arm broke away from parent Arthur Andersen in January 2001, and renamed itself Accenture.

In the two decades since its inception, what began as a small consultancy has mushroomed into one of the largest services firms in the world, offering not only technology consulting but also management consulting and outsourcing. In 2007, Accenture's revenue reached almost $20 billion, marking the sixth year of record-breaking revenue since going public in 2002. The firm boasts a 16 per cent compound annual growth rate over the past 17 years, and counts over 178,000 employees who work in 49 countries in the Americas, Europe, Asia Pacific, the Middle East and Africa. Of those employees, 15,000 are dedicated to management consulting services.

Rocky start

Accenture is raking in revenue now, but a rosy financial future wasn't always a sure thing for the firm. As it broke off from its well-established parent company, industry skeptics predicted the firm would falter on its own. Its independence was established during an economic downslide that resulted from the dot-com crash in 2001. In July 2001, former CEO Joe Forehand took the consultancy public on the New York Stock Exchange in a $17 billion IPO, and followed up in May 2002 by raising an additional $93 million in capital. Thanks to the influx of cash, along with steep staff cuts between 2001 and 2003, Accenture finally began to recover. Though business was slow through 2002 and 2003, the firm picked up speed in 2004, and brought on some 20,000 new employees that year.

Sandy shores make a nice home

Though the firm covers the globe in terms of clients and services, it isn't based in one of the global capitals that first comes to mind when you consider a firm of this size. Accenture is incorporated in sunny Bermuda, which it claims to have chosen for the island's neutrality. Upon incorporation, critics pointed to the fact that the offshore home base would allow the firm to avoid US taxes. In October 2002, the Congressional General Accounting Office identified Accenture as one of four publicly traded federal contractors incorporated in a tax haven. However, Accenture, unlike the other three companies, had been incorporated in Bermuda since its inception in 1989. The GAO eventually concluded that the firm had in fact always been "operating as a series of related partnerships and corporations under the control of its partners through the mechanism of contracts with a Swiss coordinating entity", and therefore was not accused of any sneaky tax schemes.

Chart-toppers

In 2007, *BusinessWeek* ranked Accenture the 50th most valuable global brand. The consultancy also placed No. 1 in the information technology services category on *Fortune's* 2008 Most Admired Companies list. Among its clients are large corporations, including many of the FTSE 100 companies, over two-thirds of the Fortune Global 500, and public-sector organisations and governments. Accenture claims its customers are a loyal bunch, stating that 85 of its top-100 clients, based on revenue, have been repeat clients for at least a decade.

Consulting at the core

Consulting makes up the bulk of the firm's business, bringing in $11.86 billion in revenue in 2007. Within consulting, Accenture offers strategy, customer relationship management, finance and performance management, talent and organisation performance, and supply chain management. The consulting division advises multinational clients such as Siemens, Barclay's, Bank of Ireland, Pfizer, Vodafone, ING and BP. It also works increasingly with emerging market multinational clients, such as Brasil Telecom, Tata Steel and China Construction Bank.

Accenture divides its consulting business into a number of operating groups: communications and high tech, financial services, products, government, resources and other sectors. The products and communications and high-tech groups account for the largest portion of revenue, together comprising 48 per cent of overall revenue in 2007. The operating groups are further broken down into 17 industries, as follows: communications, electronics and high tech, media and entertainment, banking, capital markets, insurance, automotive, consumer goods and services, health and life sciences, industrial equipment, retail, transportation and travel services, chemicals, energy, natural resources, utilities and government. Geographically, business is split regionally among the Americas, Europe, the Middle East and Africa (EMEA), and Asia Pacific, with the EMEA region bringing in the largest chunk (48 per cent) of overall revenue in 2007.

Tech talent

Smaller in revenue scale but no less important is the firm's IT business. Its technology capabilities cover a broad spectrum, including research and development, enterprise solutions, technical architectures and business intelligence, to name a few. In June 2007, Accenture announced that it would be making a $250 million investment over the next three years to expand its technology consulting services. According to CEO William Green, the investment will help the firm meet an increase in client demand. Specifically, the investment is meant to focus on helping clients with IT strategies, IT infrastructures and applications, implementing web-based applications and utilising service oriented architecture and other cutting-edge technologies.

As part of that investment, in January 2008, Accenture opened an innovation centre at IT partner Oracle's UK headquarters in Reading. The centre's goal is to promote development, delivery and commercialisation of business solutions based on Oracle technology. It will serve as a European hub for joint business development, and will help Accenture expand its Oracle applications offerings to customers. The facility will also provide joint support for Accenture-Oracle client projects across Europe, to streamline support through all phases of an Oracle implementation.

Gaining momentum

Accenture's outsourcing business is the newest of its service divisions, but it has quickly picked up speed. In 2007, outsourcing brought in $7.4 billion in revenue—a 16 per cent increase over 2006. The group covers application outsourcing, infrastructure outsourcing, business process outsourcing and bundled outsourcing, which consolidates multiple business functions with a single service provider. Recently, Accenture has snapped up a number of outsourcing contracts worldwide with clients such as BP North America and the London

> ❝ There are 'broad career opportunities—from management consulting to IT and outsourcing'. ❞

Stock Exchange. In February 2008, UK water supplier South West Water tapped the firm for a 10-year outsourcing agreement. Under the terms of the deal, Accenture will provide customer care and billing services, and will manage the company's back-office operations.

In November 2007, the consultancy was awarded a $400 million outsourcing contract with European travel firm Thomas Cook Group. Over the course of the project, Accenture will provide application management, technology infrastructure management, finance, accounting and human resources services. The firm also inked a BPO deal with telecoms provider BT in September 2007, to provide financial and accounting services to its UK operations through Accenture's delivery centres in India. And in July 2007, Accenture, along with partner company Capco, scored a three-year outsourcing and consulting deal with French financial firm Calyon, to support its capital markets business through onshore and offshore development resources.

Accenture provides outsourcing services to clients through its global delivery network, made up of 50 centres and 76,000 employees stationed around the world. The newest delivery centre opened in April 2008, when the firm's existing Casablanca location was integrated into its delivery network. The centre supports French and Spanish clients with technology outsourcing needs. In January 2008, Accenture opened another facility in Mississauga, Canada, specialising in outsourcing for clients in the telecommunications, financial services and utilities industries.

Trouble in the UK

Along with its contract successes, the consultancy has suffered some negative publicity for two UK contract failures recently. In May 2008, Accenture became the focus of a £182 million lawsuit by British Gas. The gas company claims the firm's £300 million billing system, rolled out in 2006 and 2007, had "fundamental errors" that resulted in a negative impact on its customer service operations. Accenture maintains that it delivered the billing system on time and to specifications, and points to a third party, Centrica—which took over responsibility when the system went live—as being the cause of problems that came about after it was up and running.

Accenture was also the subject of criticism for its decision to walk away from £2 billion in contracts for the overhaul of the UK National Health Service's IT system. The project had been slated for completion by 2010, and was meant to link 50 million patients with doctors and health care providers, as well as to automate booking for patients and put patient records online. Though the debacle reduced Accenture's net revenue by $339 million in the fourth quarter of 2006, it didn't seem to hurt overall results, as net revenue for the quarter was still up $40 million year over year.

Buy and build

Accenture seems to recognise that to stay on top of the industry requires constant broadening of its capabilities and expansion into new markets. One way it has done this is through acquisitions that have bulked up strategic areas of business. In May 2008, Accenture entered into an agreement to acquire Origin Digital, Inc., a company that provides digital media services. That same month, the firm strengthened its freight and logistics consulting business with the purchase of AddVal Technology Inc., a shipment management products and services company. In January 2008, meanwhile, Accenture completed the purchase of Gestalt, a US defence consultancy, which was preceded by the October 2007 addition of Corliant, an Internet protocol network specialist that provides voice, data, multimedia and other services through a single technology infrastructure. Also that month, Accenture purchased H.B. Maynard, a workforce development and software company, to strengthen its consulting capabilities.

On the horizon

Since 2006, Accenture has targeted Asia as a critical market for growth. As of 2008, the firm counted 3,000 staff in Greater China in its three delivery centres. In that country, it has served clients such as the Bank of China, China National Offshore Oil Corp. and Lenovo. In the Philippines, the consultancy plans to eventually expand beyond its existing eight delivery centres and 15,000 employees who provide management consulting, technology services and outsourcing. Accenture strengthened its presence in Japan with the April 2008 acquisition of SOPIA Corporation, a privately held, Tokyo-based consulting and information technology solutions firm. SOPIA expands Accenture's Oracle capabilities and customer base in Japan, where its enterprise resource planning business is taking off. And in January 2008, the firm won an outsourcing contract with Japanese pharmaceutical firm Eisai Ltd. to provide clinical data management services through its delivery centres in India.

India rising

Accenture has had a presence in India for 20 years, but only in the past decade has it been concentrating on the country as a crucial business focus. The firm opened its first delivery centre in Mumbai in 2001, and now operates six facilities across the country. In fact, with a headcount of 37,000, India has become the country with the highest number of Accenture employees. In April 2008, the firm announced its intention to add an additional 60,000 employees in India over the next year. Also that month, Accenture teamed up with the Indian School of Business to launch the Accenture Management Development Academy in India, an effort to cultivate much-needed local talent. The programme features online, classroom and on-the-job training designed to develop leaders from Accenture's midlevel management employees in India. CEO Green has indicated that the hiring spree will help meet expected mounting outsourcing demand as more companies—especially in Japan and Europe—make an effort to streamline operations and cut costs.

In India, Accenture is also is also looking beyond outsourcing toward more traditional consulting services, such as merger integration, supply chain and HR performance. To bulk up its consulting services, in December 2007, the firm opened a management consulting centre of excellence in Gurgaon. It plans to open similar facilities in Bangalore, Mumbai and Chennai to serve domestic business in India as well as global clients.

GETTING HIRED

Three long rounds

Given that Accenture "interviews 3,000 people and takes on 400", an insider warns, it's perhaps no surprise that the firm's hiring process is "terribly slow". In fact, as one longtimer puts it, "The only time the company moves slowly is in respect to its recruitment process." Specifics of the process vary, but it generally involves "three rounds" of interviews, likely including an initial "CV review" and/or telephone screen, an "HR interview", and an interview with a senior executive or partner. One or two case study interviews are also the norm, and may involve something along the lines of an "assessment of a software vendor's entry strategy into an international market". Certain candidates may also encounter some additional testing; for example, we're told that applicants in the technology consulting field will likely come across "written assessment tests", and that "fresh graduates are usually asked to partake in several online tests." A staffer in London also mentions that one round may involve a group exercise, such as "spotting mistakes in a document". And an experienced hire in France notes that he encountered an "English test in each interview".

Some insiders say Accenture focusses its recruiting efforts on the "best business schools and engineering schools", but others insist the firm is active at "all and any" schools, since ultimately the process is "more about attitude and potential than degree, background or discipline".

Smile and nod

Others note that "knowledge of the consulting environment is helpful during interviews," and explain that "interviews assess skills, competency and ability to integrate into a consulting environment." Plus, one consultant advises, "Be smiley and talkative." A recent hire in Belgium recalls that in his experience, the "questions from HR focussed mostly on soft skills (communication, presentation, etc.), language skills and motivation for joining Accenture," while the "senior manager's questions focussed more on concrete experience and skill sets". Specifically, he shares, "I was asked to describe two difficult situations I (or my team) faced on previous projects, as well as the way we dealt with these. I believe this question was asked to gain insight into the complexity of previous projects, as well as to evaluate management skills and ability to mitigate and/or escalate as required. Furthermore, I was asked the size of teams I had managed previously and in which capacity."

Another source recommends, "It is important to look the part and meet the consultant at eye level. Do not be nervous. Prepare your answers in advance." He adds, "Use the SAR, ie, the situation action result framework, and you will be OK." Questions to consider before coming into the office include: "Why do you want to work for Accenture? Why do you want to be a consultant? What are our latest projects? Tell us about a time when you were innovative. What about when you failed at something? When did you persuade someone?"

OUR SURVEY SAYS

Living large

Respondents say that because of Accenture's large size, the "ample opportunities" it offers "to move around and experiment mean it won't be hard to find your niche". There are "broad career opportunities—from management consulting to IT and outsourcing", and everyone is involved in a variety of projects and is able to "work with different clients across different areas". A manager in London advises, "Be prepared to be exposed to strategy, operations, technology, resourcing, etc. Also be prepared to work with different workforces (consulting, technology, outsourcing) at senior levels." And a consultant in Brussels remarks that Accenture offers an "inspiring/refreshing diversity of profiles within one strong business vision", leading to a "feeling of achieving something new and big during projects".

Focus on performance, for better …

Most staffers also praise Accenture's "culture of performance and success", and its "highly challenging environment", in which "growing and developing is mandatory." A business consultant in Brussels insists that there's plenty of "team spirit", as well as ample "coaching from leadership". An analyst in Madrid adds that his colleagues "have a positive attitude, are willing to help and are open to new thoughts".

… or for worse

On the downside, a manager in London warns that the "large-firm mentality" can be "very delivery-focussed, with an emphasis on delivering high shareholder returns", making the firm "very margin-oriented on engagements". A co-worker is disappointed that the "culture within the UK can be very much a work-hard, drink-hard mentality", and others agree that the "performance-driven culture" can be wearing. At such a big firm, though, there are many "different kinds of colleagues", notes a consultant in Germany. Some are "very open-minded", while others are "very reserved and only interested in their own advantage".

The growth continues

Despite its already formidable reputation and size, Accenture's various European branches are "growing rapidly". A staffer in Madrid reports that at his office, the "growth rate is high and the future is positive". A colleague in London echoes that the firm's "business outlook is good, with the firm reaching record revenue." In Belgium, we're told, "the consulting workforce has nearly doubled over the past few years." Helsinki has a similar story: An analyst there says his office "doubled the number of its employees in the last year and at the moment, all consultants are basically sold out". He adds, "Dozens of new employees are hired every month, and it doesn't seem to stop." Overall, an executive raves, Accenture is "a firm with strong financials, excellent client relationships and high growth potential."

An emphasis on diversity

With its wide international presence, its no surprise that insiders also emphasise Accenture's "global mentality and culture", and "very diverse environment, with many consultants from other countries working on projects". One London-based manager reports that represented nationalities in his office include "Asians, Brits, Europeans and Americans", as well "Aussies and Russians". When it comes to specific diversity initiatives, respondents say the company "is doing a great job of promoting ethnic minorities and provides liberal benefits to women", including "nine months' full-pay maternity leave, with an additional 13 weeks unpaid".

Putting in the time, all the time

It's a good thing new moms have some time off, since reported work hours can be as high as 80 per week—although they do vary widely, and can also be closer to 40 or 45. It's worth nothing that the "general rule of thumb is that face time is important", a manager points out. Plus, there's very little downtime: "If you are unchargeable, you have opportunities to work on business development (ie, proposals, presentations, etc.)."

While some staffers complain about the "long working hours", many say it's still possible to maintain a healthy work/life balance. A Brussels-based consultant who works 55-hour weeks believes that balance is "really taken into consideration" by the firm. A cohort in London agrees that "the firm has policies in place to support work/life balance," and that, "where business needs allow", it aims "to satisfy any requests for flexible working". Even a manager who spends 70 to 80 hours on the job acknowledges that "the firm is trying to experiment with several initiatives around work/life balance." He adds that although "projects require long working hours," the late nights are "compensated for by the fact that few people work weekends". Overall, he remarks, Accenture is "taking steps" in the right direction, "but there is a long way to go". Still, he adds, "Be glad that the firm will recognise additional effort." A cohort in Brussels notes, "With approval of project management, overtime can be compensated in the form of additional holiday and/or payout."

Get ready to go

One hindrance to balance is that staffers must "be prepared to travel out of town," therefore "mobility is key." "Travel is an essential component of consulting, so one has to be ready for it," says a senior source who adds, "Many projects require out-of-town travel for a whole week, essentially living life out of a suitcase." In fact, notes a staffer, some employee contracts state that "you may be required

> ““ The firm maintains a 'global mentality and culture'. ””

to work abroad for up to 60 per cent of your time," though he adds that "this is always discussed with HR first." And a respondent in Spain explains that "people who speak English will systematically be sent overseas, which means taking a 1:30pm flight every Monday and flying back on Thursday."

On the positive side, others add that the travel "can be exciting, as you have the opportunity to visit new places, you don't have to see the same faces and you stay at good hotels". An insider in Germany insists that the "international perspective" at Accenture is a plus, stating, "I really like that they support consultants in extending their international career." And a colleague in Spain agrees: "Accenture Spain has many European projects, so you can get the chance to travel a lot, which is good financially and also for experience." In all, "If you are comfortable travelling frequently, then you will generally love the work," reports a higher-up. Besides which, a consultant in London adds that although she regularly spends "three nights a week away from home", she "normally work[s] Fridays from home or the home office".

Paid to do the job

And as one oft-travelling consultant says of spending time on the road, "I'd rather not, but it's what I'm paid to do." Many staffers are pleased with what they consider a competitive compensation package, which includes a "company share purchase plan", in which staffers can "purchase shares at 15 per cent off the fair market value".

Benefits include "full insurance packages", as well as 20 to 30 days of vacation a year. Bonuses are dependant on "ranking versus peers", but may be around 10 per cent of salary before taxes. And an analyst in Spain adds that at the end of the year, the firm pays "a retention rate, which means that if you don't leave the company, you will receive that. This is to make the employee turnover a bit slower." In addition, through a "performance award programme", a business consultant explains, "I can already reward my team members for their strong performance by providing bonuses (gifts, vouchers, etc.)."

Newer hires tend to be less satisfied with their salaries and tell us that "if you are a fresh graduate, they don't pay too much," and there is "no sign-on bonus at the analyst level". However, raises are generous: "After three years", a source shares, "my salary has already doubled."

Not too shabby, but not exactly Google

Accenture perks vary by location and job level, but may include a "car allowance" with an "unlimited European fuel card", a laptop, a partially- or fully-paid cell phone and a subsidy of "50 per cent of gym fees"—or, in the case of Helsinki, the "opportunity to use the gym located in the same building free of charge". Offices tend to be "centrally located with access to shops and restaurants". A manager in London reports that there are "hot beverages available all day long (self-service) with a cafeteria serving breakfast, lunch and snack (you have to pay, though, unlike at Google!)".

The firm also offers staffers "three charity days a year" to devote to community activities of their choice. Accenture also sponsors "pro bono consulting within the UK and within developing countries".

Move up, or try something else

When it comes to climbing the ladder at Accenture, most staffers agree that the promotion policy is "up or out, with some flexibility". In particular, one insider notes that if it is "not possible to continue to grow in consulting, people often get opportunities in other divisions, such as technology or outsourcing, where the career path is different and may fit better with the employee's expectations."

For those who remain on the consulting track, there are "five levels to become partner". A manager explains that "it generally takes two years to progress to consultant (from the entry-level analyst role), three years to progress to manager, three to four years to senior manager and four to five years to senior executive." In Brussels, we're told that "two opportunities to get promoted are given during the eligible year of promotion," but in

Finland, one disappointed analyst states, "Performance reviews are just once a year, which means that if you are a promotion candidate but you don't get a promotion, you have to wait one more year for the next promotion round."

Get noticed

Some respondents note that "there are many opportunities for fast career progression" and that "excellence is rewarded." A London insider explains, "Opportunities for advancement are good, as long as you work hard and are willing to put in the long hours. If you do, you can see yourself at a good management position within five years." And a manager agrees, "Partners remember names of analysts and consultants, so it's good to have visibility." He advises that "being flexible is key to success within the firm. Partners will appreciate your flexibility and will request your services long after you have rolled off."

But it's largely up to employees to get themselves noticed. A source in London warns, "Accenture is pretty much a company where you need to drive your own career forward, as the internal career management is not particularly effective," adding, "You will require a good dose of luck, as well as hard work, to get rapid promotion and good salary increases." He continues, "Generally speaking, there is plenty of opportunity after you establish yourself to drive your career in the way you want it to go."

The buddy system

We're told that, "following promotion to the next level", staffers attend a "core training, usually held in Chicago". And overall, insiders say Accenture's training programme is strong. New hires "get a buddy assigned to help them integrate, as well as a career coach who will help them with personal development, training and staffing decisions, etc.". And a source in Brussels reports that he is allotted "120 hours yearly training time", plus an "extensive training budget for both internal and vendor trainings". Others warn that "it is sometimes difficult to book trainings due to project requirements," but an "eLearning tool is also available with thousands of courses". In addition, we're told there are "many initiatives, events—such as breakfasts, dinners, workshops, net-meetings, etc.—to discuss and learn informally from peers and senior people", and there's also plenty of "daily coaching and feedback". Plus, an analyst in Spain notes that the firm's "knowledge management system" is a great resource. "It's amazing how they gather and categorise data for reuse, and you can also learn a lot from the existing knowledge base in the company."

A manager in London reports that it's also possible to end up on the other side of the classroom through "opportunities to teach as faculty on core skills or on other training programmes". ☐

51, rue François 1er
75008 Paris
France
Phone: +33 (0)1 55 74 29 00
Fax: +33 (0)1 55 74 28 03
www.adl.com

The Stats

Employer Type: Subsidiary of Altran
  Technologies
Ticker Symbol: ALTRAN TECHN
  (Paris Bourse)
Global CEO: Michael Träm
2008 Employees: 1,000
2007 Employees: 1,000
No. of Offices: 30

Practice Areas

Automotive & Manufacturing
Chemicals
Energy & Utilities
Financial Services
Healthcare & Life Sciences
Operations & Information Management
Strategy & Organization
Sustainability & Risk
Technology & Innovation Management
Telecommunications, Information, Media
  & Electronics

Employment Contact

www.adl.com/careers

European Locations

Paris (HQ)
Brussels • Cambridge • Düsseldorf •
Gothenburg • Lisbon • London • Madrid •
Milan • Munich • Paris • Prague • Rome •
Rotterdam • Stockholm • Vienna •
Wiesbaden • Zagreb • Zurich

Pluses

• "Recent growth dynamics, high-profile
  joiners"
• "Strong industry expertise"
• International community
• "High degree of freedom and
  responsibility already at the
  analyst/consultant level"

Minuses

• "High turnover rate"
• Not much interaction between
  practices
• "Not a top-three player"
• Disappointing compensation

THE BUZZ
WHAT CONSULTANTS AT OTHER FIRMS ARE SAYING

• "Great name"
• "Unclear profile"
• "Family-friendly"
• "Old bird trying a revival"

THE SCOOP

ounded in Boston in 1886, Arthur D. Little lays claim to the dual titles of first and oldest management consultancy in the world. The pioneering spirit of the founder who lent the firm its name is the stuff of legend, as is the firm's continued survival, despite a serious restructuring that led to it being acquired by France's Altran Technologies in 2002. So while Arthur D. Little himself may be long gone, the firm that bears his name is still going strong. The 1,000-plus consultants it employs today find themselves spread across 30 countries, offering tailored services to clients in industries including automotive, chemicals, energy and utilities, financial services, health care, manufacturing, private equity, public service, telecoms, information, media, electronics, and travel and transportation.

Founding fathers

Arthur Dehon Little was only half of the partnership of chemists that founded the firm. The other half was his fellow MIT student Roger Griffin, and together the pair set up as researchers-for-hire, pioneering the concept of process improvement through outsourcing research. If it seems a little unfair

> " A corporate training program [is] open to all consultants. "

that the firm is named after only one of the founders, fear not. Its original name was Griffin and Little, but Griffin's name was dropped following his untimely death in 1893, when an experiment went awry.

As his firm grew in size and capability over the years, Little developed something of a genius for eye-catching PR stunts, which served no small role in increasing the firm's visibility and, thus, client base. Among the stunts designed to prove Little's maxim of "Who says it can't be done?" was his literal transformation of a sow's ear into a silk purse, as well as a competition among a group of staff in the 1970s to make a lead balloon fly—both of which were achieved to considerable acclaim.

Those feats brought some visibility to the company, underscoring the unusual measures it was prepared to take to get the job done, and establishing Little as a leading name in the field by the 1960s—a position it maintained until the late 1990s.

After the boom

After a corporate restructuring in 2002, Arthur D. Little sold off parts of its business (and reduced its workforce by almost half) to firms eager to buy into the well-known brand. Altran Technologies bought the core management consulting business, as well as the Arthur D. Little name. This change led, perhaps unintentionally, to increased attention on business affairs in Europe, rather than in North America. In September 2006, this refocussing was formally confirmed by the shift of the firm's world headquarters from Boston to Paris. Moreover, German-born Michael Träm, formerly from A.T. Kearney, replaced Richard Clarke as the company's CEO.

Executive shuffle

As part of the continued reorganisation, Arthur D. Little has made some appointments in top positions of late. In September 2007, the firm appointed Paco Hauser and Markus Stöckli as director and senior manager, respectively, for the financial services market in Switzerland. The pair previously worked as a team for several high-powered financial institutions. In July that same year, Franck Herbaux was appointed as director in the operations management practice in Paris. Herbaux was promoted from within the firm, having joined in 2004 as a senior manager.

> ❝ Our internal monitoring shows we are well above the national average in terms of diversity. ❞

Perhaps the most significant appointment made by the firm in 2007, however, was that of Petter Kilefors, who was promoted to become ADL's global head of strategy and organisation, the largest of the firm's practices. Among other things, under Kilefors' guidance the practice will help the firm's clients deal with challenges presented by the continuing expansion and emergence of markets in Brazil, Russia, India and China.

Little publications

ADL consultants are recognised as industry experts in the fields they serve, and the array of reports, articles, case studies and books they produce goes a long way toward justifying that reputation. Recent reports include an examination of the challenges faced by the automotive industry in meeting "the CO_2 challenge", as well as a report analysing "IT rightsizing", which deals the prospect of cost-cutting brought on by the credit crisis, and the effects that may have on a firm's IT capabilities.

In addition to those reports, Arthur D. Little also publishes *Prism*, a biannual journal that has been operating since the company's founding. Primarily covering developments in strategic thinking in the business world, recent subjects have included sustainability—for example, how integrity and innovation can lead to sustainable performance—as well as more work on CO_2 in automotives, and how to drag that particular industry toward sustainability.

Carbon concerns

ADL appears to be committed to solving the carbon crisis, or at least helping its clients to do so. A December 2007 report by the firm identified "the carbon margin" as an opportunity for companies to generate an additional revenue stream. Carbon margin is ADL's term for the room between permitted carbon levels and those achieved by companies. ADL consultants posit that, should a firm achieve carbon savings through use of carbon-reduction techniques, the opportunity exists to avoid future environmental taxes on emissions, as well as cost savings on reduced energy costs.

That eco-friendly approach is also being seen on the domestic level. In December 2007, the London Development Agency, in conjunction with ADL's UK wing, unveiled a new type of home, aimed at reducing the city's carbon dioxide emissions to some 60 per cent of 1990s levels by 2025. With the address of 1 Lower Carbon Drive, the specially equipped house will tour the UK with a panel of experts who will demonstrate and explain some of the sustainable solutions that consumers can implement to reduce their carbon footprint.

Back in fashion

Throughout its considerable history, the firm has never attracted the "run-of-the-mill" tag, and it remains unique among its peers to this day. Its unusual corporate culture and approach to business is perhaps best summed up by one of its own staff—Rick Eagar, managing director of the UK office. "Arthur D. Little may not be the easiest global firm to manage, but it will never become one of the 'grey' consulting firms where everyone gets brainwashed into behaving the same way and delivering the same products—unthinkable," Eagar wrote in a 2006 overview of the firm's history. "The firm's great strength is its people and its culture. More Vivienne Westwood than Chanel—vive la différence!" Vive, indeed.

GETTING HIRED

Interviews aplenty

To identify potential hires that live up to the firm's nine key values (clients first, quality, independence, integrity, sustainability, teamwork, leadership, concern for staff and pride), Arthur D. Little's hiring process can be stringent, although perhaps not out of the ordinary. "I think our recruiting process is generally in line with other management consulting firms," says an insider in the Rome office. Others report slightly differing experiences with interviews, depending on location and position, but the one thing all had in common was multiple interviews in one day, followed by a case study. For a senior position in Düsseldorf, one insider reported "one to two advance interviews, then three interviews in one day with senior managers or directors", as well as a "small presentation of case study". Snagging a senior position in Stockholm, however, required "six interviews".

There's no hanging around waiting by the phone, either, with one recent hire reporting a "fast response—if successful, you get an offer after one day with two to three interviews".

Key qualities

Despite being described as "not an effective process", there is a purpose behind all that interviewing and case studying—the chance for the firm to assess a candidate's skill set. A far as that goes, the consensus for what ADL's managers are looking for is perhaps best summed up by a Rome source: "Focus is given to communication skills, both verbal and nonverbal (presentation, facilitation, etc.), soft skills (resilience, performance in stressful conditions, etc.) and hard skills (logic, mathematics, etc.)." A cohort notes that book smarts are less important than demonstrating the ability to get the job done: "Knowledge of business/industry tools is given a lower priority," he reports, adding, "Of course you need to know your Porter's model, etc., but don't expect academic questions."

Presumably that approach is taken because academic credentials are a given, as the firm concentrates its recruitment activities on "main institutes of technology and schools of economy". In the German-speaking zone, according to a senior consultant, those "major universities" include the likes of "European Business School, Technical University Darmstadt, Technical University Karlsruhe, University of Mannheim, St. Gallen and Wirtschaftsuniversitat wien."

OUR SURVEY SAYS

Stars of the second tier

With "low hierarchical barriers" and a "flexible, open environment", ADL consultants in Düsseldorf reckon the firm is a good place to work, particularly if you're interested in pursuing "topics of personal interest". Quite what those topics are isn't made explicitly clear, but rest assured that, if desired (presumably within some sort of sphere of relevance), they can be pursued. A source in a sister German office, meanwhile, proffers the opinion that "Arthur D. Little Germany is a good place to work. It still has a very strong brand name in Germany, as well as in most other European countries." Presumably that list also includes Sweden, where a Stockholm-based colleague waxes lyrical about the "open, friendly, collegial, professional and caring" environment.

On the downside, however, some feel that the firm's "corporate culture has changed over the years." So, even though it "is well positioned as a second-tier management consultancy for strategy and operations" where "working hours, dress code and opportunities for advancement are fully comparable to any other renowned management consulting firm, nowadays, Arthur D. Little is very performance-oriented, with a more or less rigid up-or-out" policy. To put it another way (as a London insider does), "Billability and utilisation is everything and is obsessively managed." Such criticism is effortlessly flicked away by a Rome-based staffer, however, who says that "corporate culture depends on the office; in Italy it is rather open and informal."

Working 9 to, um, 9

The average workweek for an ADL consultant falls somewhere between 50 and 60 hours—par for the course in consulting, but insiders reckon that the firm at least tries to help them balance their lives. "Work/life balance is generally good when based in the office," says a Londoner. "However, on foreign assignments, minimal effort is made to achieve a good work/life balance." A colleague, meanwhile, notes that, depending on the type of case, his office "allows experienced staff to work from home one to two days a week". But that's not the case at other European offices, with grapevine buzz reporting that "the Paris and Stockholm offices have a reputation for working excessive hours, whilst the Cambridge office is totally laid-back and staff probably do no more than 40 to 45 hours a week there (but then it is a different kind of consulting)." An Italian ADLer estimates his hours at an average 60 per week, but adds the caveat that "working hours really depend on the type of assignment and the project manager. When working for due diligences, the barrier of 70 hours per week is broken more often than not. But when working for a longer operation management assignment (often abroad), the working hours are significantly lower."

As for those projects abroad, it would seem that they depend on practice area and location as well. For example, one respondent points out that "ADL London has been very successful at selling large implementation and strategy projects overseas (to Romania, Saudi Arabia, etc.), and these long-term projects create an excessive travel load on the energy practice in the London office. Other practices have far less travel." And it's not only other practices that affect the travel variable—according to one Stockholm staffer, the amount of travel required by the firm is "very varied, depending on industry, casework and position in the firm." For that staffer, for example, "travel is very much part of my work as an international energy professional," while a colleague in Düsseldorf counts himself lucky that, of late, he has had "some projects with office work and only travel to meetings. So I cannot complain, but this is really hard to predict."

Pay cheques debunked

There seems to be a body of opinion among insiders that ADL "is generally not a good payer", with one London-based source going so far as to use his research skills to make that case. "According to industry benchmark (eg, Woodhurst salary surveys), ADL pays in the bottom quartile for management consulting/strategy firms in London." However, the respondent does take into account that "we don't work quite as many hours as the other firms." In addition, an insider in Düsseldorf feels that the "compensation has recently been increased significantly." Perks and benefits, meanwhile, include a profit-sharing bonus, private pension contributions, insurance and health care.

One thing the firm is unlikely to try and sell prospective employees on, however, is the quality of its offices. Several European offices are damned with the faint praise that they are "functional" with "good locations", but unfortunately "not high luxury". ADL's London office is particularly criticised for its "uninspiring open-plan layout", although a consultant there does offer the crumb of comfort that they "may move to alternative accommodations later in the year".

Pace yourself

Life at ADL can be lived at a fairly relaxed pace, at least as far as career progression is concerned. The culture is "not up or out", which means that "we have people who have been in their career grade for several years and who will continue to work within ADL," explains a London-based manager. For those who wish to scale the consulting ladder, however, typical time frames are broken down as such: "business analyst to consultant: one to two years; consultant to manager: two to three years; manager to senior manager: three to four years. After that, it becomes a political appointment."

To aid its staff in climbing that hierarchy, ADL provides "both official and unofficial training", including "a corporate training programme open to all consultants" and "at least two one-day trainings and one weeklong training per year in a nice, sunny location".

On par for diversity

Diversity isn't an issue that garners too much attention with ADL staffers—perhaps because the firm keeps an eye on it. "Our internal monitoring", according to a manager in the know in London "shows we are well above the national average in terms of diversity, while we have more women than other companies. A third of senior managers are women, and this proportion is constant throughout the organisation (except at the director level where there are no women)." Still, there will always be room for improvement, as one of the firm's Swedish consultants points out. As far as female employees are concerned, "We can improve!" says the source, as they make up just "20 per cent of the Stockholm office." In terms of racial diversity, we're told that the "Sweden office is rather homogenous". ☐

Arthur D. Little

IBM GLOBAL SERVICES

IBM Espana S.A.
Santa Hortensia 26-28
28002 Madrid, Spain
Phone: +34 (0)91 397 66 11

IBM Suisse
Vulkanstrasse 106, Case postale
8010 Zurich, Switzerland
Phone: +41 (0)58 333 44 55
www-1.ibm.com/services

The Stats

Employer Type: Division of IBM
Ticker Symbol: IBM (NYSE)
Senior Vice President, GBS: Ginni Rometty
Senior Vice President, GTS: Michael
   E. Daniels
Managing Partner, Northeast Europe:
   Bridget van Kralingen
Managing Partner, Southwest Europe:
   José Luiz Rossi
2008 Employees: 200,000
2007 Employees: 189,000
2007 Revenue: $54.1 billion
2006 Revenue: $48.3 billion
No. of Offices: 300

Practice Areas

Global Business Services
   Application Management Services •
   Consulting • Systems Integration
Global Technology Services
   Integrated Technology Services •
   Maintenance • Outsourcing Services

Employment Contact

www.ibm.com/consulting/careers

European Locations

Armonk (Global HQ) • Madrid (Southwest
Europe HQ) • Zurich (Northeast
Europe HQ)
Austria • Belgium/Luxembourg • Bulgaria •
Croatia • Cyprus • Czech Republic •
Denmark • Estonia • Finland • France •
Germany • Greece • Hungary • Ireland •
Italy • Lithuania • Netherlands • Norway •
Poland • Portugal • Romania • Russia •
Slovakia • Slovenia • Spain • Sweden •
Switzerland • Turkey • United Kingdom

Pluses

- "Opportunity to try a variety of job roles"
- "This is the place where you can close really
  large and transformational deals"
- Lots of flexibility

Minuses

- "Very large company with a horrifying
  infrastructure"
- "It's not worth the money you get for
  all the extra work you put in"
- "Sometimes the focus on the internal
  company work is more important than
  a satisfied customer"

THE BUZZ
WHAT CONSULTANTS AT OTHER FIRMS ARE SAYING

- "Ability to deliver"
- "Big is not always beautiful"
- "Good work/life balance"
- "Struggling to balance technology and
  consulting"

THE SCOOP

I n terms of corporate recognition, few companies in the world can match the ubiquity of IBM and its stripy blue logo. Having morphed from computer hardware manufacturer into globally integrated mega-corporation, the firm targets the point where technology and business collide, integrating its three main offerings—software, systems and financing, and services—to help its clients cope with the ever-changing demands of the global marketplace. Consequently, separating out the tech work from the firm's consulting arm can be something of a challenge—particularly as IBM seems bent on further integration of both its own key business units and the systems and business performance of its clients. That approach can see the firm's consultants recommend IBM software or systems to a client, further blurring the lines in the process.

Nevertheless, IBM's Global Services unit does exist as a separate entity within the firm, and is split itself into two main units—Global Business Services (GBS) and Global Technology Services (GTS). Together, the two units generated some $54 billion of the parent company's $97.9 billion in revenue in 2007. That represents a year-on-year increase of around 10.8 per cent for Global Services, compared to 6.9 per cent for IBM as a whole, meaning that the unit is not only the biggest at IBM, but also the fastest growing. And little wonder—its consultants serve some of the largest companies and organisations in industries including aerospace and defence, automotive, banking, chemicals and petroleum, consumer products, education, electronics, energy and utilities, financial markets, government, health care, insurance, life sciences, media and entertainment, retail, telecommunications, and travel and transportation.

> ❝ The work opportunities are almost endless. ❞

Separate together

The differences between IBM's GBS and GTS divisions are relatively simple to grasp: GBS specialises in application management services, consulting and systems integration, and pulled in $18 billion in revenue in 2007. While that list of specialities may sound tech-ish, GTS takes it up a notch, raking in $36.1 billion in 2007 through its expert capabilities in integrated technology services, maintenance and outsourcing services. In the grand scheme of things, the two units are both after the same thing: Both work to identify and solve problems for IBM's customers under the Global Services umbrella, and are committed to the "global integration" mantra that is at the heart of the company's current ideology.

The firm's previous identity, of course, was as a manufacturer of computing systems and PC hardware. Following the historic $1.75 billion sale of that side of the business to Chinese manufacturer Lenovo in 2004, however, the firm has almost exclusively focussed on business service provision, with a particular slant toward technological services and solutions. The first major clue that IBM was heading down that path arrived in post-Enron-scandal 2002, when the firm emerged from the feeding frenzy of Big Four accounting firms, grasping the prize of the PricewaterhouseCoopers consulting arm. IBM managed to maintain and win back a good number of PwC's clients during the transition, a factor that quickly led to success in the consulting and business services field.

Euro success

Since the PwC purchase and the Lenovo sale, IBM has continued down the path toward service provision, with its Global Services unit steadily assuming an ever-greater prominence. The division now operates in every major European market, and in 2007 posted a staggering 36 per cent revenue growth in the EMEA region. While some of that was attributable to currency fluctuations (the firm reports financial results in the ever-weakening US dollar), it still represents a significant increase in business for the firm in its second-largest overall geographic region. Much of the growth in that area was driven by Russia—one of the countries, along with Brazil, India and China, on which the firm is pinning its major hopes for future expansion—but the firm posted more than 10 per cent revenue growth in at least a dozen countries in Europe throughout 2007, including Ireland, Spain, Poland, the Czech Republic, Slovakia, Slovenia, Ukraine, Belarus, Romania, Bulgaria and Greece. As that list suggests, the majority of IBM's new business is in developing nations, rather than in the established major European economies.

That's not to say, however, that the firm has no presence in Western Europe—the parent company does maintain a global research lab in Zurich, along with a regional headquarters in the same city and another in Madrid. The firm is expanding where the new business is, however, and for the time being, that would appear to be in developing nations—a move exemplified by the $6 billion investment in India that it announced in 2006.

New signings

Rather in the manner of a football team, IBM refers to new contracts as "signings"— and 2007 was a good year for getting its clients to put pen to paper. Global Services saw its new signings increase by 1 per cent, to almost $50 billion. That breaks down to around $22 billion in short-term signings (a 5 per cent increase) and almost $28 billion in longer-term deals, a decline of around 1 per cent. Somewhat confusing is that the longer-term deals were of a shorter duration than usual, suggesting that the overall value of the deals increased. In summation, short-term deals are up, long long-term deals are down, but short, long-term deals are up. Simple, right?

Getting a leg up on innovation

The company's future outlook depends greatly on a much-maligned buzzword—innovation. The Global Services web site contains a tool for leaders to use for help in gauging their organisation's capabilities in, yes, innovation. The results are based on benchmarks established by the firm's global CEO study, meaning that any organisation (or casual visitor, for that matter) can measure their performance

> ❝ When deciding on assignments, 'managers take your private life into consideration.' ❞

and results against those achieved by some 765 CEOs in 20 different industries across 11 worldwide regions. Once said leaders (or casual visitors) have taken the tests, they can contact IBM to find out what its experts can do to help.

Global Services consultants have also positioned themselves as "thought leaders" in the area of business value. The company's Institute for Business Value provides strategic insights and recommendations on challenges to help its clients capitalise on new opportunities. Among the areas where IBM claims it can be of use are some usual consulting suspects: global business, industry change and how to design metrics for success.

GETTING HIRED

Working your way in to Big Blue

"IBM has a well-known brand name," says one insider focussed on the obvious, a fact that doesn't help the average job hunter much, except to call attention to the fact that getting a foot in the door at Big Blue is likely to be "difficult". In fact, a goodly number of respondents tell us they were either headhunted or brought in by outsourcing agreements. Many do work the hiring channels directly to get in, however, experiencing some "two or three interviews, and then an offer", according to a source in Amsterdam.

Those two interviews, says an Eastern European source, are likely to be split between HR and a manager, along with a test to "check skills"—something a colleague in Milan refers to as an "IPATO [Information Processing Aptitude Test] test", and which will involve demonstration of ability largely in numbers, particularly pertaining to "matrices, series and problems". Likely questions, according to our insiders, include old chestnuts such as, "What do you hope to achieve within five years?" and "What do you consider as your pros/cons?", as well as the potentially limitless, "Is there something you consider important that I should know?"

OUR SURVEY SAYS

The sky's the limit

Current IBMers seem pretty happy with the range of job functions their positions offer them, and for good reason. "As this is a large company, the work opportunities are almost endless. You can change job role and speciality a lot," says one Stockholm-based consultant. The firm's size has other advantages, too: "We have contacts with all major firms," says an insider in Amsterdam, who also appreciates that the firm "is unique in the sense that IBM can bundle all components of a total solution for a client". Not only that, purrs another Stockholmer, but "when you meet the customer and he wants help, you can always say 'Yes, I (we) can do that.' Not when, not how long it will take, but it can be done. I have over 300,000 people behind me!"

With some firms, big might mean impersonal, but at IBM that's not necessarily the case, with insiders in several different locations commenting on the overall "positive climate", with "a lot of great people working here, who gladly share their knowledge with others". In addition, the firm is lauded as being "friendly and supportive", and for showing "investment in skills growth and innovation". Still, an insider in Amsterdam claims the environment is "quite sales-driven", while a colleague in Zurich offers the opinion that "only quarterly numbers count—long-term commitment to customers is not what we care for."

A decent balancing act

IBM appears to pay more than lip service to the concept of work/life balance. When deciding upon assignments, "managers take your private life into consideration," reports one insider in Oslo. That statement is backed up by colleagues across the continent, with one in Amsterdam expressing that "IBM is very open to working from home." Another insider praises the firm's family-friendly ways: "I have been working part time (80 per cent) for seven years, working full weeks and taking days of in the school holidays (five weeks in the summer, three weeks in the autumn/Christmas and two weeks in the winter/spring). To be able to work from home also makes it easier to balance work and family life." Despite efforts at balancing workloads, there are still "periods of high intensity", says a consultant, "where I am not able to balance".

(Kitchen) clock-watching

The average IBM consultant works somewhere between 40 and 50 hours a week, some of which, as seen above, can be done from the comfort of their own homes. And there's no bar on doing more than the minimum, for there's rarely a shortage of work. "Normally, you can work as much as you want and more," says a source in Stockholm. "A lot of people work overtime." Working the minimum is certainly not recommended, though. As a colleague points out, progression depends on commitment: "If you want to have a career, you need to show that you are able and willing to put in that extra time."

Getting around

Despite all the flexi-time work from home, site visits for clients are not a thing of the past, and there's no guarantee that a project will be convenient for consultants, or how long it will last. Despite lauding the firm for giving assignments close to Oslo, an insider in that office still takes "two hours each day to travel to the client, where I have been for the last two years." In Amsterdam, meanwhile "Some travels to Belgium are part of the routine, because the Netherlands and Belgium are in one region." Others don't seem overly concerned, conceding that travel "is part of the job, and I was aware of this when I started".

Onward and upward

There seems to be some dissent over the existence of an up-or-out policy when it comes to promotions. A consultant in Zurich, for example, believes the policy is in place, and a like-minded source in Oslo states, "Promotion is strictly organised. Consultants do not quickly advance." However, some staffers in Amsterdam, Stockholm and Genoa refute that, with the Genovese going as far as to point out that "middle managers don't have a history as consultants." Another source even claims that "a promotion policy is totally lacking," with a co-worker noting, "You can find your own way to do a career." One thing consultants do seem to agree on, however, is the career path itself, which management uses to "encourage you to grow". The path provides "education for a lot of specified roles, for example project manager, consultants, IT architect, etc.", and apparently involves "a lot of e-learning".

Advancement at the firm, meanwhile, "is based on your results", both in training and on the job, "which you'd have to present in a thesis presented to a profession board who would determine your advancement in the profession". The speed at which consultants climb the ladder, says one respondent, "is really up to you, how quickly you learn and what you are willing to put into your engagement". A source in Amsterdam, however, states that "normally it will take about four years to go up to the next level."

Exemplary corporate citizens

"IBM contributes to literally hundreds of groups, initiatives, conferences, organisations, and community programmes and activities," a consultant tells us. Those include such minor affairs as the Nobel Prize and the Olympics, as well as the commitment of "worldwide leadership to environmental protection", says a source based in Milan—a fact that has implications for all IBM employees. "In addition to complying with applicable environmental laws and regulations, every employee must comply with IBM's environmental policy and the corporate directives and requirements that support that policy." So don't forget to recycle!

All's fair in love and more

A source in Stockholm comments that IBM has a "strong commitment to diversity, with local variations". A staffer in Amsterdam confirms that "we have diversity programmes in place," while reports from Oslo suggest that "women are treated the same way as men." Whether that treatment is good or bad remains to be seen, but at least it's "equal". Overall, there seem to be few complaints about male/female diversity issues, with the main concern—lack of females—reflected in the comment from a respondent in Zurich: "We speak about it, but only 13 per cent of us are women."

The firm's consultants seem similarly unconcerned about diversity in other areas; an insider in Amsterdam expresses the opinion that the level of diversity concerning GLBT colleagues is "much more than you would expect from a company like IBM". □

CAPGEMINI

Place de l'Etoile
11 rye de Tilsitt
75017 Paris
France
Phone: +33 (0)1 47 54 50 00
www.capgemini.com

The Stats

Employer Type: Public Company
Ticker Symbol: CAP (Euronext Paris)
CEO: Paul Hermelin
2008 Employees: 83,500+
2007 Employees: 78,000
2007 Revenue: €8.7 billion
2006 Revenue: €7.7 billion
No. of Offices: 300+ offices in 35
  countries

Practice Areas

Consulting Services
  Customer Relationship Management
  Finance & Employee Transformation
  Global Sourcing
  Operational Research
  Supply Chain
  Transformation Consulting
Local Professional Services
Outsourcing Services
Technology Services

European Locations

Paris (Global HQ)
Austria • Belgium • Croatia • Czech
Republic • Denmark • Finland • France •
Germany • Hungary • Ireland • Italy •
Netherlands • Norway • Poland •
Portugal • Romania • Russia • Slovakia •
Spain • Sweden • Switzerland • United
Kingdom

Pluses

• A people-oriented culture
• Formal training opportunities offer a
  real advantage

Minuses

• Little cultural consistency between
  offices
• Compensation is not up to par

Employment Contact

www.capgemini.com/careers

THE BUZZ
WHAT CONSULTANTS AT OTHER FIRMS ARE SAYING

• "Innovative and hardworking"
• "Too IT- and outsourcing-focussed"
• "Good, reliable, mainstream"
• "Too big to be sexy"

THE SCOOP

F ounded in 1967 as the Société pour la Gestion des Enterprises et le Traitement de l'Information (mercifully shortened to Sogeti), Capgemini has had several identities over the 30-odd years it's been in existence. When Serge Kampf founded the company in Paris, he created a company to focus on data processing and enterprise management. Since then, that company has morphed into one of the premier global names in information technology consulting, employing more than 83,000 people in 36 countries around the world.

Capgemini offers four main services—consulting, outsourcing, technology and local professional services—and each plays a role in the larger, integrated support system it provides to assist clients in dealing with the ever-changing landscapes in technology and business. Those clients, incidentally, are not constrained by any single business sector, spread across industries as diverse as finance, health care, life sciences, telecoms, utilities and more. In 2007, the firm's

> " Everyone watches out for each other. "

revenue increased some 13 per cent, from €7.7 billion to €8.7 billion, driven partially by the acquisitions of both Software Associates and Kanbay in 2006 and 2007, respectively. The increased revenue, meanwhile, didn't come to the party alone—it brought with it an increase in operating profits of around 50 per cent, up from €293 million in 2006 to €440 million.

The name game

Capgemini's current name is the result of two acquisitions made during the early 1970s. In 1973, Sogeti picked up a controlling interest in CAP, a provider of IT services based in Europe, while the following year it brought US-based Gemini Computer Systems into its stable and onto its nameplate, bringing the vowel-tastic Cap Gemini Sogeti into fruition. That identity stuck for almost three decades, as the firm sought to gain recognition in a different way—through acquisition and extension of its offerings.

The firm extended its US operations in 1981, acquiring Wisconsin-based data conversion specialists DASD Corporation, before adding CGA Computer's consulting arm five years later. As the 1980s progressed, the firm took its first steps into the world of outsourcing, acquiring French firm Sesa in 1987 and UK-based Hoskyns in 1990. Those purchases marked the Capgemini's first foray into the outsourcing sector that has since become its main business vector. Several more acuisitions and a 1996 rebrand saw the consultancy exit the millennium with all of its subsidiaries (which, by now, included US firms United Research and the Mac Group, as well as Gruber Titze and Partners and Bossard in Europe) operating under the shiny new Cap Gemini name and logo.

Time for new stationery (again)

Maybe it was Y2K. Maybe it was fear of losing out to a rival and suffering declining market share. Or maybe the opportunity to acquire Ernst & Young's consulting division just seemed like a good idea at the time. After all, it did offer the opportunity to treble the firm's business in the US, while also adding to its European holdings. Whatever the reason, the $11 billion deal has arguably cost Capgemini more in effort than it's gained to date, and the spectre of it still hangs over one of its organisers, CEO Paul Hermelin, who took over the hot seat in 2001, the year after the deal went through. As he told the Financial Times in February 2008, it was "not the right acquisition at the right time", and it consequently led to years of cost-cutting and layoffs, as well as another rebranding (the firm had changed its name to Cap Gemini Ernst & Young, only to change it to—surprise!—Capgemini in 2004). In 2005, meanwhile, the firm sought to stem the financial bleed it was experiencing by selling its US health care division to Accenture for $175 million—a decision that saved it from the threat of buyout that many had supposed was its only route out of the mire.

Capgemini's horoscope: outlook positive

After a rocky period in the first half of the decade, Capgemini seems to be on the rise again. It got back in the acquisitions game in 2006, with a special focus on increasing its footprint in India. In September of that year, it acquired some 51 per cent of Unilever India Shared Services Ltd. (Indigo), a provider of finance and accounting shared services. In October, meanwhile, the firm agreed to a $1.2 billion fee for Chicago-based Kanbay International, a global IT services firm that has a significant foothold in India. Kanbay, which specialises in providing support to companies in the financial sector, allowed Capgemini to double its employee base in India, bringing the total to 12,000 when the deal was finalised in February 2007. By the end of that year, the firm had increased its staff numbers on the subcontinent to 18,000, a figure that represents just a fraction of the 45,000 employees CEO Hermelin is hoping to have there by 2010.

That resurgence was underscored not only by the 13 per cent revenue hike the firm enjoyed in 2007, but also by deals with some major organisations over the course of the year. Perhaps the most significant (in terms of client prestige) was the announcement in September 2007 that Capgemini would be partnering with Google to supply Google Apps—billed as an alternative to Microsoft's Office software—to businesses around the world. The partnership allows Capgemini to add the applications to the suite of desktop solutions it already offers to the 1.1 million desktop users that number among its clients.

A friend in need

French bank Société Générale called on Capgemini in January 2008 to standardise the IT systems of its retail banking subsidiaries. Whether or not the deal is linked in any direct way to the €5 billion that rogue trader Jerome Kerviel is alleged to have lost in speculative trading that same month is uncertain, as the bank has been attempting to standardise the systems for a number of years. Requiring a partner with the capability to operate in territories in Europe, Africa, the Mediterranean and French overseas departments and territories (and all in the local languages), SocGen called on Capgemini to finish the job—a project that will utilise one of its service centres in Hyderabad, India.

> " There is a great deal of pride and emphasis on training. "

They cap emissions too

Also in January 2008, Capgemini became one of the first firms in the consulting sector to sign up for the United Nations Caring for the Climate initiative. Aimed at advancing commitments by businesses to developing corporate strategies and practices to reduce carbon emissions, the UN launched the strategy in June 2007. By joining the initiative, Capgemini has agreed to disclose as much of its carbon footprint as it is possible to calculate, and to attempt to minimise that footprint.

Driving forward

Of late, the consultancy has greatly expanded its position in the automotive sector. In February 2008, Capgemini announced deals with US firms Tenneco and Affinia, as well as Dutch firm tedrive. The firm will be exhibiting its broad range of services on these engagements, conducting applications management, solutions development and asset management services for Tenneco, while at Affinia a "business driven, IT transformation roadmap" will be the order of the day. In Holland, meanwhile, tedrive chose Capgemini to provide all of its IT services for a period of five years.

That same month, rumours including the words "Capgemini", "acquisition" and "India" once again began circulating in business circles. The only difference this time was that Capgemini was the alleged target, with Indian software giant Infosys mooted as the potential buyer. The possibility so alarmed Capgemini executives that they took the unusual step of invoking France's "Breton warrants", which allow companies to launch a share buyback to ensure that they control enough of the firm to stave off any unwanted advances.

The determination to protect the business isn't the only evidence that Capgemini sees a big future ahead. Given the parlous state of the US dollar, Hermelin has set his sights on some bargain basement shopping to augment his firm's operations on the other side of the Atlantic. Speaking to the *Financial Times* in February 2008, Hermelin commented that, "with $2.5 billion in revenues, we are a sizeable player but not a tier-one player in the US. We have a portfolio of strengths but could gain from adding a few others." That doesn't sound much like a firm that's giving up the ghost.

GETTING HIRED

Young at heart (and in body)

At Capgemini, apparently "there are a lot of younger people (ie, under 30), and lots of energy and enthusiasm." Part of that—in the UK at least—can be attributed to the firm's graduate recruitment scheme, in which firm representatives travel to university campuses around the country. The road show, which typically commences in October each year, seeks to introduce Capgemini to job seekers, and vice versa. Chief among its concerns is introducing candidates to its focus on training and career advancement. Additionally, the firm offers "insight days" for recent/soon-to-be graduates—a two-day process that allows candidates to visit the consultancy and take part in exercises, case studies and networking sessions to get a taste of life as a Capgemini consultant. And in addition to paying travel expenses, Capgemini even throws in a free lunch. Little surprise, then, that the firm earned a spot in *The Times* of London's 2007 Top Graduate Employers Survey.

While that recruitment experience holds for the UK, it is worth noting that it may not be reflective of the experience throughout Europe, as the firm's recruitment and hiring is managed on a regional basis. To counter that sense of regionalism and provide would-be Capgeminites with a more cohesive, international picture of the firm, Capgemini's web site offers profiles of employees in different locations throughout Europe, and provides links to regional sites that include details of how to apply for positions in each locale, for both graduate recruitment and experienced hires. Recruitment activities run at different times, depending on the region, and information on where and when to find events is also posted on regional sites, as appropriate.

OUR SURVEY SAYS

Fragmented firm, split opinions

Knowing the score at Capgemini depends very much upon whom you should happen to ask. A consultant in London, for example, feels that "of the major management consultancies, Capgemini is probably the most people-centred—a legacy of its French roots and emphasis on collaboration." Make it as far as Telford, however, and you can turn up the opinion that it's "very much a consultancy—lots of talk, not much action". Not only that, but some argue that there's "no direction or leadership", either. Perhaps the reason for all that is the "variation between departments", a situation that means "some people have a great environment and some don't," a source points out. While that's perhaps an inevitable by-product of some of the acquisitions the firm has made in Europe recently, some staffers still feel that "there isn't enough effort to get consistency." For further evidence, consider that in Malmo a source reports that "everyone watches out for each other," while in Lisbon the culture can be "extremely political".

More discordant notes ...

Almost everything sources report on at Capgemini bears the mark of that fragmentation. While some respondents say they are able to balance their work and life, others indicate that the ability to do so "is due to my specific job". Indeed, according to one respondent, the situation varies to the degree that "some people have worked 52 weekends and some have worked none", something that is put down—in Lisbon at least—to the fact that "top management defined working after hours as an objective."

Career progression falls prey to a similar spate of inconsistency. While an insider in Lisbon reports a culture that is "strictly up or out", a colleague in the same office offers the opinion that it is "not strictly up or out. There are quite a lot of horizontal movements." An Amsterdam-based consultant, meanwhile, reports promotion to "a higher grade about every two years". Even that, though, is up for dissent, with another source complaining that "promotion relies on being calibrated during a closed, unminuted meeting by your peers. So if you ever fall out with someone, you are stuck." Not only that, but there's apparently "no formal feedback process—so you have no knowledge of why you were not promoted".

... and some much-needed harmony

Just when you thought they couldn't agree on anything, the issue of training comes along to save the day. Capgemini is "good at training", says one staffer. A cohort in

205

London agrees, saying, "There is a great deal of pride and emphasis on training, including attendance at the Capgemini University near Paris."

Further consensus breaks out among UK-based employees over another key issue— that of salary, which one insider describes as "fairly rubbish". A consultant agrees that "Capgemini is not the best payer in the market, and will not give interim increases even to keep valued staff."

Community values

Capgemini seems to be committed to its community, and its role as a responsible corporate citizen, according to respondents. Among the charitable projects that it has undertaken are "using employees' professional skills for UNHCR and building a web site for collecting gifts to support tsunami victims". A Swedish source adds, "This year, instead of giving away Christmas presents, the money went to secure education for 100 young girls in India." □

Tamesis, The Glanty
Egham
Surrey TW20 9AW
United Kingdom
Phone: +44 (0)1784 431 611
www.gartner.com

The Stats

Employer Type: Public Company
Ticker Symbol: IT (NYSE)
CEO & Director: Eugene A. Hall
2008 Employees: 4,000
2007 Employees: 3,800
2007 Revenue: $1.18 billion
2006 Revenue: $1.06 billion
No. of Offices: 75

Practice Areas

Benchmarking
Go-to-Market Strategies
IT Risk & Security
Performance Optimization
Program Management
Sourcing Execution & Management
Strategy & Architecture

European Locations

Egham (European HQ)
Austria • Belgium • Denmark • Finland •
France • Germany • Ireland • Italy •
Netherlands • Norway • Portugal •
Russia • Spain • Sweden • Switzerland

Pluses

• "High-impact projects; well-known
  brand in the IT/telecoms space"
• "Flexibility in choosing assignments"

Minuses

• "As a US-based firm, it has occasional
  difficulties understanding local market
  conditions"
• Salary erosion over time

Employment Contact

www.gartner.com/it/about/
careers/index.html

THE BUZZ
WHAT CONSULTING AT OTHER FIRMS ARE SAYING

• "Cutting-edge IT research"
• "Too focussed on one industry"
• "Respected analysts"
• "Bookish"

THE SCOOP

G artner is a publicly traded IT consulting and research company that has been providing solutions for technology companies since 1979. As a former IBM employee and tech securities analyst, Gartner's founder, Gideon Gartner, was the perfect candidate to start an IT consulting firm. And his experience paid off—the small company rose in prominence in the early 1980s, and soon thereafter went through a series of key transitions that helped lead it to its place of dominance in the market today.

Gartner knows IT

In 1986, Gartner went public on the New York Stock Exchange. Its success on the market drew the attention of British advertising giant Saatchi & Saatchi, which purchased the consultancy in 1988. Gartner gained its independence again in 1990 through a leveraged buyout and then opted to go public again in 1993, this time listing on the Nasdaq stock exchange. In 1998, Gartner switched back over to the NYSE, where it is currently traded under the symbol IT.

Gartner provides four main services for its clients: research, consulting, events and executive programmes. In the consulting arena, the firm provides benchmarking, cost optimisation services and consulting services in the fields of business, comparative analytics, programme management, architecture and critical technologies, and sourcing. The events team designs exclusive symposia for senior

> " The project style allows preparation and post-processing of workshops to be done at home. "

technology professionals, where attendees can learn about cutting-edge research technologies and network with their peers. The executive programme consists of a specialised organisation where CIOs can access Gartner's services and knowledge about the challenges executives face in the information technology field. The biggest area of operations for Gartner, however, is its research team, which offers information through its database system Gartner Dataquest. The firm serves over 60,000 CIOs and other senior IT executives at 10,000 different organisations.

It's all in the numbers

One only has to look at a few of Gartner's key stats to understand its dominance in the fields of research and consulting. Its 650 analysts receive nearly 600 media inquiries per month and are quoted in top publications like *The Wall Street Journal*, the *Financial Times* and *The Economist* approximately 70 times a week. Sixty-five per cent of the world's Fortune 1000 companies and 80 per cent of the Global 500 are Gartner clients. Approximately 44,000 people per year attend Gartner events, and 3,600 CIOs are members of its executive programme.

A good year

The firm posted solid results in 2007—revenue grew 12 per cent to $1.18 billion, and net income increased by 26 per cent for the year, coming in at $73.6 million. Each of the company's business practices showed marked growth. The greatest source of income came from the research department, which boasted a revenue of $673.3 million, representing an 18 per cent gain from 2006. The consulting division brought in $235 million, an increase of 6 per cent for the year, and representing about 27 per cent of the firm's total business. The events department held 78 events with 44,216 total attendees during the year—delivering a revenue of $180.8 million.

> ❝ There is 'no strict up-or-out policy'. ❞

New man in charge

Gartner announced in its annual earnings report that it had appointed a new leader to its global consulting business. Bob Patton, the former head of the unit, stepped down to take a top management position at Ernst & Young. His successor is Per Anders Warn, a senior executive in the firm's European and US offices, who has been with the firm for 10 years. Warn moves to the position from his former post as the leader of the global core consulting team.

Leaving behind Vision Events

In February 2008, Gartner completed the sale of its Vision Events group to media and marketing solutions company CMP. Vision earned approximately $21 million in 2007 and hosted 16 events. Still, Gartner felt that the unit didn't have the ability to compete with its other content-driven events teams. With the sale of Vision Events, Gartner lost approximately 44 employees. CMP is a subsidiary of United Business Media, a consultancy based in the UK that is traded on the London Stock Exchange.

Exiting Asia

Further paring down its operations, in May 2007, Gartner closed down a portion of its consulting operations in the Asia Pacific region, laying off approximately 18 employees. The majority of the employees that were laid off—75 per cent—were based in Australia. The rest came from the firm's Hong Kong operations. A Gartner insider told *Computerworld* at the time of the announcement that the move had to do with size and competition: "It's all down to a size issue really. To compete with some of the other IT services companies out there you need to have a fair sized team and we only have a small team in this region. We would have to invest a hell of a lot more people and resources, which we just don't have." At one time the firm's Asian team (excluding Japan) had more than 50 staff members.

IT stable, but not growing

Gartner completed a study in April 2008 that showed that IT budgets have not shown significant decline or growth in the past few years. Its conclusions were drawn from a survey of 1,011 chief IT officers. Sixty-two per cent of respondents said 2008's budgets showed no significant change from past years. Overall, Gartner found that the growth rate of IT budgets has slowed from an annual increase rate of 3.1 per cent to 2.3 per cent. In a separate study, the news was more positive for those working in the IT industry: The firm predicted that by 2010, two-thirds of the Global 1000 companies will have "formalised technology innovation processes".

GETTING HIRED

Question time

Gartner prefers to receive applications through its web site, which is equipped with a portal for submitting CVs. Before applying for any positions listed on the site, it's worth taking a look at some of the other information the firm has posted there, including its interview tips section, which contains some solid advice on what to do before, during and after any interview with Gartner. Although most of the advice is common sense (for instance, "Be clear about which role you are interviewing for and why it is the right role for you"; "Ask clarifying questions"; "Acknowledge the people who met with you through a follow-up letter or e-mail"), it never hurts to brush up on every aspect of the company and what differentiates it from others in the industry.

Insiders who have been through the interview process report having faced "two interviews" and a "case study". One source reports, "I received a case study two weeks in advance and had to prepare a client presentation on an ERP roadmap project proposal." Among the types of questions to expect on the case study, meanwhile, a colleague provides these examples: "How should the cost of the new

IT infrastructure be justified? What parts of IT should be outsourced? How will IT and business influence one another? What strategies should be followed to provide an IT solution for changing needs? Which IT management challenges should be tackled first, and why?"

OUR SURVEY SAYS

Central command

Gartner insiders report working in an environment that is "cooperative and congenial", albeit one that comes with some frustrations, due to the centralised decision-making processes at the firm. "All relevant decisions are made at corporate headquarters," according to one source, who adds that "local management is not empowered to make decisions or adapt policies to local requirements." That approach has some employees worrying that the flexible workplace they're currently enjoying may become a thing of the past. Currently, "the project style allows preparation and post-processing of workshops to be done at home," says a staffer in Germany. "However, the attempt to do larger projects and to become more like a traditional consulting firm might change this."

Among the other effects that the move toward "traditional consulting" has had is a policy in Europe that "demands coach class flights", rather than the business class that was available before. While consultants don't complain of an onerous travel load at the moment, there is a sense that that, too, will change. "The majority of the travel is one-day trips to clients, but there is pressure from management to do more on-site client work, hence travel requirements will increase," a consultant remarks. And that's not the only travel bugbear at the firm, with some respondents expressing unhappiness that travel time is not billable.

Incentives to ... stay put

Gartner may prove to be the perfect choice for those who wish to work in a less competitive environment, however. According to sources, there is "no strict up-or-out policy", with one positing that "you might even ask for a demotion." The reasoning for that strange statement is provided by a colleague in Germany who explains that "a promotion has a negligible effect on compensation (only about 3 per cent increase), but the workload increases by 20 per cent, so there is little incentive to work toward a promotion." Perking consultants up, however, the firm does provide a "company car, also for private use", which includes petrol, as well as a "stock option programme" for employees. □

Gartner, Inc.

12-18 Grosvenor Gardens
London SW1W OH
United Kingdom
Phone: +44 (0)207 730 4040
Fax : +44 (0)207 730 9665

100, Ave. Raymond Poincaré
75116 Paris
France
Phone: +33 (1)44 17 78 78
Fax: +33 (1)44 17 92 08
www.marsandco.com

The Stats

Employer Type: Private Company
Chairman & CEO: Dominique Mars
2008 Employees: 280
2007 Employees: 250
No. of Offices: 6

Practice Area

Strategy Consulting

European Locations

London
Paris

Pluses

- Work/life balance
- "More and more women have been hired during the last two years"
- Managers have a lot to teach

Minuses

- "No clear rules" on promotions
- "Poor HR and career management"
- Community involvement is rare

Employment Contact

London
Patricia Bahs
E-mail: ldn.recruiting@marsandco.com

Paris
Laurence Fouasnon
E-mail: par.recruiting@marsandco.com

THE BUZZ
WHAT CONSULTANTS AT OTHER FIRMS ARE SAYING

- "Boutique, high-end"
- "Autocratic"
- "Treats its employees very well"
- "Not international enough"

THE SCOOP

A disagreement between Dominique Mars and his fellow partners at The Boston Consulting Group led to the formation of Mars & Co in 1979, and probably helps to explain the war-like lexicon the firm employs to describe its business. Having failed to convince his BCG partners that forming exclusive relationships with one client in each area of industry was the way forward, Mars left the firm and made that idea the founding principle of his own organisation. Guaranteeing an exclusive relationship with each client within its specific industries, Mars & Co today views its clients' rivals as "enemy forces", and promises to help "dissect" them on the business "battlefield".

Given the exclusive nature of the business it conducts, Mars & Co's clients are a closely guarded secret, although it is rumoured the list is composed of only Fortune 100 companies and top global corporations. One thing's for sure, though: Once on the inside, consultants won't have too much difficulty memorising

> ❝ Mars looks favourably upon balanced individuals who thrive on teamwork. ❞

them all—Mars' stated goal is to serve no more than 30 or 40 clients with a total of some 400 to 450 Mars employees. At present, the firm is roughly halfway to that point, according to its CEO.

Spanning the globe

Dominique Mars founded his firm in his native France, in Paris, before adding a second office in 1982 in the greater New York City area (Greenwich, Connecticut). Come 1986, the consultancy set up shop in London, and followed up with a new office in San Francisco in 1994. The firm moved into Asia in 2000, adding an office in Tokyo, and expanded its sphere of influence there in 2005 when it moved into Shanghai. Despite the scattered nature of the half-dozen properties, Mars operates under a "one-office" policy, meaning that any consultant from anywhere can be assigned to work on a project for a client, putting the company's full resources at the disposal of all.

Prosper on merit

Mars, working under an apprenticeship format, remains committed to the idea of meritocracy for its staff. While both associate consultants and senior associate consultants join the firm from colleges/universities or industry, and business

215

school graduates are hired as consultants, the firm never raids competitors for talent. Higher-level positions are exclusively filled by internal promotions. All told, there are eight steps on the Mars ladder: associate consultant, senior associate consultant, consultant, senior consultant, project manager, vice president, senior vice president and executive vice president.

GETTING HIRED

Brilliant generalists

Mars hopes candidates will do a little research on the firm before applying. Aspiring consultants are encouraged to reach out to junior staffers to get their opinions on what it's like to work at the firm. Come interview day, which takes place at the firm's office, candidates meet with Mars' most senior consultants, who assess candidates' potential and leadership qualities. One source recalls "three case interviews with VPs or project managers, in addition to one HR interview". During the interview process, the firm seeks to determine whether otherwise-brilliant analysts can become catalysts for change in major organisations.

Mars looks favourably upon balanced individuals who thrive on teamwork. Because the firm does not specialise by function or industry, it's most attracted to generalist consultants who can develop practical strategic recommendations from detailed analyses of clients' competitors and market conditions. Candidates must demonstrate strong quantitative skills in addition to energy, maturity, creativity and common sense; a sense of humour also helps.

Typically, the most promising candidates have degrees in engineering, math, economics or one of the hard sciences. Mars considers both MBA and undergraduate applicants from "big-name French, British and US schools". Applicants are asked to send resumes directly to their office of choice. ☐

BEARINGPOINT, INC. MANAGEMENT & TECHNOLOGY CONSULTANTS

1676 International Drive
McLean, Virginia 22102
United States
Phone: +1 (703) 747-3000
Fax: +1 (703) 747-8500
www.bearingpoint.com

The Stats

Employer Type: Public Company
Ticker Symbol: BE (NYSE)
CEO: F. Edwin Harbach
2008 Employees: 16,000+
2007 Employees: 17,000
2007 Revenue: $3.46 billion
2006 Revenue: $3.44 billion
No. of Offices: 148

Practice Areas

Asset Management • Customer Relationship Management • Enterprise Resource Planning • Enterprise Strategy & Transformation • Finance Advisory • Growth & Innovation • Human Capital • Information Management • IT Strategy & Transformation • Managed Services • Merger Integration • Operational Excellence • Oracle • Performance Management • Risk, Compliance & Security • SAP • Supply Chain & Sourcing • Systems Integration • Technology Infrastructure

European Locations

McLean (Global HQ)
Amsterdam • Barcelona• Berlin • Brussels • Bucharest • Copenhagen • Dublin • Düsseldorf • Frankfurt • Geneva • Graz • Hamburg • Helsinki • Leipzig • London • Lyon • Madrid • Moscow • Munich • Oslo • Paris • Stockholm • Stuttgart • Vienna • Walldorf • Zurich

Pluses

• Reasonable hours
• "Excellent" training

Minuses

• "Frequently changing leadership"
• Little-known brand

Employment Contact

bearingpoint.com/careers

THE BUZZ
WHAT CONSULTANTS AT OTHER FIRMS ARE SAYING

• "Respected in niche markets"
• "Large and not fast enough"
• "Good work/life balance"
• "Don't know where they want to be playing"

THE SCOOP

B ased in McLean, Virginia, BearingPoint's 16,000-plus employees serve over 2,100 clients around the world, including government organisations, Global 2000 companies and midsized businesses to boot. The government organisations include all 15 of the US's federal-level cabinet departments, while the consultancy also works with the top-10 global technology hardware manufacturers, banks, and drug and biotech companies. Those companies, meanwhile, are spread across a range of industries from A to, um, T. Automotive to technology, that is, with just about every conceivable industry sector that requires management and tech consulting expertise thrown in along the way.

Picking up the pieces

The firm has been around in one form or another for well over 100 years—back when it was founded in 1897, it traded as Peat Marwick, before coming under the control of Big Four accounting firm KPMG. In 2000, it was spun off as KPMG Consulting, and went public on the Nasdaq stock exchange in February the following year.

The good news for BearingPoint watchers is that in 2007, for the first time since 2004, the company filed its financial reports on time—bringing in $3.46 billion in revenue, to be exact. The bad news? It's still taking considerable losses, posting a net loss of $362 million for the year. That represents the fifth negative return on the bounce for a firm that is one of the biggest management and technology consultancies in the world.

A decent RAP

BearingPoint's unique selling point is its commitment to RAP. Not to worry, though, you can cast aside the cringe-worthy image of besuited execs trying to freestyle some lyrics at the Christmas party—Bearingpoint's RAP is about results, approach and people. The results component involves being able to measure and sustain improvements in the performance of its clients, while the firm's approach is to find a solution that works for the client through collaboration, rather than trying to fit the client to a preconceived model. Finally, the firm places its clients in the hands of its consultants (people) who are both passionate and experienced in their roles ... and who solemnly promise to never, ever attempt to bust a rhyme.

Partnering up

In order to broaden its offerings, the firm partners with certain technology and software companies to create greater value. Among BearingPoint's newly established partners are

BearingPoint, Inc. Management & Technology Consultants

219

the likes of i2, Symantec and Texas Instruments. One step up, meanwhile, are preferred partners—companies with which BearingPoint has had an alliance for some time (and, needless to say, expects to continue with in the future). These companies include Cisco Systems, EMC and Google. At the top of the chain are strategic partners—a group of five companies with wxhom the firm's consultants work "hand-in-hand" to solve business challenges for clients. In no particular order, the elite five are HP, SAP, IBM, Microsoft and Oracle. Just to demonstrate the closeness of BearingPoint's relationships with its clients, meanwhile, former BearingPoint CEO Harry You now serves as CEO of EMC, and was formerly employed as CFO at Oracle.

Fiscal woes

Harry You was brought into the company as CEO in March 2005 to steady the ship after the sudden departure of predecessor Randolph Blazer. You inherited a company that was reeling from the discovery that it had counted a wide range of inventory items from a 2003 acquisition twice, an oversight that led to the filing of unreliable financial statements with the Securities & Exchange Commission (SEC). As a

> " The firm is 'just the right size so that you are not going to get lost'. "

result, the firm was required to restate its financials for 2003—a move that backed up its accounts department through 2004, 2005 and 2006, during which time the firm filed every annual report late (and posted losses in each of them).

A new leader, with a different accent(ure)

Under You's leadership, the firm got to the point where its financials were close to being delivered on time, but the honour of being the CEO that officially oversaw the first on-time filing since the debacle began went to F. Edwin (Ed) Harbach, who was appointed in December 2007, shortly before the documents were submitted to the SEC. BearingPoint had brought on Harbach, a former managing partner at Accenture, in January 2007 as COO and chairman—roles he has vacated since taking over the CEO's chair. In his place as COO is David Hunter, who joined the firm in March 2008, and who also boasts previous experience at Accenture, having served there as global senior partner prior to joining BearingPoint.

Changing the tides

In its 2007 financial report, the firm noted, "In 2008, we must show significant progress toward becoming profitable and improving our cash flow." To do that, leadership outlined a three-point plan, which involves attracting and retaining world-class employees, striving for operational excellence and, perhaps most importantly, leveraging the firm's global brand.

The latter of these aims represents a considerable departure for a firm that spent much of 2007 considering a sell-off of its European, Middle Eastern and African holdings (EMEA) to its EMEA managing directors. Having knocked that idea on the head, however, BearingPoint appears committed to going forward as a global entity, with the EMEA division one of the leading revenue generators for the firm. Indeed, that sector is second only to BearingPoint's US public-services sector in terms of revenue, having brought in $791 million in 2007. That figure represents an increase of 12.5 per cent over the previous year's figures, while the firm's overall revenue increased by just 0.3 per cent in the same period.

GETTING HIRED

Looking for experts

During the BearingPoint interview process, candidates will "meet with three to four" different people over the course or two or three interviews, and should expect to meet a range of people, "from peer-level to managing director". Some candidates will begin the process with the human resources department "to confirm CV information and answer general background questions on the firm". Second-round interviews are designed "to assess whether the candidate can do a top job on client delivery". And final rounds normally dig into topics such as "culture, motivation and career potential". A source notes, "There can also be a case study presentation if it is felt that we need to understand more about the candidate." In years past, BearingPoint had a tendency to hire people "primarily for their industry experience", but current recruiting efforts focus "more on consulting skills", we're told.

The firm has "no preferences" when it comes to where you went to school, as "the tendency is to hire more from industry or individuals with sector expertise."

Worth the wait

Although sometimes "a little too elongated in the decision-making process" for new hires, BearingPoint's interviews leave candidates feeling impressed. One consultant remarks, "I liked the honesty and directness of the managing director who interviewed me. I was new into consulting, and he told me what it would be like and the risk I would be taking in helping set up a new team." Others chose this firm over others because they were attracted to the firm's culture and "the opportunity to work on client-side advisory and supply-side solution delivery". In addition, they appreciate its stance as a "combination of local startup and established firm."

OUR SURVEY SAYS

Being small has its advantages ...

In BearingPoint's "entrepreneurial" culture, there is "no them-versus-us type of partnership model". Respondents tell us that the firm's structure is "very flat", and communication is "open and transparent". One source says, "Life does not revolve around a 'partner elite' and 'staff'." The firm offers a "good workload, good pay and good mix between technology and business consulting", and staffers get excited that their workload is balanced out with some fun: There is a "great social club that organises nights out", which helps forge "lots of close relationships" among colleagues. As one consultant puts it, BearingPoint feels "just the right size so that you are not going to get lost". In fact, insiders say, there are "more opportunities" and "lots of freedom" at this "relatively small firm", compared to some of its larger competitors.

... and disadvantages

The flip side is that the firm's small size means consultants work on "fewer projects at a time", and projects are "not as diverse" as at other firms. Other downsides to BearingPoint's smaller-scale operation are that "administration and infrastructure are not always top." A consultant complains, "Administrative processes are not designed to support the client-facing staff." In addition, there is some "uncoordinated internal bureaucracy" that may be a result of "a few CEO changes over the past few years that have affected the culture". These "continued changes" have led to a sense of "confused leadership in Europe".

Inconsistent travel demands

Many BearingPointers "live away from home during the week", though travel demands vary among consultants and projects. One source says of the heavy travel, "It doesn't allow me to keep the same level of contact with the people that are part of the firm, as I am mostly out on client site." For some Londoners staffed on projects closer to home, "the worst travel is the commute in and out of London on the Tube." Things can sway "from extended periods away to no travel for weeks or even months" at a time, but the bottom line is, "you have to go where the work is."

BearingPoint, Inc. Management & Technology Consultants

Keeping it all in check

Despite times of intense travel, BearingPointers give fairly high marks to the work/life balance afforded by the firm. As one consultant explains, "Consulting is one of those professions where [workload] swings and roundabouts. There are times when there is no work, and times when personal life is impinged upon to meet deadlines and deliver quality conclusions to projects or products." Overall, though, workloads are "very acceptable", with most consultants clocking between 40 and 50 hours per week. Working remotely is "often possible", which allows "flexibility to ensure that work is completed while still seeing the family". Most sources report working just a few weekends per year and, on average, projects run for three to six months.

Bonuses not cutting it

Compensation gets average marks from respondents. Base salaries are "very good for the industry", but the bonus scheme is "well below the standard". Bonuses amount to "4 per cent of salary if you 'exceed expectations' on the performance review", an insider details. The firm's equity share plan is "not particularly generous" either. Staffers get more excited over the "group pension scheme with contribution matching", and the "great private health plan" that covers families and includes dental. And while the firm's "US-type package covers the bases, people would prefer cash", a consultant remarks.

BearingPoint is reportedly generous when it comes to community service initiatives, and supports charities, including Make-A-Wish Foundation, and lends a hand through pro bono work. It also supports consultants' "individual commitments to local work". Some sources say the firm "could be better" at community involvement, but in the last year, "a lot of opportunities have come up."

Solid training

A great deal of training at BearingPoint is unofficial, but there is a lot offered in the way of official training as well. Overall, insiders claim, there is a "very good mix". Consultants are "required to do a set amount of training per year", and most of what's available is "online, in-house training". In addition, there are "opportunities to do courses relevant to your grade", although high demand for these courses can make it "difficult to get on them in a timely fashion". There are also some "excellent instructor-taught courses" that take place off site and are usually five days long. We're told that these "face-to-face courses are good," while online training can be "very variable". One respondent comments, "You get to a certain level and personal development is driven by the opportunities you create and the support you get from subject matter experts and senior management."

Mixed bag on promotions

At BearingPoint, promotions are "based on merit". For those who "actively seek promotion," the average time for advancement is "within two to three years". Fortunately, consultants say, the firm's policy is "not strictly up or out at all", as "they accept people who want to stay as they are." As such, progress is "flexible, depending on your impact on the business". One source says, "If you can make a name for yourself in terms of expertise, achieve high utilisation and have good communication skills, you can rise very quickly." Others sense that promotions are "based on tenure for lower grades and ability for more senior grades".

Some staffers tell us advancement can be "sometimes subjective, as certain measures are out of your control". These factors, such as "getting on suitable projects where you can contribute", can hinder or facilitate promotion prospects, and lead some sources to classify promotions as "too slow". The firm clarifies that promotions are based on individual performance and being able to perform at the next level above in some competencies at the time of promotion.

Equal opportunity employer

BearingPoint is "not a male-dominated" environment; rather, insiders estimate a 50/50 split of men and women. "Hiring occurs on ability," and the firm "looks forward to welcoming women to the senior management team". And as far as ethnic diversity, BearingPoint's London office is "probably one of the most international offices in consulting that you can find", a source claims. The office has "a huge mix of people from all backgrounds", and there are "no issues with promoting minorities". Staffers give high marks to the firm's treatment of the GLBT individuals as well. ⬚

2000 Town Center
Suite 2400
Southfield, Michigan 48075
United States
Phone: +1 (248) 358-4420
www.alixpartners.com

European Locations

Southfield (HQ)
Düsseldorf
London
Milan
Munich
Paris

The Stats

Employer Type: Private Company
Chairman of the Board: Philip
  Hammarskjold
CEO: Frederick Crawford
2008 Employees: 750
2007 Employees: 700
No. of Offices: 13

Plus

• Great reputation in its niche focus

Minus

• Excessive travel

Practice Areas

Bankruptcy Claims & Estate Management
Bankruptcy Reorganization
Business Performance Improvement
Corporate Turnaround & Restructuring
Financial Advisory Services
IT Transformation Services
Litigation Consulting Services
Litigation Technology Services

Employment Contact

See the careers section of the firm's
web site

THE BUZZ
WHAT CONSULTANTS AT OTHER FIRMS ARE SAYING

• "Restructuring experts"
• "(Too) tough"
• "Small, but well positioned"
• "Pretty senior approach"

THE SCOOP

When the debilitating malady of corporate misdirection and operational weaknesses are threatening to make an ailing company even sicker, AlixPartners is there to help put the patient back in the pink. Widely known throughout the consulting world as the fix-it firm when things are going or are already firmly awry, AlixPartners has made a name for itself by providing solid counsel in corporate restructuring, operational management and financial advisement to global automotive, retail, manufacturing, health care, power generation and financial services organisations.

The doctor is in

Founded in 1981 by Detroit-area CPA Jay Alix, AlixPartners has proven itself again and again as the go-to consultancy for corporate turnarounds. The company first made international headlines in 1984, when Alix relentlessly searched for assets at the failed auto manufacturer DeLorean Motor Company, and in the process unearthed an additional $10 million for its creditors.

Since then, AlixPartners' client roster has grown to include some of the world's biggest players, including BP, Bruno Magli, Calpine, Enron, General Motors, Henkel, Jarvis, Karstadt Quelle AG, Kmart, Narita Airport Authority Corp., Oxford Health Plans, Refco, Stolt Offshore and Toys "R" Us.

Eyes across the water

In its 27-year lifespan, AlixPartners has grown at a consistently healthy pace. Over the course of the last handful of years, the company has broadened its reach significantly in Europe and Asia. In 2000, it had just three offices, all of which were based in the US. With its headquarters still based in the Detroit area, AlixPartners today has North American offices in Chicago, Dallas, Los Angeles, New York and San Francisco, with European offices located in Düsseldorf, London, Milan, Munich and Paris. The company also has Asian offices in Shanghai and Tokyo.

Cooperative leadership

To better manage its rapid global growth, AlixPartners created an organisational hierarchy of cooperative leadership. Company founder Jay Alix serves on the consultancy's board of directors. Philip Hammarskjold sits as chairman. Leading the firm day-to-day is New York-based CEO Frederick Crawford. Reporting to Crawford are two co-presidents: Stefano Aversa, who heads AlixPartners' European and Asian operations, and Peter D. Fitzsimmons, who leads the company's North American operations.

These managing directors, along with the company's approximately 750 employees, all have equity stakes in the company via a recapitalisation deal struck in 2006. Here, San Francisco-based private equity firm Hellman & Friedman made a significant investment in the private firm to hold a controlling interest, while enabling AlixPartners' employees to share in the interest as well.

One-stop turnaround shopping

AlixPartners' menu of consulting products and services comprises business performance improvement, corporate turnaround and restructuring, financial advisory services, information technology transformation services, litigation consulting services, litigation technology services, bankruptcy claims and estate management, and cross-border Chapter 11 reorganisation.

The company, which many say coined the term "turnaround", also provides numerous studies, reports and indices to help companies better prepare for the future. One of its more recent offerings in this realm is the AlixPartners European Turnaround Index, which polls leading bankers, lawyers, fund managers and other experts throughout Europe on corporate debt default, insolvency, restructuring and turnaround predictions.

SWAT team dives in

But what continues to set AlixPartners apart from competitors is its core consulting strategy, which is results-driven from the outset. For its clients, rather than provide problem-solving advice via 10,000-foot-view observational assessments, AlixPartners sends in small teams of senior executives, who themselves immediately go to work solving operational problems. Sometimes serving as interim CEOs or CFOs, AlixPartners executives work directly with a client's existing staff to dive deep into root causes of operational weaknesses, and then work together to stop cash bleeds and start restructuring efforts.

AlixPartners' accolades

AlixPartners' consistently solid work hasn't gone unrecognised. Its 2006 International Turnaround of the Year award from the Turnaround Management Association stands as a testimony to the company's successful work with infrastructure support services group Jarvis plc. The firm was also honoured in 2008 with the Turnaround Consulting Firm of the Year distinction from The M&A

Advisor. In addition, AlixPartners, along with its client Remy International Inc., was nominated in 2008 by The M&A Advisor for a Chapter 11 Reorganization of the Year, in recognition of the firm's success in bringing the auto supplier out of bankruptcy. Founder Jay Alix gets his day in the sun, as well. In May 2008, he was named an inaugural inductee to the Turnaround, Restructuring and Distressed Investing Industry Hall of Fame. The Hall of Fame was created by the Turnaround Management Association to preserve the legacy of those who built and supported the turnaround industry. Future inductions are planned for every five years.

And though AlixPartners still is recognised as the premier turnaround firm, over half of the revenue it generates today comes from serving healthy companies that are looking for sound performance improvement, IT transformation and financial advisory services.

GETTING HIRED

Aiming for experience

AlixPartners includes little information online regarding open positions in Europe. Its English web site focusses on opportunities in the US, but it does mention that candidates interested in working in Europe should mail a resume to the Milan address listed at www.alixpartners.com/EN/Careers/tabid/135/Default.aspx.

The firm also maintains web sites in German and Japanese, which are specific to its operations in those countries. For those interested in working in Germany, the country-specific site explains that you'll need "at least six to eight years" of work experience with "demonstrable success" in a managerial role. A background in economics or engineering is preferred, and fluency in both German and English are required. Resumes and cover letters, in both English and German, can be e-mailed to sschreier@alixpartners.com or sent via snail mail to the address listed at www.alixpartners.de/DE/careers_fs.html.

Insiders say qualified candidates can expect "psychological tests" as well as approximately "six interviews". ▫

PA CONSULTING GROUP

123 Buckingham Palace Road
London SW1W9SR
United Kingdom
Phone: +44 (0)207 730 9000
Fax: +44 (0)207 333 5050
www.paconsulting.com

The Stats

Employer Type: Private Company
CEO: Alan Middleton
2008 Employees: 3,000
2007 Employees: 3,400
2007 Revenue: £364 million
2006 Revenue: £374.4 million
No. of Offices: 40+

Practice Areas

Business Operations Consulting • Cost
Reduction & Corporate Turnaround •
Decision Sciences • Identity & Security
Solutions • Information Technology &
Systems Integration • Market Analytics •
People & Organizational Change •
Program & Project Management •
Solution Builder: Design, Delivery &
Support of Software Solutions • Sourcing
Consulting • Sourcing, Shared &
Managed Services • Strategy & Marketing
• Supply Chain & Procurement •
Technology & Innovation: Product &
Process Development

European Locations

London (HQ)
Denmark • Germany • Ireland •
Netherlands • Norway • Sweden •
United Kingdom

Pluses

- "Strong UK/European brand"
- "An adult environment"
- Transparent performance
  measurement system
- "Interesting and diverse projects"

Minuses

- "Not big enough to play the game with
  American competitors"
- "Old-fashioned management style"
- "Awkward culture—difficult to feel like
  you really belong"
- Lack of flexibility

Employment Contact

www.paconsulting.com/joinpa

THE BUZZ
WHAT CONSULTANTS AT OTHER FIRMS ARE SAYING

- "Emerging"
- "UK-focussed"
- "Jacks of all trades"
- "A dull version of Accenture/
  Capgemini"

THE SCOOP

L ondon-based PA Consulting Group performs a wide variety of consulting services, from preparing companies for public launches, to implementing security systems, to supporting delivery of defence projects worth billions of dollars. Forty per cent of its revenue comes from public-sector clients. It has a presence in more than 35 countries on five continents, with full-fledged offices in 14 of them. Industries served include defence, energy, financial services, government services, health care, international development, manufacturing, postal, professional services, retail, sustainable tourism, telecoms, transportation and water. In recent years, the firm has made a particular push toward being on the cutting edge of IT developments. Although it has faced some dark financial times, in recent years the firm has been flying quite high indeed.

From housewives to global dominance

In 1943, with the war-ravaged UK facing worker shortages in the munitions industry, three Englishmen—Ernest E. Butten, Tom H. Kirkham and David Seymour—started the company Personal Administration to help out. They began by teaching housewives to build Lancaster Bomber tail gun sections so that more men would be available to join the military. After the war, PA rode the crest of the world economic boom, setting up offices across the globe, and within 20 years, it had more employees than any other management consultancy in the world. However, that superiority began to wane during the 1960s and 1970s, as American and German consulting firms began spreading more aggressively. By the early 1990s, PA almost went bankrupt and nearly half of its staff was laid off.

The phoenix rises

A major overhaul was obviously necessary, so the firm brought in Jon Moynihan as CEO in 1992. When Moynihan joined PA, the firm's finances were in dire straits. Creditors almost immediately sent him a 12-day notice to pay back loans. One of his first major changes was to give each employee a vested interest in the firm, so that even the cleaning staff had a stake in it. To make sure C-level staff were as committed as he was, he made each of them buy at least £100,000 worth of shares with their own money. (To this day, the firm remains employee-owned.)

Moynihan's changes paid off. Five years later, PA began actively growing again, and by 1999, it was opening new offices overseas. Its focus on raw restructuring during much of the 1990s left it with little time to join the dot-com cult, which helped insulate it against the bursting of that bubble. In 2000, the firm won its first Platinum Award from the Management Consultancies Association (MCA). This was the beginning of a run of four Platinum Awards in seven years, including the 2006 award for the best overall consulting firm. Additionally, each year from 2004 to 2007, the firm announced record financial results; in 2007, it raked in £100 million in consulting operating profits. PA is certainly bullish about even more growth in 2008 and beyond, having spent much of the year expanding its London headquarters to make room for future staff.

So what exactly does it do?

The company's projects vary widely depending on the industry and the client's needs. In one engagement, Nissan contracted PA to help it improve the efficiency of output at its facilities in the UK. The firm created a new scheduling system that allowed Nissan to build a third vehicle model at the same time as the two models already being produced. Through this system, PA claims to have given Nissan a 30 per cent increase in potential plant throughput. It also helped financial services firm Storebrand put together an advanced system for remunerating shareholders in Scandinavia. PA annually conducts the Managing for Shareholder Value survey of around 700 companies, and used the information from this survey to help Storebrand create its own MSV remuneration scheme. On a public-sector project, the consultancy worked with the government of Singapore to create the first completely competitive market for electricity in Asia. PA's primary involvement concerned programme management, market design and IT system development.

Virtually consulting

PA has worked hard to reverse an initial lack of involvement in the latest technological innovations. It was one of the first consulting firms in the UK to embrace mobile technology, providing its professionals with early laptops, and many of its current subsidiaries are focussed on IT products and services. As another example, following the March 2007 retirement of CEO Bruce Tindale, the firm promoted its head of IT strategy, Alan Middleton, to fill the CEO chair. All the same, the firm doesn't believe that unbridled IT is the answer. Middleton has said: "I'm a fan of IT, but I'm still a bit cynical." He says companies should invest in IT to connect people, not to keep them apart.

PA was the first major consultancy to establish itself in the virtual world of *Second Life*. This unorthodox move was met with skepticism in many circles; however, it has won the firm a number of clients, from telecommunications company Telenor to the Hong Kong Jockey Club. The firm uses *Second Life* as a way to interact with and procure clients, build prototypes of real-world solutions, and help clients build their own presences in Second Life. For example, PA built the Hong Kong Jockey Club's *Second Life* facilities, and have used the virtual world to provide training to oil tanker drivers and emergency services employees. In addition, the online community has proved to be fertile ground for the firm's recruiting.

The public zone

In 2007, £150 million of the firm's £364 million in revenue came from the public sector. This reliance on the public sector has occasionally caused some worries within the firm; although the UK government under Tony Blair was enthusiastic about hiring consulting firms, the current administration has been less so. In early 2008, the UK government began a formal investigation into the true value of all the consulting for which it was paying—the British National Audit Office estimated that more efficient use of consultants could save the government £540 million a year. In response to the investigation (and its implication of wasted public funds), PA admits that clear-cut monetary returns on investment are rare in public-sector consulting, but emphasises the secondary benefits, such as improvements in processes, essential innovations and the transfer of skills and knowledge from its consultants to public-sector employees.

Nothing ventured, nothing gained

In the past, PA engaged in the development of venture capital subsidiaries, primarily manufacturers of software and other products. In June 2008, however, PA staff shareholders agreed to a demerger of the ventures business (now known as Ipex). Ipex is independent from PA and has its own management team, led by Martin Stapleton. The latest subsidiary was created in January 2008—Auto-txt Ltd., which develops location and tracking software products and services for the automotive industry. Other past PA venture subsidiaries include HR consultancy Cubiks, wireless communications company UbiNetics and pharmaceutical delivery company Meridica.

GETTING HIRED

The long haul

According to insiders, PA recruits at the "usual suspects"—that is, "top-notch international universities, LSE and the like". That includes Copenhagen Business School, KTH and the School of Business Economics (HHS) in Sweden and "classic consultancy" favourites "Oxbridge and the red bricks" in the UK. Still, one source in Germany says "school is not as important as career, skills and expertise." Others note that headhunters play a significant role in PA's hiring, which may result from the fact that the firm "usually recruits experienced hires". PA keeps an up-to-date list of its campus recruiting events on its web site.

The hiring process is "extensive, and rightly so", according to one respondent. Another describes recruiting as "long-winded", but admits, "it is thorough." "Long and tedious" is another consultant's assessment; "I went through two telephone interviews, various tests—numeracy, reading comprehension, psychometric and an Excel test—and 10 in-person interviews. The whole process took seven months." Others note the lengthy time frame as well, saying the process "can easily take four months". A source who's been with PA for four years adds that "the interview process can be too long for junior ranks; we tend to lose a few during the application process. Senior ranks should expect a tough interview process."

Multiple rounds, many tests

So what's involved in this lengthy process? "Each practice is different," a principal consultant explains. "Within the project management practice there are three rounds. Within the three rounds, a candidate takes both verbal and numerical reasoning tests, and undertakes a group case exercise." Another source says junior consultants should expect "a first round of two interviews—one is a case interview—and a second round of an aptitude test, group case, senior interview, junior interview and an individual case interview". Most rounds are sprinkled with "math and verbal tests and psychometric (working preferences) assessments".

> ❝ The firm is 'focussed on respect, fairness and high standards'. ❞

"Case studies are scenario-based, with background information, and the candidate is asked to put himself in the position of the PA assignment manager and inform the interviewer how he would go about conducting the assignment described," an insider reveals. Others report a mix of problem-solving questions, like: "If you had two minutes with Tony Blair in the lift, what three things would you tell him to do?" "Describe the value chain for a ping-pong ball," and "How many ATMs are there in Sweden?"

Adds a longtime staffer, "If I'm interviewing, the thing I try to measure is whether the candidate can think straight and interact constructively. Doesn't matter if his first answer is wrong; but can he contribute to a team collectively figuring its way forward?"

Thin intern pickings

PA offers limited internship opportunities, including a 48-week industrial placement programme in the UK and summer internships in Germany and the United States. The latter two are, according to the firm's web site, "aimed at graduate students in a master's or MBA programme". German internships are available throughout the year at the firm's Frankfurt office; they last a minimum of three months. Candidates are required to be master's students in economics, information systems and technology, industrial engineering or organisational psychology. They must also be fluent in German and English.

In the UK, 48-week intensive placements are offered in several business areas, including systems integration, government services, IT consulting, decision sciences, financial services, training and development, and human resources. All are based at PA's London headquarters, and there are no summer or short-term placements available. Candidates seeking a short-term placement in another PA office are advised to contact the regional recruiter via e-mail (contacts may be found on PA's web site).

A senior partner calls the firm's internship programme a "good base for recruitment". "In addition, it gives us unique branding at their schools," he adds. According to PA, approximately 65 per cent of its interns accept full-time positions at the firm.

OUR SURVEY SAYS

All grown up

"Changes over the past year to PA's organisation and leadership have resulted in a confused brand and culture," an insider claims. "It really depends on the practice that you are working for, varying from hierarchical and strict to collaborative and supportive." Common threads that can be found in PA's culture include an "ethical and very professional" spirit, and a sense of being "focussed on delivering value to clients", as well as "focussed on respect, fairness and high standards".

Some call the PA culture "mature and pragmatic", whereas others describe it as "old-fashioned", "controlled and conservative" and "risk-averse". The firm can be "very cost-conscious, with strict internal control systems", says one source, adding that these policies are, "at times too bureaucratic, but effective in controlling the business".

And although things can get "fairly hierarchical at senior levels", most consultants find PA to be a friendly place: there's "very little internal competition between consultants", a source in Oslo notes. Overall, a consultant explains, it's "a perfect platform for individuals with an entrepreneurial spirit".

Travel varies

As for travel, "it's an inevitable part of the job," shrugs a principal consultant. "Consultants are expected to work at client sites, which usually means travel—either commuting on a daily basis or travelling on Sunday night and returning on Friday night," adds another insider. But most sources say there's a wide range of travel requirements: "It depends on the project," is a commonly-echoed phrase. Says one respondent, "I have worked on assignments that have been weekly commutes, and on others based near or in my own office. I know others who have been abroad for stretches of a few weeks to a month without returning home." A senior staffer estimates that time spent in transit "adds 15 hours to my working week".

Still, sources agree there are ways to minimise the demands of travel. For many based in the UK, "assignments are based in and around London. This means most people based out of the London office are home most evenings." A colleague says that even outside London, "most of the travel is within the UK, and is not long haul," and many believe arrangements can be made "so travel has as little impact as possible" on consultants' personal lives. And while logging long hours in the air is inevitable for international assignments, "You will usually have some choice as to the clients and sites that you work at."

Work more if you want

"PA doesn't require any more or less hours than other firms," an insider remarks. "However, those striving to climb the ladder are welcome to put in extra hours— and most high achievers generally do." Another agrees that while "there is rarely an expectation of weekend work", most people will "choose to work hard when it suits them and when there is a need to". Having a "degree of flexibility to work from home for the odd day on some assignments" helps, as does the ability "to negotiate directly with the client regarding working from home, and arriving and leaving early as required". "For a consultancy, PA is exceptionally good in terms of work/life balance—although this does vary by practice and project," a principal consultant says. One complaint is that "work is often allocated late, and hence time management is difficult."

Keeping a work/life balance "is always a challenge", but one senior partner finds "the opportunity is definitely there." He adds, "I have managed to raise three children and keep my marriage for 20 years now." A PA workweek is "around 45 hours, on average, but 60 at peaks", with more or less time depending on travel and deadlines. Project duration "varies so much, from three weeks to over a year". A consultant explains, "In a typical year, you'll do three different client assignments— but it might be one long project or seven or eight smaller ones." "I have been with the same client for about two years, but was involved in seven different projects lasting from two months to 12 months," a source in Copenhagen notes. One thing of note, from a principal consultant: "The longest hours are worked when you're not billable, as the firm tries to get value out of you while you are not earning fees."

Anti-perks

PA consultants don't rave about their compensation, though they do like to make it known that the firm is "fully owned by staff". Accordingly, "shares and equity in the company" are frequently cited perks. But this system has its detractors: "A minimum of 10 per cent of our bonus is issued in shares that we cannot cash for three years," a principal consultant says. "I would prefer the cash."

Back on the subject of cash, one insider puts it bluntly: "I don't think the base salary is generous compared to competitors," and another agrees that "salaries are probably falling behind the market average." He adds, "There is a belief that the share option scheme compensates for this, but I do not think this is the case anymore." One Glasgow-based source gripes that "non-London staff earn up to 33 per cent less than London-based staff."

Calling extraneous perks "counter to management culture", respondents say they receive travel allowances and interest-free loans for share purchases, as well as private medical insurance and "a decent set of flexible benefits"—but not much else. However, some Norwegians express satisfaction over the firm's paid maternity and paternity leave. "The company pays an additional 20 per cent of salary so that you receive 100 per cent pay when on maternity/paternity leave (the state pays 80 per cent)."

Fixer-upper

Office amenities aren't winning any rave reviews either. PA headquarters in London has "a good central location", though one consultant rarely gets to enjoy it, saying, "I am only in the office once every few months." Others have more gripes: "Open plan, hot-desking, not enough work space or personal storage," sums up a source. However, the "tired" spaces "are being refurbished", which Londoners hail as a welcome change. And, adds a firm veteran, "The offices in Cambridge, Copenhagen, Stockholm and Dublin are much better."

Trying, not succeeding

While some say PA "is not very diverse", others claim "there is absolutely no discrimination" and the firm promotes a "colourblind" culture. Still, an insider believes there is "a bit of a boys' club mentality to be overcome", and another in London describes the firm as "mainly white male British". One consultant says, "Although there is a firmwide diversity drive again, it depends on the practice you are in."

Specifically with regard to gender balance, a Stockholm source declares, "We still have to improve on retaining women so we get a better balance on higher ranks," and a peer in London agrees that although there are "no barriers in place", there are still "disproportionately more men than women in senior positions". "A lot is said and done about diversity for women," a principal consultant explains, "but it has not resulted in many women reaching partner or higher in the firm." In other words, "The intentions are there, but reality does not always follow."

Pro bono efforts

The firm's Giving Back and Volunteering initiative lets consultants "spend time working for charities [they] nominate", as well as tackling "larger pro bono projects for the likes of the Prince's Trust and the Red Cross". Some call this a "very good scheme", though others suggest it's merely doing "token service". "In practise, any voluntary work that one is given time off for must cease immediately if one is required for an assignment, regardless of the impact on the charity," explains an insider. The company reports that employees are entitled to three days of paid leave for pro bono work, but any days over three will be at their own expense.

> 66 For a consultancy, PA is exceptionally good in terms of work/life balance. 99

Client opportunities

Sources say "the vast majority of people at PA are down-to-earth and very approachable," and "this includes senior management." However, one consultant says the management structure is concentrated at the top, with some line managers being less hands-on: "Managers are not real managers in the business sense. The partner calls the shots and the manager is the messenger."

As for client interaction, "It does take some work to get to interact with top-level management," a principal consultant suggests, adding that "you can build your way up if you have the right approach." "PA gets people out to the client site very early in their career, and encourages everyone to take on relationship-building responsibilities early," another source notes. "The unkind would argue that this takes the place of formal top-down development. The independent-minded will thrive."

Free to climb, or not

Most training is "formal and internal", and respondents label these offerings "excellent". However, "on-the-job training could be improved," and "there is only limited opportunity for attending industry-recognised external training."

Promotion-wise, "this is definitely not a strictly up-or-out culture," says one consultant. "There is no hard and fast rule for how long you must stay at each grade," a co-worker agrees. "Guidance suggests approximately two years, but it really does depend upon performance—that's a real motivator." The ability to "perform well", and "the networks you make within the company", will help determine the rate of advancement. "You go for it when you're ready," is how one source puts it. Internal "performance improvement programmes for nonperformers" help people catch up—or decide to leave. One staffer calls the policy "up or wait", and notes that "some employees have even stepped down, eg, from partner, to reduce their work commitments." □

NERA ECONOMIC CONSULTING

50 Main Street, 14th Floor
White Plains, New York 10606
United States
Phone: +1 (914) 448-4000
Fax: +1 (914) 448-4040
www.nera.com

The Stats

Employer Type: Subsidiary of Marsh & McLennan Companies, Inc., a Public Company
Ticker Symbol: MMC (NYSE)
President: Dr Andrew Carron
2008 Employees: 630
2007 Employees: 600
2007 Revenue: $4.9 billion (all Oliver Wyman Group divisions)
2006 Revenue: $4.2 billion (all Oliver Wyman Group divisions)
No. of Offices: 22 offices in North America, Europe and Asia Pacific

Practice Areas

Antitrust & Competition Policy • Commercial Litigation & Damages • Communications • Employment & Labor Economics • Energy • Environment • Financial Risk Management • Healthcare • Intellectual Property • Market Design • Mass Torts & Product Liability • Postal Services • Regulation & Public Policy • Securities & Finance • Statistical Sampling & Analysis • Survey Research, Design & Analysis • Transfer Pricing • Transport • Valuation • Water

European Locations

White Plains (HQ)
Brussels • Frankfurt • London • Madrid • Paris • Rome

Pluses

• "Honesty and transparency toward clients"
• "Robust economic analysis"
• Growth opportunities

Minuses

• "Unsupportive attitude from execs" when it comes to work/life balance
• "Work can be repetitive"
• "No integration between offices"

Employment Contact

www.nera.com/NERA_Challenge.asp

THE BUZZ
WHAT CONSULTANTS AT OTHER FIRMS ARE SAYING

• "Economics at its best"
• "Quanty"
• "Specialised, academic"
• "Economists, not businesspeople"

THE SCOOP

N ERA Economic Consulting is a 600-strong team comprised largely of economists specialising in one thing, and one thing only: how markets work. Spread across 22 offices in 11 countries, the firm promises clients "integrity and the unvarnished truth" from its economic analysis and advice. Its clients are drawn from governments, corporations, law firms, regulatory agencies, trade associations and international agencies—anyone, in short, who could possibly benefit from detailed economic analysis of markets on a scale ranging from local to global.

Given the high-brow nature of the firm's work, it comes as little surprise to find that many of NERA's employees are distinguished academics, including current President Dr Andrew Carron, an alumnus of both Harvard and Yale. Under his leadership and economic know-how, the firm currently offers its expertise in 20 core areas that form an A to, um, W of economic analysis—everything from antitrust issues to water. That industry research, meanwhile, is governed by the firm's four key founding principles—focus, independence, defensibility and clarity—each of which helps to ensure that NERA's work is unbiased, reliable, of high quality and easily digested by its clients.

While Rome burned, NERA ... figured out the cost

The consultancy's roots go all the way back to the 1961 founding of an economic think tank by two Americans: Dr Jules Joskow and Dr Irwin Stelzer. Thus was National Economic Research Associates born, an entity that later became NERA Economic Consulting, once it started offering consulting advice based on its specialist econometric analysis. Consulting consortium Marsh & McLennan came a-calling in 1983, and NERA joined its ranks, the purchase placing it within the fold of the Oliver Wyman consulting division. Today, that division—which pulled in some $4.9 billion in revenue for fiscal 2007—also includes management and strategy, financial services and organisational design consulting firm Oliver Wyman, and design and brand strategy consultants Lippincott. Other sibling companies under the Marsh & McLennan umbrella, meanwhile, include the likes of Marsh, Mercer and Kroll.

A multilingual concern

To work at any of NERA's six European offices, knowledge of more than one language is almost a necessity. In the London office (located in one of the least polyglot countries on the continent), language capabilities among the 50-strong staff include Danish, English, French, Georgian, German, Italian, Russian and Spanish, among others. The need for that level of multilingualism is driven by the nature of much of the work the firm carries out in Europe, including competition and regulatory issues, as well as analysis of EU policy and legislation for corporate and government clients. Indeed, the fact of an office's location within Europe is scant guarantee that the work done there will focus on the same continent—beyond EU member states, the London office alone conducts business in over 70 countries throughout Eastern and Central Europe, as well as Asia, Africa and Latin America.

Over in Brussels, meanwhile, the need for language skills is, if anything, even higher, given that the office is located in close proximity to, and derives much business from issues related to, the European Parliament. On that front, NERA's staff make frequent presentations at oral hearings of the European Commission, as well as notifications under the EC Merger Regulation and Articles 81 and 82. Those same experts have also published articles in some weighty publications, including the European Economic Review, Journal of Industrial Economics, and Research Policy and Economics Letters.

Going once, going twice

Nothing spells success quite like being asked to act as the auctioneer in a charity event—which is nothing like the role that NERA's Madrid office played in auctions of energy supply for Spain and Portugal (although it is arguably close in terms of prestige gained). Early in 2007, the firm was selected by Spain's Comisión Nacional de Energía to conduct a series of auctions of bilateral contracts for regulated energy supply in Spain and Portugal (CESUR auctions). Between June 2007 and March 2008, the firm conducted four such auctions, overseeing the sale of thousands of megawatt hours of energy to distribution companies in both countries. A fifth, meanwhile, was scheduled for June 2008. The oversight of the auctions reflects the consultancy's reputation for economic expertise and process management, and is arguably the most significant (and certainly the most high-profile) piece of business it has conducted within Europe of late.

Publish and be ... recognised

Not surprisingly, for a company boasting a plethora of academics, NERA's consultants like to publish their findings in formats that range from journal and magazine articles to white papers and books. The most recent title in the latter category was the 2008 *K&L Gates–NERA Global Telecom Review*. Taking a look at the recent past and projected future in the heady world of telecoms, the book was co-edited by NERA Vice President Christian M. Dippon and Martin L. Stern, a partner at law firm K&L Gates. Published in April 2008, the book is billed as a tool that will benefit everyone concerned with the future of the industry, from lawyers to investors and corporate executives.

242

NERA Senior Consultant Sébastien Gonnet provided an overview of the scope of the new German tax law and its potential business impact on companies operating from Germany in the article "La loi allemande surles 'Business Migrations'" ("The German Law on 'Business Migrations'"), published online in February 2008. The article explains how, as of January 2008, all operations, activities and functions—as well as risks and opportunities—transferred by a German company to a related foreign company will be taxed in line with new German regulations.

New places and faces

In March 2008, the firm established its presence in New Zealand for the first time, opening new offices in Auckland and Wellington. The offices focus on competition policy practice, as well as an established portfolio of clients in the energy, securities and finance industries. They will also strengthen NERA's ability to serve the Australasian and Asia Pacific market, a key region as the firm seeks to expand globally.

GETTING HIRED

Hard core about economics

NERA's "nonbureaucratic" hiring process consists of four or more interviews spread over two to three days, "plus an economic knowledge test". The interviews and test are designed to assess "technical ability". The first round normally lasts about an hour-and-a-half, while the second "can be long", and involves "lots of case study and technical questions". The firm also "checks references".

Candidates are recruited from "major universities in countries of interest." For US schools, NERA looks "predominantly at the Ivy Leagues", while European target schools are those in the "top tier", including Oxford and London School of Economics. Sources tell us the firm's "excellent" internships provide interns with "real case involvement". Teams generally are "extremely open to input" from interns.

OUR SURVEY SAYS

Tolerant environment

As one insider states, NERA's "excellent culture is supportive and tolerant". The firm is "flexible to the working and career preferences" of its consultants, while encouraging them to "work hard" and strive for "perfection of work". In the Madrid office, sources say the "corporate culture is low-key," and consultants are "cordial and respectful". According to one Madrid-based consultant who used to work in the firm's New York office, there is "much less unnecessary stress and pressure" in Europe. In all NERA offices, however, "there is a culture of the highest honesty and professionalism toward the client," a respondent notes.

We're also told that NERA is "very diverse" firm, "especially in terms of having foreigners in its offices". There are "few women", but those who are there are "treated equally", consultants assure us. Staffers feel that the higher number of men is primarily due to the fact that "economics attracts more men", rather than an internal bias. In addition, there is "no judgment in favour or against" gay and lesbian employees, as the firm has a "completely accepting attitude". As one insider points out, "The general GLBT presence is still pretty low, but this is almost certainly not due to any voluntary action on the part of the firm."

Balance differs for everyone

Work/life balance at NERA "can be team-specific", sources explain. Most say travel requirements have a "minimal impact" on their lives, as projects are "mostly on a national basis". That said, some complain of "high workloads" and "long hours". Others claim work hours that are "not necessarily overwhelming, but extremely random". Perhaps owing to the unpredictability of hours, there is no real average workweek, as consultants report working as few as 40 hours a week and as many as 70. One Madrid-based source says, "I am usually here from 9:30am till 8:30pm every day, with a one-hour lunch break."

Fortunately, in most offices, "there is flexibility and a very helpful attitude to any domestic problem." Although "the occasional weekend is necessary," consultants tell us they "can have a personal life with family". According to an insider, "I am allowed to plan when I get my work done and am never made to do work overtime." And when travel is called for, the firm is "accommodating so that business trips can be combined with leisure". Project length also varies greatly, ranging "from one week to two years".

Good economics

Most NERA consultants give decent marks to their compensation packages. We're told that annual bonuses can amount, for some upper-level staff, to "around 50 per cent of base salary", and employees are entitled to "equity of parent company MMC at a favourable rate". Other benefits include "private health insurance" and "integrative pension funds". Consultants have "access to resources, including IT staff, academic journals and research staff", and in Madrid, a "kitchen with great coffee, tea and snacks". Staffers are happy to receive "gifts at Christmas and tuition reimbursement". As for the offices, respondents describe the Madrid space as "spacious and in a prime location", while things can feel a bit "crowded and noisy" in London.

Growing up at NERA

Consultants say NERA offers a "good mixture" of both official and unofficial training. "Good-quality training activities abound, including seminars and courses," a staffer notes. But some feel "formal training on specific issues would be desirable, as most training is unofficial and on-the-job."

The firm's promotion policy is not up or out, but rather, is based on time in the position and merit". Opinions vary on how long it takes to advance your position, with some saying the average is two to three years, and others putting it closer to three to five. One source explains the progression: "Entry level is research officer, then analyst, then consultant," and for those who earn it, "progression can be quick." □

HORVÁTH & PARTNERS
MANAGEMENT CONSULTANTS

Rotebühlstrasse 121
70178 Stuttgart
Germany
Phone: +49 (0)711 669 190
Fax: +49 (0)711 669 1999
www.horvath-partners.com

The Stats

Employer Type: Private Company
Chairman: Dr Péter Horváth
2008 Employees: 400+
2007 Employees: 330+
2008 Revenue: €70 million
2007 Revenue: €64 million
No. of Offices: 11

Practice Areas

Expert Solutions
  Management Accounting & Controlling
  Process Management & Organization
  Strategic Management & Innovation
IT Expertise
  Business Intelligence
  Corporate Performance Management
  Solutions
  IT Realization
  IT Strategy
Management Training
  In-house Training
  Specialist Seminars

European Locations

Stuttgart (HQ)
Barcelona • Berlin • Bucharest •
Budapest • Düsseldorf • Frankfurt •
Munich • Vienna • Zurich

Plus

• Highly organised methodology

Minus

• Less name recognition outside
  Germany

Employment Contact

See the career section of the firm's web
site for recruitment/HR contact details

THE BUZZ
WHAT CONSULTANTS AT OTHER FIRMS ARE SAYING

• "The balanced scorecard guys"
• "Only local"
• "Up-and-coming"
• "Good reputation, but only in the
  accounting field"

THE SCOOP

German-based management consultancy Horváth & Partners describes its consultants as "performance architects", a term based around the firm's ability to reconstruct the business results of its clients. That improvement is delivered through a variety of methods that includes consulting services across three main fields—strategic management and innovation, process management and organisation, and management accounting and controlling—as well as expertise in IT and management training, to ensure that solutions are applied effectively and integrated across the full breadth of a client's business. That approach, the company claims, makes it "No. 1 in performance management—worldwide". The "worldwide" portion is something the firm is still working on, however, at least in terms of office locations—currently there are just 11 Horváth & Partners offices, five of which are in Germany, and only one of which can be found outside of mainland Europe, in Atlanta.

The firm's clients, meanwhile, are drawn from both the public and private sectors, and from an extensive range of industries, although the company boasts expertise in the following key sectors: automotive, chemicals, oil and pharmaceuticals, consumer and industrial goods, financial industries, media and telecom, public management, transportation and utilities. Among those industries, Horváth serves a broad client list, which, unsurprisingly, is composed of many major German firms, including Audi, BASF AG, Bayer, Lufthansa, Pfizer, UBS and Volkswagen.

The finer points of modelling

Unlike some in the consulting world, Horváth & Partners didn't just snatch its marketing shtick out of thin air—its "performance architect" references are based on the model it uses to bring about improvement for its clients, and which is laid out (the theory goes) rather like an architect's blueprint, with one process following on from another. The three-pronged model, described above, starts with the concept, follows on to IT realisation and ends with standard setting and corrective action. Moreover, solutions applied in any single field are integrated throughout all categories. In this way, the firm promises to deliver integrated, sustainable growth to its clients, taking care of all the details, like finding the best IT systems and training staff in how to use them.

Eye on expansion

Horváth & Partners got its start in Stuttgart in 1981, when two university professors—Péter Horváth and Eric Zahn—got together with businessman Hans-

Georg Winderlich to found the IFUA Institut für Unternehmensanalysen GmbH. Mercifully, for all who would come to write about the firm in later years, it changed its name to its current iteration some time later, following the retirement of Zahn and the death of Winderlich. It wasn't until 1990 that the firm expanded, however, with its Budapest office making a foray into Péter Horváth's country of birth. By the turn of the millennium, however, the firm had developed into a genuine international concern (albeit a largely German-speaking one), adding offices in Vienna, Munich, Düsseldorf, Berlin and Zurich. More were to follow in the post-millennial period, as the consultancy crossed the Atlantic for the first time, establishing a subsidiary in Boston (which would move to Atlanta in 2005), and expanding into Spain and the Czech Republic by 2003, the latter through an alliance with a local firm. Come 2006, Horváth's leaders saw an opportunity in another emerging market in Europe—Romania. Seeing an explosion of business within the country, the firm decided to open an office in Bucharest to bring its expertise in managing growth to a fresh audience. In June 2008, a new office in Frankfurt was opened with a focus on clients in the financial services sector.

Team dynamics

All through its expansion, which has seen the firm grow to more than 400 consultants, Horváth has maintained its independence, and its commitment to partnership. According to the firm, its partners are expected not only "to embody the competences and the values of the Horváth & Partners Group", but to provide the entrepreneurial spirit and drive to take the company forward. At last count, the firm had 26 such partners, some of whom are also members of the managing board, and four of whom were appointed as recently as April 2008. Three of those appointments were in Munich, with Axel Borcherding and Dr Ralf Sauter being appointed head of the chemicals, oil and pharmaceuticals, and consumer industrial goods "competence centres", respectively, while Werner Stegmüller will head up the finance supply chain integration business segment. In Düsseldorf, meanwhile, Kai Grönke was appointed to lead the entire office.

In addition to appointing managers of its own, the consultancy also supports clients by developing the abilities of others through its management training wing. To bring managers (or potential managers) up to speed on current issues and techniques in the corporate world, the firm offers specialist seminars on a range of topics and skill sets, and also offers in-house training that can be tailored to fit the needs of the individual or company. Horváth prides itself on the fact that its trainers are also consultants, which allows for less of a jump between the "classroom" and the real world—sometimes blending the two together, so that managers learn from trainers as they tackle real issues within their own organisations.

The (global) buddy system

In a bid to add further international flavour to the Horváth table, the firm has developed an alliance of like-minded firms around the globe. Known as the "performance architects alliance", the list currently includes Atlanta's North Highland, Paris-based Oresys, UK firm Qedis, Twynstra Gudde in the Netherlands, Italy's Bonfiglioli and Prague-based Point Consulting.

GETTING HIRED

Variety is the spice of life

Horváth & Partners is open to hiring recent graduates as well as experienced professionals. In addition to graduates of economics and business administration programmes, the firm also accepts candidates with engineering or IT backgrounds. To advance through Horváth's hiring process, candidates must demonstrate excellent achievements in their studies and, ideally, specialised knowledge in a certain field— but those qualifications alone will not impress interviewers. Horváth is keen on hiring people with enthusiasm, common sense, teamwork skills, creativity and humour. In their interviews, candidates also should demonstrate analytical thinking, unconventional ideas and initiative. The consultancy values international and industry expertise from experienced applicants, but will only extend offers to those who are excited about steadily gaining new knowledge. Candidates can search current job opportunities, organised by level of experience, and can view contact information for Horváth's HR and recruiting team on the firm's careers web site.

Attractive opportunities for students

Horváth offers plenty of opportunities for students. Throughout the school year, the firm hires students to support its consulting teams. After an initial training period, students have the opportunity to work their way up to a project assistant position. In this capacity, assistants actively participate in projects, gaining in-depth understanding of practical consulting. Horváth is fully supportive of university studies as a student's main priority, so assistants have the freedom to stipulate on a monthly basis when and for how long they wish to work for the firm.

The firm also offers internships, through which interns may be fully involved in projects from day one. Participants in the internship programme learn the manifold tasks of a consultant in a dynamic working environment, provide active support for the teams and eventually run smaller project phases on their own. Horváth supports interns who want to write their bachelor's or master's thesis based on their experience at the firm. Senior consultants help soon-to-be graduates prepare papers on subjects selected from Horváth's variety of consulting activities, and stand-out students can become members of the Horváth Student Club, allowing them to stay in contact with the firm and be coached in their studies.

Continuing development

Once hired, staffers are granted access to a variety of training and career development services: In-house training based on hierarchical level and needs (public speaking, project management, leadership and others) is offered, as is external training. For further academic development, the Horváth scholarship programme offers sponsoring of doctorates, MBAs or other relevant degrees. The programme becomes available after a two-year tenure with the firm, and includes financial support and leave for up to one year, depending on the field of studies. Another highlight is the Horváth & Partners University, an internal training event occurring twice annually at an off-site location and featuring diverse workshops, knowledge-sharing forums, sporting events and get-togethers. □

AAM Management Informati

Alvarez & Marsal • Arup • At

Consulting • Commercial Ad

Value Associates • Detica • Di

Consultants, Inc. • Droege &

Logica • Mott MacDonald B

• Proudfoot Consulting • PRT

• Simon-Kucher & Partners

Towers Perrin • Value Partn

Wipro Ltd. • XLENT Consulti

Management Information Con

Marsal • Arup • Atkins • Can

• Commercial Advantage Cons

• Detica • Diamond Managem

• Droege & Comp. • Infosys

THE BEST OF THE REST

AAM MANAGEMENT INFORMATION CONSULTING LTD.

59-61 Pannónia Street
H-1133 Budapest
Hungary
Phone: +36 (06)1 465 2070 or
 +36 (06)1 465 2071
Fax: +36 (06)1 465 2078
www.aam.hu
www.aamtech.hu

The Stats

Employer Type: Private Company
Partner & President: Dr Gábor Kornai
Partner & CEO: Zoltán Szűcs
2008 Employees: 220+
2007 Employees: 200+
2007 Revenue: €16.3 million
2006 Revenue: €14 million
No. of Offices: 7

Practice Areas

Business Efficiency Improvement
EU & Worldbank Project Management
IT Organisations Advisory
IT Systems Implementation Support
 (Client-side Support, Feasibility,
 Quality Assurance)
Overall Programme Management
Project Procurement Management
Strategy Change Management
Technological Solutions

European Locations

Budapest (HQ)
Belgrade
Bucharest
Pécs
Sarajevo
Skopje
Sofia

Plus

• Good reputation within Hungary

Minus

• Lack of overseas opportunities

Employment Contact

aam.hu/en/jobs

THE SCOOP

AAM Management Information Consulting Ltd.

AAM Management Information Consulting got its start in Budapest in 1994, not long after the fall of the Soviet Union allowed private companies to set up shop. Since then, the management and IT consulting specialist has grown exponentially, surpassing 1 billion HUF in revenue for the first time in 1999, and 3 billion HUF in 2006. Employing over 200 professionals, the firm is one of the largest consultancies in Hungary, and has an avowed aim of expanding its horizons beyond the country's borders. To this end, the firm created a Romanian subsidiary in 2006, and is planning more offices in the region.

AAM's primary clientele includes large public administration institutions and the top-200 of the private-sector corporations. Its public-sector clients include several government departments in Central and Southeastern Europe, as well as educational institutions. In the private sector, the firm serves clients of the stature of E.On, Hungarian Telecom and MOL across a range of industries that includes finance and insurance, energy, industrial, transport, public utilities, media and telecommunications. The fundamental offerings of the company include client-side consulting and technological solutions. AAM additionally delivers off-the-shelf products, though it remains independent from any single supplier.

Integration specialists

Drawing on its own country's knowledge of integrating a nation within the European Union, one of AAM's specialties is in providing consulting services to countries undergoing similar transitions. The firm won an EU-funded contract in August 2007, for example, to advise the Serbian government on the creation of a more transparent financial system. The contract, which is worth some €2 million, is scheduled to run until 2009, although it is unclear how Kosovo's recent declaration of independence and the ensuing tensions may have affected that time line, or AAM's involvement in the region.

Among AAM's other specialty offerings is its ability to help companies comply with ever-changing (and sometimes Byzantine) EU regulations. This is especially helpful for organisations seeking to win EU contracts that may otherwise not have had the means or wherewithal to navigate the sea of strict regulations involved in the process.

Tech savvy

At some point, there is a crossover between offering IT consulting and IT support. Savvy consultancies, upon realising this, offer both, and AAM is no exception. Understanding that there was demand for the provision of the sort of software and system development it was recommending to its clients, the firm set up AAM Technologies Ltd in 2001 as a subsidiary. Offering its services across four major technology platforms, the firm specialises in Oracle- and Java-based application developments, implementation of IBM, BEA and Seebeyond integration utilities and related developments, as well as Microsoft .NET-based developments.

Looking forward

In 2006, AAM launched a 10-year strategy based around international expansion. The first stage involves spreading the firm geographically into between eight and 10 countries outside of Hungary—many of which seem likely to be in Central Europe and developing European nations. Obviously, this will require employees at the firm to be fluent in more than one language, and for the moment, AAM is envisioning conducting most of its business in English and through a network of independent subsidiary companies, each pulling in around 20 to 30 billion HUF annually.

To keep up with this expansion, AAM will also need more employees, and it is planning to up its numbers to between 1,500 and 2,000 professionals by 2015. The vast majority of these hires are likely to be foreigners (ie, non-Hungarians) with a fluency in more than one language. When it reaches the international level, however, the official language of the company will be English. Its offices abroad will operate as legally independent subsidiaries and profit centres. On the client front, the consultancy anticipates offering the same type of services to a similar range of clients, and splitting its energies evenly between public and private enterprises.

GETTING HIRED

Testing, testing

Landing a job at AAM requires as much in the way of language skills as it does consulting skills, not to mention a general ability to fit with the existing team. Most positions require English skills, and the firm's avowed aim of expansion into Eastern Europe means there will be opportunities for those with skills in other languages as well. The consultancy's web site maintains a list of vacancies, complete with job descriptions, and AAM also offers a summer internship programme—aimed at giving current students a taste of the consulting industry prior to embarking on a career in the field. One former intern found the experience particularly useful, admitting that he "decided to be an IT consultant, and not an electrical engineer, after my internship".

To land the job, candidates can expect to "interview with HR, then interview with a consultant", before moving onto the skills tests. For a position requiring English, a current employee faced an "English and personality test", followed by an "oral presentation in English". The consultancy recruits candidates from several Hungarian universities, and an insider points out that "there is no strict rule, but we like to recruit from BME (Faculty of Electrical Engineering and Informatics), Corvinus and the University of Pecs."

AAM Management Information Consulting Ltd.

ABOLON

90 Long Acre
Covent Garden
London WC2E 9RZ
United Kingdom
Phone: +44 (0)207 849 3006
Fax: +44 (0)207 849 3200
www.abolon-consulting.com

The Stats

Employer Type: Private Company
Managing Director: Dr Thimo L.
  Sommerfeld
No. of Offices: 2

Practice Areas

Corporate Finance/M&A
Finance/Accounting
Marketing & Sales
Operations
Organization & Organizational
  Capabilities
Strategy

European Locations

London
Munich

Pluses

- "High-caliber clients"
- "Challenging and interesting projects"
- "Performance-related pay"
- Consultants have "more influence" here than at larger competitors

Minuses

- Long working hours
- "Weak infrastructure"
- Little opportunity for those without industry experience
- "Relatively high turnover"

Employment Contact

www.abolon-consulting.com/
  recruiting.htm

THE SCOOP

A bolon Ltd. is a London-based consultancy that serves companies in the health care industry, helping with strategy development, operational improvements and corporate M&A. Abolon holds the bar high for its senior consultants, who are required to have a background in both management consulting and in health care. Abolon executives feel that experience working in the health care industry is a strong asset for potential employees because it helps to build relationships with key clients. Within that industry, Abolon focusses its operations on prescription pharmaceuticals, medical devices, health care service providers, diagnostics, animal health, over-the-counter medicines, crop sciences and biotechnology. The firm operates out of its offices in London and Munich.

Wide reach, wide range

Though Abolon may focus exclusively on health care, it offers a wide range of services for its clients. The firm operates across four geographic sectors: Japan, North America, emerging markets and, of course, Europe. Through these regions, Abolon provides advice in the areas of corporate finance and

> ❝ Consultants are given 'much room to bring their own ideas'. ❞

M&A, strategy development, finance and accounting, marketing and sales, operations and operational improvement, and organisation and organisational capabilities.

Closing the sale

One of Abolon's particular strengths is strategy development, where the consultancy is in continuous and direct competition with its older and larger competitors. The firm has built a knowledge base in this area through its consultants' years of experience within the innovative, specialty and generic pharmaceuticals, and various segments of the medical devices, diagnostics and crop sciences industries. Abolon also helps its clients access licenses for new products, and advises on the research and development process for the strongest possible launch of new products.

The firm has also made a name for itself as a commercial due diligence advisor for private equity and venture capital firms. Examples include the sales of medical consumables company ConvaTec for $4.1 billion (in May 2008), Merck Generics for $6.7 billion (May 2007), acute care hospitals Hirslanden Kliniken for $2.4 billion (February 2007), and medical device company BSN for €1.03 billion (February 2006).

Fixing the system

Though European health care is often touted by many Americans as being flawless, the reality remains that in the UK, national health care budgets often force payers and providers of medicine to raise prices and cut costs while attempting to maintain the high standard of care to which their clients are accustomed. Abolon tries to find creative means to achieve these seemingly insurmountable goals by advising on everything from marketing strategies to risk management.

Abolon serves the sectors of both over-the-counter and prescription medications. When it comes to OTC meds, the consultancy recommends to its clients an aggressive marketing and sales campaign that is more akin to consumer goods. Prescription pharmaceutical consulting can be a little more complicated. Abolon helps its clients access licences for new products, and advises on the research and development process for the strongest possible launch of new products. Pharmaceutical companies also often regularly utilise the firm's expertise in the field of M&A.

> " Meritocracy defines the level of interaction with senior clients. "

Nice niches

The consultancy also has its hands in other health-related fields. In animal health, Abolon offers services of more efficient marketing for animal pharmaceuticals, while also searching for situations in which human products can be applied to animals as well. It also provides acquisition and licensing services in the biotechnology niche, and the firm's services in this field extend to advisory for companies in advance of an initial public offering.

Making the grade

With the latest statistics showing that more than half of all corporate merger and acquisition transactions have a negative effect on value, M&A consulting has increasingly become one of Abolon's most important tools for attracting clientele. In the course of its short history, the firm has advised on six transactions to date—and always in the sector its advisors understand better than others, health care.

Recently, the firm advised a US pharmaceutical client in the takeover of a Western company, with positive results in the incorporation of transaction process management and financial advisory. Another recent case where Abolon made measurable gains was in the area of operations. Consultants helped a chemical plant reduce costs by 40 per cent by improving efficiency and developing operations strategies that optimised performance.

GETTING HIRED

M&A skills give an edge

Since many of Abolon's consultants joined the consultancy after starting their careers with McKinsey, followed by several years in operational line roles or in the financial services industries, it's no surprise that its "McKinsey-like" hiring process involves "several interview rounds with senior-level consultants and partners". There are "not more than three interviews", each of which is "between one and two hours long" and involves "cases and brainteasers". Interviews are looking to assess "a range of skills", including "numeric, general business and interpersonal skills, along a range of subdimensions". And because Abolon does M&A advisory and a lot of work for financial investors, "both numeric skills and commercial judgment might play a larger role" than they do in competitors' hiring processes.

One consultant provides a detailed sample interview question: "A pharma company's women's health business has observed shrinking growth rates in Russia. I would like you to explore why that is and, in a second step, develop recommendations to reinitiate growth. I would like to see how structured you are in your approach. I will play the business unit manager for Russia; please ask me whatever you believe will help you diagnose the situation and develop recommendations." Abolon "only" recruits at "European business schools", we're told, such as INSEAD, and at "leading universities," like ETH Zurich.

OUR SURVEY SAYS

Fun on the job

Abolon's culture is "nonhierarchical and open", and consultants are given "much room to bring their own ideas". The firm's "entrepreneurial spirit" attracts people who are "fun, yet very professional", and who are "focussed on excellence and client service". And staffers make sure to integrate fun into their assignments. A contact says, "Gaming is an important aspect around transactions, so we have a number of competitive games going on at any point in time. For example, the person with the estimate that comes closest to the final transaction value will win a bottle of champagne."

Abolon also is big on recognising hard work. Consultants are awarded "fun prizes for the highest client impact during a given year". The firm has "no formal programmes in place" to promote diversity, but according to one insider, "Due to the notorious shortage of skilled professionals, nobody here can afford to not involve a diverse group of individuals."

Lifestyle dependencies

Work/life balance at Abolon is "mostly OK", respondents tell us. Consultants work between 50 and 70 hours per week on projects whose length is "very much dependent on the type of assignment". Commercial due diligence assignments normally range "from three to six weeks", while strategy gigs run closer to "three to 12 months". For M&A engagements, "time lines are very tight," which can result in longer working hours. Still, Abolon consultants appreciate that they "work less than M&A banks, but get involved in as many transactions". (A source remarks, "This is the most transaction-related consulting firm I am aware of.") On the whole, the firm is "flexible", and there are "quiet times between projects that balance the high workloads during tight project situations". In addition, there are "large degrees of freedom to work over weekends and to take time off during the week". For new parents, part-time work is an option, and "projects can be selected" to accommodate their lifestyle.

Abolon consultants also have travel to take into account. For well-organised consultants, "there are no downsides" to the firm's travel requirements. Travelling is in "the nature of the business", and this firm's demands are "not more or less than other consultancies'". On average, staffers are on the road "two days per week", which some say is actually "limited, relative to other consulting firms". We're told that travel is "not on a regular basis", but consultants "have to be flexible to go on a trip for two continuous weeks at short notice". Indeed, much of the firm's project work offers "limited planning possibilities".

Content with comp

Abolon consultants give very high marks to their pay packages. One insider remarks, "This is the first time in my life that I am fully satisfied with my compensation." The firm is "open to discuss equity", and treats its teams to "parties at Christmas and other special events". When on the road, consultants "stay in good hotels", and when at home, they kick back in "apartment-like" offices, designed as such because the firm "values direct interaction between consultants".

The firm is also generous in its charitable leanings: In 2007, Abolon "transferred a "four-digit USD amount to the Children with Leukemia charity".

Consulting with a twist

Abolon consultants feel fortunate to be exposed to "a wide range of projects", including M&A advisory and "typical management consulting projects". A contact says, "As M&A advisors, we have closed four health care transactions during the last 18 months, more than some European investment banks." And a colleague says of the firm's client demands, "Stringent conclusions are required, based on detailed sector insights across the entire range of the health care sector and across numerous jurisdictions." Consultants are expected to contribute to Abolon's "superior bottom-line offering to clients".

But exposure to those clients' senior personnel isn't always a given. Abolon works at a "broad range of levels with strategic clients and financial investors". With financial investors, there is "limited opportunity for more junior professionals to get involved", a consultant reports, since these clients "tend to be hierarchical". However, when working on strategic projects, "meritocracy defines the level of interaction with senior clients." And, since many of the firm's consultants "have a long track record and have spent time with Abolon competitors", they have enough experience to "spend an over-proportionate percentage of their time with senior people".

Learn it and earn it

Promotions at Abolon are "in line with the timing of competitors", but they typically have a "slightly more commercial aspect". Insiders tell us the firm considers the following metrics before promoting someone: "How much value was created for clients? How many projects have resulted from a professional's activity? How good is the judgment of a consultant when recommending an investment to a private equity firm?" In this "meritocracy, specialist expertise is valued highly". A source notes that in the early stages of a career at Abolon, the promotion policy can be "quite rigid". "Without a 'spike', there is limited opportunity to find a role in the mid- to long term."

To help get staffers to where they need to be, the firm offers "only unofficial training". Consultants don't feel shorted by this system, though, as it is a "structured, on-the-job" effort—the firm "stresses this kind of learning a lot". □

ALVAREZ & MARSAL

One Canada Square, 10th Floor
Canary Wharf
London E14 5AA
United Kingdom
Phone: +44 (0)207 715 5200
Fax: +44 (0)207 715 5201
www.alvarezandmarsal.com

The Stats

Employer Type: Private Company
Co-CEOs: Tony Alvarez II & Bryan
   P. Marsal
2008 Employees: 1,200
2007 Employees: 1,100
No. of Offices: 36

Practice Areas

Dispute Analysis & Forensics
Financial Industry Advisory
Healthcare
Performance Improvement
Tax Advisory
Transaction Advisory
Turnaround & Restructuring

European Locations

London (Europe HQ)
New York (Global HQ)
Amsterdam
Frankfurt
Madrid
Milan
Munich
Paris

Pluses

• "Personal time is valued"
• Promotions are based on merit
• Junior consultants work directly with
  partners

Minuses

• "Very little formal training"
• Travel demands are quite high
• "Nothing special" in regard to perks

Employment Contact

www.alvarezandmarsal.com/europe/
  en/careers.aspx

THE SCOOP

A lvarez & Marsal founders Tony Alvarez II and Bryan Marsal refer to themselves and their company as "corporate doctors", providing a remedy for a special type of illness that plagues the corporate world. The two have been administering their care to a wide variety of businesses for 25 years now. With operations in North America, Europe, Latin America, India, the Middle East and Asia, A&M is spreading the cure worldwide.

Mr Fix-its

Like many of the great business plans of the 20th century, the idea for Alvarez & Marsal was hatched out on a golf course. In the early 1980s, the founders forged a friendship working together at Norton Simon. Over the course of 18 holes one day, the two realised that combining their skill sets as "in-house Mr Fix-its" might prove lucrative if they started a consulting firm together. The goal was to focus on both the tactical and strategic aspects of consulting, with hands-on implementation as a key differentiator. Alvarez & Marsal opened in 1983, and is still privately owned by the two men and the firm's partners today.

In Europe, the firm focusses on helping clients achieve the optimal solutions in the following areas: performance improvement, turnaround and restructuring, financial industry advisory, health care, transaction advisory, dispute analysis and forensics, and tax advisory.

European presence gets a boost

Since the opening of its UK office in 2000, under the leadership of Antonio M. Alvarez III, A&M has rapidly expanded throughout the continent, launching operations in Paris, Frankfurt, Munich, Madrid, Milan and Amsterdam. The work the company has done in Germany is some of its finest. In fact, A&M was recognised by the Turnaround Management Association for the International Turnaround of the Year in October 2007 for its restructuring of Treofan Germany GmbH & Co. KG. It was the second consecutive time that A&M had taken home the honour, after winning in 2006 for its work with Ihr Platz GmbH. In both cases, A&M was singled out for its innovative approach to turnaround solutions.

Extending the winning streak

That award turned out to be just one of several prestigious honours bestowed upon A&M in 2007. In October that year, it was voted Turnaround and Restructuring Firm of the Year by *Private Equity News* at the publication's annual Awards for Excellence in Advisory Services. The firm also received the award for Most Outstanding Restructuring Adviser from a field of five nominees, as judged by a panel of 40 judges drawn from across the private equity community. A&M accepted the award in October at a ceremony hosted by *Private Equity News* in London.

Branching out

A&M expanded another branch of its business in Europe with the launch of a new dispute analysis and forensics (DA&F) practice headquartered in London. In conjunction with the opening of the new business, A&M appointed Merryck Lowe as managing director of the European DA&F team. Lowe comes to A&M from accounting firm PKF, where he most recently had been a partner. He brings extensive experience in the field of dispute and investigations in the UK and abroad, having also served in a senior management position with the forensic services business at Ernst & Young.

A-list clientèle

A&M's client roster in Europe includes some of the most recognisable name brands in the world, including Levi Strauss & Co., Bridge Information Systems, Treofan Germany, Schefenacker plc and TMD Friction. The size of these companies ensures that A&M has the confidence to crunch big numbers and come up with large-scale solutions.

An example of that in action is the firm's work with Levi Strauss Europe, a company that has more than $1 billion in annual revenue and over 4,000 employees. A&M was tasked with helping the company boost sales and decrease operating costs. The company took an active role in managing the business, with A&M professionals assuming interim management roles such as CFO and CEO of Dockers Europe, CFO of Levi's UK & Germany, and restructuring adviser to the board of Levi's Europe. The work paid off—as a result of A&M's involvement, Levi Strauss Europe was able to streamline its product offerings and increase profitability.

A&M Taxand goes to the UK

In addition to its turnaround and restructuring, performance improvement, and dispute analysis and forensic services, Alvarez & Marsal is part of an independent network of tax advisors called the Taxand Global Network. The company was instrumental in the formation of Taxand, which was launched in 2004 as a response to the fallout from the bad tax practices of mainstream accounting firms that failed the system in the Enron case. Formed in 2005 by a small group of tax firms, Taxand has since grown to more than 2,000 tax professionals, including 300 international partners based in more than 40 countries.

Under the leadership of Robert N. Lowe Jr., A&M Taxand, LLC, serves as the Taxand member firm in the US. In 2007, Alvarez & Marsal expanded its presence in the Taxand Global Network, forming Alvarez & Marsal Taxand UK LLP to replace former UK representative firm Chiltern Plc, which was acquired by an audit firm and, therefore, no longer eligible to maintain its membership. Chiltern CEO David Pert joined the A&M Taxand UK team, serving as managing director along with Shiv Mahalingham and Kevin Hindley. The transition was a natural one for Pert, who said in the press release accompanying the move, "This feels a lot like coming home. Shiv, Kevin and I have been serving clients and working closely with our tax partners at Alvarez & Marsal and Taxand for years, so this transition has been seamless."

Business bonanza

Alvarez & Marsal took full advantage of Wall Street's lack of liquidity in 2007, stepping in as the white knight to restructure businesses that failed to meet their loan obligations. The company has worked to stem the bleeding for these credit-challenged firms with sometimes drastic, but necessary, measures such as layoffs,

> " Weekends at home are guaranteed. "

overhead cuts and liquidation of assets. A&M's restructuring clients have included the portfolio companies of private equity firms, Medicor and Interstate Bakeries.

The firm now has plans to capitalise on the mortgage-related woes of the market. In December, A&M's turnaround and restructuring practice, which was reported to be representing several large US homebuilders at the time, formed a new group dedicated to the homebuilding industry. In late January 2008, the company announced plans to open a complementary practice within its real estate group, specialising in distressed commercial real estate.

Bad news, big gains

Bad news translated into big gains for A&M well into 2008. In April, the firm was handling the bankruptcy case of media company Movie Gallery, which went belly up after competition from companies like Netflix rendered its services all but obsolete. Movie Gallery paid the firm upwards of $1.3 million to help with its turnaround.

A&M was also hired to help with the sale of the Canadian bathroom fixture company Maax, which had amassed approximately $500 million of debt since it was acquired by private equity firm J.W. Childs in 2004. The beleaguered Canadian company faces an uphill battle due to falling revenue and decreased confidence in its ability to make money.

GETTING HIRED

Experienced team players wanted

Alvarez & Marsal's "rigorous and efficient" hiring process involves a "minimum of three interviews," although we're told the "number can vary". Most candidates spend at least "one day with senior staff" and may meet as many as "four different managing directors". According to one source, "All joiners are interviewed by at least one MD." The process is "100 per cent interview-based" and involves "no special tests". Technical questions are asked, and some candidates may be asked to complete a case study based on real project work. A contact says, "We tend to use real cases we are working on, on a no-name basis." Interviewers are interested in hearing about "how you changed things in your previous job". The firm tends to gravitate toward "tried and tested personnel", which can make it "unlikely for people with no employment history" to receive an offer. Above all, displaying a "team-player mentality is mandatory" throughout A&M's "quite detailed hiring process". Some say the process can feel "a bit disorganised", but interviewers are reportedly "decisive" and offer "fast feedback".

Candidates are considered from "all main European universities" and "most big MBA programmes", including London School of Economics. The majority of consultants come through "recruitment agents or via personal recommendations".

Good first impression

Insiders say they chose Alvarez & Marsal over other "high-profile institutions" because it's "less hierarchical", so you are "not held back by middle managers". A&M is "the best at what it does" and offers consultants "the ability to learn and grow", and to be surrounded by "high-quality people". Those who interview at this "results-driven" firm often leave with a "great feeling about the people" they met in the process.

OUR SURVEY SAYS

One big happy, results-driven family

"Founded over drinks following a round of golf", A&M is an "open-minded" firm with "entrepreneurial zeal". Respondents say their firm, "unlike others, is uniquely

268

action-oriented and fact-based". It's also a "family-oriented" environment, which comes with "all of the advantages and disadvantages of a close family". There can be "some politics" and sometimes an attitude of "every man for himself". But more often than not, the atmosphere is "supportive" and "close-knit". A&M "takes care of its employees, even in difficult situations". Things can at times feel "relaxed", but A&M is a "driven, practical" place that is "committed to results and devoted to development". A contact says, "We focus on value creation and don't hang around billing the client once we have delivered our value proposition." Leadership is "transparent and straightforward", and junior consultants are "given responsibility" early in their careers. A&M "very much carries the reputation of the founders and senior MDs, who are keen to provide their advice and guidance, and focus on quality across all jobs, especially those in restructuring".

Personal values

A&M's entrepreneurial approach "allows employees to manage their time when not working on a project". Things can get "extremely intense" when it's busy, but when there's downtime, "employees are encouraged to maximise family time." Unless you're starting a new project or dealing with something urgent, the "firm's recommendation is to devote time to family, hobbies and sports." And although "working on a project basis can make life unpredictable," work/life balance is attainable "if you properly manage your time". Consultants report that A&M ensures a "high level of flexibility" by refusing projects for which it does not have sufficient resources, and that flexibility extends to consultants, who have the freedom to work from home whenever possible. In addition, "weekends at home are guaranteed."

Planes, trains and automobiles

Although A&M is good about prioritising personal time for its employees, travel demands can at times be "quite high". This is "especially true for specialists and more senior staff, which can mean working away from home a lot." Many consultants endure "long weeks, often ending a Friday evening in a foreign country". This "can eat into personal time" and can be "very mentally exhausting, especially during the early stages of a restructuring or crisis management job." Although the travel demands are "part of the job" and are "implicit when you join", travelling so much can really "impact a wife's life standard", a source notes. Some colleagues spin the story another way, claiming that as the firm's "European practice is growing", the intense travel "provides great opportunities to pick up experience in multiple European countries". And anyway, "when you chose consulting, you can't assume that your clients will always be based around the corner from home!"

Assignments vary in length

Although travel demands are high, "there is a level of flexibility" regarding work hours in general. "People are not expected to work excessive hours," a respondent comments. Most average between 50 and 60 hours per week, with "low overtime". However, "in crisis, workloads are high, and those who deliver exceptional work will tend to be those who have worked harder and longer." The "average assignment length varies from six weeks to six months," and "restructuring cases tend to be longer than performance improvement cases." One source explains that "a typical year might include one or two long cases, and perhaps a couple of smaller assignments."

Bonuses and perks could use a boost

Compensation at A&M is "competitive with mid- and upper-mid-bracket private equity firms," though some feel the "reward mechanisms could be more generous." According to one contact, "On the face of it, the package seems good, but bonuses have yet to live up to expectations." The compensation scheme for the most part is "transparent", but there can be "a number of end-of-year adjustments".

Beyond some "terrific off-site trips and events", A&M offers few additional perks. Consultants are granted health insurance and pension funds, and senior staff members, "once they have proven themselves and demonstrated commitment and fit with the culture", are entitled to a "very attractive equity package". The firm also accommodates new parents on a "case-by-case" basis.

Impressive encounters

A&M consultants have the opportunity to work with "good partners", and generally enjoy "challenging but fair relationships" with their supervisors. A source says "senior staff make a lot of time to develop junior staff and share their experience." Junior and midlevel consultants are often "involved at a high level, working directly with partners", and they have the "opportunity to interact with top-level staff at the client very early on". The bottom line, insiders say, is that A&M provides the chance to meet "outstanding professionals" and be exposed to "very interesting cases".

D.I.Y. training

Staffers give low mark to the firm's training efforts. Although close interaction with senior-level managers and clients provides "high quality on-the-job training", options are limited when it comes to formal learning. "Training is unofficial and on the job," with "some in-house days". Fortunately, "peer learning is without parallel," and sources tell us some "new, more structured sessions have been planned".

Merit rules

Promotions at A&M are "only dependent on performance"—the firm has "no automatism or fixed-time schedule" for advancing people. At this "meritocratic" firm, "if you are successful, you can move up fast." For underperformers, it's "not strictly up-or-out, but quite close to it, particularly for intermediate staff." A contact quips, "If you were not moving up, you yourself would want to move out." However, sometimes "people are allowed to progress very slowly," as sometimes it can be "all about who you know". Moreover, it seems that not everyone is hoping to rise to the very top: "A&M careers can peak at director, senior director or at MD level without any stigma."

Comfortable environment

A&M Europe has offices in "some of the most prime locations in Europe". The London office is centrally located "in the main tower at Canary Wharf", which "is a nightmare to get to". Once you get there, though, employees enjoy "well-stocked kitchens" in an office that is "light and quiet". The Munich and Frankfurt offices are "extremely well located in the financial centres of the city".

Regardless of location, A&M operates "entirely on merit", which means that "across Europe, staff from different national backgrounds operate side-by-side with no prejudice of any kind." Many offices have "good multicultural teams", and "there is absolutely no sense of any obstacle to developing female staff." Although applicants are "still predominantly male", applications from women are "certainly looked on favourably". That said, "no special allowances are made for women." □

Alvarez & Marsal

ARUP

13 Fitzroy Street
London W1T 4BQ
United Kingdom
Phone: +44 (0)207 637 1531
www.arup.com

The Stats

Employer Type: Private Limited
  Company
Group Chair: Terry Hill
Global Consulting Chair: John Miles
2007 Employees: 10,000
2006 Employees: 9,000
2007 Revenue: £572 million
2006 Revenue: £475 million
No. of Offices: 92

Practice Areas

Business & Management Consulting
Civil Engineering
Design
Economics
Engineering
Environmental & Project Management
Planning

European Locations

London (HQ)
Denmark • Germany • Holland •
Ireland • Italy • Poland • Russia • Spain
• Turkey • United Kingdom

Pluses

• A good place to develop young talent
• "Many opportunities to work on
  interesting, large-scale projects that
  help develop technical skills"

Minuses

• Long hours are "becoming a
  prerequisite for career advancement"
• "Career advancement is extremely
  slow"

Employment Contact

www.arup.com/careers.cfm

THE BUZZ
WHAT CONSULTANTS AT OTHER FIRMS ARE SAYING

• "Respected in niche markets"
• "A bit limited outside the UK"
• "Innovative"
• "Strong in engineering but weak in
  management consulting"

THE SCOOP

Having started life as an engineering consultancy before extending its expertise into other areas of the built environment, Arup today is a multifaceted concern that consults on everything from project management to economics, while the list of areas it specialises in goes from acoustics to wind engineering, and runs to around 85 different specialties. To keep up with such a broad knowledge base (not to mention the 10,000 projects it can have going simultaneously), the firm needs people power, employing over 10,000 staffers in 37 countries around the globe.

Among the landmark projects Arup has worked on are the Pompidou Centre in Paris, the Scottish Parliament Building in Edinburgh and London's Millenium Bridge. In addition, Arup has consulted on much of the work being done in preparation for the 2008 Olympics in China. For the Games, Arup consultants have worked on everything from the recently opened Terminal 3 at Beijing Capital International Airport to the innovative Water Cube (or National Aquatics Centre, as it's officially known) that will host the event's swimming and diving competitions.

A rare influence

Ove Nyquist Arup founded the firm in 1946 as an engineering consulting concern, having previously run a construction company with his cousin. The new firm, known as Ove N. Arup Consulting Engineers, went on to become one of the most recognisable names in the construction and engineering business, and earned its Anglo-Dane founder a knighthood in 1971. One year prior to receiving that award, Arup made a speech that has come to define the firm and its ideology, and still holds sway some two decades after his death in 1988. Known as "the key speech", it is required reading for all new Arup hires, and deals with such weighty matters as corporate and social responsibility, the pursuit of happiness and a philosophical approach to salaries and profit taking.

Perhaps the most famous passage from the speech, and one still espoused by the firm's management, concerns Arup's thoughts on the two ways of pursuing happiness: "One is to go straight for the things you fancy without restraints, that is, without considering anybody else besides yourself. The other is: to recognise that no man is an island, that our lives are inextricably mixed up with those of our fellow human beings, and that there can be no real happiness in isolation. Which leads to an attitude which would accord to others the rights claimed for oneself, which would accept certain moral or humanitarian restraints." Arup, both the individual and the firm, claims to "opt for the second way."

Employee-owned

Having undergone several shifts in identity over the course of the 20th century, Ove Arup became Arup Group Ltd in 2000. Although still a private limited company, the firm is now known simply as Arup. Followers of UK business law will know that a private limited company is one in which shares of the company are issued, but are not for sale on the open market. Arup chose to follow that model as opposed to going public so as to keep control of the firm. In addition to allowing the company to shape its own future free from the demands of the stock market, being private has allowed it to live up to another tenet of Sir Ove's theory—that of keeping the firm's shares in trust for its employees.

When is a consultant not a consultant?

Due to the nature and volume of the projects Arup takes on, there is something of a blurring of the lines between what portion of its work counts as consulting, and what portion is, well, just work. Given that the firm has specialists in so many different areas, and that they can combine on any number of projects, it is entirely possible—and indeed often the case—that Arup is called in to consult and work on a building project from start to finish. Thus, its consultants help identify a need or solution for a client. To provide that need or solution, Arup's design team helps come up with the blueprints, which can then be handed off to its project management specialists, who contract the work out and supervise it. For this reason, Arup consultants tend to be highly specialised in their fields, and the firm has a strong leaning toward those with engineering and hard science backgrounds. There is, after all, a reason that company literature proclaims that its "strength lies in the endless combination of skills and services we can provide from a single source".

> ❝ The firm leans toward those with engineering and hard science backgrounds. ❞

A perfect example of Arup's all-in-one approach was honoured at the 2008 Financial Services Technology Awards, where the new Citi Data Centre in Frankfurt was handed the Data Centre Excellence Green Energy Efficiency award, and the prize for overall winner at the 2008 awards. The building, which is scheduled to open in late 2008, has so far seen Arup's engineering influence in the architecture, structural, mechanical, electrical and public health elements, while its specialist consultancy units provided services in acoustics, environmental, facade, facilities management, fire, geotechnics, logistics, materials, project management, risk and security.

GETTING HIRED

Take your pick

There are four roads that head to Arup, depending on your interest and academic standing. As the company explains on its web site, its UK graduate programme is looking for recent grads with fewer than 12 months' continuous work experience, excluding any mid-degree placements. A minimum of three C grades or equivalent to A level is expected, as is a relevant degree with a 2.2 or higher (or equivalent). Candidates with more than 12 months' work experience should consider open postings listed in the careers section of the site.

For those about to begin a university degree in engineering, Arup's pre-university scheme provides a nine-month gap year placement. Running from September to May of each year, it's aimed at students who have completed A levels but who wish to spend some time on the job before moving on to higher education. Successful completion of A-level maths and science is required; those who complete the pre-university scheme will be eligible for Arup's degree sponsorship programme. They will also be considered for summer placements during each year of their university studies.

Engineering students who have completed two or three years of their degree may apply for a mid-degree placement, which the firm says is an opportunity to take a year off from school and gain hands-on industry experience. However, Arup warns, there may only be "a small number of mid-degree placement vacancies available".

ATKINS

Woodcote Grove
Ashley Road
Epsom
Surrey KT18 5BW
United Kingdom
Phone: +44 (0)137 272 6140
www.atkinsglobal.com

The Stats

Employer Type: Public Company
Ticker Symbol: ATK (LSE)
Chairman: Ed Wallis
CEO: Keith Clarke
2007 Employees: 16,800
2006 Employees: 14,900
2007 Revenue: £1.26 billion
2006 Revenue: £1.05 billion
No. of Offices: 200

Practice Areas

Asset/Facilities Management
Design
Engineering
Environmental Services
Management Consultancy
Planning
Programme Management
Project & Cost Management

European Locations

Epsom (HQ)
Czech Republic • Denmark • Finland •
Greece • Hungary • Ireland • Italy •
Netherlands • Norway • Poland •
Portugal • Romania • Sweden • Turkey
• United Kingdom

Pluses

• "No pressure to work silly hours"
• "In a growth stage and creating a new market"

Minuses

• "Lack of opportunity to influence how the firm is run"
• "Limited feedback"

Employment Contact

Graduate Recruitment Team
Phone: +44 (0)121 483 6233
E-mail: graduates@atkinsglobal.com

THE BUZZ
WHAT CONSULTANTS AT OTHER FIRMS ARE SAYING

• "Top engineering"
• "Inflexible"
• "Aspiring"
• "Excessive commercial approach"

THE SCOOP

WS Atkins plc was founded as an engineering firm in 1938 by William Atkins. Based in Westminster, London, the organisation grew quickly after World War II, branching out into new areas such as design, planning, architecture and project management. Over 70 years later, Atkins now employs almost 17,000 people in 200 offices spread across the UK and Europe, the Americas, the Middle East, India and China. It now stands tall as the largest engineering consultancy in the UK, the largest multidisciplinary consultancy in Europe and the fifth-largest design firm in the world—testament to its consistent internal growth as well as that of corporate acquisition.

Over the last few years, Atkins has made numerous acquisitions, including the project cost management consultancy Faithful & Gould, a move which in turn added Hanscomb to the Atkins family in the US. It also acquired the Lambert Smith Hampton commercial property and real estate agency, which it then spun off in 2007. During the same year, Atkins purchased Boreas Consultants to further its reach in offshore oil and gas markets; Advantage to bolster its work in

> " Most people go home at 5:30pm. "

defence; and Intelligent Space, a consultancy that specialises in providing pedestrian movement advice and analysis to the transport, health care and urban development markets. At the end of 2007, Atkins announced its intention to acquire Dutch aerospace consultancy Nedtech to complement its work in aerospace and defence systems engineering.

Seven arms of outreach serve the biggest of the big

Operationally, the firm divides its areas of service offerings into the following categories: design and engineering solutions (27 per cent of its business), highways and transportation (20 per cent), rail (19 per cent), management and project services (15 per cent), Middle East and China (8 per cent), equity investments (7 per cent), and asset management (4 per cent).

Catering to both the private and public sectors, Atkins serves many markets, including aerospace, buildings, defence, education, energy, environmental, health, industry, oil and gas, telecommunications, transport, urban development and water. Its client roster includes heavyweights such as Anheuser-Busch, British Airways, British Telecom, BP, Cadbury Schweppes, Hilton Group, Prudential Corporation, ExxonMobil and Unilever, to name but a few.

Revenue growth a cat's meow ...

And delivering solid work for the likes of such powerhouses does, indeed, have its rewards. When its fiscal year ended in March 2007, Atkins reported revenue of £1.26 billion for the period, a 20 per cent increase from the previous year's £1.05 billion. Much of this increase came from significant growth in its Middle East ventures, solid performance from its design and engineering solutions, as well as its highways and transportation arms, and recovery in workload of its rail segment.

... but cash in hand dogged by Metronet

Atkins Chairman Ed Wallis said that cash performance continued to be strong in 2007, with the company ending the year with net funds of £199 million. He added, though, that these results were adversely impacted by an exceptional loss of £121.3 million related to the long-ailing London Underground maintenance project, Metronet, in which Atkins was partnered in consortium with Balfour Beatty, Bombardier (Canada), EDF Energy (France) and Thames Water. Metronet dogged Atkins and its partner firms for several years after going more than £1 billion over budget (Metronet declared bankruptcy in 2007).

Prowess garners high-profile contracts

Despite its struggles with Metronet, however, Atkins' rail business has flourished elsewhere, most notably with its ambitious multidisciplinary design and programme management of Dubai's metro rail system, the largest of its kind worldwide. Other high-profile projects include a "green" scheme design of Chinese developer Shimao's hotel in the Sheshan Mountain area of Songjiang, near Shanghai—a project awarded in early 2008, to be completed in 2010; the design of Durrat Al Bahrain, a 20-square-kilometer, 45,000-person resort comprising 13 man-made islands (to be completed in May 2009); planning and infrastructure support for the London 2012 Olympic Park in the UK (completed in just five months in 2007); wing design and analysis for the Airbus A350 XWB aircraft, a project started in December 2007; project management and cost estimating for the construction of the World Trade Center Memorial and Visitors Center in New York (2006); and development oversight of the next generation of medium-weight armoured vehicles in the Ministry of Defence's Future Rapid Effects System programme (awarded in 2004).

More trophies in the case

And, lest you worried that Atkins' work was going unnoticed, fear not. According to the NCE Consultants File, Atkins continues to lead the ranks among UK engineering consultancies, as it has for the last 10 years, and has been ranked in the top 10 over the last 13 years. *The Sunday Times* placed Atkins among the 20 Best Big Companies to Work For in 2007, not to mention ranking it in 2006 among the Top 100 Graduate Employers and The Top 50 Companies Where Women Want to Work (for the second straight year). Atkins also was the sector winner in the Target National Graduate Recruitment Awards for both 2006 and 2007.

Showing its green thumb, Atkins also racked up recognition for its environmental practices from the UK Centre for Economic and Environmental Development. In 2007, the firm walked away with the National Energy Award in the educational awareness category, and was crowned by edie.net as the Environmental Excellence Awards winner, the best consultancy to work for, best consultancy for contaminated land, best consultancy for waste and recycling, and best environmental consultancy award winner. Additionally, the firm won the Best Places to Work in IT and Best of the Best in the construction and mining category awards from *Computer Weekly*.

GETTING HIRED

A question of fit

Atkins' "straightforward" hiring process involves "two interviews and a case study". The firm is "in a growing stage", so is "employing a lot from other companies", in addition to new hires culled from universities. Recruiters look to "a large number of schools", including "universities in Sweden", due to Atkins' "spread of offices". Recent graduate candidates go through "a daylong interview process" that involves "a variety of tests, interviews, presentations on the company and team exercises". Here's an example of typical question: "What would you do to reduce carbon emissions from our office building?" Insiders say interviewers are looking at "skills, but also at social skills". It's crucial for candidates to demonstrate that "they fit in with the team."

OUR SURVEY SAYS

Not *that* Atkins

Atkins is filled with "friendly people", insiders tell us. The "old-fashioned British culture is very supportive," and presents "lots of possibilities for varied and challenging business opportunities". According to a respondent, consultants are offered "so much autonomy to do what they think is right". This "family sort of culture" allows for "personal and professional development"—a contact says,

"People are always willing to help you when you or your project needs it." Co-workers place "very little blame, unless you ask for help too late". Part of what drives these consultants so hard, according to one insider, is that "we always think other companies are better than us, so we are constantly looking for ways to improve." The firm reportedly offers a "good balance" of unofficial and official training, but promotions can be "slow". "You have to do excellent work to grow," a source comments.

Plan on lots of personal time

Atkins has "no culture of presenteeism", meaning, there is no pressure to stay at work late just for the sake of being seen. In fact, "most people go home at 5:30pm." Moreover, consultants "can work from home" if they please, as the firm grants "external access to databases and a company mobile". One source reports, "I can arrive late or leave early. There is give and take in terms of working hard sometimes and then allowing people a bit of slack at other times." Work hours vary, with some logging between around 40 hours, while others put in "50 hours, plus maybe 20 hours where you think about your projects". Those who work long hours do so by choice, insiders say—they are "not forced by the firm".

Travel presents "no problems" for Atkins consultants. Some "need to visit other offices and construction sites on a frequent basis", and they're thankful that costs are "fully covered by Atkins". Those who travel by train, the firm's "main method of travel", consider it "fairly stress-free".

"Blood, sweat and tears"

Since Atkins is "in a building stage", consultants are "not earning that much money yet". For the time being, "it's much blood, sweat and tears" from the firm's "out-of-date" London office. In an attempt to make up for any shortcomings, Atkins does offer profit sharing, and consultants consider the "international knowledge and experience" they are gaining as a form of compensation. One consultant remarks, "I have been offered more by other firms, but I stayed with Atkins because I still think they pay well." In addition, employees get "access to some good theatre and museum tickets", and "you can buy extra holidays, from the normal five weeks up to eight weeks." Atkins also offers a "return-to-work bonus after maternity leave".

Recognising a need

Percentages of women at the firm are "small" and "drop as you increase the level". But insiders say this is a broad "industry problem", and "Atkins' internal figures on salaries and employee satisfaction show no difference between genders." The firm has "a number of initiatives in place to encourage women" to come onboard, as "there is full realisation that more women are needed to ensure diversity of talent and skills." Similarly, Atkins is "trying to ensure that its offices reflect the percentage of ethnic minorities in the various towns in which they are based". Minority religions are "accommodated, and information is available about other religious holidays and customs". Respondents say their firm is the kind of place where "everyone is recognised equally for their contribution and performance."

In an effort to give back to the community, Atkins does "pro bono work as teachers and consultants for the public sector", and consultants are "encouraged to fund raise for charities". That said, some feel the firm's community efforts are "nowhere near enough". ▢

CANDESIC LIMITED

New Zealand House
80 Haymarket
London SW1Y 4TQ
United Kingdom
Phone: +44 (0)207 096 7680
Fax: +44 (0)207 206 9383
www.candesic.com

The Stats

Employer Type: Private Company
Founder: Dr Leonid Shapiro
2008 Employees: 20
2007 Employees: 20
No. of Offices: 3

Practice Areas

Consumer Goods & Retail
Financial Services
Healthcare
Private Equity
Technology & Telecom

European Locations

London (HQ)
Madrid
Paris

Affiliates in 20 cities worldwide

Pluses

- "No real hierarchy"
- Very close relationships amongst colleagues
- "Flexibility" makes lifestyle "unbeatable"

Minuses

- "Unpredictable project pipeline"
- "Down months with no income"
- Little name recognition

Employment Contact

E-mail: talent@candesic.com

THE SCOOP

F ounded in 2002, Candesic Limited attempts to offer a more flexible and cost-effective way of solving problems for its clients. To wit, the firm is arranged around a central core of 15 experts spread across its three offices in London, Madrid and Paris, supported by a small group of analysts. Roughly 150 more consultants are available to the firm, however, through a network of affiliates it has established in 20 locations around the world. The associates work on a part- or full-time basis, but are not employed permanently by the firm, nor do they require Candesic to supply them with office space. Because of this, even as a boutique firm, Candesic is able to offer a broad suite of services with significantly less overhead than more heavily staffed outfits. The firm offers its services

> " There are 'no barriers to getting ahead' at Candesic. "

across a range of industries, with particular specialities in financial services, health care, private equity, technology and telecoms. Under the ever-popular "Other" category, meanwhile, the firm also provides a range of services in the luxury consumer goods, energy and utilities, aerospace and defence, and chemicals industries.

The Candesic difference

Dr Leonid Shapiro founded the firm after spotting a gap in the market during the bursting of the dot-com bubble. Realising that there was a place for firms that could solve a client's problems in a more flexible and cost-effective way, he put together a team comprised of fellow former McKinsey colleagues and consultants from other top firms, and began doing things his way—based on that vision of low overhead and a network of affiliates. Given that the firm started out conducting business for around one-third cheaper than many of its employee-intensive rivals, Candesic quickly became the consulting firm of choice for many firms that had been sideswiped in the tech crash and were looking for fast and affordable assistance in getting back on track.

Planting seed

Evidently the firm's approach was something of a success, as within two years of its founding, Candesic was able to expand into new territories. In 2004, the city at the other end of the Eurotunnel (or Paris, as it's usually known) saw Candesic set up shop, as the firm positioned itself to meet the increased international demand for its lower-cost services. Back in London, meanwhile, Candesic also formed a health care due diligence unit in 2002, aimed at companies in the medical field (biotech, medical devices, pharmaceutical spin-offs and the like). The move was a good fit for a firm that boasted several trained medical doctors on its staff—including founder Shapiro and Dr Victor Chua, who heads the unit and is a fellow McKinsey alumnus.

Come 2007, the time was right for further expansion, as the firm opened a new office in Madrid—a move that furthered Candesic's international standing. The company's offerings are consistent across all three locations—which is to say there's no guarantee Candesic will take on a project that it doesn't think is in its clients' best interests. Candesic's modus operandi when it receives a prospective client engagement is for its three partners (Shapiro, Chua and Marc Kitten) to assemble a team from among its in-house and affiliate consultants that meet the appropriate areas of expertise required. Due to the global nature of the firm's affiliates, there is the potential for consultants from all over to work on a single project. Once that team has met, if Candesic feels that it has something to offer the client, it proposes possible solutions and an engagement plan. Should the partners feel that the project is not in the client's best interests, however, it'll turn the engagement down—a threat that's been carried out in the past.

Money, money, money

Candesic's expertise in finance isn't just restricted to cutting costs and maximising value for clients. Its financial services wing is headed by Marc Kitten, a financial markets expert and former vice president at Deutsche Bank Global Markets. Under his watch, the unit offers strategic, organisational, marketing and operational advice to institutions and individuals including investment banks, brokers, private banks, asset managers and retail financial services. All told, Candesic consultants have served or worked for more than half of the top-30 banks in Europe, be they universal, commercial or retail, as well as a number of top private banks.

GETTING HIRED

Don't get too comfy

Candesic's hiring process is "similar to any other firm", consultants tell us, in that it normally involves "a CV screening, plus one interview with partners and managers, including a case study and a brain test". But under Candesic's model, consultants are brought onboard on a project-by-project basis. Candidates who impress the firm's partners are asked to work on a project. A source explains, "If goes OK, you get asked to join formally." "The advantage we have is we can employ someone on a trial basis to do a project, and if they aren't good, we just don't use them again," a colleague remarks. Job seekers who are up to the challenge should "know what a case study is," and "be ready to discuss what strategy consultants do." According to one insider, "A clear idea of the day-to-day job is important for entry-level positions." An example of a typical interview question is: "Try to figure out the weight of a sugar cube without any help apart from office equipment."

Candesic recruits from "London-based business schools", including Cambridge and Oxford. The firm also looks for candidates at INSEAD and ESCP-EAP. And, insiders say, it's not uncommon for candidates to be asked to produce "many references from former employers".

OUR SURVEY SAYS

McKinsey-lite

Candesic's "freewheeling and entrepreneurial" culture attracts consultants who are looking for a vibe that can be described as "McKinsey-lite". It's like the big-name firm, respondents say—"All the partners and the majority of everyone else was originally trained there"—but "without the corporate baggage". Many view the firm as an opportunity "to get in on the ground floor", and they relish in the "freedom, lifestyle" and "greater independence" offered at Candesic.

Consultants label their firm "informal", and describe their colleagues as "down-to-earth and friendly, while still intellectual and professional". The culture is "extremely pleasant", as the firm's consultants comprise "a very earnest bunch focussed on client service". Candesic's "unique model", by which contract consultants are "free to work on other projects", provides employees with "flexibility and a very rich atmosphere". Co-workers are able to learn from each other, as there's "always a lot of give and take", a source notes. Respondents also say that while the firm has experienced some "growing-up pains in the past year", Candesic remains "a great place to work".

Most nights at home

Since "most clients are in the home city," a Londoner explains, travel for Candesic consultants is "not an issue". Some partners do "a lot of work in Europe, and one of the managers spends his life on a plane", but that is "not the case for most". A source comments, "Our clients are almost always London-based, and when we do an operational piece, it's more of a diagnostic and may be one to two days a month instead of three to four days a week at the client site." Overall, staffers tell us, Candesic has a "fair and flexible travel policy, and always accommodates working from home".

On your own time

Thanks to limited travel requirements and "very flexible" policies about work hours, "the work/life balance at Candesic is incredible for the industry." There is a "focus on delivery rather than face time", so consultants are "able to work from home" and are given the "option to mix personal pursuits with flexible work patterns". In addition, the firm's "project-by-project focus" makes it possible to "take time off and socialise more during less busy times." During a "typical four-week project", a consultant explains, hours can get "very intense, but outside of that, we are free to work or not work as we please". Others admit that while on a project, balance is "not always easy", but according to one insider, "We all like and respect each other enough such that an individual's most important plans can be respected."

The benefits of this project-based model are apparent in a positive work/life balance and heightened flexibility, but it also has its downsides. Sources point out that, "especially in slower times", there can be "little work or no projects" at all. This creates "a greater uncertainty or risk factor" than you'd have at a larger firm. One contact remarks, "Even in 'good times', the real choice about when to work and not to work can be limited."

Clocking in

Weekly hour requirements are "highly variable", with consultants logging "anywhere from zero to 100 hours per week", depending on what stage of a project they are in. Many report working between 40 and 50 hours per week, on average. One consultant details, "About a third of the time, hours are excessive, at a (real) 70 hours a week. Another third of the time, it's about 50 hours a week, and the remaining third is at a regular 40 hours a week." Since face time requirements are "nonexistent, no one looks twice if you get in at 9am and leave by 6pm". The "average project length is three to four weeks," we're told, with some "slightly longer for corporate strategy projects". A source says, "Assignments tend to be short and intense, so working weeks are demanding. However, gaps between projects compensate for this."

Comp peaks and valleys

Candesic consultants "don't earn a base salary"; instead, they "share project revenue based on their commercial contribution and execution". Overall compensation for

Candesic Limited

experienced consultants is "very competitive", but what junior analysts take home is "slightly below the market average", a consultant remarks. A partner claims, however, that "total compensation is similar to McKinsey at the partner level, and superior at the consultant level." Unfortunately, though, there are sometimes "cash flow issues", when consultants have to "wait to get invoices paid". Moreover, since there are "periods of no projects", that means "no income during that time"—another drawback to the project-based model.

On top of regular pay, consultants are treated to "numerous team dinners" and "cocktails in the office", including "a glass from one of the partners' sparkling wine collections every time we sell a big project". There's also "lunch paid for by the company", which is "particularly attractive to junior staff and interns, as it saves them money and time". An insider adds that

> ❝ Consultants 'share project revenue based on their commercial contribution and execution'. ❞

"consultants have by far the most vacation days of any firm I know." As an additional (unofficial) perk, two of the firm's partners are trained doctors, so consultants often get "medical advice, rather than bothering to see a general practitioner".

To-die-for view

Candesic's London-based consultants work from "beautiful" offices with a "fabulous view of Buckingham Palace, St. James Palace, Clarence House, Pall Mall and Haymarket". As one respondent puts it, "Not many people can say they bring their friends and family back [to work] on a Friday night to admire the view." As for the office's interior, the "open, friendly" layout can feel "a bit Spartan". The office was "recently refurbished" with "new carpet, which is a big improvement", insiders tell us. And one source says, "Collectively, we are incredibly untidy, so our otherwise fantastic offices are let down a bit"—a fact that really makes an impact when, "to get to client meeting rooms, you have to go through office space." The firm's Paris and Madrid offices also are in "central and pleasant locations".

Getting more formal about training

Candesic has "limited official" training opportunities, but offers "lots of learning on the job"—thanks to "real availability of all partners". The firm is "increasingly organising formal training schemes, particularly for analysts and junior consultants". Recently, Candesic "started offering institutional training", for which "initial feedback has been very positive." The current norm is "one week of training per year", and these sessions are "very well prepared", respondents note. One source recalls an "official two-day training session that covered material very similar to the standard offered at top consulting firms".

Forcing the issue

Candesic's size means that there's plenty of opportunity to "work with top people". One junior consultant remarks, "After a month working on a project, I was able to come to a top-level client meeting, which was an amazing opportunity for someone at my stage." It's also an advantage that consultants are able "to pick and choose who you work for, in a way you wouldn't be able to in another firm". Internally, Candesic consultants have "daily contact with MD-level professionals". Supervisors and consultants have "very open and direct relationships with each other", and they "know and trust each other pretty well". One staffer cites a "healthy—albeit sometimes hidden!—streak of humility in the partnership, which helps build loyalty".

Not your average promotion time line

Candesic is reportedly "pragmatic and flexible" about promotions—the firm "doesn't have structured positions or fixed career progression like larger firms". There's "no up-or-out" policy, insiders say, but "if associates aren't good, they don't get hired again on the next project." Advancement is based on "merit and is flexible". A contact explains, "It's the Candesic spirit that you can find your niche and develop as far and as fast as you wish." It's also "OK to sit at one level, if needed". There are "no barriers to getting ahead" at Candesic, and no secrets of success either, as advancement policies are "transparent". Promotion is "automatic and rewards a combination of commercial success and team spirit", an insider states. As a colleague points out, though, "It is not clear yet how easy it would be to become a partner, since Candesic is still not quite old enough to have bred its own."

Too small to judge

Candesic may be "too small to make any sensible comparisons" about diversity— but it's still worth noting that the firm has "few women, if you're not counting the interns" (but out of a staff of 15 in London, that's not too shabby). This is not a reflection of the firm's willingness to them bring on, however, as Candesic is "keen to recruit women".

The proportions in the ethnic diversity category are more balanced. There is only one native English person in the London office, which "demonstrates tremendous diversity of all races and religions". One contact interjects, "We could do with more

English people, as there's a general shortage in London." Sexual orientation is "left to individual privacy", but is "respected" by Candesic. A consultant remarks, "I had an associate working for me who was openly a lesbian. Apart from that, we prefer not to pry into sexual preference, so it is difficult to calculate how many we employ."

Showing support

Candesic consultants are "expected and encouraged" to participate in community initiatives outside of work, which are "often charitable or educational" in nature. Some partners "do their own work in these areas" as well.

At times, Candesic is also charitable toward its junior employees. For instance, the firm "tutors interns and analysts" to prepare them for "interviews in whatever industry they choose". A source reports, "One of our analysts who has worked with us since 2005 wanted to work for an investment bank, so we helped him through the process." □

Candesic Limited

CELERANT CONSULTING

Avalon House
72 Lower Mortlake Road
Richmond
Surrey TW9 2JY
United Kingdom
Phone: +44 (0)208 338 5000
Fax: +44 (0)208 338 5002
www.celerantconsulting.com

The Stats

Employer Type: Private Company
CEO: Ian Clarkson
2008 Employees: 600
2007 Employees: 600
2007 Revenue: €111.6 million
2006 Revenue: €115.9 million
No. of Offices: 11

Practice Areas

Asset Management
Business Performance Management
Innovation
Integrated Supply Chain
Management
Organisational Effectiveness
Private Equity
Process Excellence
Revenue Generation

European Locations

Richmond (HQ)
Amsterdam • Brussels • Copenhagen •
Düsseldorf • Helsinki • Oslo • Paris •
Stockholm • Zurich

Pluses

- "Chance to grow fast within a dynamic company"
- Diversity of assignments, both in topic and location
- "Entrepreneurial spirit is supported and encouraged"

Minuses

- "Remuneration is not equally distributed in the value chain"
- Some processes are too informal
- "100 per cent result focus sometimes causes need for compromise on values"

Employment Contact

www.celerantconsulting.com/Careers/
careers.aspx

THE BUZZ
WHAT CONSULTANTS AT OTHER FIRMS ARE SAYING

- "Hire only the very best"
- "Small player"
- "Very hands-on"
- "Cost killers"

THE SCOOP

Celerant was first launched in 1987 under the name Peter Chadwick, the middle names of its two founders, Quentin Baer and Ian Clarkson. Over the subsequent 20 years, the firm went through a series of acquisitions and adjustments that led it to its current status as a top UK-based consultancy serving Europe from offices in 11 different countries. The biggest change came in 2001 when Peter Chadwick (then operating under the name Cambridge Technology Partners) was acquired by software company Novell for $266 million. That's when Celerant adopted its current moniker and entered into a new phase of operations.

A consistent focus pays off

The partnership with Novell came to an end in 2006 when the firm shifted its focus back onto software: After five years together, Novell sold Celerant to the company's management team for $77 million. British investment firm Caledonia chipped in $30 million to acquire a minority stake. Though the firm was now

> 66 We are a more human consulting practice. 99

free from Novell, it kept the name it had adopted under its ownership, making the complete transition to the world's largest independent operational consulting company.

Over the years and all its various stages of existence, Celerant has been consistent in its service to big-name companies. Among its clients are industry giants such as Akzo Nobel, BP, Occidental Petroleum, Reuters, Rohm & Haas, RadioShack, Texas Petrochemicals, T-Mobile, Honda and Wyeth. Its expertise covers a wide variety of sectors, including aerospace, automotive, chemicals, energy, financial services, government, life sciences, health care, manufacturing, metals, mining, pulp and paper, retail, telecommunications and utilities.

Close quarters

The consultancy employs a trademarked system of working together, which it calls the Closework® approach, meaning that clients can expect extra care and attention from its staff. The approach consists of studying a company's current operating format, then challenging that format with a jointly developed and executed programme of improvement. The intimate collaboration with clients means that employees in client companies are able to take part in the operational improvement process. Celerant puts the advantage this way, "Everyone plays a part in setting targets, so they become a shared objective and a point of personal pride. Rivalry gives way to respect and teamwork."

Allowing the clients' employees to become so enmeshed in the process also helps to ensure that the changes made will become permanent.

Seeking out excellence

In March 2008, Celerant was selected by two leading European business schools to become a partner in choosing their annual Industrial Excellence Award over the next three years. The schools, INSEAD of France and WHU of Germany, recognise European companies that have "excellent manufacturing processes". The award has been running for 14 years in France and 12 years in Germany. Past nominees have included Siemens AG and DaimlerChrysler AG, Rational AG, Varta Microbattery, GmbH, Valeo Systèmes Thermiques, SAS and Fresenius Medical Care. As Celerant's director of corporate development stated, "This exciting partnership will link the great history of the Industrial Excellence Award with Celerant's 20 years' experience of running large scale programmes that have helped European manufacturing companies to become winners."

A new partner

Six Sigma, a six-step, data-driven approach to eliminating flaws in product-based business, is a big part of Celerant's business model. The firm cites Six Sigma as having helped it boost Reuters' data accuracy from 40 per cent to 99.8 per cent in some areas in May 2007. The firm hopes to spread the love for Six Sigma; in November 2007, it signed on to sponsor a web site called onesixsigma.com, which will attempt to thrust the Six Sigma approach even further into mainstream consulting. Celerant claims that there are fundamental misunderstandings about how to use Six Sigma in the workplace, proffering the web site as the best way to spread this information. Jeff Patton, capability leader at Celerant, explained, "We believe that many companies put too much emphasis on the learning, belt gaining, process of Six Sigma and not nearly enough time and effort on understanding how to apply Six Sigma and Lean in a way that tackles the major business challenges they face."

Life in the fast lane

Consulting may not be the most fast-paced profession, but the Celerant team manages to get in some heart-palpitating action by working with the Honda F1 Racing team. The consultancy completed a three-year contract with Honda in 2008, in which it worked to help the company exploit the potential of a newly built $50 million wind tunnel that would help the racing team test their newest cars. Celerant's job was to find out the most efficient way to utilise the new wind tunnel, while rearranging the organisation for optimal performance.

Using its Closework approach, Celerant delivered in a big way for Honda by cutting out 370 to 400 minutes per week of the time it takes to test cars in the wind tunnel. Consultants also lowered manufacturing processes and costs for Honda, and opened up communication with suppliers. The greatest proof as to the success of the project was the strong endorsement of Nick Fry, CEO of the Honda F1 racing team: "Our efficiency has got as good as it could be," Fry said. Celerant maintains connections with the Honda F1 Racing team by providing sponsorship for James Rossiter, one of its test drivers.

Bottom-line results, delivered

Ian Clarkson, founder and CEO of Celerant Consulting has been quoted as saying, "In the future, the only real source of value from consulting will be delivered, bottom-line results. Advice and good intentions won't cut it." The consultancy took these words to heart in the case of its work with Phillips Lighting Products in 2005. Phillips had a plan to improve operations in its Netherlands plant as a part of its "green flag" initiative, with the goal of boosting its line yield targets while simultaneously driving down costs. Celerant helped Phillips accomplish these goals with tangible results—when the engagement was completed, line yields were up and costs had been lowered by €4 million.

GETTING HIRED

Don't stress about that C in chemistry

No need to fret if you don't have a 4.0 GPA, since we're told that "individual impression and fit to the Celerant culture are more important than university grades" when it comes to getting hired. After a "CV filter" and a "phone interview", qualified "younger" applicants are sent to the firm's "assessment centre", which consists of a "second interview, role play, problem solving and presentation", as well as "a group exercise". Specialists and senior hires will generally have a "meeting with key people" instead. Insiders reveal that interview questions might include, "What has been your most successful implementation of improvements?" or "What has been your biggest challenge in your career so far?" They are thankful that the entire "process usually is very fast".

OUR SURVEY SAYS

Entrepreneurial and encouraging

Most insiders say the "work hard, play hard" attitude at Celerant is what stands out about the firm. They describe their colleagues as "genuine, interesting and not arrogant", and the culture as "results-driven and entrepreneurial", but also "people-oriented and collaborative". Sources also say the firm has a strong "focus on people growth", and provides a "good mix of official and unofficial training", with an emphasis on mentoring. "A lot of attention goes to coaching and helping others to become successful consultants," a vice president insists.

"We are a more human consulting practice," echoes another experienced staffer, which "makes it encouraging and pleasant to work as a consultant". Others add that the firm "does genuinely strive to do right for its clients and employees", and offers "great opportunities for every colleague". Plus, we're told that "people are accepted for who they are," "everyone is treated equally" and "there are no significant differences between men and women" at the firm.

Climb up or slide sideways

In addition, promotion is "very results-based", and there's no urgency to move up or out. There are "twice yearly appraisals", and "if you deliver, you might climb a step a year at the lower levels." A longtimer reports, "The firm prefers to push people up, rather than recruit from outside. In that sense, advancement can be fast for good performers." Alternatively, we're told, "people can move sideways as long as they are good at what they do." A respondent with more than a decade's experience at Celerant explains, "A project manager who does not want to become a senior project manager can remain on the level of his/her best comfort, ie, an older colleague continues as a project manager until retirement (and feels great sharing his experience without being burdened with too much responsibility and pressure)."

> ❝ The firm prefers to push people up, rather than recruit from outside. ❞

Travel keeps things interesting

When it comes to the daily grind, some workweeks are "very hectic", while others are "very quiet"—but on average, putting in around 60 hours per week is the norm. Few of these hours are spent in the office, however, since almost all staffers are travelling four or five days a week. We're told that junior staffers tend to travel within "local geography", while seniors are sent all over Europe and "typically travel a lot more". One project manager says he spends only "two to five days a year" in his local Düsseldorf office. That may be just as well, since respondents say many offices are "in need of a revamp" and are "not very prestigious". Plus, as a senior staffer notes, although the travel is demanding, at least "you don't get bored"—especially since there are "always opportunities" to work in "exotic locations like oil rigs in Alaska, refineries in Oman and construction sites in Egypt", not to mention on assignments in Asia, Africa, the US and Latin America.

Relax on the weekends

Another plus, says a senior project manager, "I came from a job with extensive travel over the weekends, which my wife didn't like. Now I'm home every weekend." Another agrees that his mantra is, "Work hard during the week, relax and enjoy over the weekends." On the other hand, a colleague explains, "I work on weekends because it helps me step back from the transactional work during the week," however, he agrees, "Celerant colleagues do not encourage weekend work."

Still, warns a manager, "It can be hard to strike the right balance of travel and work when assignments are in lots of different countries." But Celerant is reportedly willing to work out special arrangements for those who request them. A staffer in London reports, "I have a small child and work four days a week," adding that the firm has been "very flexible". Nonetheless, the source spends those four days on the road and says that ultimately, "going back to work and being away from home with a very small baby is hard."

Gas up the company car

Some respondents say their salary is high enough to make it all worthwhile, but others think compensation levels should have a "better link to merit" and would like to see "better tax-friendly remuneration". One source warns that a "bonus is not always given." Extras include a "leadership team award", commission, a shares programme (for senior project managers and above) and a "team selling bonus". Plus, some mention getting a "decent company car that can be used privately", as well as a "phone provision". A senior project manager adds that there are also "incredible parties, both with and without the client, and sometimes with our families".

Celerant also supports community involvement by matching "the employee contribution for all charity work it knows about". And in lieu of generating a Christmas card mailing, the firm donates the money it saves to "a good cause". Says one insider, "There is an accepted culture of personal charity challenges and sponsorship being requested over e-mail."

COMMERCIAL ADVANTAGE CONSULTING

5-11 Lavington Street
London SE1 0NZ
United Kingdom
Phone: +44 (0)207 902 9850
Fax: +44 (0)207 902 9851
www.commercialadvantage.com

The Stats

Employer Type: Private Company
Chairman: Emyr Williams
CEO: Aidan Bocci
2008 Employees: 25
2007 Employees: 25
2008 Revenue: $9 million
2007 Revenue: $8.2 million
No. of Offices: 1

Practice Areas

Ambition Development • Building
Capability • Brand Development •
Brand Renovation • Business Planning •
Category Rejuvenation • Change
Management • Commercial
Transformation • Corporate Strategy •
Cost Reduction • Customer & Channel
Strategy • Customer Presentation •
EDLP Management • Field Sales
Effectiveness • Innovation • M&A •
Market Due Diligence • New Product
Launch • Pricing Strategy • Product
Portfolio Management • Promotion
Effectiveness • Sales & Marketing •
Strategic Decision Making • Trade
Marketing • Trade Spend
Effectiveness • Turnaround

European Location

London (HQ)

Pluses

- Interesting and varied work
- "Being among friends"
- "Good exposure to the whole business"

Minuses

- "A lot to do and not many bodies to do it"
- Narrow client base
- "Lack of recognition in the industry"

Employment Contact

www.commercialadvantage.com/
careers/index.asp

THE SCOOP

H aving undergone a rebranding exercise in April 2008, Commercial Advantage has gone from being a firm that claims, "We make people," to one that promises to help bridge the gap "from what to how". At heart though, the company remains unchanged, with its core value—"We make ambitions braver, sharper and real"—still intact. Translation? Commercial Advantage does what it has always done: help clients in the consumer goods industry enable their employees to break free from inhibiting practices, take risks and find new paths to success. In essence, it helps clients go from identifying "what" they need to do to "how" they're going to achieve it.

Meet the chief

At the helm of Commercial Advantage is Aidan Bocci, a former Procter & Gamble employee who partnered with current Chairman Emyr Williams to create a company that cut through the blue-sky, outside-the-box culture they saw pervading many consulting firms in the 1990s. Offering a fresh take on the consulting world, they eschew "off-the-shelf" strategies in favour of an approach

> ❝ Personal commitments always come first. ❞

where only proper execution justifies whether or not the strategy was the right one in the first place. This means that, rather than trying to fit a theoretical framework onto a company and figure out what parts work, Commercial Advantage does what it can to deliver results.

Among the companies that CA has done business with are such heavyweights as Coca-Cola, Kimberley-Clark, Nestlé and Diageo. And while the majority of its work is within the UK, the consultancy also operates in Central and Eastern Europe, Africa, the US and Asia.

Mapping the route

The firm's speciality is in helping consumer goods companies achieve better performance by building better business strategies and a culture of high performance, and by maximising return on investment—in money and people. It does this by taking clients on a journey, using a series of tools to help companies get from their starting point ("what") to their destination ("how")—a journey that, hopefully, will see a client's employees become empowered to make decisions, overcome barriers, execute objectives and achieve results.

Results, however, don't come along just because a consultant says they will. Commercial Advantage appears to be very aware of that fact and has therefore developed a process known as "ambition setting", a series of workshops that aid clients in arriving at a collective idea of where they're heading. Once that's achieved getting there together becomes the target, and decision making on how to do that becomes the order of the day. Enter another trademarked process—"decision logics"—to help companies get to where they need to be. The process involves workshops that demonstrate how clients can approach problems from the same viewpoint, avoiding "analysis paralysis", and enabling faster, more efficient decision making.

Serious gamers

Each of these processes is designed to help Commercial Advantage deliver on its ambition-fulfilling credo, and is backed up by something the firm calls decision simulations—basically a game setting that teaches the business decision-making process in a nonthreatening (ie, non-real world) environment. The process, the firm says, helps clients develop and streamline new approaches to decision making, allowing them to quickly make organisational changes.

Beyond improving a client's ability to make decisions, CA stresses the importance of learning through results. Given that the consultancy's take on business is that results are the only things that matter, this is hardly surprising. Neither is the firm's suggestion that "nothing drives results like results"—a mantra that supports its focus on feeding back results to further shape an organisation's direction and aid its decision making.

PIMPing ain't easy

Commercial Advantage's commitment to its employees, it says, is evidenced by its willingness to PIMP them out. Rather than a tawdry term to describe the oversight of the selling of one's flesh, however, CA's PIMPing is confined to bringing out the best in its employees through training and development—otherwise known as the Process for Internally Making People (see the acronym?). The unusual moniker for the process shouldn't detract from the intent behind it; like the approach the firm takes with its clients, it is committed to individually tailoring professional development to each and every staff member, rather than providing a one-size-fits-all structure.

In addition, the firm has also set up an institution known as the CA University, a learning forum for staff where, once a month, they are encouraged to "take a step back" from client responsibilities and meet to discuss a prepared topic such as brand renovation or core skills needed in the consulting trade.

GETTING HIRED

Experience required

Commerical Advantage's interview process involves "three rounds", insiders tell us. The first is with the HR manager, "to suss out if you are the right kind of person for the business". HR is looking to determine if a candidate is a "people maker, someone who will understand the firm's unique approach to helping clients get to the answer". The second interview is "usually with the firm's head of practice, who will interrogate your industry knowledge and the appropriateness of your skills to becoming a consultant". At this stage, candidates must be able to show that they can "think on their feet". The final round is a "panel interview". A consultant explains, "It is a live gig, where candidates are given an hour to prepare a response to a case study. They then give a 20-minute presentation to three people from the business. This is normally followed by a 20-minute Q&A session." A typical interview question might be the following: "What current issues are most prevalent in the fast-moving consumer goods industry? Prioritise the top three and share your approach on how you would go about helping a client mitigate them."

Sources say that Commercial Advantage "does not recruit graduates". Normally, "people join the firm with at least three years of consulting or industry experience." One insider notes, "Around the interviews, consultants often chat to candidates to help them work out if it is the right business for them." One insider says of his decision to join the firm, "It's a young company, so I get a chance to be an individual rather than a number, and help shape the company."

OUR SURVEY SAYS

Individuals on the same team

Commercial Advantage's "truly unique" approach to consulting attracts "fun, down-to-earth, intelligent" people. The firm's consultants are "lively and youthful", yet still "professional", insiders report. It's a "hands-on" culture in which consultants are "empowered to help out on anything to do with building the company from within". The firm has a "culture of approaching problems in a different way, and it is accepting of individuals rather than a set approach". In this "nonhierarchical" environment, things are "extremely merit-based", we're told. In addition, respondents say the consultancy fosters an atmosphere in which people "work together to solve big, real business problems". "We're all friends, and we care about each other and our clients," a source remarks.

Colleagues enjoy "being part of shaping what the company becomes", and they're "always willing to offer a helping hand". Communication channels are "open", but "without the politics that you'd associate with this industry."

Staffers are also pleased to report that the consultancy is quite diverse. There is a "60/40 split between women and men, with more women than men overall, and equal numbers in the more senior positions", a consultant states. In addition, Commercial Advantage employs "people from all over the globe" and "would never discriminate" against anyone.

Free to be

Commercial Advantage consultants tell us they're "largely in control of their own work/life balance". Assuming client deliverables are met, a source explains, the firm allows people to "work from home and plan their own travel requirements". A contact says, "The firm acknowledges the importance of maintaining a life outside of work. Consultants won't be expected to work at nights or on weekends." Most staffers log between 45 and 50 hours per week, and projects range in length from six weeks to three months. Staffers "work late when needed", especially at the end of projects when demands escalate, but a source notes that there is "flexibility and team support when you have commitments you want to keep". One insider says, "I'm definitely the first to leave work out of my friends with other consultancies."

> " There is a '60/40 split between women and men'. "

Cozying up to clients

One of CA's "core principles" is that "clients own what they help to create." For this reason, consultants "work closely with clients on a regular basis, usually at their offices". "Travel is necessary to do a good job," a respondent comments, but the firm is reportedly flexible on this point. One consultant remarks, "Personal commitments always come first, so if someone can't get somewhere, we find a way of working around it." And when they're on the road, staffers "get looked after well", which means they "don't really have the stresses that other firms have". Additionally, since "half of the client work is based in the UK," travel requirements are "relatively low compared to other consulting firms".

Working with "large, global, blue-chip consumer goods companies", consultants are exposed to "a variety of work", which means "there is always a new challenge." In addition, the firm's "flat structure and small teams" allow for "good relationships with senior management", and "more than enough" interaction with clients. An insider explains the consultancy's approach to client work: "There is a healthy disregard for consultants here! We focus on execution, not just blue-sky theory, and have techniques to help clients get to the answers themselves, rather than give an analysis that shows them everything they are doing wrong."

Welcome to CA University

Commercial Advantage offers "a balance between official and unofficial training", insiders say. There is a "dedicated day each month for internal training known as CA University, which helps to formalise some aspects of training". These monthly sessions are dedicated to "codifying our approach and learning what it is that is so different about us". In addition, consultants have "personal training budgets to spend on anything we'd like, as long as there is a perceived personal or business benefit". Some say they "rarely have time to use" the allowance, however, which makes them appreciate the "loads of unofficial training".

Take it and run with it

We're told that promotions are "managed uniquely to individuals". In CA's current "fast growth mode, there is no clear progression". According to one respondent, "The promotion policy is not really a policy. If you're ready to go to the next level and have expressed an interest to the directors, you'll get promoted." By the same token, "if you're happy to stay where you are, that's fine, too." Consultants say it's possible to advance from junior to senior consultant "very quickly", but all moves are "based on merit and client feedback".

Don't come for benefits

Sources also feel fairly well looked after when it comes to compensation. Since Commercial Advantage is "a young company, it does not yet have an established pension or health care scheme", but that is "taken into consideration when figuring basic salaries", a source explains—the firm is "working on setting these things up". But as perks stand, we're told that staffers are treated to regular social events, such as "wine tastings on Friday nights", as well as gifts for longevity of service, like "cufflinks or a pendant with the company logo for your third anniversary". Insiders appreciate CA's "active involvement in SIFE", or Students in Free Enterprise, and it efforts in "tutoring and mentoring up-and-coming entrepreneurs and business students".

Commercial Advantage's office is in a "good location" in London that's "easy to get to" for many staffers, and the "open office space" contributes to the firm's "collaborative and honest culture". One consultant remarks, "Our offices are not what you'd expect from a strategy consulting firm that competes with McKinsey, but they reassure our clients that they're not paying for expensive overheads." In short, the vibe is "not flashy, but comfortable enough". □

CORPORATE VALUE ASSOCIATES

6th Floor
Kinnaird House
1 Pall Mall East
London SW1Y 5AU
United Kingdom
Phone: +44 (0)207 559 5000
Fax: +44 (0)207 559 5099
www.corporate-value.com

The Stats

Employer Type: Private Company
Founder & Managing Partner:
  Paul-André Rabate
2008 Employees: 300
2007 Employees: 200+
No. of Offices: 16

Practice Areas

Fast Moving Consumer Goods
Financial Services
Government
Healthcare
Mining Resources
Packaging
Pharmaceuticals
Retail & Distribution
Stock Exchange
Telecommunications & Logistics
Transport
Utilities

European Locations

Amsterdam • Berlin • London • Milan •
Paris • Vienna

Pluses

• "Diverse assignments"
• Flexible about work hours
• "Enterprise culture"

Minuses

• "Far too few women"
• High travel demands
• Limited community involvement

Employment Contact

For country-specific recruitment
contacts, go to:
  www.corporate-value.com/join/
  cva_join_working.asp

THE BUZZ
WHAT CONSULTANTS AT OTHER FIRMS ARE SAYING

• "Quite good in their (small) domain"
• "Too small"
• "Interesting, good quality people"
• "A lot of calculation"

THE SCOOP

Corporate Value Associates

H aving celebrated the 20th anniversary of its founding in 2007, Corporate Value Associates employs more than 300 consultants in 16 offices, offering its "boutique" solutions across a range of industries in more than 30 countries.

Spreading its wings

The firm was started in 1987 by three French consultants, with the express intent of becoming an international player by offering a value-focussed methodology for improving the businesses of its clients. Having established offices in Amsterdam, Boston, London and Paris in its first year, and broadening its international footprint ever since, there is little doubt that the firm has evolved into the multinational, multicultural affair it set out to be. Today, its facilities include six offices in Europe, seven in the Asia Pacific region, two American offices (one of which is the home of its US affiliate Dean & Company) and a single African office in Morocco.

Of the dozen practice areas CVA serves, it claims to be a "major player" in two— health care and pharmaceuticals. In addition, it identifies itself as a top-10 player in segments of the transportation and fast-moving consumer goods sectors, specifically in airlines and brewing, wine and spirits, and luxury goods. For the remaining sectors in which CVA does business, it identifies itself as a top-three player.

Value, value and more value

CVA's core tenet is that client value is created at the customer level. As a result, CVA offers a "customer-centric" approach, and does not shirk its responsibilities when it comes to solving clients' problems. To do so, the company has generated a methodology that is based around four key elements: quality of people (including high levels of partner involvement); providing methodologies (the firm has developed proprietary frameworks to help meet its clients needs); a joint team approach (working together with clients rather than, say, taking over a project to achieve success); and having a global mindset (ensuring that people and ideas are moved freely between offices to benefit all corners of its operations).

CVA sets out to differentiate itself from its competitors by stressing that its methodologies do not provide off-the-shelf solutions to problems, but rather a systematic approach to identifying and solving problems that will help each client arrive at a tailored solution.

Inside the mind of the customer

One way that CVA helps clients derive more value from the customers they serve is by helping them get inside their customers' minds. CVA's proprietary Customer Centric Value Enhancement (CCVE®) metric analyses customer behaviour by examining the relationship between a customer's needs and the economic implications of meeting those needs. This is a fancy way of saying they figure out how much a customer is willing to spend for goods or service, and what can be done to affect that amount. And it's something the firm takes seriously, as evidenced by its development of a marketing lab in Berlin, where market research is combined with neuroscience to try and better predict the purchasing decisions of consumers. Now that's the way to get into their heads!

GETTING HIRED

Must have brains and personality

CVA has a "classical, case study-based hiring process, with candidates normally going through "three rounds of two one-on-one interviews"—each about 45 minutes in length, we're told. First rounds are with "consultants and senior consultants", and second rounds are with "associates and managers". Applicants who make it to the final round meet with the firm's partners. A consultant explains that interviews "focus on quantitative skills" and involve both "brainteasers and case studies". A colleague offers an example of a possible stumper: "If it is a quarter past three, what is the angle between the hands?" Current staffers say the firm uses "very interesting" case studies. Candidates will also be assessed on "structuring skills and self-presentation". Above all, however, CVA is looking at "personal fit", so interviewees should expect several "behavioural and resume questions" as well.

CVA "accepts applications from all schools", but due to its small size, it only "actively engages the Oxford and Cambridge campuses". For positions in the Paris office, recruiters look to the "top-three business schools and top-three engineering schools in France".

Sealing the deal

Candidates who do not hail from these schools—or target school students looking for a leg up—might consider participating in CVA's "extremely positive" internship programme. Insiders say the position is "open but challenging", and that participants will face a "steep learning curve". One former intern shares, "My summer internship was the reason for my decision to work for CVA."

OUR SURVEY SAYS

Does size really matter?

CVA consultants work in a "highly motivating and stimulating" environment. Colleagues are generally "friendly, relaxed and down-to-earth, and everybody gets on pretty well". Consultants are granted a lot of "trust and freedom", and the firm fosters a "family kind of culture". One insider says, "Among the consultants, it is less a group of colleagues than a group of friends. There are absolutely no elbows in sight." Some say this "very informal" and "international work environment" can become "too personal", but most give positive reviews to CVA's "easygoing culture". Indeed, the firm's "very centrally located offices in top European cities encourage a lot of exchange on know-how and marketing across offices."

And while CVA's small size provides "opportunities for senior engagement and broad experience of industries, methodologies and geographies," it also "means that the support infrastructure is not as advanced as it could be". Consultants "must be self-starting about things like booking travel and organising diaries". At times, the firm's "high speed and innovation causes structure and organisation to become overloaded." One insider complains, "We need to fix IT!" Furthermore, although the firm's small size prevents consultants from "becoming pigeonholed into an industry practice, it can sometimes be difficult to choose the projects on which they work."

The friendly—and frequent—skies

Travel requirements at CVA "very much depend on the project", but most consultants tell us they're on the road a lot. A respondent remarks, "It's the usual consulting deal. If you're staffed abroad, you fly out on Monday morning and come back on Thursday evening." For these staffers, "working at the client is the norm, which means most cases require being at the client, and often abroad, four days a week." Some travel weekends as well, while others manage to stay closer to home, since CVA has "a lot of London-based projects". More representative of a job at CVA, however, is the head of the firm's Asia Pacific region, who, insiders say, "was the most frequent flyer on two airlines simultaneously in one year".

Tough, but not excessive

Spending so much time on the road "can be a great opportunity to discover another country and live a very intense experience", but, as these consultants find, it can also be a "complication in building a life back home". "Naturally, if you are abroad during the week, your private life takes a dent," a source comments. However, "apart from travelling and its consequences on personal life, the work/life balance is very good," notes a colleague. There is "no face time required" and, for the most part, "casework is managed so that consultants leave the office at reasonable hours." Most respondents tell us they log an average of 50 to 60 hours per week, although in Berlin, a "culture of late nights and weekends has become too ingrained". In that location, "65 hours-plus is the norm." There is "no general rule" on project length, but most fall in the range of three months. More recently, though, the firm has "tended to do longer-term engagements".

Most consultants say they deal with a "generally high level of work", but note that it's "not excessive". And if things become too much, "partners intervene and help."

> ❝ The firm offers 'opportunities for juniors to interact with senior client members early'. ❞

Overall, CVA is a "very flexible company", and "the measure of how well you do your job isn't the time you spent on it, but how the client and partner perceive it." Staffers are given "the freedom to work from home, and to start later or finish earlier, if necessary". And, like the correlation between eating your veggies and getting dessert, if your work is done, "you can spend time with your family."

A different kind of travel

Most insiders give high marks to their compensation packages. In general, "remuneration is in line with other top consulting companies," and consultants "always receive a good bonus", though there is "no pension fund". Additional perks are "all pretty standard", but sources give especially high praise to the firm's "breakout travel and retreats". To celebrate the consultancy's 20th anniversary, "all the staff from the 16 global offices gathered in Namibia." Staffers enjoyed a "safari, cruise, sandboarding and flights in chartered planes". Clearly, CVA went "full out for this amazing trip". Something similar takes place "every one to two years", we're told—in 2006, everyone went to Dubai.

In addition to great off-site activities, consultants get "gym membership contributions and health insurance", and in the Berlin office, staffers are treated to a "regular informal dinner". New parents are offered the "possibility of several months' sabbatical and/or part-time work."

Hit-or-miss management

Management at CVA gets mixed reviews. The firm's management style is "not homogenous, so sometimes the fit [between supervisor and subordinate] is great, and sometimes not". Some feel interoffice communication, "particularly from the partner and manager level to consultants", could use improvement. On the bright side, CVA is the kind of place where "you can talk to everyone, regardless of their rank." A consultant says of the firm's leaders, "They will tell you everything about their life, not just what is going on in the business."

In addition, insiders enjoy "very good and long-lasting client relationships". The firm offers "opportunities for juniors to interact with senior client members early". And since CVA "mostly works on growth projects", client interactions are "very pleasant", a respondent comments. One particularly "fun" client, we're told, is the government of Mauritania.

Training needs improvement

Sources say there's a "lack of continuously structured training" at CVA—most learning is unofficial and takes place on the job. A consultant remarks, "It is a worry whether you will attain the skills you need on the job, as it's purely luck and there is no formal route." A colleague adds, "Not much is done for people with basic skills to improve on things like Excel and PowerPoint." On rare instances of formal training, which normally amount to about "one week every one to two years", staffers are taught "CVA methodology and teamwork", while specific training on various software programmes is offered on "a case-by-case basis".

To each his own pace

Sources appreciate that CVA does not have an up-or-out promotion policy, as the firm is "strictly a meritocracy"—consultants "can advance quickly if they are good". There is "no set quota for different work levels", which insiders have found "reduces competition among the consultants". Time between promotions is "very variable", with some employees moving up "incredibly quickly" and others experiencing "stagnation". On average, "promotions happen roughly every 18 months." As one consultant explains, "Promotion is truly based on merit, and strong performers advance quicker than others. Consultants who need a little bit more time to progress at some stages are given it." The downside to allowing people to "develop at their own pace", however, is that "the review process isn't done very professionally," a respondent notes. According to a colleague, "Managers forget to give you reviews or spend time with you talking about how you can improve." This can make the process feel "nontransparent and arbitrary at times".

Trying to attract women

Although CVA is "very receptive" to hiring women, there's a "lack of candidates", which results in few female consultants at the firm. That said, the firm hires a "pretty healthy amount of female consultants", but representation "thins out as you get to the top". Respondents assure us that there is "no discrimination" toward women at the firm, and insist that the numbers are "partially improving each year". CVA is "trying very hard to become more attractive to women, with several good mechanisms in place"

When it comes to ethnic minorities, CVA is, in a word, "indifferent". According to a source, "The firm hires without any positive or negative discrimination." As a general rule, "it doesn't matter where you are from, only what you do." Similarly, the consultancy takes a "relaxed attitude" toward gay, lesbian, bisexual and transgender employees, and there are "several members of the staff who are openly gay". □

DETICA

Surrey Research Park
Guildford
Surrey GU2 7YP
United Kingdom
Phone: +44 (0)1483 816 000
Fax: +44 (0)1483 816 144
www.detica.com

The Stats

Employer Type: Public Company
Ticker Symbol: DCA (LSE)
CEO: Tom Black
2008 Employees: 1,538
2007 Employees: 1,464
2008 Revenue: £203.2 million
2007 Revenue: £156.1 million
No. of Offices: 12

Practice Areas

Business Consulting
Operational Support
Project Management
Software & Hardware (Electronic
  Engineering)
Systems Development & Integration
Technology Consulting

European Locations

Guildford (HQ)
Amsterdam • Gatwick • Geneva •
Gloucester • London

Pluses

• Not a cutthroat environment
• "Decent pay for decent work/life
  balance"

Minuses

• "Sometimes pushed to perform
  unfamiliar roles"
• Internal adjustments as the firm
  transitions into a global entity

Employment Contact

www.detica.com/careers

THE BUZZ
WHAT CONSULTANTS AT OTHER FIRMS ARE SAYING

• "Up-and-coming"
• "Process geeks"
• "Narrow but technically successful"
• "Small fish"

THE SCOOP

I n a world where keeping information safe is about more than locks and keys, UK-based Detica has carved its niche. A specialist business and technology consultancy, the firm excels at security, fraud containment, risk management, regulatory compliance and customer management. Counting government agencies and several major financial institutions among its clients, the firm does everything it can to keep critical information where it's supposed to be, and even aids law enforcement departments in bringing offenders to justice.

In fiscal 2008 (ending in March), some 61 per cent of Detica's revenue was earned through its government contracts. On the commercial side of the business, banks—one of its main groups of clients—have had a well-documented, torrid time of late, and they are seeking to curb spending across the board. One of the ways they are doing so is by reining in spending on security consulting, a fact

> " Most travel is daily return trips, rather than overnight stays. "

that seems set to hit the Detica books hard—especially given the fact that some 25 per cent of the £203.2 million it pulled in throughout fiscal 2008 was from financial services clients such as HSBC, Barclays and Lloyds TSB. The remainder of fiscal 2008 revenue (£28 million) came from the telecoms, media and technology business area, which advises such clients as BT, Vodafone and Sony.

Growing in stature

Detica's roots go all the way back to 1971, when research services firm Smith Associates was founded to provide data analysis within the UK defence sector. A name change in 2001 preceded a flotation on the London Stock Exchange in 2002 led by CEO Tom Black, then in his fifth year in charge of the firm, and his 18th since joining in 1984. Still in charge today, Black has held almost every senior management position at the consultancy at one time or another, and now has over a quarter of a century's experience with Detica.

With all that experience under his belt, Black is in a unique position to appreciate exactly how far the firm has come in recent years. Under his leadership, Detica has followed an expansionist agenda, opening offices and buying the occasional complementary company along the way. One recent purchase was the £8.4 million acquisition of financial sector IT services provider Evolution Consulting in January 2006, a deal Detica paired with the September 2006 acquisition of M.A. International

Limited, a consultancy with a focus on capital markets. Also known as m.a. partners, the firm's 130 staff were based largely in the financial centres of London and New York, while it also had several European offices. The £34.7 million acquisition was intended to increase Detica's capabilities in the financial services world.

Other acquisitions, meanwhile, have included Inforenz Limited, a provider of specialised computer forensic services to private- and public-sector clients, including law enforcement, in July 2006, and Extraprise UK, a consultancy and systems integrator focussing on the CRM market, in April 2005.

Infiltrating US security

The most significant expansion of the firm's footprint of late came in early 2007, when it purchased Washington-based security consultancy DFI for some £22.5 million, a deal that created Detica Federal Inc. in the US. DFI specialised in using IT-derived intelligence for national defence; Detica Federal today focusses on policy, analysis, knowledge management and IT—expertise applied in the fields of defence, Homeland Security, IT security and fraud.

The acquisition brought in many more contacts within the US intelligence community, largely thanks to the influence of General John A. Gordon, a former homeland security advisor to the Bush administration and retired four-star Air Force general. As chair of DFI's US national security business, Gordon played a key role in bringing the two firms together, and was rewarded with a nonexecutive directorship at the merged entity.

The move paid off immediately for the consultancy. The new Detica Federal division announced in September 2007 that it had signed a contract to provide advanced analytics services to an unnamed "major US government client involved in counterterrorism activities". Under the terms of the deal, the firm will enhance existing analytics services with new advanced tools and methods developed in the UK, in order to improve the client's ability to provide more rapid and effective intelligence aimed at curbing terrorist threats. That same month, Detica was tapped as part of an 11-member team led by Scitor Corp. to provide a range of services for the US Department of Defense.

Keeping the home fires burning

Even as it begins to find success abroad, Detica continues to pick up contracts in its home market. In November 2007, Trusted Borders—a consortium of firms led by Raytheon and including Detica—signed a deal with the UK Home Office to develop and implement the nation's e-Borders programme. Under the "advanced border control and security programme", which is expected to be operational within two years, Detica will provide intelligence and analytics services. The original contract was worth around £50 million to Detica, but an addendum signed in January 2008 added a further £25 million in value, and is being subcontracted to the firm by Raytheon. Other firms involved in the consortium, meanwhile, include Accenture, Capgemini, QinetiQ, Serco and Steria.

Early in 2008, the firm picked up a couple of contracts in its own right, securing a deal in late March worth £18.1 million to provide and support operational PDAs, mobile data terminals and other infrastructure for the Metropolitan Police Service. In April, meanwhile, the firm was selected—in partnership with Atkins—to provide cryptosecurity capabilities for the Ministry of Defence, a project worth £2.3 million.

Revelations

The firm has also been picking up business in the financial sector, thanks largely to one of its most popular solutions—Detica NetReveal®, a fraud detection technology that helps identify fraudsters within social networks, rather than in individual transactions. The consultancy's method helps track down fraudsters using multiple identities to defraud organisations, such as those in the financial and the insurance industry. In January 2008, HSBC Bank Plc signed up for

> ❝ Detica has transitioned from a white public school environment to a diverse company. ❞

NetReveal after a test pilot of the software proved successful. RBS Insurance followed soon after, signing a deal in late February, just weeks before Detica unveiled the latest generation of the software—version five, for those who are counting. The business NetReveal has attracted to Detica is clear evidence that the software works—in August 2007, the UK Insurance Fraud Bureau announced that NetReveal had enabled it to expose insurance fraud networks leading to 74 arrests.

Reportage

In addition to doing business, Detica also publishes research in its areas of expertise, much of which—surprise!—suggests that there is greater need for its products and knowledge. In March 2008, for example, the company responded to recent rogue trading scandals (Monsieur Kerviel was the name on many lips at the time) with research that urged financial institutions not to tighten internal controls, but rather to shift to a networked approach to operational control. The fact that Detica specialises in such an approach is surely just a coincidence. Other information published by the firm, however, involves spending a lot less money. One such example was its November 2007 statement that suggested a novel method for companies to save on data storage—encouraging employees to delete personal e-mails. Detica found that companies that blamed regulators and new compliance rules for "data glut" often overlooked the enormous toll exerted on their storage capabilities by employees failing to delete old e-mail. There was no word, however, as to whether Detica was setting up a specialist e-mail deletion unit.

GETTING HIRED

Let's talk aspirations

Insiders tell us Detica has a "two-stage interview process". The first is "generally just a run-through of the CV to understand the applicant's motivations and decision making". This initial meeting, which normally lasts one hour, is also "an opportunity for the candidate to find out about the firm". The second interview is "a bit more in depth", and "typically lasts about two hours". This round focusses on "fit to culture and technical ability", and assesses the "softer skills of consulting". During the second round, candidates give a "20-minute presentation on any topic of their choosing". There's also "a case study exercise to assess a candidate's method of working things through". Case studies are "typically based on a past project", we're told. A source says, "There are no right or wrong answers, but the case generally works through the project life cycle, exploring what information may need to be gathered and how the design is put together, following through to implementation and support." In addition, notes a respondent, candidates should plan for "plenty of discussion of aspirations".

Detica recruits from "most of the top-end universities", including Oxford, Cambridge, Durham, Bath, Southampton and Imperial. A source comments that consultants are "encouraged to return to their stomping grounds to pick up new hires".

OUR SURVEY SAYS

Small firm on the rise

Staffers say Detica's "inclusive" culture is made up of "hardworking, ambitious" consultants with "good senses of humour". One source states that the firm is filled with "friendly, intelligent people working together to achieve success for a growing business". Insiders are also "willing to have fun", and, in fact, the firm has a "strong sports and social scene". Respondents also appreciate that Detica maintains a "small-company feel despite having 1,500 employees", probably because the firm "treats employees as individuals, not just resources". Some say there have been some "growing pains" as the consultancy has gone from "being a small firm to a global firm"—"the internal processes, tools and systems are struggling to keep up"—but its "flat structure is easy to navigate", thanks to managers and directors who are "approachable and in touch with the staff".

Team-based approach to hours

Most Detica consultants report working between 45 and 50 hours per week. People "often work over the contracted 40 hours", but it is "not part of a 'last man standing' attitude". It's more that "everyone is chipping in to succeed." There is "no pressure to work weekends or extended hours, but it is part of the culture and teamwork spirit that drives everyone to deliver". In return, Detica offers "flexibility for working from home or working alternative hours". For instance, an insider explains, consultants are "able to alter their working days around child care commitments". A colleague says, "I am empowered to manage my own time, so I can choose the appropriate points to balance work and life." Most consultants say they "can commit to evening activities, and rarely miss appointments" due to work.

Travelling does not impose on work/life balance either, because "most travel is daily return trips, rather than overnight stays." What also helps is the fact that most of the firm's clients are based in London and the South East of the UK.

Benefits of choosing Detica

With regard to monetary reward, Detica employees can participate in a "share ownership scheme", which is taken "from pre-tax salaries and includes an option with every share purchased". A respondent tells us Detica makes "excellent pension contributions at the principal consultant level". The firm also offers "ad hoc bonuses" as well as an "inconvenience allowance for travel over three hours a day". In addition to car allowances, which are grade dependent, consultants are given "flexible benefits", providing the opportunity to choose "differing levels of life insurance, health care, dental insurance and pension contributions". Employees also have the "option to buy/sell holiday days", and the "ability to take a period of unpaid leave".

Other fringe benefits include child care vouchers, "bike-to-work support", gym membership, "first-class rail travel for long journeys", "good coffee" and, not to be missed, "free Kit-Kats". New dads are granted three days' paid paternity leave.

Training is a work in progress

At Detica, "the majority of training is on the job." However, "if formal training is required for a project or desired by an individual for a career aspiration, then consultants are free to find a suitable formal training course." A contact says, "Individuals are empowered to find and book training courses to meet their needs." The firm "supposedly offers a week of official training per employee per year, but most people are too busy to arrange training". Fortunately, "senior staff are eager to mentor and coach on an informal basis." The consensus amongst insiders is that Detica's is "not a particularly mature training programme".

Advance as you please

The consultancy's promotion policy is "not at all up or out". Staffers "advance on merit, rather than time served, and they can get promoted very quickly if they are overachieving". And, as one source puts it, the firm offers "plenty of opportunities to shine". Under Detica's "formal grading structure", consultants are "graded individually and moderated against their peers". All new graduates join the firm as consultants. Then it typically takes "two years, based on individual performance assessed every six months" to move to senior consultant. Advancing to principal consultant takes "another three years", on average. An insider notes, however, that "there is a gap between the rate of advancement in the business versus the technical side of the company, which is not in the technical side's favour." The firm disagrees on this point, however, noting that the companywide competency framework should ensure that all employees are assessed in a consistent manner.

Looking for proportion

At Detica, we're told, "all people are treated fairly." However, the firm has a "very low percentage of women", a fact that's "particularly true at the senior levels". But, respondents say this is no fault of the firm's; Detica hires "as many as can be", a staffer claims, and "the numbers of women go up every year." That said, they remain a "tiny minority".

The proportions are a bit more favourable when it comes to ethnic diversity. Detica has "plenty of people from all kinds of backgrounds, both indigenous and from abroad, where security clearance permits". According to one consultant, "Detica has transitioned from a white public school environment to a diverse company over the past few years."

The firm also initiates "lots of community involvement", including "a charity of the year and various events and promotions to raise funds". It also "runs a young enterprise scheme in schools and organises teams for contest". Consultants have participated in such events as the Microsoft Challenge and the Prince's Trust Challenge. □

Detica

DIAMOND MANAGEMENT & TECHNOLOGY CONSULTANTS, INC.

Orion House, 10th Floor
5 Upper St. Martin's Lane
London WC2H 9EA
United Kingdom
Phone: +44 (0)207 959 7700
Fax: +44 (0)207 959 7710
www.diamondconsultants.com

The Stats

Employer Type: Public Company
Ticker Symbol: DTPI (Nasdaq)
Chairman: Mel Bergstein
President & CEO: Adam Gutstein
2008 Employees: 518
2007 Employees: 610
2007 Revenue: $169 million
2006 Revenue: $145 million
No. of Offices: 6

Practice Areas

Complex Program Management •
Customer Value Management • Data
Strategy • Digital IQ Diagnostic •
Enterprise Resource Planning • Global
Sourcing Advisory • Growth Strategies •
Information & Analytics • IT Cost
Management • IT Governance •
Marketing Strategy • Multichannel
Integration • Operations Improvement •
Private Equity • Risk Management •
Strategic Enterprise Architecture •
Supply Chain Management •
Technology Strategy & Transformation

European Locations

Chicago (HQ)
London

Pluses

- "Great people—smart, practical and easy to get along with"
- Innovative, entrepreneurial
- "Sense of belonging"
- "One can expect to get involved in all aspects of the firm, from hiring to business development"

Minuses

- "Lack of recognition within the industry"
- Long projects lead to more and more execution work
- "US-centric policies and world view"
- "Lack of choice over projects and locations"

Employment Contact

ukrecruiting@diamondconsultants.com

THE BUZZ
WHAT CONSULTANTS AT OTHER FIRMS ARE SAYING

- "Good specialists"
- "Lost all strategy direction with the sale of the Cluster part"
- "Good people"
- "Yesterday"

THE SCOOP

D iamond Management & Technology Consultants' London office provides— what else?—management and technology consulting services to C-level executives at firms in the consumer packaged goods, financial services, health care, insurance, logistics, manufacturing, public sector, retail and distribution, telecoms and high-tech industries. Headquartered in Chicago, the firm also maintains offices in Mumbai, as well as in New York, Washington, DC, and Hartford, Connecticut.

The firm has undergone a couple of shifts in identity and focus since its founding in 1994. Starting out under founder Mel Bergstein as Diamond Technology Partners, the firm also operated as DiamondCluster International before settling on its current identity in 2006, following the sale of one of its units.

First cut

Having spent four of his 20 years at Andersen Consulting (now Accenture) as managing director of its worldwide technology division, followed by executive management roles at Technology Solutions Company and Computer Sciences Corporation, it's little surprise that when Mel Bergstein chose to

> ❝ You have to work hard, but the hours are less intense than other consultancies. ❞

found his own consulting firm, he opted to make technology his niche market. He co-founded Diamond Technology Partners with the aim of providing computing solutions for Fortune 1000 companies in the financial services and health care industries.

Bergstein's timing could hardly have been better, given the surge in technology that ensued throughout the second half of the 1990s, and he took his firm public in 1997. Three years later, having opened an office in London, Bergstein also oversaw a $300 million merger with Barcelona's Cluster Consulting—a move that created DiamondCluster and established the firm on a global scale.

Losing its sparkle

The bursting of the dot-com bubble in 2001 caused problems right across the tech sector, and DiamondCluster was no exception, watching revenue slide by a third in a single year—from $307 million in 2001 to just under $203 million in 2002. The

Diamond Management & Technology Consultants, Inc.

following year brought little comfort as income disappeared. The firm sought to stem the tide by slashing salaries, as well as over a third of its workforce. Leading by example, CEO Bergstein even forfeited his own pay for a full six months, and the firm finally saw revenue grow again in 2004.

In a further bid to cut costs for the long term, meanwhile, the firm began a restructuring effort in 2005. Out went offices in Düsseldorf and Lisbon, as well as some 6 per cent of the company's global workforce—including members of the significantly downsized Barcelona office. That was enough to signal a 25 per cent increase in revenue for 2005, but a corresponding drop in income the following year signalled that more drastic measures were required.

Cluster buster

In July 2006, DiamondCluster International performed the business equivalent of shaking hands and walking away from a dysfunctional relationship. The firm announced that it was selling its operations in Continental Europe, South America and the Middle East (the part of the company known as Cluster, for all intents and purposes). The buyer, Mercer Management Consulting (now part of Oliver Wyman) acquired those interests for some $30 million, while Diamond emerged shorn of half its name. Mel Bergstein shifted seats in the boardroom, handing over the CEO-ship to fellow company founder Adam Gutstein and assuming the role of chairman.

> " Consultants advance every year, with a title change every two years. "

Gutstein brought a couple of new approaches to the pared-down company. While Diamond continues to promote largely from within its own ranks, Gutstein instituted a few external partner hires. In 2007 alone, the firm brought in four new partners from outside the firm; Kevin J. McGilloway joined Diamond's financial services division in January, bringing years of experience garnered from stints at Lehman Brothers and Equitable Life Assurance; in London, veteran retail and consumer goods consultant David Oliver came onboard in April; and Richard Findlay, a 25-year veteran of the health care field, joined the firm in September.

Diamond's commitment to hiring experience goes all the way to boardroom level as well. In February 2008, 70-year-old Dr Michael Moskow was named the firm's 12th director. His appointment is no small feat for the firm—Dr Moskow is a former president and CEO of the Federal Reserve Bank of Chicago, and previously served in five separate roles in the US government, including deputy US trade representative with the rank of ambassador, under secretary of labor, and senior staff economist at the Council of Economic Advisers. Upon his appointment, Gutstein enthused that "the depth of his experience, his broad global perspective, and his integrity are great assets that will serve Diamond, its clients, its employees and its shareholders well in the years ahead."

Writing up business

One way Diamond keeps its clients informed of trends and developments in their respective industries is through its publishing activities—its consultants frequently publish white papers, articles and (less frequently) books on business and technology trends. The publications also help drum up business for Diamond—after all, there's nothing like telling a company what they're missing as a means of persuading them to hire you to fill that void. In the UK, London insurance industry Partner Scott Bauer published a white paper in April 2008 on how insurers there should think about transforming their legacy information technology systems. Other recent publications include a treatise on how companies are ill-prepared to meet the needs of baby boomers as they approach retirement, and Diamond Fellow Dan Ariely's *Predictably Irrational: The Hidden Forces That Shape Our Decisions*, published in February 2008.

Ariely presented some of the book's findings at the company's DiamondExchange— a membership-based forum for executives and business leaders aimed at spreading understanding of how to use technology to gain competitive advantage. Ariely's findings include the insight that irrelevant influences can drive consumers to make irrational purchases.

Focussing on expansion

Following the 2006 reorganisation, Diamond has increasingly focussed on expanding its offerings in its current areas, rather than attempting to expand geographically. In London, Diamond has grown in its core industry sectors of financial services, private equity, retail and consumer packaged goods, with many top-tier firms appearing on its client list and coming back for repeat business. Along those same lines, the firm established the Diamond Information & Analytics Center in Mumbai in 2006 to offer more information and data analysis to its clients—a move that had been requested by clients themselves. Among the services offered by the centre are analytics to uncover and realise new revenue and cost savings, tracking and measurement of key strategic business metrics, and information strategy, which boils down to finding ways to increase competitive advantage.

These new developments seem to be pushing Diamond in the right direction. Net revenue for the first three quarters of fiscal 2008 was up 11 per cent compared to the same period in 2007. That's on top of a 16 per cent increase in full-year revenue between 2006 and 2007—a year that saw the firm boost its customer base by 30 per cent. Looking ahead through 2008, meanwhile, CEO Adam Gutstein is hoping for revenue growth of 15 per cent overall—a figure the firm may still be on track to achieve, despite an increasingly difficult economic climate.

Feeling groovy

Having watched its share price drop precipitously in recent years, however, the firm evidently feels that it is still undervalued—in February 2008, company directors authorised an increase of $25 million to Diamond's existing stock repurchase programme, a development that brings the total authorisation to some $56 million. That's not a move usually made by a company that feels bad times are ahead, and Diamond's confidence has been bolstered by several long-term contracts. For example, in May 2007, the firm was awarded a five-year management, organisational and business improvement services contract with the US General Services Administration. Under the terms of the agreement, Diamond will provide a variety of strategic consulting and programme management services to US federal agencies. Indeed, the deal was such a big one for the firm that it broke its habit of not announcing the identities of its clients to broadcast the news.

GETTING HIRED

Come prepared for cases

Securing a position in Diamond's UK practice reportedly requires a "very lengthy interviewing process", involving "case-based interviews and fit-focussed interviews". For recent graduates, "Diamond has two to three rounds of interviews," the first of which "consists of one interview, including a case study." This interview is normally "one-on-one and roughly 30 minutes". Typically, "first-round interviews for undergraduates and MBAs take place on campus." The second round is what's known as "Analyst Day, which takes place in the London office with up to 16 candidates". During this round, "there are case study interviews, a group exercise and a numeracy test, followed by a dinner with several Diamond consultants at all levels." The final round is with a partner, and is "usually confirmation that you're the right choice". MBA-level applicants also go through "three rounds of interviews, which include cases". Experienced hires may "not have any special tests", but should still come prepared for "a mixture of business and technical case studies".

Diamond Management & Technology Consultants, Inc.

Candidates may be asked such questions as, "Can you calculate the size of the market for X type of product within the UK?" or other "standard consultancy case study questions" such as, "How many light bulbs are in the UK?" and "How many passengers ride on the Millennium Wheel per year?" The firm recruits from a "range of top universities," including Oxford and Cambridge for undergraduate recruiting, and London Business School and London School of Economics for graduates. Diamond, we're told, "participates in the major graduate career fairs in London".

Smaller is better

Most Diamond consultants say they chose this firm over others because it is a "smaller firm, which makes people feel less like a small cog in a big machine". Plus, "the size of the practice makes it easier to interact and get to know other members of the firm." A contact says of his decision to join Diamond, "I wanted to make more of a difference to the bottom line." Diamond consultants have refused offers from competitors in order to be a part of the firm's "personal-touch" culture. An "impressive client list" and "intellectually challenging work" are also a draw. Diamond affords consultants "the opportunity to combine business and technology strategy", as well as "freedom and room to operate."

OUR SURVEY SAYS

Small-firm feel

Diamond's UK office is filled with "great, smart people who are easy to get along with." It's a "close-knit group that likes to have fun". This "collegiate, inclusive" firm "values people", insiders tell us, and treats employee and client relationships with "a personal touch". There's a "good sense of community", and "principals and partners are very approachable." In addition, the firm's small size allows it to stay "innovative, entrepreneurial and agile". Consultants are attracted to the "small-office feel", which allows for an "extremely flat and friendly environment". Sources explain that Diamond consultants are "highly cooperative", as well as "hardworking and efficient". There are "regular social events", and many co-workers know each other "on a personal level".

But Diamond's size also has its downsides: At times, the "smaller office and organisation results in being more susceptible to external factors, such as failing client relationships". But most consider the firm's culture one of its "greatest assets". It's a place where junior consultants are able to have "high-profile impact at clients" and "can expect to get involved in all aspects of the firm, from hiring to business development". Generally speaking, "people are collaborative, friendly and always willing to go out of their way to assist with requests." In the words of one consultant, there is a "real feeling of cooperation that comes with a firm that is smaller than its rivals".

No one left behind

Due to the small size of Diamond's European operations, consultants enjoy "lots of interaction" with clients and supervisors. "Diamond cannot afford to have analysts beavering away in the back office." Instead, "the whole team is on site and seen by the client." Consultants enjoy working with "very good quality people at all levels", and there is a "great opportunity to work with the clients' C-level executives." Internally, "partners' doors are always open." In the UK, the majority of Diamond's clients are "big names within the financial services industry." As one consultant notes, "Sometimes you get staffed on projects you are not interested in," but the work is "varied" and provides "a lot of exposure" nonetheless.

A day at the beach

At Diamond, we're told, "you have to work hard, but the hours are less intense than other consultancies." Project length varies, but the "average is about three-to-six months," insiders explain. Most consultants log between 50 and 60 hours per week. According to one respondent, "When I am not staffed on a project, I tend to work 9am to 6pm. While on projects, work hours tend to be longer and normally peak closer to an important deliverable."

Due to Diamond's small size, the firm has "above-average beach time". Insiders say this is because the firm's "resourcing pipeline is hard to predict". While some projects are as short as six weeks, there is "some potential to be involved in long-tailed execution projects", and at times, there is the "challenge of trying to do too many things and cover too many fronts, resulting in overambitious objectives and people spread too thin across many fronts". This is particularly true "on nonclient-related initiatives."

A healthy balance

The bright side to long-term projects is that "it enables you to set your pace and work the hours that best suit you." Overall, "there is a very good respect for people's family time, and support from senior management to ensure balance." "Managers usually help protect your weekend." And for nights or weekends that do require extra hours, insiders say that Diamond is "very flexible" and allows people to "head home to complete work on their laptops." Work/life balance can "depend on the type of project you have," a consultant notes, but "the fact that chargeability is not a key metric for consultants alleviates a bit of the pressure." One source explains, "Ultimately, any job in consulting will result in work infringing into personal life, but at Diamond, this is kept to a minimum." A colleague agrees, "Don't expect to be able to get to your 6pm class, but at Diamond, I never feel robbed of my time." There is "no face time" required at the firm and "a good balance between work and free time is definitely considered as important."

Staying close to home

Also contributing to a favourable work/life balance is that, unlike at many consultancies, Diamond's UK practice does not demand much travel. Most projects are "London-focussed", which "results in minimal travel". Consultants "travel a lot less now than we used to in the telco-heavy years". Average time spent on the road is "20 to 30 per cent", consultants say, and "often only within

> " Diamond has a GLBT network and offers equal opportunities to all. "

Europe". Projects that do require travel abroad "usually involve four days a week away and one day back in the office", typically Friday. For those who desire travel, "there are often opportunities to work on projects in the US, across Europe or even in the Middle East and Asia." For the most part, however, "work is primarily London-based."

The compensation breakdown

Diamond consultants give overall high marks to their compensation packages. Employees receive "restricted stock upon joining" and many receive "sign-on bonuses". The breakdown for bonuses is typically "50 per cent cash, 50 per cent equity"—some feel, though, that "the proportion of the equity and cash should be reviewed." A consultant explains, "Given that the equity is given in the form of restricted stock, people cannot use their bonuses straight away." Overall, pay at Diamond is "not exceptional, but competitive", and some say bonuses are "low compared to the market and to what they should be". There is opportunity, however, for "rapid increases in pay". The firm explains that, on average, compensation raises range from £3,000 to £8000 per year as analysts move from analyst to associate in their first three years. As successful consultants progress to the level of senior associate, their salary typically increases another £21,000.

These increases correspond to Diamond's "transparent promotion policy", which allows for "rapid advancement", we're told. Typically, "consultants advance every year, with a title change every two years." Sometimes, though, "consultants spend an extra year to develop and demonstrate that they are ready for more responsibility." The firm has a "fairly flexible up-or-out" policy, as "the rate of progress can vary a bit" from person to person. The norm, however, is "two years at each level", with a "12-year path to partner". A contact says, "We don't have a strict up-or-out policy, but it's informally expected that Diamond consultants should be striving to move upward every year." Most agree that "if you perform well, you will be promoted rapidly."

Lots to be thankful for

Diamond offers "the usual lot" of perks and benefits, insiders report. Employees get "private medical insurance" and "travel insurance", and "mobile phone bills are covered up to £45." The firm is "generous with travel benefits, such as decent hotels and business-class flights for long-haul travel". Consultants have "four weeks holiday" in addition to "bank holidays and carry-over days", and the firm also allows "disconnecting days"—six days a year, taken on a Friday or Monday, to "connect onto weekends to make long weekends". These can be taken "every two months". As for benefits come baby time, Diamond offers "two-to-three weeks of paternity leave", and women typically take "three-to-six months of maternity leave". The firm is "quite flexible about arrangements for new parents, from ensuring limited travel to offering four-day working weeks."

Perhaps the most raved-about perk at Diamond is the thrice-yearly All Hands event, held in Chicago. Insiders say the event is a "great opportunity to interact with your peers and to share great, fun moments". Diamond also holds "subsidised annual ski trips", as well as "company-sponsored social events every other month in London" and off-site "office days' four times a year.

Diamond also grants "special time allowances" for community involvement. The firm has a "corporate citizenship programme that allows employees to spend one or two working days per year working for a charity". There's also "a charity donation matching scheme". Diamond offers "financial sponsorship of individuals doing fund-raising sporting events, and encourages participation in community events". Despite these initiatives, some say the firm's corporate citizenship programme has had a "hard time gaining traction".

Location, location, location

Most respondents also consider the firm's "cool London location", complete with a "kitchen loaded with breakfast goodies and healthy snacks", as a major perk. Insiders say the office is a "comfortable, pleasant and conducive working environment," and welcome the facility's open plan and foosball table. Consultants note that Diamond's London office is "central and in a very attractive area, with access to plenty of good restaurants and shops." A contact explains, "The office is located right between SoHo and Covent Garden, which is great for drinks after work on a Friday!"

It's what you make of it

Diamond recently has made "lots of improvement in the area of formal training," but insiders say there is "still some ground to cover to reach the level that a top-notch consulting firm should have". The firm offers official training, "typically taking place in Chicago" for five to seven days. In addition, "there are training courses that take place in London that tend to be one-day or half-day courses." Led by senior consultants, sources deem these sessions "very useful". However, formal training "depends on project commitments, and you are unable to go if on a project." Fortunately, there is "a lot of on-the-job coaching" as well, and "funds for external training are available." Diamond places a "strong emphasis on mentoring", but "it is up to the consultant to seek out their training needs and make it happen."

Receptive to everyone

Diamond has a "very good proportion of ethnic minorities", with consultants from "many countries across Europe and Asia". According to one source, "At last count, there were 12 nationalities in an office of 45 people," including "consultants from India, the Philippines, Malaysia and Peru." In fact, some claim there are "probably as many minorities as locals". At this "very diverse" firm, insiders are proud to say, minorities are "not treated any differently by fellow consultants".

In addition, the firm is "very committed" to providing a welcoming environment for gays, lesbians, bisexuals and transgender individuals. "Diamond has a GLBT network and offers equal opportunities to all, regardless of sexual preferences." The firm's leadership is "accepting" and employs people "regardless of sexual orientation". These individuals are "highly respected and totally open about it".

On the gender front, sources agree that there are "not enough women in senior management". There are "loads of women in the office", but "most are at the junior level." Still, there is "proportionally a good ratio of women for a consulting organisation", and the firm offers a "global women's network that provides mentor matching and other support". Respondents say the firm remains "very receptive" to female employees and all are given "equal opportunities to male counterparts". □

DROEGE & COMP.

David-Hansemann-Haus
Poststrasse 5-6
40213 Düsseldorf
Germany
Phone: +49 (0)211 867 310
Fax: +49 (0)211 867 311 11
www.droege.de

The Stats

Employer Type: Private Company
Managing Director: Dr Christian Horn
2007 Employees: 300
2006 Employees: 250
No. of Offices: 15

Practice Areas

Corporate Systems/IT
Financial Consulting
Innovation/R&D
Maintenance/Facility Management
Marketing
Organization/Management
Personnel
Post Merger Integration
Production/Supply Chain Management
Public Private Partnership
Purchasing/Sourcing
Sales
Turnaround Management/Restructuring

European Locations

Düsseldorf (HQ)
Bucharest • Budapest • Hamburg •
London • Lucerne • Moscow • Munich
• Paris • Vienna • Warsaw

Plus

• Competitive salaries

Minus

• Limited diversity

Employment Contact

Follow the careers link at
www.droege.de

THE BUZZ
WHAT CONSULTANTS AT OTHER FIRMS ARE SAYING

• "Niche player"
• "Lost magic touch"
• "Solid but not exciting"
• "'The firm is your family' culture"

THE SCOOP

D roege & Comp.'s motto encourages its employees to practise the "art of consulting", which requires a delicate and intricate knowledge that comes together in the "unity of conception and action". These German consulting artists have been colouring the landscape since 1988, when Walter P.J. Droege started the firm with aspirations of elevating the level of consulting. The firm's strategy is to boost efficiency quietly and to produce tangible results with a process that appears effortless. With offices across Europe, as well as in the United States and Asia Pacific, Droege has built a distinctive footprint.

The company's consulting practice covers strategy and portfolio management, operational excellence, organisational and leadership improvement, finance management, turnaround management, and change and communication strategies. It draws 51 per cent of its clients from the industrial sector, 31 per cent from the financial services sector and 18 per cent from other service-based companies. Droege's employees have expertise in the automotive, banking, chemicals and health care, energy and utilities, retail and consumer goods, high-tech and telecoms, mechanical and plant engineering, insurance and transport sectors.

Five steps to success

The consultancy outlines five central principles to its strategy for success. The first is "implementation right from the outset", which means that clients can expect the firm to get to work right away. The next principle is speed, a value that helps keep Droege in the game with an increasingly large pool of competitors. In addition to helping it best its competition, Droege also believes that speedy delivery actually produces better results. The third pillar of Droege's business is its payment structure, under which the company will only get paid if clients see results. Droege then emphasises the virtue of trust, which it strives to build with clients to encourage repeat customers. So far, this has paid off handsomely: More than two-thirds of the firm's business comes from former clients. Lastly, the firm believes in "implementation in accordance with the state of the art", meaning that Droege consultants utilise the most modern and complex tools available to them.

Making mergers and acquisitions work

With German M&A business booming, Droege & Comp is working to smooth the transition for companies in motion. In February 2007, the firm released a study that aimed to dispel commonly held beliefs about the M&A process that hinder the integration of newly merged companies. Many of these myths come from a specific "playbook" that companies believe they must follow when merging. Droege insists that common misconceptions include "a deal is a deal," "10 per cent is a magic number" and "we need to let at least 300 employees go." The consultancy also predicts that extra liquidity in the Asian markets might make German companies the targets of future acquisitions.

Sights set on Southeast Asia

Much of Droege's international expansion efforts are directed toward the burgeoning economies of Southeast Asia. Its headquarters in Asia is located in Singapore and covers a wide territory, including Malaysia, Indonesia, Vietnam, China and India. The firm's research team recently completed a study of German companies in Singapore, with mostly positive findings: The country's stock market has been prosperous for five straight years, and continues to show room for growth. However, Droege is concerned about the inevitable inflation that comes with a booming market. In November 2007, the firm invited more than 400 German companies to size up the challenges and opportunities in the Singapore market. Droege summarised the main points of the conference as follows: Local product development is key to sales opportunities; German companies must partner with Singaporean companies for success; Vietnam and Malaysia are the next frontier of outsourcing; and the biggest challenge to German firms in Asia is the inability to retain skilled personnel. Time will tell how these findings will affect Droege's future expansion in the region.

> ❝ Droege takes an 'implementation-oriented approach' to projects. ❞

Moving into Mumbai

The consultancy expanded its business into India in April 2007 with the launch of an office in Mumbai. The firm plans to provide a bridge between Europe and India by providing advice to both German companies who wish to invest in Indian businesses and vice versa. The sectors that Droege plans to cover in India include automotives, pharmaceuticals, engineering and manufacturing. Asia currently represents a significant portion of Droege's total international revenue, and with the launch of the Mumbai office, the company is expecting that number to increase to 50 per cent. At the time of the expansion, Managing Director Christian Horn said, "We started our Asian operations 10 years ago and with our entry in India we look forward to be[ing] a frontrunner for German companies who want to invest in India, as the interest for investment in India is increasing in Germany."

GETTING HIRED

You better have it all

On its web site, Droege emphasises that the "main prerequisites" for starting a career with the firm are expertise, enthusiasm, creativity, a winning presence, confidence and leadership skills, sensitivity in dealing with people and a track record working abroad. Oh, and by the way, candidates should also have "an honors degree in economics, engineering or science from a reputed university". A doctorate or MBA is even better.

That's not to say that there aren't options for fresh university graduates. Entry-level candidates can get a foot in the door through Droege's fellowship programme, a two- to three-month internship. One former intern recalls that the programme gave him a "chance to gain real consultant experience", including "direct contact" with clients, and that "people were very supportive." Sources say Droege recruits at schools such as University of Mannheim, TU Darmstadt EBS, TU München and Unversität zu Münster, among others.

One-day turnaround

Interested parties can apply for either a consultant or fellow position by completing an online application form and submitting a cover letter, CV and references. Those who fit the bill for a consultant position will be contacted "within 10 working days" and brought in for a first round of "four interviews". These meetings may include "brief applicant presentations" as well as case studies. If all goes well, a second round includes interviews with two partners. Fellowship applicants go through just "a single round of interviews". And there's no need to wonder for long as to how the meetings went: At each stage, applicants will get feedback "on the next working day" regarding whether they are "still in the running".

Those who wish to know more about Droege before applying are encouraged to inquire about recruiting events by contacting a recruiting coordinator through an online form.

OUR SURVEY SAYS

High points

On the whole, insiders praise Droege as a "top management consulting" firm with an "implementation-oriented approach" and a culture that is "very open" and "down-to-earth". Training opportunities abound in the "Droege & Comp. Academy", which is "staffed with external professionals". Other perks include "direct insurance", car leasing and offices in "great locations" filled with "great art". On top of that, a happy staffer in Düsseldorf insists that the "team, project and company events are really great." ☐

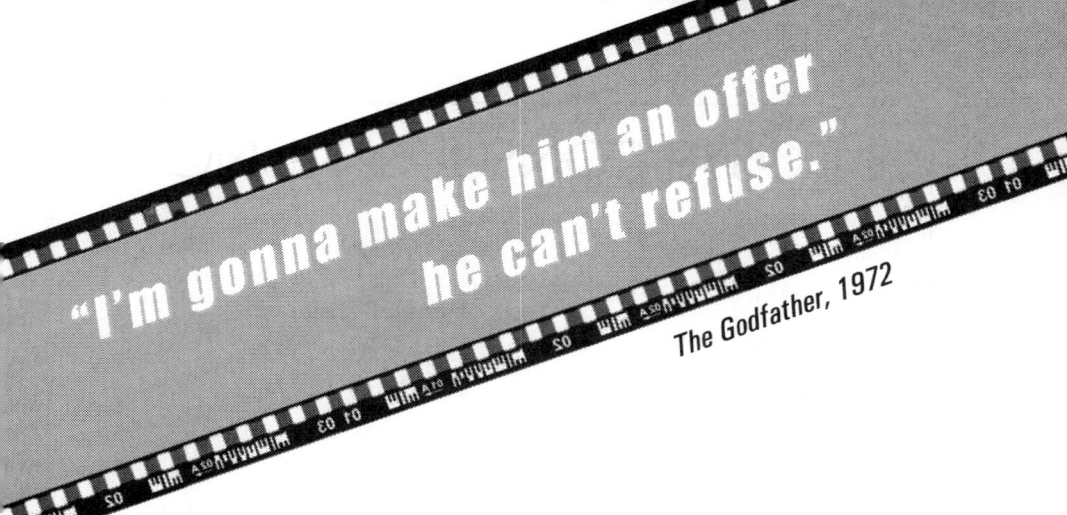

"I'm gonna make him an offer he can't refuse."

The Godfather, 1972

Find a job. Ace the interview.
Get a job you can't refuse.

Search the Vault job board.

Browse thousands of vacancies by industry, function or location.

Sign up for Vault's weekly Job Newsletter and receive jobs directly to your inbox.

www.vault.com/europe

INFOSYS CONSULTING INC.

14th Floor
10 Upper Bank Street
Canary Wharf
London E145NP
United Kingdom
Phone: +44 (0)207 715 3300
Fax: +44 (0)207 715 3301
www.infosysconsulting.com

The Stats

Employer Type: Public Company
Ticker Symbol: INFY (Nasdaq)
CEO (Infosys Technologies Ltd.):
  S. Gopalakrishnan
CEO (Infosys Consulting Inc.): Stephen
  R. Pratt
Nonexecutive Chairman of the Board
& Chief Mentor: N.R. Narayana Murthy
2008 Employees: 91,100+
2007 Employees: 80,500+
2008 Revenue: $4.18 billion (global
  revenue for all Infosys)
2007 Revenue: $3.1 billion (global
  revenue for all Infosys)
No. of Offices: 42 offices worldwide

Practice Areas

Aerospace & Defense • Banking &
Capital Markets • Communication
Service Providers • High Tech &
Discrete Manufacturing • Insurance,
Healthcare & Life Sciences • Media &
Entertainment • Resources, Energy &
Utilities • Retail, Distribution &
Consumer Packaged Goods •
Transportation Services

European Locations

Fremont, CA (HQ)
London

Pluses

- "Growing at an aggressive pace"
- "Open culture that allows constructive dissent"
- Diverse client roster

Minuses

- "Multiple business units are often poor in collaborating as one"
- "Blind focus on billability"
- Materials and experience not always properly reapplied to new projects

Employment Contact

www.infosysconsulting.com/
  join_the_ team.htm
E-mail: recruiting@infosysconsulting.com

THE BUZZ
WHAT CONSULTANTS AT OTHER FIRMS ARE SAYING

- "Growth company"
- "Not seen in Europe"
- "Best for leadership development (or so they say)"
- "Outsourcer trying to enter the strategy scene"

THE SCOOP

nfosys Consulting was created in 2004 as a means of expanding Indian tech outsourcing giant Infosys' business offerings. Based around a model that offers increased value for its clients, IC is committed to making companies more competitive, and is prepared to leverage all the contacts its parent firm has to make this happen. A good deal of the firm's strategy is tied up in offering consulting on a global scale, in much the same way that Infosys helped pioneer global outsourcing—there's no reason that strategising and technical analysis of a company needs to take place on the client's premises, after all. And if it's going to happen on IC's premises, then why not their premises in India? Oh … and if IC's consulting activities should happen to coincide with the need for some outsourcing to help a client become more efficient? So much the better—Infosys can take care of that, too.

A chip off the old block

Infosys is a $3 billion a year enterprise that started up in India in 1981, specialising in providing technological solutions for firms. In its early years, the firm offered IT services to the domestic Indian market, but was soon branching out to non-Indian clients, and scored GE as one of its first major successes. From there, the firm gathered top clients from an array of industries, including American Express, Boeing, Apple and J.C. Penney.

Infosys' revenue topped $100 million in 1999, the same year it became the first Indian company listed on the Nasdaq stock exchange. Within five years, that figure shot up $1 billion, as more and more companies sought its expertise and outsourcing capabilities, especially as the bursting of the tech bubble in the early years of the millennium caused many to look for ways to slash costs.

Come 2004, Infosys decided to expand the range of services it offered clients, creating subsidiary firm Infosys Consulting to help muscle in on a seemingly lucrative business area; "seemingly", as the subsidiary has yet to turn a profit for the group. Not that it's held the Infosys juggernaut back any—the group's $3 billion in revenue in fiscal 2007 represented a tripling of that particular figure in just three years, and grew to $4.18 billion in fiscal 2008. Global headcount now exceeds 91,000, up from 80,000 in 2007.

Heads up, big guys

"We specialize in making companies more competitive. That is our singular focus." So sayeth the company literature, in an attempt to do for IC a portion of what it proposes to do for its clients—creating "strategic differentiation" to show how the firm is different from competitors in its field. The other half of the equation is in figuring out how to run the firm better than its competitors—something IC calls "operational superiority". And, as every schoolboy surely learned in consulting class, operational superiority plus strategic differentiation equals competitiveness.

Having scooped up 20-year consulting veteran Stephen Pratt as its CEO and managing director from rival firm Deloitte (where he had served as senior partner for 12 years), the consultancy has steadfastly followed a policy of recruiting the top-10 per cent of consultants from the top firms, offering commensurate salaries and benefits to seal the deal. As further proof of the strategy, IC also lured Managing Directors Romil Bahl, Raj Joshi and Ming Tsai from EDS, Deloitte and IBM, respectively. Those consultants, and many more, are in turn helping IC compete for business with the very firms they were recruited from, establishing IC as a major up-and-comer in the consulting world.

24/7—literally

One of the ways in which Infosys Consulting delivers operational superiority to its clients is by utilising a global delivery model. In much the same way as its parent became known for being able to turn around software solutions and provide outsourcing by utilising foreign locations (not to mention lower-cost labour), IC uses centres in China and India to conduct work it generates in the UK and US. So when it's nighttime in the West, there's no need for the consulting and solution making to stop—it can go on in the East, and be ready for the clients when they arrive at work in the morning.

If there's one area where IC could use a boost, it's in its European dealings—it's somewhat light on the ground on the continent, generating most of its business across the Atlantic in the US. While that's not necessarily a problem, given the size of the US market, it does leave IC exposed to fluctuations in the value of the dollar. Perhaps because of those concerns, IC was linked with a takeover of European giant Capgemini in June 2007, which ultimately proved to be little more than speculation that fizzled when Capgemini acquired Indian firm Kanbay International in October that year—a deal that took the consultancy into Infosys' territory instead. But given that IC and its parent company have both tended toward organic growth rather than growth by acquisition in the past, the mooted deal with Capgemini had never seemed likely to many industry analysts.

When less is more

Infosys Consulting's approach is perhaps best summed up in the words of its own executives. CEO and Managing Director Steve Pratt told *BusinessWeek* in April 2007 that the difference between his current firm and his previous one was that "at Deloitte, a good day was to get a client to pay more. We'd high-five each other. But at Infosys a good day is when we can figure out how to charge the client less. And we'd high-five each other for that." If that's not evidence of a shift in direction, then how about the sentiments of Managing Director Romil Bahl? In July 2007, *Consulting* magazine named him one of its top-25 consultants of the year. In an interview with the publication, Bahl stated, "We absolutely want to eradicate some of the abuses of the consulting industry." Abuses? In consulting? Yes, says Bahl, abuses like "walking into a client and within 10 minutes tell them how to run their business." According to Bahl, "those days are over. Now, the client absolutely expects and demands delivery." And Infosys Consulting is trying to ensure that the client gets it.

GETTING HIRED

More selective than Harvard

Visitors to the Infosys online careers page are greeted with an excerpt from a *Fortune* magazine profile of the company, comparing Infosys' acceptance rate of applicants to that of Harvard. The firm actually puts Harvard to shame, accepting a mere 1 per cent of applicants, while Harvard claims to admit a whopping 10 per cent. Candidates willing to put their resumes to the test have the option of creating a profile and browsing job openings online. Opportunities can be narrowed down to country, sector, title and area of technical expertise. That fortunate fraction of candidates who are chosen (labelled "Infoscions" by the company) are promised "a place where people work in a campus-like facility and culture, are unafraid to voice new ideas" and "where there is minimal hierarchy", says the firm.

When under consideration, applicants are subject to a "rigorous" hiring process, according to a senior principal, who describes an "average of four to five interviews—a combination of phone and face-to-face". Another source describes the experience as consisting of "one telephone interview and one office interview with one to two partners and one to two senior principals. I would say the interview process is friendly but comprehensive." An insider in London recalls the questions as being "the usual—leadership, teamwork, drive—but also questions like, 'What makes you interesting to work with?'"

A solid first step

The company sponsors an internship programme known as InStep. It is a global and highly organised undertaking, providing students with airfare to India, room and board, transportation once settled and a stipend. Interns, encompassing undergraduate, graduate and PhD students, are placed on live projects, and serve with the company for eight to 24 weeks. To accommodate all possible academic calendars, the programme is active year-round. As with the firm's open positions, hopeful interns can apply for InStep online.

OUR SURVEY SAYS

True to its country of origin

Even in locations abroad, the firm is very much an Indian company. A consultant in London reports that the "population is largely Indian in the office, approximately 90 per cent. The rest are local hires." The corporate culture is heavily influenced by the technical employees, since the consulting side of the business is still in a "nascent" stage, says the source. "Hence," a colleague points out, "working in consulting may not be that lucrative in terms of recognition. The delivery (technical people) call the shots." Some consultants are far more comfortable, however. Another Londoner calls the culture "quite open and value-based", while others attest to the firm's "entrepreneurial" nature.

On your own

Maintaining a favourable work/life balance at Infosys is possible, but certainly requires effort. As an insider explains, "Due to client commitments, time spent on activities like building new methodologies, go-to-market strategies and toolkits, and recruiting require work outside normal working hours." Accepting the reality of these commitments means "balance is a personal objective," according to a co-worker. "The firm does not hinder work/life balance," the contact adds, but "probably should do more to promote it". It's important to know your personal limits, but luckily, as a principal has found, "If you say no, they listen!" Most respondents report working 50 to 60 hours a week.

Travel also plays a big part in these consultants' lives. As a source says, "The London office is small and covers a large chunk of Europe—travelling comes with the territory." Voyaging can take its toll, as it's "not good for social life, but good for work output". As with other balance issues, though, an insider believes the travel is, in a word, "manageable. If it gets to be a problem, you just make clear what is OK and let the management sort it out." It will also vary depending on the assignment and circumstances. For one insider, "Travel has been minimal in my specific case, as I've been on an in-town assignment for most of my tenure. Infosys was extremely flexible, however, in allowing me to work from Germany for a number of months before I moved to the London office."

Pass the popcorn

Regarding compensation, to which most give middling marks, respondents are more excited about the perks. In addition to a typical benefits package, the company awards discretionary spot bonuses. An insider considers it "a small thing, but endearing—we receive 'popcorn' awards anytime we do something above and beyond what is expected of us. For example, when I worked a weekend on a proposal, my partner awarded me £100 to have a nice dinner with my wife. This was very well received." There is also a pension plan, allowing 6 per cent employee contributions with 6 per cent matching.

The self-taught will thrive

The promotion track at Infosys is "reasonably outlined", according to one staffer, and most agree that it's entirely merit-based. A principal observes, "Consultants advance only when they've demonstrated certain capabilities." Another agrees, calling the process "performance-driven". The firm may not recognise contributions immediately, however. A source remarks, "Sadly, you advance about one year after you are ready."

And all this readiness will have to be of your own making. A senior principal claims "training is virtually nonexistent." Colleagues agree, finding there is "no clear process for obtaining training" and "very little formal training, but good on-the-job training." A principal suggests the firm's small size may be a factor in the lack of formalised instruction.

It's a man's world

Gender diversity is scarce at Infosys, which one source calls "male-oriented, but not by policy". A cohort agrees: "Just looking at the ratio between men and women—I would suggest this could improve!" Still, this is not an automatic sign of discrimination, as the nature of the business can lead to some disproportionate numbers of men, respondents explain. A consultant insists, "I think women are treated fairly and at the same level as men." □

Infosys Consulting Inc.

LOGICA

Stephenson House
21 Hampstead Road
London NW1 2PL
United Kingdom
Phone: +44 (0)207 637 9111
Fax: +44 (0)207 468 7006
www.logica.com

The Stats

Employer Type: Public Company
Ticker Symbol: LOG (LSE,
   Amsterdam Euronext)
CEO: Andy Green
2008 Employees: 39,000
2007 Employees: 40,000+
2007 Revenue: £3.07 billion
2006 Revenue: £2.4 billion
No. of Offices: 90+

Practice Areas

Application Management • Business
Process Outsourcing • Consulting
Services • Enterprise Asset Management •
Enterprise Resource Planning • Finance
& Accounting • HR/Payroll Services •
Infrastructure Management •
Outsourcing • Security • Testing •
Wireless Enterprise Solutions

European Locations

London (HQ)
Belgium • Czech Republic • Denmark •
Estonia • Finland • France • Germany •
Hungary • Luxembourg • Netherlands •
Norway • Poland • Portugal • Russia •
Slovakia • Spain • Sweden • Switzerland •
Ukraine • United Kingdom

Pluses

• "Good management consultancy
  branding"
• "It's rarely boring, and we get to tackle
  really hard problems"
• Flexible work-from-home policy

Minuses

• "Dealing with Bangalore"
• Training opportunities are insufficient
• Poor sales and marketing

Employment Contact

Go to the Careers section of the
company's web site for a full list of
European employment contacts by country

THE BUZZ
WHAT CONSULTANTS AT OTHER FIRMS ARE SAYING

• "Good but narrow"
• "Technologists, not business analysts"
• "State-of-the-art"
• "Systems- not client-oriented"

VAULT career library

THE SCOOP

L
ogica has been around (and defying expectations) in one form or another since 1969, when it was founded as a systems integration business in the breathtakingly futuristic world of computing. These days, the company is a leading IT and business services provider that has incorporated several other brands—most notably its former rival, CMG—under its wing. Indeed, the firm formerly known as LogicaCMG dropped the CMG from its title as it formally rebranded all of its holdings under the Logica name in February 2008.

Scale and scope

Logica's 39,000 employees are distributed throughout 36 countries, offering solutions and services in the following market sectors: automotive, defence, energy, financial services, manufacturing, pharmaceutical, public sector, space, telecoms and media, transport, travel and logistics, and utilities. The firm also maintains new operating segment, outsourcing services, created as part of an ongoing review of its operations, the results of which were released in April 2008 and are detailed below.

The firm offers services covering everything from consulting to business process outsourcing, meaning it can not only do research and make recommendations to its clients, but it can also follow up on them by providing some of the services itself. The scale of the company's operations is such that anyone who has sent a text message, bought a ticket from a machine to ride the London Underground or transferred money between bank accounts internationally has probably used a system designed by Logica; little wonder, then, that it cleared £3 billion in revenue in 2007.

Growth—they've got IT covered

Starting out in the UK, Logica has steadily expanded its global presence over the years, making several acquisitions along the way to speed the process along. While the firm has a presence on all six continents, however, the vast majority of its holdings (and therefore its revenue generation) are in Western Europe. Many of these holdings were acquired during the 2002 merger with telecoms consulting specialist CMG—a move that was pilloried on Fleet Street, but which ultimately proved a winner for the firm. Critics of the deal pointed to the fact that there would be major integration issues between the two firms, and that neither was adequately equipped to provide the levels of outsourcing some were claiming.

In what must surely be a first, the journalists and commentators seem to have got it wrong. Rather than falling apart at the seams, LogicaCMG continued to grow and make further acquisitions throughout the early years of the new millennium, primarily within Europe. In April 2005, the firm acquired some 60 per cent of Edinfor, a supplier of IT services based in Portugal, before buying up the remaining 40 per cent in March 2008. In early 2006, meanwhile, the firm snapped up French IT services entity Unilog in a deal worth some €930 million, before expanding its Nordic offerings in October that year with the €1.3 billion purchase of Sweden's WM-Data.

The one area where Logica has failed to impress, however, is in the stock market. Years of underwhelming performance led investors to oust longtime CEO Martin Read in May 2007. After a search that lasted several months, his successor, Andy Green, was unveiled the following October. Green joined the company from BT, where he had been serving as head of strategy, and had been tipped to eventually take over as CEO.

> ❝ We're often fun to work for, and we do get to do the interesting stuff. ❞

Evidently the challenge of turning around Logica's business (not to mention a generous compensation package) was enough to lure him to the consultancy, and he officially took over the reins in December 2007.

European core

Logica's revenue is divided by region, which gives an accurate picture of exactly where the company makes its profits. Unsurprisingly, the single most valuable country for the firm is the UK, where £662.5 million in revenue represented some 22 per cent of the firm's total for 2007. That figure was down from the 30 per cent generated in 2006, however, a drop of some £56 million from the £718 million posted in 2006—results that were ultimately blamed for putting pressure on outgoing CEO Martin Read.

The only region that generates more revenue for Logica is the combined Nordic countries, which together pulled in some 27 per cent of revenue in 2007. This represents an increase of 19 per cent in the Nordic region's contribution from 2006—a figure almost entirely attributable to the addition of WM-Data in 2006. Other Western European revenue generators are as follows: Germany (6 per cent), Netherlands (16 per cent) and France (19 per cent). Perhaps the most surprising figure is the general "international" reporting segment, which consists of everything not in Western Europe, and includes operations on six continents. In 2007, that category generated only 10 per cent of total firm's revenue, down from 14 per cent in 2006.

Under the radar, but not for long

Despite being one of the biggest tech consulting firms in the world, Logica tends to go unnoticed due to the unspectacular nature of some of the work it carries out. To combat this, the firm issues regular reminders of some of its crowning achievements, which also serve as an indicator of just how big a concern it is. Headline stats include the revelation that Logica's financial systems for banks transfer the equivalent of the USA's annual GDP every single day, while its software supports around a third of the world's satellites. Some of Logica's key clients include blue-chip titans such as Ford and Shell, as well as government departments such as the UK Defence and Justice Ministries.

There are signs, however, that the new management at the firm is more interested in both recognition and spreading the business globally. Speaking in February 2008 about the decision to brand all the companies under the firm's aegis with the Logica name, CEO Green explained, "We are committed to providing our customers with excellent local services, whilst at the same time combining this with the innovative capabilities and expertise of a 39,000 strong global organisation." Green then backed this statement with actions, hiring a new chief executive of global operations in April 2008. Craig Boundy opted to leave his post as COO of Cable and Wireless' business in Europe to take over the running of Logica's global delivery, a position that includes consolidating processes across the firm, and managing its offshore outsourcing capabilities in India, Morocco and the Philippines.

In addition to key personnel, the firm also took the step of creating an outsourcing division in early 2008—a decision aimed at consolidating its existing offerings and examining the potential for further expansion of this service in the future. As part of this effort, Logica announced the opening of a new facility in Chennai, India, in June 2008, which will add some 1,500 staff in the region and further increase the firm's stated aim of relating to customers locally, but offering cost savings by utilising international expertise—or cheap labour, as it used to be called.

Self-awareness helps bring about improvements

All of the recent changes are part of a wider review of operations that the firm announced in January 2008, and delivered the following April. After the review, Green released two lists that will be crucial to the future direction of the firm—the first is of things he likes about the firm (or "positives", as the firm called them), while the second is billed "areas for improvement". On the former list are the company's staff and customers, its strong local operations, blended delivery methodology and the fact that the consultancy operates as a key partner for many of its clients. Needing improvement, however, are the firm's focus on sales, growth at the group level (which will require investment), cost of overheads, size of the delivery model, the fragmented nature of the firm and lack of implementation on the "service" front. To counteract these, the firm has already taken some steps (to wit, the rebrand, global expansion and international outsourcing), and is working on strategies to improve its performance in other areas.

GETTING HIRED

Awards for presentation

Having garnered a recent award for the careers portion of its web site, there are few better places to start looking for information about careers with Logica. Along with phone numbers and e-mail addresses for recruiting contacts in each of the countries the firm operates in, the site contains a database of current vacancies, and allows candidates to apply by submitting a CV.

The company's graduate recruitment scheme is aimed at—guess who?—new or soon-to-be graduates, offering entry-level positions with a strong focus on project and teamwork, as well as the opportunity to work in different areas of the firm to find the best career fit. Logica is committed to helping new recruits make the transition from university to working life, and wants to make sure applicants are aware of the fact that frequent travel may be a part of the job from the outset. Interested parties can check out a series of testimonies on the site from recent graduate training alumni.

Experienced hires, meanwhile, will find the application and interview process to be a relatively simple affair. Following a CV screen, any candidate under consideration will be asked to participate in a 30-minute pre-interview online screening test. Should the test results prove the candidate's skills to be as advertised, the next stage of the process is an on-site interview with a manager from the business line to which the candidate has applied. A one-day affair at most, the interview isn't the only fast part of the process—applicants can expect a decision within a couple of days of the interview.

OUR SURVEY SAYS

Career liftoff

Folks at Logica seem genuinely proud of not only what they do, but how they do it. "We're often fun to work for," says one insider, "and we do get to do the interesting stuff, if that's what gets you out of bed in the morning." If "stuff" seems a bit vague, one source offers as an example the fact that "we do the software for all European

346

interplanetary space missions—it really is rocket science." Top that off with the "very strong team feeling", reported by a source in Amsterdam, as well as a decent work/life balance, and you have a fair summary of the bits staffers most appreciate about their firm. The work/life balance is made possible—for some—by the firm's commitment to "flexibility". That commitment allows a London-based consultant, for example, to be "in the office around two days a week, which I like, as I'm far more productive at home".

Must try harder

The one major drawback that staffers point to is the difficulty in climbing the corporate ladder. According to a source in the Netherlands, "promotion is a bit difficult," due to "strict and difficult rules for reaching other levels". That opinion is borne out in a testimony from a London-based cohort who reports that "one of my colleagues is grade 6, and has been doing the same consultancy job for 20 years. I've had the same grade for five years and don't expect to advance—there's only a handful of higher-grade consultants, and they tend to be management."

Another area where sources tick "room for improvement" on the Logica report card is in its approach to training. What training there is tends to be "heavily overbooked", according to one source, who also reckons that "useful trainings are scarce." That can be explained away a little, however, by a respondent in London, who tells us "there is no training course for the sorts of things I do." Perhaps that's why the source feels comfortable with the admission that he "went on a training course in 1994 and didn't like it, and haven't been on one since." □

MOTT MACDONALD BUSINESS & TECHNOLOGY CONSULTING DIVISION

St. Anne House, Wellesley Road
Croydon
London CR9 2UL
United Kingdom
Phone: +44 (0)208 774 2000
www.managementconsultancy.
 mottmac.com

The Stats

Employer Type: Subsidiary of Mott
 MacDonald Group
Managing Director, BTC Division:
 David Cox
2008 Employees: 122
2007 Employees: 118
2007 Revenue: £10.5 million
2006 Revenue: £10.3 million
No. of Offices: 10

Practice Areas

Business Process Re-engineering
Business & Systems Assurance
Commercial & Value Management
ICT Solutions
Organisational Change Management
Programme & Project Management
Public/Private Sector PPP/PFI Advisory
 Services
Risk Analysis & Management
Strategic Business Case
Strategic Procurement

European Locations

Croydon (HQ)
Belfast • Bristol • Cardiff • Edinburgh •
Glasgow • Leeds • London •
Manchester • Reading

Pluses

• "Interesting workloads"
• "Small-company feeling"
• Lots of opportunity for junior
 consultants

Minuses

• "Lack of mentoring, training and
 orientation into the basics of
 consulting"
• "Muddled structure creates internal
 politics"
• "Poor provisions for young families"

Employment Contact

www.careers.mottmac.com
E-mail: jo.kitt@mottmac.com

THE SCOOP

Mott MacDonald Business & Technology Consulting Division is, as the name suggests, a division of Mott MacDonald Group, a titan of the engineering and consulting world. Based in the UK, the parent company was created in 1989 as the result of a merger between two firms—Mott, Hay and Anderson, a transportation engineering firm, and the water consultancy outfit Sir Murdoch MacDonald and Partners. Founded in 1902 and 1921 respectively, the companies brought with them a history of working on large-scale projects such as the London Underground (Mott) and the Channel Tunnel (MacDonald).

These days, Mott MacDonald operates all over the globe, providing services from some 150 locations in 140 countries. Given the scale of its operations, it's sometimes difficult to separate exactly where the engineering consultancy ends and the business and technology consultancy begins, except that the latter appears to be confined to UK shores. Specialising in management strategy in 10 different practice areas, the firm serves a variety of sectors, both private and public, including central and local government, defence, education, energy, health care, property, telecommunications, transport, utilities and more.

> " The ambitious will rise, but the unambitious are not penalised. "

Mott's not-so-little black book

Mott MacDonald Group has worked on some prestigious engineering projects all over the world (Heathrow Terminal 5 or Dubai's Mall of the Emirates, anyone?), and has served some major clients. Operating mainly within the UK (but not afraid to take on global projects either—it is part of a global consultancy, after all), the BTC division has garnered some suitably impressive clients of its own, including BAE Systems, Shell and Barclays Bank in the private sector, and government departments including the Home Office, the Ministry of Defence and the National Health Service.

The BTC division is an accredited member of the Management Consultancies Association, while Mott MacDonald Group as a whole joined the Association for Consultancy and Engineering (ACE) in November 2007. Both memberships appear calculated to gain greater visibility and representation for the firm within the consulting field. Upon joining the ACE, Mott Managing Director Keith Howells commented, "We welcome their initiatives on seeking fairer terms and conditions of engagement for consultants, which currently often put disproportionate levels of risk onto consulting firms."

Expanding the grand Schema

In April 2007, Mott MacDonald announced that it had acquired fellow UK management consultancy firm Schema. Founded in 1989, the firm specialises in advising the technology, media and telecoms industries, and has worked on the advent of broadband and digital TV throughout Europe. Given the size and variety of Mott MacDonald's overall operation, it is unclear exactly where Schema will fit into the overall shape of things, but there seems little reason to doubt that the BTC division will benefit from the acquisition. At the time of the deal, Tom Allen, head of Mott MacDonald's information, communications and media business, expressed his enthusiasm at the potential for expanding the firm's reach throughout emerging telecoms markets. "With deregulation of the telecoms markets now progressing at a rapid pace across Africa, Asia and Latin America," he said, "our joint teams will be in an ideal position to advise international operators on the expansion of their operations to these markets."

Another awards ceremony?

The words "awards", "recognition" and "Mott MacDonald" appear together on a fairly regular basis, usually for the company's work on high-profile engineering projects around the globe. In May 2008, the firm won the Best Technical Adviser award at the Public Private Finance Awards for the third time in four years. Several months earlier, the company picked up another piece of kudos that has become almost habitual—recognition on *The Sunday Times'* list of Best Companies to Work For. Landing at No. 8 on the Top 20 Big Companies list, the firm improved on its 2007 ranking by three places, and was the top-ranked consultancy of its kind on the list. The reasons? "One in four workers has been with the management, engineering and development consultancy for at least a decade," according to the paper, which also noted that "staff believe they can make a valuable contribution to the success of the organisation and that the experience they gain is valuable for their future." To top it all off, "Mott MacDonald employees say they would not leave tomorrow if offered another job (74 per cent, a score bettered by just three other organisations) and would strongly recommend the company as a place to work (75 per cent)."

GETTING HIRED

Tailored interviews

Mott MacDonald's BTC division, insiders say, has a "basic interview process that's varied to suit the needs of the position or individual." The norm is two interviews, and style "varies from one-on-one to panel interviews". Typically, "the people who you will be working with" conduct the interviews, though some meetings also are "attended by HR for monitoring purposes". Respondents tell us there are "no fixed questions", but most interviewers are looking to ensure that "the interviewee will fit into the team". A consultant explains that interviews tend to be "very informal" and involve "no tests". The firm employs "strictly competency-based interviewing". Candidates should come prepared "to discuss technical issues" and may be faced with questions like, "What can you offer the company if hired?" Interviewers might also want to hear an "example of a time when you've worked under pressure", a source advises.

Mott MacDonald does not conduct campus recruiting, opting instead to look for candidates via its "web site, student vacation placements and agencies". The firm also finds prospects through "personal contacts" by way of its recruiting-bonus programme. A source explains, "The company advertises posts nationally and also encourages networking, and will target specific individuals."

OUR SURVEY SAYS

One big family

"One of the largest employee-owned firms in Europe," Mott MacDonald has a "family feel with big-company backing". The BTC division's "encouraging, forward-looking" culture attracts "responsible and caring" people, an insider states. According to a colleague, "Mott's is a great culture, with lots of opportunities for young staff to excel." There are "good relationships within the teams and quite a lot of people who have been with the company a long time". It's the kind of place where, "if you work hard, you get rewarded." The firm is "open and inclusive", and holds "regular team meetings and social events". Staffers say that Mott's consultants and managers are "supportive of everyone who wants to flourish and develop". This "entrepreneurial" firm is "risk averse and technically sound", though at times, its "low-key" vibe can feel "slightly disjointed".

Flexible, as long as the job gets done

In Mott MacDonald's BTC division, a consultant explains, "the emphasis is getting the job done, not the number of hours it takes you to do it. How that is achieved is down to you, providing you are managing your time and the job successfully." There are "some long days", but those are usually "balanced by shorter days when in the home office". A source says, "There are generally peaks and troughs of workload, and you tend to know when you have a busy period coming up." In addition, there are "people around to help out if a lot of unexpected things crop up at once". A colleague notes that sometimes "work beyond the basic hours is required to meet client expectations, but there is flexibility to take time off at other times." This sort of flexibility makes it "possible to balance work and life." Still, some feel the firm's work/life balance policies "still need work", as "the annual leave allowance is a bit pathetic." Fortunately, "there is no pressure to work weekends," and according to one consultant, "There is the option to work at home when the plumber or some other tradesman visits my house. I also find it quite flexible when my children have been ill."

BTC consultants are contracted to work 37.5 hours per week, but most report logging between 40 and 50 hours in an average week. This "varies throughout the organisation". According to a contact, "Some offices work long hours and some don't. You can control it to suit you, with a bit of effort." Project length also "varies a lot". A consultant details, "I have been involved in projects lasting a few years, long-term secondments (six months to one year) and other projects that last a couple of weeks." Others claim there is "no such thing as an average assignment, as project durations range from weeks to years".

Accessible by train

Travel requirements "depend on specific projects", with some requiring consultants to be "away all week for months at a time". As one respondent puts it, the "company ethos is to work with the client", so some consultants find themselves doing "a lot of travel". That said, most sources claim that travel is "not a problem", though some are admittedly hit harder than others. A staffer says, "Many employees are reluctant to work away from home, so those who are willing travel excessively." The good news is that "work outside the office is normally within a reasonable travelling distance to be able to be home no later than normal"—most clients are "within the London area". However, the firm's "policy to travel by train can lead to excessively long journey times" when travelling to distant clients. A consultant notes, "British roads and transport systems in winter slow the course of work and adds to project work time."

Nothing to write home about

Repondents say that at Mott MacDonald, "base salary and the pension scheme are poor," though the firm does offer "share ownership for those above a certain grade". The option currently applies to "grade F and above", but "the scheme is being extended to allow nominated grade E consultants to buy into the company." A large percentage of compensation comes in the form of "profit-related pay", we're told, which is usually "fair and regular". The firm explains that all staff get 14 per cent PPS on top of base salary, and honoraria is discretionary. And as an added bonus, the firm makes "additional uplift payments" to those who undertake "extra travel". Mott also offers a "bonus for recommending someone else who ends up being employed".

As far as extras, the firm provides a "car allowance" and pays some commuter costs for London-based employees. There is a "health care contribution scheme," as well as "child care vouchers". Mott's social committee provides "subsidised events", including "sports days, hill walking, theatre trips and beer festival trips". A consultant explains, "A sports event is held every year, where people come from all over the country to participate in a variety of events. It is a fun, but still highly competitive, weekend."

Cramped quarters

Respondents say the London office is "nice and has everything you need", but some find it "quite an impersonal, intimidating environment that is not conducive to sociability". The Berkshire space is "currently overcrowded", while the Glasgow office, "currently undergoing refurbishment," could be faced with a similar problem: According to a source, "Recruitment targets, if reached, will mean space is tight." A colleague in Leeds feels the same way, stating, "More space is required due to the increase in employees. We also need more parking facilities." In Bristol, "space and support services are OK, but facilities and actual infrastructure are poor," and the Croydon location is described as "dated and cramped". A consultant based in that location grumbles, "We do not have voicemail, which results in quite a lot of embarrassment when dealing with clients."

"Hey boss, remember me?"

Overall, managers in the BTC division get high marks, with some consultants reporting "excellent rapport" with their supervisors. One source says, "I feel comfortable that my ideas are well received and that I am making an impact and impression on the future direction of this division." However, some find that the "management structure is very confusing and dynamic." According to one consultant, "There are no line managers, and the annual reviews are performed by someone who does not operate out of my office or interact with me." The respondent adds that it can sometimes feel like "senior management is many hundreds of miles away," assuming an "out of sight, out of mind" attitude. A colleague remarks, "Typically, supervisors are too busy maximising their own utilisation to spend any significant time mentoring or supervising."

Could use more guidance on training and promotions

Most training at Mott MacDonald is "official", we're told, and some insiders say there is "not enough on-the-job training and mentoring". Instead, the firm offers "a wide selection of training courses, both classroom and web-based", and the selection of available courses and training plans is determined at the board level, the firm explains. Attendance at company-run training days is "encouraged if they are relevant", and external courses can also be attended, "if necessary". Staffers say each employee's training needs are "assessed and planned at the annual review".

Sources lament that the BTC division does not have the same structured promotion policies of many other consultancies, though the firm notes that it's working to address this issue. There is "no formal promotion policy, and employees get promoted based on grades". You can "apply for jobs in the higher grades as they become available," but insiders say it can be "very tough to get up to or past the consultant level, unless you are over 35 to 40" years old. A consultant remarks, "People are challenged to find their place. The ambitious will rise but the unambitious are not penalised." The good news is that promotions generally happen "based on merit as opportunities arise". But many feel the "progression routes are not very clear." For this reason, "some people get stuck and eventually leave as a result." Similarly, a contact claims, "criteria are extremely unclear," which makes it seem as though "individuals are mysteriously promoted against no particular criteria."

Changes are happening slowly

Regarding diversity, Mott MacDonald "does not discriminate and takes this policy very seriously". The firm's "engineering history leaves it with a male-dominated senior management team", but insiders say that is "slowly breaking down". Since the firm has built up its management consultancy, "more women have been brought into the division." There is "no evidence of positive or negative discrimination" toward women, sources insist, and female employees are offered the "same promotional tracks" as men. Still, "there are few women at the high levels," despite the fact that "hiring is fine."

The firm also shows "lots of enthusiasm for people across all ethnic groups." A consultant explains that recruitment efforts are "based on capability, so there is no 'positive discrimination'". The fact remains, however, that there are "few minorities at the high levels", respondents admit. As for the consultancy's receptivity to gay and lesbian employees, one source remarks, "I have never once heard any adverse comments about hiring GLBTs in all my time here."

Doing its part

The BTC division's contribution to surrounding communities "depends on the local managers". A staffer explains that some locations conduct "excellent community service activities, including mock interviews for schools, mentoring high school kids and raising money for local charities". One staffer notes, "We have a corporate social responsibility system encouraged by the company, and regular and enthusiastic fund raisers. Charitable activities are given high profile within the company's internal publications." In addition, the firm also has "a responsible attitude about its carbon footprint".

PROUDFOOT CONSULTING

10 Fleet Place
London EC4M 7RB
United Kingdom
Phone: +44 (0)207 710 5100
Fax: +44 (0)207 710 5101
www.proudfootconsulting.com

The Stats

Employer Type: Subsidiary of
  Management Consulting Group
Ticker Symbol: MMC (London Stock
  Exchange)
Executive Chairman: Alan Barber
CEO: Luiz Carvalho
2008 Employees: 480
2007 Employees: 425
2007 Revenue: £73.6 million
2006 Revenue: -£88.7 million
No. of Offices: 19

Practice Areas

Asset Management • Call Centres •
Energy • Energy Management •
Organisational Effectiveness • Process
Improvement • Procurement •
Productivity • Sales Performance
Improvement • Supply Chain
Management

European Locations

London (HQ)
Budapest • Frankfurt • Madrid• Paris •
Prague • Vienna

Plus

• Strong, team-based approach to
  problem solving

Minus

• Travel five days a week is a given

Employment Contact

Go to the Careers section of the firm's
web site

THE BUZZ
WHAT CONSULTANTS AT OTHER FIRMS ARE SAYING

• "Strong specialists"
• "Low profile"
• "Good people offerings"
• "Pushy"

THE SCOOP

Let's start by getting something straight: Proudfoot Consulting is a subsidiary of Management Consulting Group (MCG), which has previously operated as Proudfoot Consulting PLC, Proudfoot PLC and the Alexander Proudfoot Company. So it's a subsidiary of itself—simple, huh? The firm adopted the MCG moniker in 2001. This was to avoid confusion between the parent company (which holds several consulting brands, but is not a consulting firm) and the Proudfoot Consulting brand, which most definitely is a consulting firm—and a licensed brand— and operates in some 15 countries across six continents.

Proudfoot's motto is a simple one ("We add value"), but one that sums up everything the firm is about. Using its proprietary Co-Venture® system, the firm focusses on three main areas to create that added value for its clients: process improvements, people solutions and management operating systems. The list of clients, meanwhile, is almost as exhaustive as the industries they operate in (and that's not counting

> 66 Proudfoot consultants analyse each client's existing organisation, management systems and leadership behaviour. 99

those served by the other MCG subsidiaries): automotive, chemicals and pharmaceuticals, construction, distribution and transportation, electronics, financial services, food and beverage, health care, manufacturing, mining and metals, oil and gas, paper and natural resources, retail, services, telecommunications and high tech, and utilities.

Founded by Alex P., PhD

The firm got its start back in 1946, when Chicago native Alexander Proudfoot realised the potential for a new kind of consultancy, one that—gasp!—would offer clients results that far exceeded the cost of gaining them. To this end, he created a proprietary programme for analysing the businesses he dealt with, and would only work for a company if he was given full control over installing that programme. That programme, known as Lost Time, focussed on cutting the amount of time wasted by employees at the workplace—a methodology that still has value some 60 years later. Indeed, Proudfoot monitors and reports annually on workplace productivity around the globe, each year identifying the gains and losses made by respective nations in their commitment to keeping workers focussed on the task at hand. In 2007, for example, the firm's analysis found that, between 2003 and 2006, the top-three locations for high labour productivity were France, Australia and the US, while the UK appeared in the bottom three, marginally ahead of Spain and Canada.

In addition to the consultancy's productivity reports, meanwhile, it also puts out its own magazine, *P3*. Typically containing interviews with executives from its own clients, the magazine serves as something of a marketing tool for Proudfoot, while also offering business insights to a wider market.

Don't venture alone—Co-Venture

Proudfoot's clients are a wide-ranging bunch, but many have something in common: their willingness to provide testimony that the firm's Co-Venture system has helped their business. Representatives from smaller companies to industry luminaries such as Bayer AG, BP America and ING have all declared their satisfaction with the

> 66 Proudfoot looks for results-oriented candidates who demonstrate an affinity for teamwork. 99

firm's services. The Co-Venture technique aims to improve business by helping clients maximise their knowledge of their own companies. Once this is achieved, Proudfoot works with the client to figure out where value can be added and profitability enhanced.

And just to prove it's serious, the firm offers a no-penalty get-out clause at any time, provided its clients give just two weeks' notice.

The joys of parenting

Parent company Management Consulting Group PLC—based in London—is a fan of the Co-Venture approach as well. Having sold its Japanese holdings at the turn of the millennium, it licensed the Proudfoot name so that the firm still has representation in that country. It took a similar approach in South Africa, meanwhile, selling some 51 per cent of Proudfoot Consulting Africa to Vuya! Investments and Chrims Investments—a deal that made it the first black-owned consulting firm in the country. MCG also owns several sister firms to Proudfoot, including financial management consultancy Parson Consulting, Asian market specialists Salzer Consulting, and the multi-industry Ineum Consulting.

MCG had a busy year in 2007, meanwhile, acquiring two more consulting firms, and creating a third. In June, it established a corporate strategy consultancy, Viaduct, before merging a new acquisition, CBH Consulting, with Parson in September. That same month, the firm shelled out around $125 million to acquire Kurt Salmon Associates, a US-based solutions provider to the retail, consumer products and health care industries.

GETTING HIRED

Put your proudest foot forward

To help client companies become proficient in developing solutions and implementing sustainable productivity improvements, Proudfoot consultants analyse each client's existing organisation, management systems and leadership behaviour. This requires close cooperation with clients, and also among the firm's four- to six-person project teams. So throughout the hiring process, interviewers are on the lookout for results-oriented candidates who demonstrate an affinity for teamwork. Another quality shared by Proudfoot consultants is an ability to multitask professional and personal life, as the majority of staffers are at the client site five days a week.

Proudfoot's careers web site lists current opportunities, detailed job descriptions for various positions and a chart mapping the typical progression of a consultant over three years. Candidates can apply online for any of the firm's available positions by filling out a brief application form and attaching a CV. □

PRTM

25 The Quadrant
Abingdon Science Park
Abingdon Oxford OX14 3YS
United Kingdom
Phone: +44 (0)1235 555 500
Fax: +44 (0)1235 554 835
www.prtm.com

European Locations

Frankfurt
Glasgow
London
Munich
Paris

The Stats

Employer Type: Private Company
Global Managing Director: Scott
  Hefter
Europe Managing Director: Dean
  Gilmore
2008 Employees: 675
2007 Employees: 660
No. of Offices: 16

Pluses

- "International mission and scope"
- No weekend work policy
- "Low consultant-to-partner ratio"

Minuses

- "Intensive travel requirements"
- Lack of notoriety
- Imbalance between short- and long-term goals

Practice Areas

Business Technology Innovation
Customer Experience Innovation
Operational Strategy
Product Innovation
Supply Chain Innovation

Employment Contact

Follow the careers link at
www.prtm.com

THE SCOOP

T he original name for PRTM was a mix of the names of its founding partners, Theodore Pittiglio, Robert Rabin, Robert Todd and Michael McGrath. But when Pittiglio Rabin Todd & McGrath became too much of a mouthful, these clever consulting strategists changed the name of the firm permanently to PRTM. Under either name, the firm has been devising strategies since 1976, offering advice in the practice areas of operational strategy, product innovation, supply chain innovation, customer experience innovation and business technology innovation.

PRTM means innovative solutions

The firm's focus on innovation in every aspect of its practice is intentional. PRTM advertises itself as the firm where "innovation operates" and promises clients that all solutions will be bold and progressive. PRTM offers new ideas for clients in the sectors of aerospace and defence, automotives, chemicals and process industries, communications and media, electronics and computing, energy, financial services, health care, life sciences, private equity, public sector and software.

PRTM is based in Waltham, Massachusetts, but operates out of three distinct regions, which are all led by separate managing directors. Michael Aghajanian is the director of the firm's Americas operations, which includes offices in Chicago, Dallas, Detroit, New York, Silicon Valley, Orange County, Waltham and Washington, DC. Dean Gilmore is the managing director for PRTM's five European offices in Frankfurt, Glasgow, London, Munich and Paris. The company's Asian operations, headed by James So, includes offices in Bangalore, Shanghai and Tokyo. All of the different branches of the business are managed by Global Managing Director Scott Hefter. The namesake members, Pittiglio, Rabin, Todd and McGrath, have all retired from the firm.

Operational strategy essentials

PRTM has five core rules of thumb for helping organise a business. The first rule is to "transform market forces into operational advantage," or to allow your company to work with the market, instead of against it. Second, PRTM encourages clients to "do one thing extraordinarily well." Next, the firm advises clients to "think end-to-end, continuous, real-time and horizontally," and then, fourth, to "drive innovation in your operations and business model," essentially stressing the importance of outside-the-box thinking in solving operational issues. The last step is to "execute relentlessly," the key element to achieving pay-off from all the planning and hard work.

Focus on frameworks

Within the product innovation and supply chain innovation practice areas, PRTM has created original frameworks that are employed to help companies achieve their goals. The Product and Cycle-time Excellence (PACE®) is PRTM's unique methodology, created in the mid-1980s, that provides clients with a multi-disciplinary approach to product innovation. PRTM puts PACE to work in the areas of cross-enterprise innovation management, environmental and regulatory compliance, product development operations, PLM transformations, and technology and IP management.

PRTM co-developed the Supply-Chain Operations Reference-model® (SCOR), and with AMR Research in 1996 co-founded The Supply-Chain Council, a global nonprofit consortium dedicated to assisting its members make dramatic and rapid improvements in supply-chain processes. SCOR is endorsed by the Supply-Chain Council as the cross-industry standard diagnostic tool for supply-chain management. The most widely accepted framework of its kind, SCOR is a process reference model that spans from the supplier's supplier to the customer's customer, enabling users to address, improve and communicate supply-chain management practices within and between all interested parties.

Performance benchmarks head south of the border

In 1998, PRTM launched a subsidiary company, the Performance Measurement Group (PMG), to deliver operational performance benchmarking services for PRTM and PMG clients. Over the past 10 years, PMG has been utilising the SCOR model to provide supply-chain performance benchmarking services to over 1,000 companies, including 50 per cent of the Fortune 500. PMG also uses PRTM's PACE framework for its product development and product life cycle management benchmarks/best practices.

In July 2007, PMG entered into a strategic alliance with Brazilian boutique management consultancy Iteology Partners. Iteology will sell PMG's supply-chain monitor benchmark service in Latin America. The supply-chain monitor is a high-level quantitative subset of the comprehensive SCOR benchmark service of PMG, and is used to help companies identify major performance gaps in areas such as delivery performance, order fulfillment lead time, upside production flexibility, cost of goods sold as a per cent of revenue, inventory days of supply, cash-to-cash cycle time and asset turns.

Stamp of approval

PRTM has established a solid reputation as a healthy workplace for its employees, ranking in *Consulting* magazine's Top 10 Best Firms to Work For for the past six years.

The magazine gives awards based on survey responses culled from consulting professionals with regard to the following categories: compensation, work/life balance, career development, job experience, firm leadership and firm culture. *Consulting* gives the firm especially high marks in the category of work/life balance. In its 2007 issue, the publication said that at PRTM, "burnout is not as high because work/life balance actually exists." The article also includes a key quote from Global Managing Director Hefter that touches upon PRTM's stance toward individuals who plan on a swift ascent up the corporate ladder. Hefter says, "This is a business where literally everyone who's here has the opportunity to make partner."

"Execute relentlessly"

As mentioned above, the last step on PRTM's list of operational strategy ingredients is to "execute relentlessly," and some recent examples of the firm's work show that relentless execution pays off. Since 2005, the firm has been working on reformatting Arrow Electronics' business strategy. PRTM helped Arrow switch to a four-pillar business model incorporating growth, operational excellence, financial stability and shared leadership. PRTM found that Arrow's weakness was a lack of insight into its clients' needs. The fix involved the Voice of the Customer (VoC) methodology, which was quickly incorporated into Arrow's everyday operations. The company was happy with the results. Arrow CEO William Mitchell stated, "VoC has become one of the real drivers of the business. We ask, 'are we doing the right stuff?' Because if what we're doing is not leading to something that's of value to our customers or of value to our suppliers ... then why are we doing it?"

Another success story is PRTM's work with Texas-based IT company ACS. ACS, a Fortune 500 company, came to PRTM with the challenge of seamlessly integrating its recent acquisitions into its business. PRTM worked with ACS to segment its external sourcing spending, and helped it achieve an expected 15 per cent in run rate savings in 2008.

GETTING HIRED

Not big on cases

"Cases don't play a big role" in PRTM's interview process. The firm is "looking for people who are a match with the working culture that is valued by our clients", so "fit interviews" are more the norm. Candidates can expect "up to six non-confrontational interviews with directors of the firm." There may be one case interview or exercise, but the process is much more focussed on finding those who "fit with the firm's values". The type and number of interviews can vary depending on level of experience, but most newbies go through an "initial HR screening", followed by a "fit and experience round" with a principal or director. Finally, there is a "one-day session with the partners". During this day, there may be one case question designed to test knowledge and problem-solving ability, and one to examine communication skills. The process is "adapted to the level of seniority". In general, interviews tend not to be "typical case study-style", but rather, "more of a dialogue, providing a great opportunity for candidates to gain insight into the firm through discussions with those at the top". Questions are "taken from fresh topics and recent examples, and are adapted to the area of expertise and experience the candidate is bringing". "Discussions are aimed at understanding the candidates' consulting skills," as well as "their industry and practice knowledge, and their interest in growing PRTM's business".

To find its future hopefuls, PRTM looks to "all major US and European business schools", including Wharton, Stanford, INSEAD, London Business School, Harvard and Indian Institutes of Management. The firm also looks to employ "the best talent from industry and other consulting firms". Overall, PRTM is "quite selective" in who it brings onboard. It's looking for "technical depth, relevant industry experience and a proven track record of exceeding expectations and advancement".

OUR SURVEY SAYS

Results with an international flair

Insiders say PRTM is an "international company" that fosters "excellent teamwork" and "truly operates as one entity globally". Small team sizes create a "do-it-yourself attitude", which gives consultants "great freedom". The firm's "friendly atmosphere promotes cooperation rather than competition". In addition, PRTM "treats everybody as individuals and does not try to enforce one style of consulting". The "open-minded culture" brings with it "little weight of hierarchy"—it's a "flat organisation" in which junior consultants have "close access to directors". The firm's "fun" yet "results-driven" consultants "truly work as a team and respect each other", and the focus is "on results and not politics", which means "communication is direct and honest." Moreover, the firm has a "very international" feel due to "cross-country staffing".

In this "hands-on" culture, a "self-starter attitude" is required. PRTM consultants perform "leading-edge work" and are proud of their "culture of excellence." A source says, "As an international firm, created in the US, there is an American sense of recognition and overall team. The work you do is recognised and rewarded." In that way, staffers consider the firm to be "extremely meritocratic and exacting on deliverable quality". At the same time, "everyone's opinion is valued." In fact, "each new hire is considered as a possible future director." PRTM consultants have "developed tough skins and are more than willing to have a discussion to make their point". It's a good thing the firm's consultants enjoy their working environment so much, because "the pace rarely, if ever, lets up."

Quality hours

Despite its reportedly frenetic pace, PRTM "leaves the consultants quite free to organise their work hours as long as the work gets done". On average, people log between 50 and 60 hours per week, with some putting in closer to 70. Weekly hours "vary from mission to mission", but "10 hours per day" is fairly standard. As a general rule, PRTM "tries to optimise quality and not quantity of hours". As a result, "there is wide personal freedom to manage work hours."

> " The work you do is recognised and rewarded. "

A typical working day starts at 8am, but "how late in the evening [you work] is very much dependent on the project phase." For example, "if we work longer in the beginning of a project, the project leader takes care that we work less in the remaining duration of the project." And for projects where the workload is higher than expected, "additional employees are assigned to reduce the workload of the other members." Normally, "Fridays are shorter working days." Project length also varies, but the norm is around three months, with "a minimum of three weeks and a maximum of six months."

Get used to airports

For PRTM consultants, travel is "the rule, not the exception." Most travel "every week" because "assignments are primarily outside of the home office." Generally, the trips provide "exposure to different working cultures without losing too much in efficiency". The norm is to be "away three to four days per week" on trips that "normally involve plane travel". Per week, most consultants take "two trips by plane on average, not more". They can usually arrange to "fly to the client on Monday morning and return on Thursday," which means "travel logistics are kept simple."

The "high travel requirements" mostly apply to the London-based team and are due largely to the fact that the firm's UK client base is limited. "There is less travel for the

French and German offices. Fortunately, UK leadership has identified this as an issue and is concentrating on building a larger UK client base so we can balance the travel requirements." And although a job at PRTM is sure to be "travel intensive", the firm has "clear policies that allow consultants to optimise travel on a personal basis". Insiders appreciate that "travel is not excessive in the sense that it only happens when it is absolutely required by the mission." Since most travelling is done "within Europe", you can normally spend "Friday in the home office and have a balanced life over the weekends".

Weekends are sacred

PRTM has a "strong focus on keeping weekends free for family and recreation." Although it can be "hard to manage your personal life when you are away from home four days a week", PRTM "strictly believes" that weekends are for downtime, and "works hard" to avoid having its consultants at the client site on Fridays. "Travel can affect family life to some extent," but if you are "very organised and willing to prioritise your family during the weekend", it can be achieved. Even for people without children, "being absent during the week detrimentally affects relationships, but only to a limited extent."

Some say the more problematic impact of travelling so much is the "stress and fatigue induced by shuttling back and forth across hotels, cities, countries and time zones". The firm tries to alleviate this by "making it a priority to support employees in managing professional and personal priorities". A contact says, "The firm's emphasis on consultants returning to the home office at the end of the week for training, networking and socialising, as well as respecting a no-weekends policy, is key to good work/life balance." If weekend work is required, consultants are encouraged to "bring partners or spouses" to the city they're working in. And during the week, "directors even tell you to go home to your family if they feel like you work too much," and consultants are given the freedom "to take off when family issues arise". The bottom line is, "the travel requirements take a toll on the private life," but generally speaking, PRTM is "quite considerate in accommodating personal lives".

Can't complain about comp

PRTM has a "nondisclosure policy on compensation", but insiders reveal that "salaries are aligned with yearly benchmarks in the consulting industry and are competitive." Bonuses, which are given "twice a year", are "based on both firm and individual performance, with excellent incentives for top performers". The firm compensates "to avoid burnout", and most sources report a very high level of satisfaction with their overall pay packages.

The firm offers medical, dental, disability, life, accidental death and dismemberment, and travel insurance, as well as paid vacation and pension schemes in each European country. Consultants enjoy a "choice of mobile phones, rather than a limited choice of company-endorsed options". There's also a "yearly Christmas party with partners or spouses, and summer picnics." The firm caters to new parents "as much as possible" through "flexible and part-time scheduling, and the ability to work close to home." Consultants "have the opportunity to take sabbaticals" as well. Still, some gripe that they "travel in coach, including on long-haul flights", and note that because the company is "focussed very much on the overall firm's profitability, there is an old-rooted austerity on all nonclient-related expenses."

Big support for community work

PRTM has a "structured programme to support communities and charities in the locality of its offices". Known as PRTM in the Community, the programme has "a fairly good participation rate". The firm also supports "individual causes" and is "open to any suggestions" for additional community involvement.

> 66 I have never experienced a more internationally and ethnically diversified company. 99

As one respondent puts it, PRTM's community involvement is "driven by individuals in the firm who want to make a difference, and the firm supports this". Currently, the firm sponsors "several charity runs and events, as well as special initiatives based on some calamity". Programmes are directed at fighting hunger and poverty, conducting medical research, and improving housing and education.

Close encounters

PRTM's "1:4 director-to-consultant ratio" provides "great learning opportunities", we're told. The "low ratio enables a lot of on-the-job training and coaching from experienced people," and consultants are given a "high level of responsibility" and "support from management to handle it". There is "excellent exposure and teamwork among all levels", and staffers "generally have very good and collegial interactions with partners."

There's also "frequent interaction directly with senior management at the client". A contact says, "I work on a daily basis with CXOs at client sites, and can call in any partner in the firm if I feel it's needed." Praising the firm's approach, a source explains that PRTM has a "huge amount of repeat business with very enthusiastic clients", despite "relatively poor brand awareness." According to a colleague, "We are not well known, but those who know us value our collaboration highly, as compared to better known firms that may have a more 'hit and run' approach."

On the job is where it's at

Respondents explain that coaching is performed with the goal in mind of "making consulting a long-term career". Sources say most training at PRTM is "on the job, but not exclusively"—the firm does offer a "wide range of training courses, such as consulting skills development, industry and practice area expertise, and firm management." There's also a "professional development programme that is supervised by a director acting as a career coach".

However, the firm's emphasis on on-the-job mentorship is "starting to break down due to recent high growth". As a result, PRTM is "starting to develop its internal training to become more sustainable and scalable". Currently, "webcasts are provided on Fridays" and "books are offered for personal training." Insiders say "time is limited for formal training", but add that "you learn a huge amount through the informal pathways."

You get what you give

In terms of promotion, there is "no up-or-out policy", but typically "consultants advance every one to four years." Most progress comes in six-month to two-year intervals, but the "pace of progression can vary from one consultant to another." Performance compensations "take place every six months, and a promotion is possible after every evaluation." On average, "development from consultant to director is a seven- to nine-year path." We're told that the firm sets "clear expectations for capabilities and competences", and these expectations are the basis for a "fair" and "merit-based promotion policy". As a general rule, a consultant notes, "If you're good, you'll make it. "The attitude is "not up-or-out at all", a staffer remarks, but rather more of a "development approach".

Well located

PRTM's current London office is a "temporary leased space", but "the other European offices are of a better standard." The Frankfurt office, for example, is "new and in a great location", offering "all the infrastructure a consultant needs". The "nice and modern office" is "very well equipped, but not overdone". Munich also has "new offices in a top location", outfitted in "contemporary design". We're told that the "downtown" digs offer "everything necessary". PRTM's Paris facility is located in "an excellent downtown location" in "one of the nicest parts" of the city. The office itself is "comfortable, with ample space and good lighting." Food and beverages are provided "at any time", and the "support staff ensures that consultants needs are met swiftly." In addition, connectivity in the office is "fast and reliable".

You won't see many women around

PRTM is "an equal opportunity employer" that "coaches and fosters women" just as it does with all employees. The firm "strives to recognise and value diversity, including gender diversity", That said, "there is an imbalance in the workforce, with more men than women." One insider has "never worked with a woman", but says that the firm "would appreciate more women". Most agree that the lack of women is due to "limited female candidates for senior-level consulting jobs", and the fact that PRTM has "a small team". A female consultant, who says PRTM is "exemplary in the sense of providing equal opportunities to men and women", says the low numbers are "100 per cent due to the very low level of demand from women." It can be "difficult to attract women to an engineering-intensive environment." That said, women who have found their way to PRTM are "treated exactly as their male counterparts in all respects—hiring selectivity, promoting, mentoring, compensating and training", a consultant insists. The firm may be "behind the curve," however, in retaining them. "PRTM does not have any official practices in place to retain women." There are "no maternity packages above the government-mandated minimum, or alternate work packages that could help retain women with children." Nor are there any mentoring groups specifically for women.

Discrimination is foreign

When it comes to ethnic diversity, however, "PRTM is probably one of the best companies to work for." It would be "completely alien" for anyone at PRTM to consider anything but performance when assessing a candidate or employee. Minorities report feeling "very comfortable" working with other people at the firm. In the London office, there are people who are "white, Caribbean, African, Pakistani, homosexual, Indian and Chinese", and they "all feel part of the same team". Most projects at PRTM are "internationally staffed". A contact boasts, "I have never experienced a more international and ethnically diversified company."

Just as ethnic diversity is a "nonissue", sexual preference is "really irrelevant". Whether someone is gay, lesbian, bisexual or transgender "has no relevance to our work, and thus does not play a role". One openly gay employee brought his partner to a company retreat in Portugal and "no one even thought twice about it." At PRTM, a source concludes, "people are just treated like people." □

QUEST WORLDWIDE CONSULTING

The Manor House
Huxley Close, Godalming
Surrey GU7 2AS
United Kingdom
Phone: +44 (0)1483 427 031
www.quest-worldwide.com

The Stats

Employer Type: Private Company
Chairman & Founder: Dr Steve Smith
2008 Employees: 50+
No. of Offices: 5

Practice Areas

Operational Excellence
People Engagement
Strategy Implementation

European Location

Godalming (Global HQ)

Pluses

- "Opportunity to work at a senior level in blue-chip organisations"
- Promotions based on merit

Minuses

- Few women, relative to other industries
- Not as well known outside of London

Employment Contact

recruitment@quest-worldwide.com

THE SCOOP

S pecialising in global change management, Quest Worldwide is the brainchild of Dr Steve Smith, who founded the firm in 1988 following stints at Chrysler, Aston University and as a director at PA Consulting Group. Now celebrating its second decade of operation, Quest has grown from a single office into a globe-spanning entity, with locations in Godalming, Dubai, Singapore, Sydney and New York.

Quest's client service model is divided into three key components—strategy implementation, operational excellence and people engagement. The company believes that sustainable performance improvement is delivered when impact is felt in more than one of these areas, but also that people drive changes in performance and culture. Hence, the company involves people at all levels of a client's business, making sure each knows how they fit into the specific direction the company is going. In order to determine how it can help both current and potential clients, the firm provides a series of online tools to evaluate clients' strengths

> 66 We prefer to work in teams, so people are rarely overloaded. 99

and weaknesses across each of the three key areas. Among those seeking Quest's guidance are global firms of the stature of Airbus, DuPont and Unilever, as well as up-and-coming entities such as Dubai's Aujan Industries, a soft drinks company that the firm is assisting in growing its business throughout the Middle East.

Making methodologies

In addition to its online tools (which assess a company's capabilities on a very general level), Quest has several proprietary methodologies it uses to identify and improve areas of its clients' businesses. The most well known of these, according to the firm, are tools known as "strategy into action", "performance culture", "lean operations", "high impact events" and "WorkSmart for results". Each tool focusses on a different area of need, but they can be used alongside one another, if necessary. Strategy into action includes training, coaching, workshops and more that are aimed at, well, turning business strategies into practical solutions for firms. The other tools follow a similar path, applying Quest's abilities in training, information dissemination and "upskilling" to a range of performance improvement initiatives.

Perhaps the most important methodology the firm has developed, however, is the one it uses to collect feedback from its clients on its own performance. Not only is Quest concerned with the performance of its clients' business, but it brings its own methodologies home to benchmark in an effort to improve upon how it helps clients improve.

Award-winning performance

Back in 2005, Quest was hired by multinational conglomerate Unilever to help it cut through a labyrinthine management structure that was stifling growth. Having worked successfully with Unilever in the past, the consultancy was asked to identify the cause of the problem and find a solution to it. Conducting a four-week global survey of stakeholders, the firm identified several problems, most of which were related to disconnectedness at Unilever—different departments employed different terminologies, and there was little evidence of a shared understanding of a common approach for taking the business forward. Quest's solution—and one that is indicative of the simplifying nature of much of the work it does—was to host a workshop for Unilever leaders to have them come up with a one-page plan for the future, which in turn was developed into a "strategy into action" plan. Once delivered, the plan was then rolled out to employees across Unilever's organisation—a process that was completed within six months. Shortly thereafter, Unilever's sales began to grow, and in 2006, surpassed a rate of growth that had not been predicted until 2010. For its part in the process, meanwhile, Quest was named Best Small Firm at the 2007 MCA Management Awards.

> ❝ Quest has a 'low level of hierarchy', and the culture is 'encouraging of its people'. ❞

Getting their names in print

In addition to aiding corporations both big and small, Quest consultants somehow find the time to produce books, articles and industry reports on their various areas of expertise. Founder and Chairman Steve Smith, for example, weighed in with *Plan to Win: Turning Strategy into Success*, a book for managers at all levels that is billed as "an accessible guide to good planning and better implementation". In addition, the firm also produces The Toolbox Collection, a series of how-to books based on Quest's core competencies. Titles in the series include *The Lean Toolbox, Make Things Happen!* and *Solve That Problem!*

To the Manor born

Founded by a UK national within the UK, it comes as little surprise to learn that Quest's global headquarters is also based in the UK. What is perhaps surprising, however, is the firm's decision to locate its headquarters outside London, in Godalming, Surrey—only an hour's drive from the capital, but not exactly handy should a client based in the Big Smoke decide to drop by for a chat. The reason for Quest's out-of-the-way location, however, is also a key part of its business—The Manor House, a run-down property the firm bought in 1993 and renovated into a headquarters that also houses a dedicated conference venue, where the firm can hold residential workshops, events and the like for its clients. Such was the success of the project that the consultancy added extra bedrooms and a new office wing to the property in 2000, and it now functions as a full-scale conference facility that is also open to outside business (ie, non-Quest conferences), and operates as a sister business to Quest.

GETTING HIRED

Meet and greet

Quest's hiring process is designed to find consultants who are committed and collaborative in their approach, and who are willing to take on challenging work with enthusiasm—all to deliver results to clients. An insider says, "Candidates are encouraged to meet as many existing consultants as possible" throughout the interview process, to get a better idea of whether Quest is a good fit. Interviews are conducted at assessment centres, which Quest uses "to simulate the consulting environment". Interviewers look for candidates with deep expertise in at least one of the firm's core service areas, but that alone isn't sufficient to make it past the threshold. Future Quest consultants must demonstrate a participative leadership style, as well as the drive and personality to inspire the firm's dynamic client roster. The consultancy is looking for experienced individuals with first-hand appreciation of the challenges facing senior management teams in large organisations. Current openings in the UK and throughout Europe can be found under the Working at Quest section of the firm's web site.

OUR SURVEY SAYS

Small-scale, global firm

Quest's European group is a "small team", but one that's "truly global" in its approach. Consultants at this "open and client-focussed" firm are given the opportunity to "make a difference"—through client assignments as well as pro bono consulting. Sources tell us Quest has a "low level of hierarchy", and the culture is "encouraging of its people". The consultancy is "positive to diversity", although, as source points out, "relatively few women apply or stay in consulting." Receptivity to gay and lesbian employees, adds a colleague, is "not an issue for us".

We're told there is "no up-or-out" policy for promotions, as moving up the ladder is "based on merit". And recently, there has been "increasingly organised training off the job".

Quest for balance

Achieving work/life balance at Quest is "not a problem", insiders say. As a consultant explains, "We prefer to work in teams, so people are rarely overloaded. And when they are overloaded, it is only for a short time, such as when working on a big client." Travel is also a big part of the job, as the firm bills itself as "an international consultancy". Many staffers, however, consider this "an advantage rather than a problem". Consultants work "all over Europe and farther, but usually for short visits". There's also "occasional leisure travel for staff and their partners". Projects typically last around three months, and the average consultant logs 45 hours per week.

To bring co-workers together and to create a sense of camaraderie, the Quest team enjoys "good staff parties", and there are often "celebrations for birthdays and new babies". ☐

SIMON-KUCHER & PARTNERS

Haydnstrasse 36
53115 Bonn
Germany
Phone: +49 (0)228 9843 0
Fax: +49 (0)226 9843 140
www.simon-kucher.com

European Locations

Bonn (World HQ)
Cologne • Frankfurt • London •
Luxembourg • Madrid • Milan • Moscow •
Munich • Paris • Vienna • Warsaw •
Zurich

The Stats

Employer Type: Private Company
Chairman: Prof Hermann Simon
2007 Employees: 450
2006 Employees: 365
2007 Revenue: €80 million
2006 Revenue: €64 million
No. of Offices: 17

Pluses

- "Interesting and international projects"
- Consultants have a lot of responsibility from the first day
- "Open to office rotation and transfers"

Practice Areas

Corporate Strategy
Marketing & Sales Strategy
Price Management
Price Strategy

Minuses

- "Salary could be higher"
- Office spaces aren't entirely satisfactory
- "Increasing bureaucracy"

Employment Contact

Attn: Dorothea Hayer M.A.
Haydnstrasse 36
53115 Bonn
Germany
E-mail: dorothea.hayer@simonkucher.com

THE BUZZ
WHAT CONSULTANTS AT OTHER FIRMS ARE SAYING

- "High reputation in the pricing field"
- "Not much more in stock apart from pricing"
- "Small, but good"
- "Care to do the same thing 100 times?"

THE SCOOP

S imon-Kucher & Partners is a worldwide leader in pricing consulting, helping its clients maximise profits by giving them the tools to correctly set prices for their products. The firm has helped price four of the five best-selling drugs in the world, and assisted over 100 companies in the Fortune Global 500. In addition to its work streamlining marketing and sales tactics, SKP also advises on M&A corporate strategy. With 450 employees and 17 offices spanning 12 countries, SKP has carried out work in over 55 countries for clients including Allianz, AstraZeneca, BMW, Goldman Sachs, ICI, Microsoft, Porsche and many more.

Name your price

The consultancy was started in Germany in 1985 by business administration and marketing expert Professor Hermann Simon (who remains as chairman of the firm today), and two of his PhD students. Believing that price is the "primary driver" of a company's short- and midterm profits, but that many manage it inefficiently, SKP began picking up business from companies eager to maximise their profit margins. The firm's approach to pricing involves extensive quantitative and qualitative analysis of market factors that boils down to one key element—identifying "what the market will bear".

Of course, there's more to pricing than simply setting a level and charging it indefinitely, however, and it is here that SKP's expertise in pricing strategy comes into play. SKP has a holistic approach that encompasses everything from competitive strategy to product positioning and sales force execution. Offering strategies and solutions for a range of possibilities over a product's lifetime, the firm encourages clients to adopt a consistent, targeted approach that anticipates the market, rather than reacts to it. At the upper end of the pricing scale, for example, the firm extols the benefits of "selling an emotion". According to Jens Baumgarten, managing director of SKP's New York office, marking down an item, even in tough economic conditions, can be disastrous for luxury consumers. "If a product is priced too low, it will have the reverse effect on the emotions," Baumgarten told *Forbes* in February, 2008.

Take it to the bank

Between its consulting work and the various white papers, reports and books it publishes, the firm prides itself on offering advice its clients can take to the bank. SKP estimates that it squeezes an average of an extra 2 to 3 percentage points of profit out of any product it works on. And if SKP doesn't think it offers what the client is looking for, it won't take the job. According to the firm, "We refrain from projects for which we do not have or cannot develop the required competencies."

Among SKP's undertakings are pricing strategies for Mercedes Benz, BMW and Porsche for their new models, and helping B2B companies improve their price setting, competitive strategy and price execution. Central to its pricing services is the company's belief that setting prices is "the area where profits are most often left on the table" and that "value pricing"—focussing on increasing the value of a product and quantifying what customers will pay for it—is more profitable than the more common cost-plus model of pricing. SKP also helps clients set prices across different countries, a complex decision-making process that often confounds companies in the international marketplace.

> “ Consultants appreciate that they're given a 'high level of autonomy'. ”

You First

It should come as little surprise that a company founded by a professor of business, and with over 50 PhDs on its staff evidences committment to professional training and development. SKP is supported in its endeavours by an international advisory board made up of academics at some of the most venerable higher education institutions around the globe, including both the London and Harvard Business Schools, Stanford University, HEC, Paris, IESE, University of Barcelona and several institutions throughout Asia.

The company's commitment to its staff—formalised in a programme known as You First—begins with an international orientation, partnering mentoring as well as a company training programme to familiarise all new hires with SKP procedures. Additional education is actively encouraged, and the firm arranges lectures by internal and external speakers. Employees are also encouraged to publish the results of their work and experience in industry journals, and to present at conferences and seminars. For a role model, consultants can look to Professor Simon himself; a renowned expert in his field, Simon has presented and published widely, including more than 30 books published in 22 languages. Those books include the best seller, *Hidden Champions: Lessons from 500 of the World's Best Unknown Companies*, published in 1996. His most recent publications are 2006's *Manage for Profit, Not for Market Share*, and 2007's *Hidden Champions of the 21st Century*, which updates the ideas first presented a decade earlier in *Hidden Champions*. It celebrates midsized companies that focus on a niche market, are willing to venture into global markets and are often privately owned—all factors that allow these companies to maximise profits ahead of market share. Those ideas were also evident in *Manage for Profit*, which exhorts managers to go after profits, rather than focus on volume of sales or market share.

Gimme a G—twice

As far as its own profits go, SKP has some fairly firm targets for the future, as it seeks to achieve both growth and globalisation—exactly the sort of advice it would offer its clients. On the growth front, the company has an avowed target of 15 per cent every year—a lofty goal that would see it double its revenue every five years. Unattainable as it may sound, the firm achieved those numbers in 2007, posting a record growth of 25.3 per cent, as revenue increased from €64 million in 2006 to €80 million in 2007. That record saw the firm's average annual growth climb to 21 per cent since 1995, a figure that means SKP is now 10 times larger than it was in that year.

Arms around the world

To continue meeting its growth target, SKP is committed to increasing its global footprint via two methods. The first involves opening offices in nations where its services are likely to be most needed, ie, those that are already highly industrialised, with an established market where SKP's expertise will come into play. The second prong of the plan is to open smaller offices in emerging markets, and grasp opportunities as they come along.

As evidence of both of these approaches, the firm opened offices in Cologne, New York and Vienna in 2007, and opened concerns in Luxembourg, Moscow and Madrid in 2008, moves that increased the number of its offices to 17 worldwide. In January 2008, SKP also added four new partners—Jens Baumgarten, who directs the financial services practice in New York; Dr Fabian Braun, part of the chemicals and construction division in Cologne; André Weber, joining the travel, transport and telecoms division in Boston; and Dr Gerald Schnell, selected for the medical devices division in the new Luxembourg facility. Total staff numbers are above 400 for the first time in company history.

Globalisation can come at a cost, however, especially if others attempt to cash in on the consultancy's hard-won successes. In 2007, SKP discovered that an unaffiliated firm in China was operating under the Simon-Kucher brand and logo, passing itself off as an SKP regional office and forcing the real firm to take legal action. The case is ongoing, but Chairman Simon is adamant that such setbacks will be overcome: "The further globalisation of Simon-Kucher will not be halted by such obstacles."

GETTING HIRED

A day to remember

SKP looks to "renowned business schools and universities" from "all over the world" to find its future consultants. Its interviews are "run on an office-by-office basis", but the process is slowly "becoming more structured", insiders say. Currently, most candidates have an "initial telephone interview, followed by a half-day process of multiple interviews and tests". This day normally "starts with a general SKP presentation by a partner". After that, candidates must take a "multiple-choice math test", after which interviews commence. The number of interviews can vary "depending on the profile", with some candidates having as many as "seven, with a lot of case studies", and others enduring only three meetings. Most commonly, though, candidates have "five interviews". Interviewers look at "case study performance, motivation and soft skills" when making their decisions. Candidates should expect to meet "partners, directors and consultants" on their interview day, which often involves "a lunch date in between the first and second interviews".

Interviewers ask "the standard stuff, with a bias towards pricing". There might also be "questions on marketing and company-specific topics". Digging into "educational background, expectations and language abilities" is common as well. A potential question could be the following: "Talk me through the potential impacts of the introduction of a new iPod model into the current range," or "How would you rate the market potential of shaving foam in Japan?" Specific questions "depend on the interviewer", but almost everyone will want to "discuss your CV" and will throw in a few "brainteasers", respondents note. A consultant explains that the goal is to "combine knowledge testing with personal talk." Candidates normally "get results pretty fast, usually within the next day".

Good first impression

Many candidates leave SKP's interview day with a "good personal impression". According to one source, "SKP's was the most convincing recruiting event I have ever attended." Consultants tell us they chose SKP over other firms because of its "superior reputation, especially in scientific areas". And those who are looking for a "focus on very quantitative consulting" are drawn to the firm's "reputation as a world leader in pricing". Some report that SKP is "more entrepreneurial" and offers a "nicer work/life balance" than other consultancies, whereas others comment on the "friendly and humane atmosphere" displayed during the interview process.

Jumping right in

SKP interns are "involved in regular project work and have direct contact with clients". Insiders say the "very positive" experience is a chance for young consultants to take on "their own tasks and project streams", and to be exposed to SKP's "friendly corporate culture". The firm's "nice atmosphere and good mentoring" leave many interns pleased at the prospect of working there full time. One former intern, who "went to nearly all meetings with the customer", remarks, "I had a very good experience, otherwise I would not be here now."

OUR SURVEY SAYS

No clones allowed

SKP has some "partner-specific subcultures", but for the most part, the firm is an "open and friendly" place that "does not have too many defined rules". Insiders tell us the firm "does not hire or create clones", so "every associate is different." Consultants "are valued as individuals, without any pressure to produce a stereotype". In addition, a source notes, SKP has maintained an entrepreneurial spirit, "despite significant growth"—the firm retains a "small-company, cosy family feeling". Sometimes, "a lack of structure and guidelines can be an issue," though, especially as "not all partners follow the same approach to work." But the majority of SKP staffers enjoy the consultancy's "down-to-earth feel". It's a place where "work/life balance is taken seriously" and "people like to have fun." A contact explains, "We make a big effort to hire people who are interesting and fun, in addition to being smart."

We're told that consultants at this "very international" firm are "not that competitive", yet are quite proud of SKP's "market-leading position" in pricing and marketing and sales consulting. The culture is "nonhierarchical", and consultants appreciate that they're given a "high level of autonomy". The firm has a "bunch of hardworking and smart, yet idiosyncratic individuals" who thrive in this "enthusiastic and flexible" environment. One source interjects that the firm is also "pragmatic and cost-conscious", which can sometimes feel "rather rigid". But overall, consultants appreciate the "honesty and freedom" that's exhibited in this "really nice and relaxed atmosphere". As one insider puts it, "People are by far the most important part of the company, and not just people by numbers—it is the individual that counts."

Relatively well balanced

Work/life balance at SKP is reportedly "project-driven". In general, believes one insider, "it is possible to balance work and private life, especially on the weekends."

Exactly how balanced one feels "depends very much on the partner" with whom one works. Some bosses emphasise work/life balance, while "some do not care." Hourly requirements per week "vary from 50 to 65 hours", with the majority of consultants logging "at least 60, and sometimes up to 70 hours", but "overall, there is little weekend work." A contact notes, however, that "prior to important presentations, long hours or weekends do occur." During these times, the real opportunities for balance "come between projects". Project length "differs a lot", staffers point out, but the "average is around four months". Fortunately for these consultants, there is no need to put in face time, and they "only stay late when there is a lot to do".

Differences in work/life balance also exist among offices, due to their "very different sizes". A source states, "More flexibility is necessary in a 10-person office than in a 100-person office." Most say SKP's balance is "acceptable for consulting, although you do have to sacrifice somewhat on exercise". At times, it can feel like "you have to fight for your work/life balance." But if you do, balance at SKP "is probably better than in most consultancies", and is "generally accommodating to personal needs, ie, pregnancy, part-time work, further education and changing locations".

> 66 SKP's 'familiar atmosphere' lends itself to 'uncomplicated, friendly interactions with superiors'. 99

Travel is not excessive

Travel requirements at SKP are also "dependent on the project". Some assignments require consultants to be "at the client site four to five days a week", while others only require travel "about once a week". For those who enjoy it, a job at SKP provides a "great opportunity to travel", and consultants are "not held back by [their] base office location". Some say "travelling has no impact on work/life balance," whereas for others, "travelling on weekends is common," which makes its effects on lifestyle more visible. And, although travel is "rarely for long periods", it can have a "bad effect on the social environment" in the office. SKP tries to temper this through its "policy to not spend more time than necessary at the client's site", a consultant explains. As such, apart from "exceptional projects", most travel is "day trips, done by train"—allowing many staffers to return to their own beds "almost every night". Most respondents consider the travel opportunities "positive, since they are not excessive".

Lackluster compensation

But SKP consultants aren't thrilled with their compensation. Entry-level salaries "differ a lot for the same position with the same education", but on average, "compensation is far below industry levels," sources say. The firm "claims to balance lower salaries with less hours", but insiders say "this is not really the case"—if the promoted work/life balance "was better enforced, the offered salary would be fair". One consultant remarks, "Because of the partnership scheme, which is great in the long run, partners are hesitant to give industry-matching salaries." At the partner level, there is profit sharing and "compensation is very attractive." Bonuses are "a percentage based on salary", and this "increases with your career path", though it is "usually a ridiculous amount" a respondent comments. Bonuses are "based solely on qualitative feedback from partners and project leaders", so "there is no connection to project or company performance." Moreover, there are "high differences in workload" among consultants, which "leads to gross inequalities on an hourly wage basis". On the upside, some divisions give "special performance bonuses to compensate for excessive travel or extraordinary achievements".

In the way of perks, the firm provides health insurance and makes a "contribution to pensions". Sources say there is also a "contribution to car leases" at the senior consultant level, but "associates do not get a company car." Consultants appreciate that "air miles can be put toward private usage." In addition, employees have "guaranteed days off for the 24th and 31st of December", and enjoy an "annual holiday party held in some of the most prestigious and historical places in Germany". In general, though, respondents feel that perks at SKP are "very limited, as the firm is really penny counting".

Head office needs a makeover

Certain of the firm's offices aren't putting any smiles on faces, either. The Bonn headquarters, we're told, has "very old furniture and looks shabby", though others reinterpret it as "nice, clean and cosy". The location is "not very attractive" and it's "not in the newest building". Sure, "all the necessary technology" exists, but as "the company is growing quite rapidly," office space is "limited, especially on Fridays" (which is why, according to the firm, it plans to move out after the lease expires). One unsatisfied consultant remarks, "The offices in Bonn are as charming as the interior of military barracks, due to grey colours, no plants and old furniture. Some chairs are very uncomfortable and bad for people with spine problems."

Fortunately, "in other cities, the offices are much better." The Zurich location is "very nice and modern", while the Paris crew works from a "unique location in central Paris, with exceptional offices with a view of the Eiffel Tower". The facility in Madrid is "basic, but well located", and the Cologne office is "beautifully located on the Rhine, in a brand-new building". There are "very poor-quality offices in London", and a Milan-based respondent complains, "The managing director of the office is stingy. He hasn't rented an office linked to the prestige of the firm." In Munich, a hungry staffer notes that there is "no cafeteria or other food supply, apart from coffee, fruit and yogurt."

Not everyone gets client contact

Most insiders tell us that SKP's "familiar atmosphere" lends itself to "uncomplicated, friendly interactions with superiors". In Paris, consultants have "total accessibility to the three partners of our 30-person office". A source in Madrid comments, "I have a very good relationship with my supervisors because there is a high level of trust, ability to delegate responsibility and, in general, a good working atmosphere."

But access to clients' upper management varies by location. A consultant in Bonn notes, "There is only very little direct contact with the client, and usually the clients are in middle management." A colleague in the same office agrees: "There are not many opportunities for a consultant-level employee to interact with top management. This is usually restricted to partners/project leaders." This is not the case in Luxembourg, where a senior consultant tells us staffers are encouraged to have a "high degree of responsibility from the beginning on". Such is the case in Madrid, too, where a source explains, "Supervisors encourage you to get involved from the beginning with clients and give you opportunities to present to them."

Formal training could use some tweaks

SKP has "structured training programmes that run throughout the career spectrum, even at the partner level". The firm "tries its best to make sure that each consultant has the opportunity to attend these trainings". According to one respondent, "There are some teething problems, such as conflicts between consultant availability with training sessions, but efforts are being made to solve this." During the first year, "each consultant has to complete a predefined set of training modules, which are offered at different point of times throughout the year." Ongoing official trainings are "mostly held internally". The quality of these events, known as SKP Universities, "varies based on the speaker, and normally, quality is medium at the max". And, an insider remarks, "training seminars offered often do not meet the needs of project work." For this reason, staffers insist that "most of the relevant training is done on the job." To that end, "experienced team members are willing to invest time in helping junior members develop."

Promotions happen quickly

Promotion at SKP is viewed as "a reward for good performance and an expectation of future performance". Respondents feel that the firm's policy is "performance-driven and fair". The structure is such that there are "four consultant levels before you reach senior consultant". A staffer explains that it is possible to "advance quickly due to strong growth of the firm—promotions generally happen within one year", but it is "realistic to move up after six months". The speed with which one advances "depends on the abilities of each person and his willingness to be promoted".

Male-dominated at the top

Sources say there are "a lot of women" at SKP, but just one female partner and few female directors. Although there are "no salary or career advancement differences between genders, most women drop out at the director level". A consultant remarks, "When it comes to top levels, we are weak. Part of this is built into the business model that combining family and consulting is hard to manage." Nor are there any "mentoring programmes or special programmes to support young mothers". One source doesn't see this as an impediment, however: "Specific mentoring does not exist, but it is not necessary anyway. They're just women—not handicapped!"

Similarly, at SKP, "it does not matter whether you are a minority or not." The firm "actively promotes" acceptance of different ethnic groups, but there are "no specific programmes" to support them. As a source asserts, "People are merited on capabilities, not cultural background." Consultants with multiple language skills are "highly welcome", and "bilingual minorities should have an advantage." One respondent points out that "minority in terms of nationality or ethnic background is not an issue; we are a global consultancy." When it comes to gay and lesbian employees, "nobody is discriminated against." Although SKP "does not actively search for gays or lesbians" during the recruiting process, there are "quite a few openly gay people" at the firm, and "there have never been any problems."

Limited community involvement

We're told that SKP has "no systematic process in place" for involving its consultants in community work. The firm does have specific projects in place "in the US, but not in Europe". Sometimes, if it is "initiated by individual consultants", the company will back them, but it is "rather uncommon" in most European offices. Targeted efforts "depend on the division", with some participating in "pro bono consulting or tutoring at universities". There are also are "some sports events" held in honour of charities. But generally speaking, SKP in Europe "does not proactively approach" community work. □

TATA CONSULTANCY SERVICES

4th Floor
33 Grosvenor Place
London SW1X 7HY
United Kingdom
Phone: +44 (0)207 245 1800
Fax: +44 (0)207 245 1875
www.tcs.com

The Stats

Employer Type: Public Company
Ticker Symbol: 532540 (Bombay Stock
   Exchange), TCSEQ (National Stock
   Exchange)
CEO & Managing Director:
   Subramaniam Ramadorai
2008 Employees: 111,000+
2007 Employees: 83,500+
2008 Revenue: $5.7 billion
2007 Revenue: $4.3 billion
No. of Offices: More than 170 offices
   in over 50 countries

Practice Areas

Business Intelligence & Performance
   Management
Business Process Outsourcing
Consulting
Engineering & Industrial Services
Enterprise Solutions
IT Infrastructure Services
IT Services

European Locations

London (Head Office, UK & Ireland)
Mumbai (Global HQ)
Belgium • Denmark • Finland • France •
Germany • Hungary • Iceland • Ireland •
Luxembourg • Milan • Netherlands •
Norway • Portugal • Spain • Sweden •
Switzerland • United Kingdom

Pluses

• Global network is unmatched
• Strong management team

Minuses

• Still building a name for itself in
  Europe
• Hierarchical environment

Employment Contact

www.tcs.com/Careers/Careers.html

THE BUZZ
WHAT CONSULTANTS AT OTHER FIRMS ARE SAYING

• "Growth company"
• "Huge, can do a lot, but not all on a
  high level"
• "Dedicated and smart"
• "Aggressive"

THE SCOOP

The largest IT services firm in India, Tata Consulting Services is just one of 96 firms that comprise the multinational conglomerate that is the Tata Group. While the latter fact may make TCS sound like a minor player in the grand scheme of all things Tata, the former, plus the impressive $5.7 billion it raked in throughout fiscal 2008, establishes TCS in the upper echelon of global consulting firms of any discipline or geographical bent. With over 111,000 consultants operating in 50 countries around the globe, the firm is well on its way to achieving its stated aim of being one of the top-10 global consulting companies by 2010.

Say hello to Tata

Having started life as a provider of low-cost employment outsourcing (a/k/a cheap labour), it should come as little surprise that one of TCS' core service offerings to this day is outsourcing. In addition to this, the firm has two further consulting strands—IT services and business solutions—which together are parcelled up and delivered through the firm's unique, proprietary global delivery model. That model is "recognised as the benchmark of excellence in software development", according to the firm.

All that capability would be wasted without clients, of course, and TCS also has these in abundance, spread across industries including banking and financial services, insurance, telecoms, media and entertainment, government, health care and life sciences, energy and utilities, retail and consumer packaged goods, travel and hospitality, manufacturing and high technology.

UK & Ireland—not "Europe"

TCS claims to have 18 offices in Europe—a figure that includes a development centre in Hungary and a private banking centre in Luxembourg, but not its holdings in the UK and Ireland, which the firm classes as a separate geographical entity to its European affairs. While that description may be appealing to certain members of the British political classes looking to turn the clock back to a pre-EU world, it seems likely that TCS' reasoning is based more on when it arrived in each theatre of operations, rather than any attempt to rewrite the political landscape of the region. While TCS has been operating in mainland Europe for around 20 years, it has an extra decade of experience in the UK and Ireland, and a considerably bigger footprint there. Indeed, while the firm employs more than 1,300 consultants out of 18 offices in "Europe", the English-speaking part of the region boasts some 3,700 staff, distributed between a network of just six offices, but also a whopping 85 client sites. Little wonder, then, that the firm chooses not to make tracking its operations there any more complicated—especially as it also owns and operates a subsidiary consulting firm in the UK, Diligenta Ltd. As for the colonialism that established English as an official language on the subcontinent, making the UK and Ireland a natural place for an Indian firm to seek global business expansion? Best to not even go there.

Within TCS' UK holdings, meanwhile, is something the firm calls an "innovation lab", located in Peterborough. Part of the UK subsidiary Diligenta, the lab is the only one of its kind in Europe, and out of 16 such facilities owned by TCS, is one of only five located outside of India. The function of the labs is to provide environments for finding solutions for TCS customers, giving them cost-effective access to a team of experts in TCS' core competencies. While each location has its own particular specialities, the Peterborough lab focusses largely on browser-based Web 2.0 technologies, as well as utility computing and RFID (chips, tags, labels, readers and middleware).

Diligenta, meanwhile, is regulated by the UK Financial Services Authority (FSA) and specialises in outsourcing services for financial services firms. TCS chose to brand the firm as Diligenta in order to keep its identity separate from its non-FSA-regulated concerns in the UK. The firm was launched in 2005, following TCS' £486 million acquisition of the Pearl Group's life and pensions operation, which has formed the main core of its business. That's not the sum total of it, though, as TCS announced in February 2008 that it had picked up a contract to provide BPO services for Standard Life—a deal worth an estimated £100 million over 10 years.

Counting the rings on the family tree

Parent company Tata Group has been around in one form or another since 1868, when Jamsetji Nusserwanji Tata founded the private trading firm that would eventually grow into India's largest conglomerate—one that generated some $64 billion in fiscal 2008. The company's roots in Europe were established even way back then, as the founder travelled to England in the 1880s, seeking ways to diversify his successful textiles industry and gain an international standing. Hitting upon steel as the answer, Tata resolved to become India's first steel magnate—a decision that met with derision from many, but which eventually paid off, albeit after the founder's death. J.N. Tata was succeeded at the helm by his son, Dorab, an occasion that marked the first in a line of familial succession at Tata that has continued almost uninterrupted to this day. Dorab (and his successors, for that matter), continued to diversify Tata's holdings, moving into hydroelectrics, luxury hotels, consumer goods and more—with "and more" including an airline, a chemical company, an engineering and locomotive concern, a science institute, an industrial concern, consumer goods, a tea company and an international export business, all bearing the

Tata family name. Eventually, in 1968, the firm broke yet more new ground, establishing India's first software services company: Tata Consultancy Services.

Its birth in 1968 was the first of many firsts for TCS as an Indian software company. In 2002, for example, it became the first such firm to surpass $1 billion in revenue. Just two years later, the consultancy went public, raising more than $1.2 billion—the largest IPO in Indian history. Along with the rest of the Indian economy, it has continued to enjoy exponential growth, although recent global economic turmoil may see TCS' growth rates slow from the 41 per cent revenue gains it enjoyed between 2006 and 2007, and the 25 per cent increase it saw in fiscal 2008.

Going global

While TCS is active all around the world, its business model is built on providing cost-effective operations for clients and, as such, tends to prosper in areas where employment cost savings can be achieved. As such, the firm has extensive operations in Asia, and a sizeable presence in South America, with Uruguay in particular operating as a booming market for the firm, as it utilises the Spanish-speaking workforce there to provide services to clients in Spain. Following this approach, recent movements in Europe by the firm have been somewhat limited, aside from the Diligenta deal, and the acquisition of some 75 per cent of Swiss software company TKS-Teknosoft in late 2006. As TCS CEO Subramaniam Ramadorai phrased it in a *Forbes* interview in May 2007, "We've integrated our global workforce and reached out to markets that are far beyond traditional non-English-speaking markets. We did it successfully in Uruguay and China. We're a global player with a global presence."

That global presence, meanwhile, relies on the firm's global delivery model, which has three integrated components: a global workforce, integrated processes and a multi-tiered infrastructure. Each of these components combines to allow the firm to deliver lower-cost results to clients by simultaneously working on projects around the globe. As evidence of the model's success, the firm points to client satisfaction ratings of 89 per cent, compared with cost variations averaging just 3 per cent.

GETTING HIRED

Log on to start

TCS' European hiring efforts are divided between continental Europe, Hungary, and the UK and Ireland—candidates can find regional employment contacts for each of these regions on the "career seekers" section of the firm's web site.

TCS claims it's looking for "top-flight professionals committed to creating and implementing innovative solutions that help transform business", and these professionals don't necessarily fit a standard academic or employment profile. As the firm explains, "TCS associates have diverse backgrounds, talents, experiences and interests, but share a spirit of teamwork, a commitment to delivering quality results and the desire to keep growing professionally." While much of TCS' recruiting is still focussed on India—and, to a lesser extent, the United States—undergraduate and graduate candidates from around the world can log on to careers.tcs.com and submit an online application form along with their CV.

Current employees can bring new hires into the fold, too, through the TCS Bring Your Buddy initiative. This online portal allows TCS-ers to log in and make referrals; then, they can check back to monitor their friends' recruitment status. □

TOWERS PERRIN

1 Stamford Plaza
263 Tresser Blvd.
Stamford, Connecticut 06901
United States
Phone: +1 (203) 326-5400
Fax: +1 (203) 326-5499
www.towersperrin.com

The Stats

Employer Type: Private Company
Chairman & CEO: Mark V. Mactas
2008 Employees: 6,000
2007 Employees: 5,400
2007 Sales: $1.57 billion
2006 Sales: $1.42 billion
No. of Offices: 81

Practice Areas

Actuarial Services
Change Management & Communication
Employee Benefits
Enterprise Risk & Capital Management
Executive Compensation
Financial Modeling Solutions
Health & Welfare Consulting
HR Function & Effectiveness
Insurance & Financial Services
Mergers, Acquisitions & Restructuring
Organization & Employee Research
Reinsurance Services
Research Surveys
Retirement Consulting
Retirement Risk Solutions
Total Rewards Effectiveness
Workforce Effectiveness

European Locations

Stamford (World HQ)
Belgium • France • Germany • Ireland •
Italy • Netherlands • Poland • Spain •
Sweden • Switzerland • United
Kingdom

Pluses

• "Early responsibility"
• Performance pay
• "Great clients"

Minuses

• "Bureaucracy"
• Sometimes lacking in strong leadership
• "Terrible time and reporting systems"

Employment Contact

careers.towers.com

THE BUZZ
WHAT CONSULTANTS AT OTHER FIRMS ARE SAYING

• "Very good tools and approaches"
• "Old style"
• "Good in their specialisation"
• "Overrated"

THE SCOOP

Towers Perrin's roots in the business world stretch back to 1931, with the launch of a Philadelphia-based reinsurance firm that had 26 employees and a first-year income of less than $200,000. The company was called Towers, Perrin, Forster & Crosby and quickly tapped into New Deal legislation that created a boom in the employee consulting business. As time went on, Towers, Perrin, Forster & Crosby quickly become an established name in the human resources consulting business. In 1965, it opened its first European office in Brussels, and just four years later, a second European office in London. In 1987, after a string of mergers and acquisitions, the firm permanently changed its name to Towers Perrin.

Today Towers Perrin is an internationally recognised consulting firm with over 6,000 employees and representation on every continent except for Antarctica. The scope of its business has expanded substantially over the course of its 74 years of operations to incorporate far more than insurance. The firm's three main areas of operations today are reinsurance, financial risk management, and human resources and benefits consulting.

Tillinghast is an asset

Towers Perrin also provides insurance consulting through Tillinghast, an Atlanta-based actuarial firm with which it merged in 1986. Tillinghast is now wholly incorporated into the Towers Perrin network and provides services including enterprise risk management, financial management, financial modelling solutions, insurance industry M&A consulting, products, markets and distribution analysis, and regulatory compliance. In 2007, Tillinghast was recognised by the press for its excellence in consulting, taking home the award for Best Consultancy of the Year from *Reactions* magazine, and Top Global Consultancy in a *Life & Pensions* survey.

Building an empire

The last 10 years at Towers Perrin have been marked by rapid expansion, including a string of key acquisitions that have augmented and strengthened its business. With these extensions, Towers Perrin has also created a more significant presence in Europe with several subsidiaries operating on the continent. For example, in 2002, Towers Perrin acquired British insurance and reinsurance consultancy Denis M. Clayton, adding even more strength to its UK practices. Following the acquisition, the company's British reinsurance operations were renamed Towers Perrin Clayton. In 2005, the German employee benefits and pension consultancy, Rauser AG, became part of the Towers Perrin family.

In 2007, the consultancy added a Stateside asset to its growing group when it acquired ISR, an employee research and consulting firm. ISR is based in Chicago, but has a global presence, including offices in London, Frankfurt, Paris, Helsinki, Madrid and Milan. Towers Perrin also currently holds alliances with several other European companies, including Abcon, a Swiss actuarial firm, Greco International, a Vienna-based benefit consultancy and—in Poland—Trio Management, an actuarial consultancy, and HRK, an HR consultancy.

Well decorated

Towers Perrin has received its fair share of praise from the press in recent years, and 2007 proved to be quite a banner year in terms of garnering accolades from a variety of publications and organisations. In August, Linda Chase-Jenkins, the managing principal of Towers Perrin's enterprise risk management practice, was recognised by *Business Insurance* as one of 2007's Women to Watch. Chase-Jenkins worked in the

> ❝ Rewards are tilted toward those who produce good results. ❞

London offices until she became a principal in 2005. In May, the consultancy was named Advisory Firm of the Year by *Energy Risk* for its expertise in "energy-related issues that range from enterprise risk management (ERM) framework development, to acquisition due diligence, to the particulars of market and credit risks as well as risk capital structure." And in April, Towers Perrin was named Best Services Supplier by communications technologies firm Nortel in an awards ceremony that took place in Beijing.

Executive comp causes problems

Towers Perrin found itself in the midst of a mini-scandal in October 2007 when a report was released by The Corporate Library showing that companies who use compensation consulting services often increase executive salaries independently of performance. When the report was published, Towers Perrin e-mailed Bloomberg with a statement that said its role was to be "part of the solution and not part of the problem", and also that "it is clear that there does need to be a better understanding about the role compensation consultants play in this process."

As the pain of the subprime mortgage collapse left its footprint on the market in 2008, executive salaries continued to be an issue. Donald Lowman, a managing director at Towers Perrin, told *Forbes* in April, "One of the great things about disclosure is that we have much more information than we've ever had about pay practices for public companies." On the flip side, he adds, "One of the problems is we've had more information than we've ever had about pay practices for public companies."

GETTING HIRED

Unrehearsed brain power

Insiders tell us Towers Perrin's interview process is "quite rigorous, involving several interviews and preparation of case studies". Recent graduates in the UK will typically have one telephone interview, a face-to-face interview and a day at an assessment centre. On this day, "candidates can expect a written test, group exercise and two interviews," says one consultant. There's normally "one behavioural and one competency-based interview". A respondent explains that the firm "does not want over-rehearsed and practised candidates", but rather, is looking for "great brain power and the right attitude". To find its future brainiacs, Towers Perrin recruits at "all tier-one UK universities", including Warwick, Oxford, London and Cambridge. Those are the schools at which the firm "proactively markets" itself, but a contact points out, "We recruit from anywhere."

OUR SURVEY SAYS

Clients come first

It's the firm's "collegiate" atmosphere and "positive, can-do attitude" that helps attracted candidates to Towers Perrin. Sources describe the culture as "supportive but hardworking", and note that it is "focussed on securing results for clients". Consultants appreciate "the chance to work with people who are famous thought leaders in their profession". One insider raves, "The smartest people work for Towers Perrin." And although the firm is "genuinely focussed on client issues", some say "this is currently under threat," in part because of the "organisation's inability to effectively change". In fact, a respondent claims, "management and leadership at Towers Perrin are generally quite poor."

Taking balance into your own hands

Work/life balance is left up to the individual at Towers Perrin. According to one consultant, "In general, I can choose when and where I do my work, as long as I get it done. Sometimes there are periods of stress when several deadlines come together, but most of the time I have no problem devoting enough time to my family and leisure." We're told that the firm "does not promote work/life balance", but fortunately, "local senior leaders do, through example." In addition, employees have the freedom to "work from home regularly". Respondents explain that Towers Perrin consultants handle "multiple projects at the same time," and are "not 'on assignment' like at other firms". A contact says of balancing multiple projects, "This helps in many ways, including with work/life balance." Most consultants average 50 hours a week, but in general, "it is up to you how hard you work." "Rewards are tilted toward those who produce good results, and I am personally motivated to do well and get involved in interesting projects, so I tend to work hard," a source shares.

Many consultants "travel quite a lot, and when it becomes too intense, it can be a chore". One source remarks, "It's tiring, and makes it difficult to keep up with other work." But the majority of respondents say travelling for the firm has "many positive benefits, including meeting people and learning different ways of doing things". Overall, travel demands are "not a problem".

Statutory comp

When it comes to compensation at Towers Perrin, "it takes a while to get to market rate, but it does get there." As one consultant puts it, "We pay pretty OK." Some staffers get equity in the firm, which can be "difficult to quantify". In the UK, "the pension is good, with a 10 per cent rate of employer contribution." Perks are "nothing better than statutory", but consultants do enjoy working from an "excellent and new office space in London". And in terms of giving back to the community, the firm offers "support of some firm-sponsored charities and several individually sponsored efforts", but staffers say that, overall, community involvement is "not really part of UK business culture".

Learning to advance

Towers Perrin consultants have the "ability to learn and advance quickly". The firm provides "excellent on-the-job training, and the experience you get through client projects is superb", a source reports. Although "there are many opportunities to learn through in-house training," some insiders feel that "investment in off-the-job training has declined in recent years."

We're also told that promotions are "based on merit". Advancement can be "rapid, but criteria can be rather narrow". A London-based source notes, "Due to talent shortages in the UK, up-or-out is increasingly a short-term view of little value." As such, most consultants "advance regularly, but you will stick at a level if you do not develop your skills".

Colourblind

Respondents say there is "a very cosmopolitan atmosphere in the London office", and the consultancy has a "strong culture of mutual respect". The firm is "very supportive of women balancing career and family life, however, distinctly fewer women than men make it through to senior levels", a staffer comments. When it comes to ethnic minorities, a colleague states, Towers Perrin is "pretty colourblind", and the firm is "very tolerant" with regard to gays and lesbians. An insider says, "There are a lot of gay people in the firm and they are treated no differently than anyone else." There are "plenty of successful gay people", another points out, because the firm's primary concern is "how well you do your job". □

VALUE PARTNERS

9 Via Vespri Siciliani
Milan 20146
Italy
Phone: +39 (0)2 485 481
Fax: +39 (0)2 485 487 20
www.valuepartners.com

The Stats

Employer Type: Private Company
CEO: Giorgio Rossi Cairo
2008 Employees: 3,000+
2007 Employees: 3,000
2007 Revenue: €380 million
2006 Revenue: €240 million
No. of Offices: 14

Practice Areas

Company Restructuring
IT Consulting
Operational Improvement Programmes
Organisational Change Management
Portfolio & Business Strategies
Product & Service Portfolio
  Development

European Locations

Milan (HQ)
Helsinki • Istanbul • London • Rome

Pluses

• "Staff turnover is very low"
• Very fast learning curve

Minuses

• Less brand awareness than
  competitor firms
• "Opaque management processes"

Employment Contact

Go to the "Work with us" section of
the firm's web site

THE BUZZ
WHAT CONSULTANTS AT OTHER FIRMS ARE SAYING

• "Nothing but excellent feedback"
• "Not international enough"
• "Said to be strong in Southern
  Europe"
• "Few very important clients"

THE SCOOP

Value Partners serves its customers through two separate companies: Value Partners Management Consulting and Value Team IT Consulting & Solutions. The management consultancy specialises in helping companies with strategy, restructuring and investment projects across many different sectors, including telecommunications and media, energy, manufacturing, high-tech and financial services. Value Team IT Consulting & Solutions has been operating since 2000 and provides large and medium-sized firms with IT consulting, systems integration, and custom projects and application management.

An Italian master

Value Partners Management Consulting was founded by Giorgio Rossi Cairo and Vittorio Giaroli in 1993. The two veteran consultants hoped to start a firm that would live up its name and provide solutions that have true value for its clients. The consultancy's rapid international expansion allowed clients all over the world to access its services, starting with the first international office, which opened in São Paulo, Brazil, in 1994. That office encountered a serious problem within its first three years of operations that threatened to close Value Partners

> ❝ The firm's 'distinct industry focus tends to attract passionate, engaging people'. ❞

Brazil operations completely. Three partners in that location betrayed Value Partners to its competitor Bain & Company, giving the rival firm access to confidential documents and planning to take all of their employees with them to Bain. Value Partners took the rats to trial, winning a $10 million jury verdict, and didn't let that incident stop its growth trajectory. The consultancy went on to open an office in Turkey in 1999 and offices in Shanghai, Buenos Aires and Beijing in 2005. In 2006, the firm made its first move in the flourishing Indian economy with the opening of an office in Mumbai. Today, Value Partners has over 3,000 employees of 25 nationalities.

The Spectrum of success

Value Partners made a key strategic move in early 2007 with the acquisition of Spectrum Strategy Consultants, a London-based new media and telecommunications consultancy that serves big-name clients like BBC, NBC, Siemens, Nokia and Vodafone. Spectrum's international presence includes markets such as Hong Kong, Singapore and Sydney, and fits in perfectly with Value Partners' recent expansion plans. Now called Spectrum Value Partners, the merged company serves as the firm's media and telecommunications practice, and its main operations include strategy, operations, licensing and regulatory advice.

Yet another partner joins the team

Value Team IT Consulting & Solutions made its most significant move toward expansion in February 2007 when it purchased Etnoteam, another Italian information technology firm. With the acquisition, Value Partners added 1,170 employees from 10 offices to its team and became the third-largest Italian information and communications technology firm. Etnoteam's services include the design of web applications, mobile VAS development as well as IT consulting. One of the key benefits of the Etnoteam buy was an even larger international presence through Etnoteam's office in Helsinki. Roberto Galimberti, chairman of Etnoteam, expressed his pleasure with the new arrangement, stating, "Value Partners and its sister company Value Team share our DNA: a client-first and innovation-oriented approach. They are also younger than us."

Emerging markets face licensing battles

A unique revenue stream for the consultancy is derived from helping companies in developing countries to successfully bid for licences for 3G mobile phone technology. In June 2007, there were 200 million 3G subscribers, and the majority were situated in Europe. The leading country for European subscription to 3G is Value Partners' home country of Italy, where about one-third of the mobile phone users have access to the service. The debate about this technology is spreading throughout the world, as developing countries such as Turkey, China and Indonesia face bidding contests for the licences to operate 3G technology. In 2007, Value Partners worked with phone companies in Brazil, Turkey, Hungary, India, Saudi Arabia and Kenya, advising them on how to overcome the challenges of introducing 3G to their marketplace. In developed locations like Hong Kong, Japan and Ireland, and also in developing markets, the firm has helped more than 40 different sources acquire operating licences.

Sideshows

Value Partners is more than just a consultancy—it also is active in the management of a successful venture capital company. The fund is named, somewhat whimsically, Golden Mouse, and invests primarily in high-tech European startups. Since 2002, Golden Mouse has invested in 10 ventures, including Funambol, UsableNet and Italian technology outsourcing firm Ingenium Technology. Institutional investors include the European Investment Fund, Italia Group and Banca Popolare dell'Emilia Romagna. So far, these investors have contributed €15 million to Golden Mouse, although the fund had only invested €7 million as of 2008.

GETTING HIRED

Searching for value

Value Partners' hiring process involves "detailed quantitative interviews", as well as interviews "to assess a candidate's commitment and coherency with the firm's values". Insiders tell us that most candidates have a "two-round interview, with each round consisting of three to four 30-minute to one-hour interviews". The first round normally entails a general CV interview; a case study interview and some testing of numerical skills come in the second round. At the end is an interview with a partner. We're told that interviewers look at "what kind of a person you are", and a source elaborates: "They want warm, natural people whom they would like to have around." Candidates will meet with "HR, managers, senior managers and partners" throughout the process.

A contact says that, typically, "cases are adaptations of current client issues". A colleague says applicants should be prepared for brainteaser-type questions, such as, "How many taxis are there in Milan?" or, "What is the fair value of the pub at the end of the street?" Here's another example: "Pretend you are the CEO of a TLC incumbent in your country. How would you evaluate

> ££ When on travelling assignments, 'the company makes it as comfortable as possible.' ɔɔ

entering this emerging market? What would be your entry strategy?" And a typical essay question might be along the lines of, "Is radio dead?" Nailing questions is a plus, but one insider offers a tip: "You should somehow impress the partner who interviews you, apart from answering his questions." For example, "speaking Italian is an advantage."

Where to get noticed

The firm recruits from "top colleges and business schools around Europe", including Bocconi, Milan Politecnico, Cambridge, Oxford, INSEAD, IESE and London Business School. Value Partners also looks to "Asian business schools", insiders report. A Milan-based source notes, "We prefer MBAs and master's degrees from Bocconi or Politecnic." The firm's Istanbul office has a college hiring day, which involves "a full-day event with games, personality tests, interviews, cocktails and dinner."

One way to get a jump on the competition is by participating in an internship at the firm, which is "not a lot of pressure, but does involve hard work". Former interns say they "learn a lot" from the programme and, often, the "very favourable" experience makes for an "easy decision to join the firm".

OUR SURVEY SAYS

Big, happy family

Value Partners' "homemade corporate culture is supportive and very friendly", a consultant explains. The company takes "good care of its employees", who are reportedly "competitive and hardworking", though the environment is "not cutthroat" and Value Partners remains "sensitive to individual consultants' needs and aspirations". The firm's "distinct industry focus tends to attract passionate, engaging people", insists one associate. The "purely results-oriented" culture is "entrepreneurial and informal", and even "intimate and fun". As one insider puts it, the "very relaxed" attitude produces a "great friendship environment". In London, there is "table football in the kitchen and a fantasy football league that everyone gets involved in". And the crew even has "Nintendo Wii in the office!" One consultant remarks, "The London office is run like a family, with a kitchen where people sit around for a break, and a Friday joint lunch meeting where every member reports his achievements of the week." As a staffer puts it, Value Partners has managed "a good merge of strictness and fun", which keeps staff turnover "very low".

> ❝ New parents are welcome back, and usually are assigned to their home office location. ❞

With growth comes travel

Travel requirements are different for everyone. Some consultants are "always on the move", travelling to "glamorous places", while for others, travel is "largely optional". Insiders say demands can be "very office-dependent", with some consultants having "very little choice about travel requirements". It also is "very dependent of the kind of project" you're working on. A source explains, "If you travel in your country, the effects are very low. But if you work in other countries or continents, it's hard without the right rest plan." On the whole, an insider states, "travel requirements are getting more and more demanding," as Value Partners continues to expand its international presence. However, "projects tend to be in London or abroad in major cities," so consultants based in those cities may spend less time on the road. On the flip side, according to a respondent, "The fact that European assignments are staffed from major hubs [in Milan, London and Istanbul] ... as opposed to having multiple offices in each country, drives a higher travel requirement." It is not uncommon to be "on an off-site client assignment for four to six months of the year", a staffer claims.

In general, though, "there is less travel than at other firms," and when you are on the road, "the company makes it as comfortable as possible." As one associate notes, projects are assigned "considering individual consultants' personal requirements", so typically, "consultants willing to travel a lot have the opportunity to do so, while consultants that prefer to stay in a given city tend to travel less."

Flexible, until the client calls

Value Partners' is a "demanding environment", but it does provide "excellent opportunities to balance work and life". Insiders say their firm is "oriented on time-to-value logic, meaning, it's not important when or where you are working, as long as excellent, on-time results are delivered". A contact says, "The firm has a high-performance environment, but as long as I deliver, the firm is remarkably relaxed about where and when I work." Specific hourly requirements "depend on the project"—sometimes "long hours are expected," but normally with "some degree of flexibility". Still, it can be "hard to make weekday evening commitments". When there are tight deadlines, consultants "make sacrifices", but once the project is done, "the sacrifice is always compensated." In addition, because Value Partners "never rejects when clients come up with extra requests", it can sometimes be "hard to keep commitments". Things typically "come in phases", though; as one consultant explains, "There will be weeks when there is no time to do anything else but work, and others when one has a lot of free time."

It is "very difficult to assess" average project length, staffers say, because assignments can vary from two weeks to three months. Most say a typical project falls somewhere around "three to six months". Longer assignments are "possible, but not frequent". And overall, hours are "no worse than at other consultancies" and are described by respondents as "very reasonable for consulting". The "average is 40 to 60 per week, with an absolute max of 100 on particularly intense projects". What helps make things manageable is that, as a general rule, consultants are "not expected to carry out work on weekends", and during the week, there's the freedom "to complete work at home if you want to leave early". On occasion, however, "weekends and holidays are at risk if the client calls."

Varying levels of satisfaction with comp

Value Partners insiders give decent marks to their overall compensation, but opinions vary on the competitiveness of the firm's offerings. Some say salaries are "competitive", while others feel they are "toward the lower end of the scale". There's also a feeling that "bonuses leave something to be desired." A source says, "Bonus amounts have dropped significantly this year, from around 20 to 25 per cent of base to 15 per cent." One theory for this drop is that "compensation is competitive for juniors," but that as you advance, "the more other consulting firms' compensation policies are attractive". But there is some variance depending on one's geography. The Istanbul crew is happy, because "Value Partners gives the most competitive consulting salaries in Turkey," and in Milan, "compensation is aligned with competitors," including McKinsey and BCG.

As for perks, the firm offers "equity for partners", and consultants get "BMW company cars", an "integrative pension plan" and "medical insurance, including insurance for your wife or husband". Value Partners equips all consultants with BlackBerries, and "allows personal use". Employees also get "free dinner in the office past 8pm and free taxis home after 9pm". And on Fridays, everyone gets "free hot lunch", endearingly referred to as "flunch". Other extras include "comfortable business travelling and nice hotels", "help with MBAs" and "excellent paternity leave of three weeks paid". A consultant adds, "New parents are welcome back, and usually are assigned to their home office location to allow them to have a normal relationship with their family."

No-frills offices

Respondents say Value Partners is a "no-frills company" that is "not focussed on offices and location". The London office is "rather shabby and needs refurbishment", insiders report. The "office location is fine and the open plan is good, but the office itself a little dingy". A contact based there remarks, "The office feels fairly uninspiring." Fortunately, the firm is "expecting to move or refurbish soon". The Istanbul office has a "wonderful atmosphere"; a staffer tells us the office is "open, with no cubicles", the lighting is "very optimal" and there are "always snacks and beverages at the office". The Rome office is "wonderful", and in Milan, there currently is "a lot of space", but that office has just moved to a new location. The new spot, says one source, is "supposed to be much better, especially concerning environmental aspects".

Mutual respect

The consultancy's "fantastic, team-focussed culture offers unmatched project opportunities in terms of both clients and client interaction", insiders say. Value Partners has "an exceptionally strong profile in the UK media sector", which provides a "genuinely excellent platform for those interested in this area". A consultant notes, "We interact with the clients' top management earlier than other consulting companies." In addition, junior consultants enjoy a "high degree of mutual respect" with their superiors. There is "minimal hierarchy", respondents tell us, and "the small-firm feel means excellent one-to-one relationships with managers and partners." In general, "partners and senior management are very approachable," and relationships are "very friendly and informal"—this collegiality apparently spans "every level of management, CEO included". As one source states, regardless of your position in the firm, "you always easily communicate with your supervisors."

On the job is where it's at

Value Partners offers a "good mix of formal and informal" training, but it is "mostly unofficial". For this reason, "on-the-job training is considered essential," and consultants receive "very careful feedback" from managers. "Everybody shows much commitment in fostering colleagues' learning experience," a respondent comments. There is an "official training programme in place, but it can sometimes feel a bit ad hoc." Insiders say the "quality of formal training still needs some work", and a contact recalls, "Training was really fun and useful in terms of getting to know the office and the people, but not useful practically." Moreover, explains a colleague, "once you become an associate, there is no more training, only unofficial training." Overall, the firm's strategy is "to train people during the assignment".

Fast tracks for those who earn it

The consultancy's promotion policy is "structured and clear, but not rigidly up or out". Advancement is meritocratic, we're told, and normally occurs in "24-month cycles". The typical progression "from associate to manager is two to three years". People advance "when they are ready, because you don't have to conform to a bell curve of people being promoted at different times". But lately, a consultant notes, standards for promotions have been "tightening" and it is "becoming more up or out now".

We're also told that for some, the "professional path moves very fast". A source remarks, "Usually, you advance faster than in other consulting companies. You can become a manager at 28 years old if you are skilled and lucky." Value Partners offers the "added advantage of exceptional opportunities to specialise earlier and to gain profile in some sectors". For this reason, "consultants often leave for amazing jobs in the media industry."

Mixed bag on diversity

Insiders feel that their firm has a "much more balanced workforce than elsewhere". A source explains, "Up until manager level, it's about 50/50 male to female. Beyond that, it's slightly more male, but we still have an almost equal male-to-female ratio at the senior manager level." One insider claims the firm "has the highest ratio of female consultants I have observed in the industry". There is "no evidence of discrimination", and the consultancy pays "great attention to maternity". In fact, "several women who have taken time off to have children have subsequently returned for part-time projects." But representation of women is "very varied from office to office", a source notes, with "some territories being much more progressive than others". In Milan, for example, "women are very few, accounting for less than 20 per cent of consultants."

We're also told that Value Partners' focus on top university graduates "limits" the number of ethnic minorities. There are "no black people", but the firm is "not actively discriminatory by any means". In fact, respondents claim that the firm is "colourblind", in the sense that "minority consultants are treated as any other." Race makes "no difference at all in terms of hiring, promoting and mentoring". Similarly, sexual orientation is "not a factor in recruiting", and it is "not an issue" in the firm's "very tolerant culture". In fact, a staffer recalls, Value Partners "had an openly gay partner in the past who brought his boyfriend to company events".

The value of community service

Insiders say the consultancy does "some pro bono work, plus various fund-raising activities". It "has an internal charity committee", which organises such things as a "Christmas hat-selling event to support schools in India". In addition, Value Partners offers "sponsorship of a village in Ethiopia" and undertakes "fund raising for African missions". It also "supports the Kennedy Foundation for Europe", and some consultants participate in "sports events to raise money". ☐

WATSON WYATT WORLDWIDE

21 Tothill Street
London SW1H 9LL
United Kingdom
Phone: +44 (0)207 222 8033
Fax: +44 (0)207 222 9182
www.watsonwyatt.com

The Stats

Employer Type: Public Company
Ticker Symbol: WW (NYSE)
Chairman, President & CEO: John J.
  Haley
2008 Employees: 7,000
2007 Employees: 6,600
2007 Revenue: $1.49 billion
2006 Revenue: $1.27 billion
No. of Offices: 104

Practice Areas

Communication
Flex Consulting
Health Care & Risk Consulting
Human Capital/Data Services
Insurance & Financial Services
International Consulting
Investment Consulting
Retirement (Defined Benefit & Defined
  Contribution Pensions Consulting)
Technology & Administration Solutions

European Locations

London (European HQ)
Arlington (Global HQ)
Amsterdam • Apeldoom • Birmingham •
Bristol • Brussels • Budapest • Dublin •
Düsseldorf • Edinburgh • Eindhoven •
Frankfurt • Leeds • Lisbon • Madrid •
Manchester • Milan • Munich •
Nieuwegein • Paris • Purmerend •
Ratingen • Redhill • Reigate • Rome •
Rotterdam • Stockholm • Vienna •
Welwyn • Wiesbaden • Zurich

Plus

• Lots of recent expansion

Minus

• Still building up a reputation in Europe

Employment Contact

www.watsonwyatt.com/Graduate

THE SCOOP

W atson Wyatt Worldwide is one of the oldest actuarial consulting firms in the world, with roots stretching back to the 19th century. Perhaps its long shelf life is derived from the fact that the firm focusses on people, treating them as individuals and not just a means to an end. Throughout its respected history, Watson Wyatt has been a human resource expert, helping companies hold onto their staff while keeping down the costs of benefits such as pension schemes and other benefits packages. Watson Wyatt's four main areas of specialisation are employee benefits, human capital strategies, technology solutions, and insurance and financial services. The company is headquartered in Arlington, Virginia, but has a massive presence all over the globe, serving companies located in 32 different countries throughout Europe, North America, the Middle East and the Asia Pacific region.

Combining Watson and Wyatt

Watson Wyatt Worldwide originated in the UK in 1878, when the original founder Reuben Watson started a small actuarial firm in London. Watson's little enterprise grew to be one of the most respected establishments in the UK through its work with the government on social insurance plans. Its reputation grew so much that by the middle of the 20th century, Watson & Sons was one of the most recognised

> " The consultancy works with 50 per cent of the UK's 100-largest corporate pension plans, and 70 per cent of British Fortune 500 firms. "

names in consulting in all of Europe. Meanwhile, across the pond, a company called The Wyatt Company was launched in 1946. Wyatt was also an actuarial consulting firm, but later expanded its services into health care and compensation consulting.

As The Wyatt Company and Watson & Sons both grew to expand their reach in a global economy, the two companies saw the opportunity for a unique alliance. In 1995, they joined forces in a partnership that separated the company into two branches covering different geographic segments. Watson Wyatt & Company was the North American and Asia Pacific branch of the company, while Watson Wyatt Partners covered the European market. The collaboration was a success: In the first year together, Watson Wyatt's earnings grew by 30 per cent. Watson Wyatt & Company's business grew so significantly over the next five years that the firm made the decision to launch an IPO on the New York Stock Exchange.

Watson Wyatt Worldwide

In October 2000, Watson Wyatt began trading on the NYSE under the symbol WW. The companies made their merger official in August 2005, adopting the name Watson Wyatt Worldwide to signify the joining of its two geographic sectors.

Solid growth

Times have been good for Watson Wyatt Worldwide since making its merger official. The firm earned $737 million in its first year together and, in 2006, revenue jumped dramatically to $1.27 billion. In 2007, Watson Wyatt continued its steady climb upward, posting revenue of $1.49 billion, essentially doubling its earnings since the merger. Net income has also increased substantially, from $51 million in 2005 to $116 million in 2007.

The stats for Watson Wyatt's fiscal 2007 year were excellent across the board. Revenue for investment consulting led the way with an increase in business of 43 per cent. The change was driven by an increased need for solid management of clients' pension funds. The firm's human capital group increased revenue by 15 per cent, due to an expanding market for compensation plans.

Old friends become family

In February 2007, Watson Wyatt completed another merger that had been in the works for many years when it acquired Watson Wyatt Brans & Co., its strategic partner in the Netherlands. The two companies had been aligned with one another since 1999, when Watson Wyatt combined its Netherlands branch with Brans & Co., one of the top Dutch consulting firms. They entered into a similar agreement under which Watson & Sons and The Wyatt Company had been operating before their official merger—the companies were allied, but not fully merged. But Watson Wyatt decided in early 2007 that the Netherlands company could achieve its full potential better if it was a fully owned subsidiary. The official addition of Watson Wyatt Brans & Co. brings 180 new associates to the Watson Wyatt family and gives the firm access to five Dutch offices located in Amsterdam, Eindhoven, Nieuwegein, Purmerend and Rotterdam. John Haley, president and CEO of Wyatt Watson, said of the acquisition, "We are delighted to bring our long-term partner in the Netherlands fully into the Watson Wyatt fold. The Netherlands, with its well funded pensions system, is a base for many multinational companies and a very important territory for the firm."

Winning the Heissmann trophy

Later that year, Wyatt Watson continued its aggressive expansion in Europe with the July 2007 acquisition of Heissmann GmbH, one of Germany's top actuarial, benefits and human resources consultancies. Heissmann has a large presence across the entire continent of Europe with subsidiaries in Ireland, the Netherlands, France and Austria. With the purchase, Wyatt Watson assumes complete control over all Heissman subsidiaries, as well as its staff of 360 employees. The acquisition will make Watson Wyatt the No. 1 pension consulting company in the UK, the Netherlands and Germany.

Nordic newbies

The string of European acquisitions extended into October 2007, when the firm purchased Oakbridge Consulting Group, a Swedish HR consultancy based in Stockholm. The acquisition of Oakbridge is a reunion of sorts for Watson Wyatt—the firm was started by a former WW staffer, Magnus Drogell. It also represents another notch on Watson Wyatt's belt in terms of its dominance in the European market. With the acquisition, the firm holds "the largest salary database in the Nordic region, with over 400 clients". Both Oakbridge and Watson Wyatt were pleased with the opportunities that the merger would present to their international business plans.

Only the best and the brightest

In conjunction with its massive European expansion, Watson Wyatt launched an advertising campaign in the UK calling for the best and brightest minds to join its team and become a part of one of the largest firms on the continent. The advertising campaign seeks to achieve a new level of name recognition for the consultancy in the UK by placing its branding on taxi cabs, railway stations, and pension and actuarial trade publications. The firm hopes to stress three main points to its potential new employees: "Watson Wyatt offers some of the most exciting and rewarding opportunities in the pension industry; Watson Wyatt offers unrivalled long-term career prospects; and Watson Wyatt is the place to work for the gifted and talented." The consultancy also stresses its current dominance of the British market with statistics that demonstrate its work with 50 per cent of the UK's 100-largest corporate pension plans, as well as 70 per cent of British Fortune 500 firms.

GETTING HIRED

Four-step process

Aspiring consultants interested in a career at Watson Wyatt Worldwide should begin by visiting the firm's careers web site. Broken down by region, the site offers detailed information on the hiring process for positions within the UK and throughout

Europe, in addition to listing current openings. The hiring process is designed to be a two-way experience, allowing both the firm and the candidate to determine if there's a good fit. The firm expects a high degree of mental agility from its consultants, who are asked daily to apply intellectual rigour to a host of different problems. As such, candidates undergo an extensive, four-stage interview process. To begin, all applicants must complete the firm's online form; simply submitting a CV will not suffice. The application form is Watson Wyatt's firm impression of a candidate, so applicants should ensure that the information provided is clear, accurate and well presented. It is also vital to fully answer all questions and give details of all qualifications, including grades where appropriate. Missing information may lead to a delay in processing an application. Watson Wyatt tries to get back to applicants within 72 working hours, letting them know whether they've advanced to the next stage. Those who advance are asked to complete a series of online verbal and numerical reasoning tests.

Candidates who pass those first two stages will then attend a brief screening interview at Watson Wyatt's London office. Conducted by a member of the firm's HR team, the screening interview involves several competency-based questions. Candidates are asked to provide examples of situations when they demonstrated certain skills and abilities. For example, an interviewer might ask, "Describe a time

> ❝ Those looking to get a leg up on the interview process might consider one of Watson Wyatt's work experience programmes. ❞

when you have had to persuade someone around to your point of view." Examples can be drawn from any environment—university, home or work experience—but the more relevant to a job in consulting, the better. The final stage of the process is the assessment centre, which lasts for about half a day and is held in the office to which the candidate is applying. Candidates who make it to this stage will be asked to complete a written exercise based on a real-life work scenario, and then discuss a similarly relevant topic with fellow interviewees. Candidates are given a presentation title a few days prior to the assessment centre and will be asked to give a brief presentation and answer questions. Also on this day, candidates are usually taken out to lunch, which provides a good opportunity to ask questions about the firm and to get a sense of office culture and future colleagues.

Invaluable experience

Those looking to get a leg up on the interview process might consider one of Watson Wyatt's work experience programmes, of which there are two. Both are designed to give candidates insight into the work and culture of the firm, but each is tailored to fulfill the needs of different groups of applicants. The summer scheme is designed for penultimate-year students (studying for either undergraduate or postgraduate degrees) and those who have already graduated. Participants get first-hand experience of one of the firm's training schemes, and also have the opportunity to secure a permanent job offer for the following year. Insight programmes are designed for anyone in their first or second year of a four-year course. These programmes also are well suited for people who are considering a career change and can only take a couple of days off to sample a new working environment. □

Watson Wyatt Worldwide

WIPRO LTD.

Doddakannelli Sarjapur Road
Bangalore, Karnataka 560 035
India
Phone: +91 (80) 844 0011
Fax: +91 (80) 844 0256
www.wipro.com
www.wipro.com/consulting

The Stats

Employer Type: Public Company
Ticker Symbol: WIT (NYSE)
Chairman & Managing Director: Azim H.
  Premji
President, Americas & Europe:
  P.R. Chandrasekar
2008 Employees: 92,000+
2007 Employees: 79,832
2008 Revenue: $4.9 billion
2007 Revenue: $3.5 billion
No. of Offices: 50+

Practice Area

Business Process Outsourcing
Consulting Services
  Business Consulting
  Process Consulting
  Quality Consulting
  Technology Consulting
IT Services
Product Engineering Solutions
Technology Infrastructure Services

European Locations

Bangalore (HQ)
Austria • Finland • France • Germany •
Holland • Italy • Portugal • Romania •
Spain • Sweden • Switzerland • United
Kingdom

Pluses

• Lots of interaction with client
  executives
• Company is growing steadily

Minuses

• Offshoring model dominates
• Little entry-level opportunity

Employment Contact

careers.wipro.com
E-mail: sudhir.nair@wipro.com (mention
"Consulting Europe" in the subject line)
or manager.career@wipro.com (for all
vacancies)

THE BUZZ
WHAT CONSULTANTS AT OTHER FIRMS ARE SAYING

• "Better and more strategic than you'd
  expect"
• "Primarily a systems integration firm"
• "A coming force"
• "IT cost-cutters"

THE SCOOP

Take a family business that produces sunflower oil. Diversify with a large handful of IT services and software solutions, mix in some IT consulting, business process outsourcing (BPO) services and a sprinkling of research and development services. Cast aside the oil, and combine the rest well, adding an infrastructure engineering firm and a lighting concern just for good measure. Nurture carefully, feeding as necessary, gradually rolling it out until it's spread across four continents. Time: around 60 years. Result: a company that serves 647 clients and supports more than 92,000 employees worldwide.

Wipro Ltd. is one of the major success stories of Indian business. One of the first technology consulting firms to compete with the established US and European firms in its home market, it has since brought the fight onto the home turf of those rivals, establishing a significant base in Europe and the US as it expands beyond the low-cost outsourcing model upon which its early success was based. The firm today is a major player in the global services provision game, offering end-to-end, largely technology-driven business solutions to an impressive list of clients with global stature. Wipro also has strategic partnerships with the likes of Cisco, HP, IBM, Microsoft, SAP and Sun Microsystems.

In addition to those tech giants, the firm offers its five major service lines (consulting, IT services, product engineering solutions, technology infrastructure solutions and BPO) to global businesses in a range of industries, from automotive to energy, health care to manufacturing, media to product engineering, and more. In order to offer such a wide array of services to such a diverse crowd, the firm maintains a slew of "centres of excellence" (more than 50 at last count) where teams of domain experts and functional architects generate solutions for clients. The firm also has some 53 development centres, including 35 offshore, which work on developing software to meet client demands. Meanwhile, in Europe alone the firm has operations in 18 countries, at which employees of 15 different nationalities can be found hard at work.

The founding father

The firm's roots go all the way back to 1945, to the founding of Western Indian Vegetable Products, a family business producing sunflower oil and laundry soap. When the company's founder (and father of current Chairman and Managing Director Azim Premji) died in 1969, the leadership of the firm fell to his son, then in his final year at Stanford University. Taking on the role at the tender ago of 21, Premji brought a fresh perspective to the business, and began casting around for ways to diversify the firm's output. He was aided by an Indian government decision in the

1970s to limit the rights of foreign-owned firms to do business in India—an event that saw several multinationals leave the country altogether. Among those firms was IBM, the top supplier of computer products to the Indian market, and it was there that Premji saw his opportunity.

By the early 1980s, Premji's firm had transitioned to the role of computer hardware manufacturer, and became one of the top tech outfits on the subcontinent, even manufacturing the first Indian microchip. Just as the firm was thinking of taking its tech expertise outside of India in the 1990s, however, another government decision hamstrung it at home, as foreign competitors were allowed back in, greatly increasing the level of competition. It was against this background that Premji made the decision to utilise the one resource his country had that the West could not compete with: its workforce.

> " Top candidates will have an MBA from a prestigious university and a GPA of 3.3 or higher. "

Outsourcing frenzy

Wipro claims to be the firm that pioneered the offshore outsourcing model in the 1990s, creating an easy way of adding value that many businesses would flock to and emulate in the coming years. Today, Wipro is the only Indian company to be ranked among the Top 10 Global Outsourcing Providers in the International Association of Outsourcing Professionals by Fortune Global 100 listings.

The company's current holdings are divided into four main groupings: global IT services and products (including BPO services); India and Asia Pacific IT services and products; consumer care and lighting; and the catch-all "other" category, which still includes laundry soap and other household goods. The first of these categories is the major business driver at Wipro these days, pulling in around $3.4 billion (around 69 per cent) out of the total $4.9 billion the firm posted in revenue in fiscal 2008. IT services and products will likely remain the company's focus as it attempts to offer a full suite of IT-related services to its customers.

Wipro's fiscal 2008 results marked the first time the firm posted more than $4 billion in revenue, a figure it has been remarkably swift to reach, aided in no small part by a period of exponential growth in the Indian economy, and the demand for outsourcing there. For each of the past 19 years, Wipro has posted double-digit revenue growth—sometimes healthy double figures, as the 32 per cent gain from 2007 to 2008 will attest.

Eating rivals for breakfast

Part of Wipro's astonishing growth has been driven by a series of acquisitions around the world—some high profile, others less so, but equally important in the grand scheme of upping Wipro's capabilities and business offerings. Known as the "string of pearls" strategy, where Wipro expands its capabilities by capturing new assets one by one, the firm has snapped up a surprising number of firms in recent years. These include 13 IT companies—nine of which have been acquired since 2005. The most recent of these was New Jersey-based outsourcer and IT service provider Infocrossing for $600 million—the largest overseas IT acquisition by an Indian firm to date. As a specialist in health plan and payer management companies, the Infocrossing acquisition gives Wipro a foothold in the infrastructure management business.

Going back further, Wipro added several more IT companies throughout 2006. In November that year, both 3D Networks and Planet PSG joined the Wipro family, increasing its capabilities in business communication solutions and professional services on voice and speech platforms. In June, meanwhile, Portuguese retail solutions firm Enabler was brought into the fold for some $52.5 million. Also that month, the firm bought Saraware Oy, a Finnish provider of design and engineering services to telecoms companies, for approximately $37 million. The acquisition of Saraware expanded Wipro's capabilities in radio networks and secure mobile platforms.

The (very big) one that got away?

From a consulting standpoint, what is perhaps missing from Wipro's roster of acquisitions is the addition of a specific consulting firm. That hasn't been for any lack of effort on Wipro's part, however—at least according to the rumour mill that linked the firm with consulting industry titan Capgemini in late 2007 and early 2008. The deal, potentially valued at around $7 billion, was met with several questions by analysts, the most pressing of which concerned Wipro's ability to fund such a takeover, given its recent acquisition spree and the then-burgeoning problems in the credit market. Whether or not there was any truth in the rumours, Wipro felt compelled to issue a statement in January 2008 scotching them. In a fairly unequivocal press release, the firm stated, on behalf of all of its interests and subsidiaries, that it "ha[s] not recently been, and [is] not in discussions with and/or in relation to Capgemini, the French Euronext listed group, on merger/takeover of Capgemini."

Focus on consulting

Despite the speculation over Capgemini, there is clear evidence to suggest that Wipro is seeking to transition toward a heightened focus on consulting as a specific business, rather than a mere by-product of its other offerings. Given the recent slowdown in the global economy, the firm faces a more uncertain future as far as growth is concerned, particularly in light of the threat of a shrinking US economy. In an April 2008 interview with the Indian publication *Business Standard*, Wipro Technologies' newly appointed joint-CEOs Girish Paranjpe and Suresh Vaswani recognised that tougher times were on the horizon for the firm. "The 35 per cent growth pattern, which the Indian software industry has been showing during the past decade, is history now," said Vaswani. "There is no doubt that there are significant changes in how clients are thinking about IT budgets."

With that in mind, Wipro recently announced an intention to "carve out a consulting vertical", as *Business Standard* put it. According to Paranjpe "the consulting element was embedded across our various businesses. What we are doing is bringing various dispersed pieces under a single umbrella. The objective of this business will include upstream business transformation consulting, building IT strategy for customers and helping clients build business solutions that leverage IT. This single consulting face will have about 1,000 consultants spread across Americas, EMEA, India and APAC."

> " Consultants are typically on the road 80 to 100 per cent of the time. "

Windows of opportunity

While the firm gets its consulting house in order, there is every sign that the rest of the business is set to carry on as normal. In April 2008, for example, the firm announced that it was expanding its strategic alliance with Microsoft—an agreement that saw two new "centres of excellence" opened in Bangalore and Mysore. The centres will focus on using Microsoft technologies to develop solutions and services for integrating various business communication tools into a single solution delivered across a range of devices and enterprises.

And there's no point being a tech-industry titan if you're not going to use the environment you create to your advantage. In October 2007, the firm launched an offshore development centre model in cyberspace as a means of meeting its hiring quotas in the future. Known as Innovation Island, the model campus is in the *Second Life* realm, and features facilities that include a client engagement centre, a learning centre, a security desk at the campus entrance gate, a press announcements hall, sports facilities and a library. Anyone interested in working for the firm can "tour" the facility and submit their resume at Wipro's virtual campus. Initially limited to Wipro BPO, the e-recruitment initiative will eventually become a core part of the firm's recruitment drive.

GETTING HIRED

Have job, will travel

Wipro's hiring process is designed to uncover savvy business school graduates with a demonstrated interest and experience in management consulting. Top candidates will have an MBA from a prestigious university, and a GPA of 3.3 or higher. Pre-MBA work experience is a plus, especially if it is in the consulting industry. The firm is also launching an undergraduate recruiting effort in both the US and Europe, starting with the class of 2008. Interviewers probe candidates to determine if they can work both independently and as part of a team, and if they are comfortable interacting with and presenting to executives and senior business leaders; consultants at Wipro are expected to take an active role in all stages and aspects of the client engagement. The firm is seeking individuals who can take a quantitative, fact-based approach to team-based problem solving, and a strategic approach to addressing issues and offering solutions. Excellent skills in all Microsoft Office programmes are required. And since potential projects typically involve business process re-engineering, ERP packaged solutions, business case requirements gathering, outsourcing strategy and organisational structure changes, and IT governance, the firm looks favourably upon candidates holding undergraduate degrees in computer science, information systems or engineering.

The firm has European offices throughout the continent, but consultants are typically on the road 80 to 100 per cent of the time, so fitting candidates will express interest in working at the client site. Applicants can view current job openings and obtain contact details for personnel handling Europe-based positions by visiting the firm's careers web site.

Those who fit in have a strong desire to learn and shape their own career paths, as well as a commitment to making a positive and lasting client impact. At Wipro, client and project direction is not always well defined, so interviewers will want to see a self-guided attitude throughout the process. □

Wipro Ltd.

XLENT CONSULTING GROUP

Regeringsgatan 67
111 56 Stockholm
Sweden
Phone: +46 (0)8 519 510 00
Fax: +46 (0)8 519 511 50
www.xlent.se

The Stats

Employer Type: Private Company
Chairman: Lennart Jacobsson
CEO: Dag Sundström
2008 Employees: 200
2007 Employees: 200
2007 Revenue: SEK 200 million
2006 Revenue: SEK 100 million
No. of Offices: 7

Practice Areas

XLENT Business Integration
XLENT Strategy
XLENT Technology

European Locations

Stockholm (HQ)
Helsinki
Hudiksvall
Örnsköldsvik
Oslo
Östersund
Sundsvall

Pluses

• "Interesting assignments"
• Culture is "not pretentious"

Minuses

• "Knowledge management is very rudimentary"
• No diversity programmes

Employment Contact

See the employment section of the consultancy's web site

THE SCOOP

Founded in 2003, XLENT Consulting Group's sphere of influence is strictly Scandinavian. Based in Stockholm, the firm has four other Swedish offices, as well as one each in Finland (Helsinki) and Norway (Oslo). Offering its services across three platforms—strategies and change, solutions and implementation, technology and maintenance—the firm claims to have the skills and tools to support and implement recommendations made by its consulting arm.

The firm came into being following the merger of Swedish consulting firms Digiscope and DataVis. The group then added IT development consultancy Crescendo to its holdings in 2005, a move that saw the firm consolidate and rebrand its holdings into the three divisions it still operates today: XLENT Strategy, XLENT Business Integration and XLENT Technology.

Customers—totally XLENT

XLENT's business model revolves around helping companies realise the full benefits of their relationships with customers and other businesses. Using a model the company refers to as "customer-centric", XLENT consultants assist clients in moving away from marketing to new customers and toward keeping and maximising the revenue they derive from existing customers. The reasoning behind this approach is research that shows that more than 100 per cent of a company's

> 66 Bonuses are based on billable hours, and advancement is based on performance. 99

profit is generated from just 20 per cent of its customer base. XLENT's theory, then, is that companies should think twice about spending the typical 95 per cent of their marketing budget on attracting new customers. To maximise profits, they should focus instead on upping the income from the other 80 per cent of their existing customers.

Each of the XLENT divisions mentioned above has its own remit within the firm, and serves clients in a different way as part of the firm's overall suite of solutions. While the strategy group helps companies identify ways of putting customer needs at the heart of their strategies, the business integration team works to develop processes, IT systems and the like to put those strategies into play. The technology unit, meanwhile, offers not only IT consultancy, but maintenance and operations support to boot.

Between them, the three units have worked on projects in industries as varied as finance, media, pension provision and telecommunications, and have served clients of the global stature of Ericsson, Vodafone and Canal Digital, as well as many high-profile firms within Scandinavia.

GETTING HIRED

Empowered from the start

According to XLENT's careers web site, the firm believes in empowered responsibility, and so looks for employees who want to shape their roles and work situations. Interviewers seek out candidates who value quality of life, team spirit and personal development. To find those consultants, insiders tell us the firm conducts "three rounds of interviews", including "one HR round". XLENT's "basic approach" to interviewing involves "one test", and is designed to assess "personality and case performance". According to one source, "We do not use ridiculous brainteasers or stress interviews." Fortunately, nor does the firm "believe in being rude or mean to the interviewees".

OUR SURVEY SAYS

Good times at work

Respondents describe XLENT's culture as "fun and entrepreneurial", noting its makeup of "clever, great people". Consultants get "a lot of freedom, as long as you deliver", and they enjoy working with "interesting clients and markets". It's the kind of place where "everyone helps everyone." We're also told that the crew at XLENT is "social and not pretentious", and staffers have a good time together; one insider says, "We play *Guitar Hero* and Nintendo Wii at our Friday gatherings!" The firm's Stockholm office, although "quite crowded at the moment, due to in-house projects", has an "open place that leads to camaraderie". With all that camaraderie, though, some say the layout can make it "difficult to concentrate".

Everything kept in balance

Sources appreciate the "flexible work hours" the consultancy affords them. A respondent notes, "You don't have to be at the office until 10pm every day. Even if there is a lot of work to do, one can go home and meet the family and continue working from home."

Colleagues are "understanding of personal situations, if you explain it to them", and there is "no face time needed". Most consultants claim to work between 40 and 60 hours per week, and projects can run anywhere from "a couple months" up to a year. Staffers say travel requirements are "minimal, even when working at the client site", because "most clients are within the greater Stockholm area." Specific travel demands can "depend on the client", but insiders assure us that at XLENT, there is "no rule of four days at the client". There is "management agreement and support" about the importance of work/life balance, so achieving it is "no problem at all".

Compensation doesn't appear to be a problem either. Over the past year, XLENT has made "a strong effort to raise salary and bonus levels". In addition to salary and bonus, employees are granted "SEK 5,000 per year for health-related needs", which can be used toward "a gym membership or yoga classes".

> " We play *Guitar Hero* and Nintendo Wii at our Friday Gatherings! "

A consultant explains that bonuses are "based on billable hours, and advancement is based on performance". We're also told that the firm's promotion policy is "not up or out". The company explains that individual performance regulates both bonuses and promotions.

Unofficial about training

On its careers web site, XLENT claims to be a knowledge-based company at which education and personal development are constantly in focus. As such, the consultancy offers both external training and individual coaching through an internal mentor programme. An insider confirms that the majority of training is "unofficial", noting, "We have certain official training days, but those only happen a couple times a year." A colleague remarks that the firm's "on-the-job training is much more effective," though "the danger is that every consultant does not get the same exposure to training."

The Swedish way

Insiders give high marks to XLENT's approach to diversity, although the firm has "no special programmes" to support minority groups. Sources say "there is no sexism in Sweden," yet it remains that there are "fewer women in the higher ranks of the organisation than in the lower". When it comes to ethnic diversity, we're told XLENT is "very diverse in ethnicities and actually encourages it in recruiting".

The firm does "not really" participate in pro bono or charity work, but, according to one consultant, "Sweden, in general, is not a country that does much of this." □

ZS ASSOCIATES

1800 Sherman Avenue
Suite 700
Evanston, Ilinois 60201
United States
Phone: +1 (847) 492-3600
Fax: +1 (847) 492-3409
www.zsassociates.com

The Stats

Employer Type: Private Company
Co-Chairmen: Andris Zoltners
   & Prabhakant Sinha
Managing Director: Jaideep Bajaj
2008 Employees: 1,000
2007 Employees: 900
No. of Offices: 17

Practice Areas

Data Management, Performance
   Reporting & Analytics
Marketing Performance Measurement
Marketing Planning
Product Forecasting
Sales Force Design
Sales Performance Management
Sales Process Development
Segmentation
Targeting & Account Planning
Territory Design
Value-Based Selling Support
Value Proposition

European Locations

Evanston (Global HQ)
Frankfurt
London
Milan
Paris
Zurich

Pluses

- "High responsibility and client
  exposure in junior roles"
- Growing fast
- "Relaxed attitude"

Minuses

- "Projects can be repetitive"
- No formal diversity programmes
- Vacation policy is "not generous"

Employment Contact

www.zsassociates.com/careers
E-mail: careers@zsassociates.com

THE BUZZ
WHAT CONSULTANTS AT OTHER FIRMS ARE SAYING

- "Strong specialists, established in their
  niche"
- "Hard-core sales analysis"
- "Friendly"
- "Long hours"

THE SCOOP

I n 2008, ZS Associates celebrated its 25th anniversary as a global consulting firm. The firm has grown in both size and prestige since its humble start by Andris Zoltners and Prabhakant Sinha, two Kellogg School of Management professors. When the partners started ZS in 1983, they hoped to hone their research skills and academic prowess into market success. Twenty-five years later, with 17 offices around the world and over 1,000 consultants working for ZS, it's safe to say they've achieved their goal.

Going global

From its small-town roots in Evanston, Illinois, ZS Associates has expanded into a company with representation all over the globe. In fact, approximately 40 per cent of ZS' business comes from outside of the United States. The firm conducts business in Europe from locations in Frankfurt, London, Milan, Paris and Zurich (which opened for business in 2008). 2008 also saw the opening of a new location in Shanghai.

ZS is most well known for its pharmaceutical and biotech services, but it serves a variety of sectors, including consumer products, energy, financial, high tech, industrial products, medical products, media and entertainment, pharmaceuticals, telecommunications and transportation. In all of these sectors, ZS focusses on sales.

Tracing an arc

Aiding ZS in its quest to help companies achieve optimal sales performance are several software programmes that the company has developed to organise data in a clean and concise manner for clients. The most notable of these are collected in the Javelin™ Software Suite, a set of tools that address issues of sales and marketing. Among the Javelin modules available are incentives, for management of incentive compensation programmes; call planning, for the design, management and effective distribution of call plans; and promotion strategy, for sales force design and territory mapping. There are additional modules based around forecasting and account management.

One of the firm's most successful programmes is Territory Designer (formerly known as MAPS), a component of the promotion strategy module. The application creates a mapping system that organises sales territories based on the sales results of each area. In Europe, Territory Designer services are available in Austria, Belgium, the Czech Republic, Denmark, Finland, France, Germany,

Greece, Ireland, Italy, Norway, Poland, Portugal, Slovakia, Spain, Sweden and Switzerland. Worldwide, the programme is used by over 500,000 salespeople in 40 different countries.

Results across the spectrum

ZS Associates does not disclose client details, but it's happy to share case studies of its past projects. In the pharmaceutical industry, ZS boasts of a case where it helped to seamlessly merge two pharmaceutical companies with tens of thousands of representatives in two months. On top of that, ZS says it helped to actually raise market share for the newly merged companies during the transition period. Another pharmaceutical case study involved boosting the sales of a leading diabetes drug that had plateaued. ZS helped the company analyse the scientific data to launch a new advertising and marketing platform for the product, which ultimately raised sales.

In the consumer products vertical, ZS explains that it helped a billion-dollar consumer products firm hone a retail strategy that represented 40 per cent of product sales. ZS conducted thousands of qualitative interviews of speciality retailers and used the data to help the company consolidate partners. Another success-

> “ Helping each other is a must and comes before anything else. ”

ful project was a sales design process for a large bank. ZS helped the bank modify its pay structure to a more incentive-based programme to encourage sales accountability. The company soon achieved its goal of boosting profitability in its mutual fund marketplace.

The best of the best

ZS' founding partners were academics, so it's only reasonable that the consultancy would hire the best and the brightest to populate its staff. In 2007, one of these talented individuals was recognised by *Consulting* magazine as one of its top-25 consultants. The recipient of the award, Michael Moorman, a former NASA engineer and current managing principal at ZS, was recognised by the magazine for his work with United Airlines, which he helped to restructure after its bankruptcy. Despite United's problems, Moorman urged the firm to invest money into its sales and marketing departments. His advice resulted in United capturing 80 per cent of Chicago's top-50 accounts, and helped to swing more than $100 million worth of business in United's direction.

Call of the conference

ZS Associates is not stingy with its brainy consultants. The firm regularly mobilises them for international conference appearances, and even academic engagements. In December 2007, company experts visited the Indian School of Business in Hyderabad to give a lecture on accelerating sales force performance. Additional presentations on sales force performance were given at conferences in American cities in February, May and September 2008. In June 2008, ZS Principals Kurt Kessler and Brian Lefebvre attended the annual conference of the European Pharmaceutical Market Research Association held in Barcelona. The three-day event, which brought together researchers, corporate executives and academics, highlighted the current trends and challenges facing the pharmaceutical industry.

Collect them all

Zoltners and Sinha continue to influence the industry with their thought leadership. The two have collaborated on a series of books on sales force, starting with *The Complete Guide to Accelerating Sales Force Performance* in 2001. That first offering, a blueprint for improving sales productivity, was followed in 2004 by *Sales Force Design for Strategic Advantage*, another practical-minded tome that expounds on the best methods of managing a sales force. Next came *The Complete Guide to Sales Force Incentive Compensation: How to Design and Implement Plans That Work*, a 2006 publication focussed on properly motivating a sales team. The next instalment of the series, *Building a Winning Sales Force*, is slated for release in late 2008.

GETTING HIRED

Don your analytical hat

ZS Associates holds "two rounds of interviews for consultants". In total, candidates will face "about five to six interviews" throughout both rounds. Sources report that the firm's interview process is "quite analytical" and "related to the pharmaceutical work" in which the firm specialises. Candidates are given "ample material" to prepare for the first-round cognitive test, which includes "numerical and analytical reasoning". A consultant advises, "Use it! Failing the test will automatically disqualify you." Second-round interviews consist of "three to four interviews plus case studies". Consultant-level hires will also view a presentation, something of a "project-like simulation that asks for more unstructured answering". One insider says of ZS' style of cases, "Cases are always subject-related. I have never heard of anyone at ZS doing silly, abstract cases, such as, 'Imagine you're on a deserted island …'" Candidates may be asked questions on "product launch, forecasting or logistic strategy". An example includes, "How many Aspirin tablets are sold today in China?" During the interview process, candidates often "get the impression that ZS interviewers want to find out about you, rather than just test you".

In the UK, ZS recruits from London Business School, London School of Economics, Oxford and Cambridge. The firm also looks to INSEAD in France and IESE in Spain. In Italy, ZS recruits "mainly from Politecnico di Milano and Università Bocconi for junior positions". Consultants are "encouraged to recommend [candidates] from other universities" as well.

OUR SURVEY SAYS

Cultural facts

ZS' culture is "fact-based" and "highly analytical", respondents tell us. There is an "extremely high level of attention paid to people and social fit within the company". The firm's "cooperative and friendly" consultants prioritise "collaboration and client satisfaction". A source says, "Helping each other is a must and comes before anything else." For this reason, there is "a lot of trust among people". In this "very informal" environment, co-workers are "easygoing and laid-back", yet still very professional. Most wear "business casual, or even casual", most days. Adding to that laid-back atmosphere is that ZS is a "flat organisation", where "independence and responsibility are key values."

Reasonable travel requirements

Travel at ZS "depends on the project and your grade", but generally speaking, it tends to be "at the lower end, compared with other consulting firms". ZS consultants "do not live at the client"—work is "mainly office-based", although there are "some projects that require short trips in Europe and, at times, one-week trips". One consultant says it's not uncommon to hop "two planes a week, for one-hour flights". That said, there are also "light periods that require no travel at all for several weeks". An insider points out, "Since we have a smaller number of offices, when you do travel it can be farther, often outside the country or continent." And for the firm's European teams, "travel is more common than in the US."

Weekends are sacred

Since ZS does the majority of work in office, it is "much easier to maintain a life outside work". One respondent says, "ZS pays much attention to employees' personal commitments. Whenever possible, work is arranged in the most flexible way, to allow time for medical visits or other required activities." Sometimes work/life balance requires staffers to "push back significantly during projects and drive the effort to bring in additional resources". That's because "the firm is unlikely to notice when consultants are overworked, due to unreasonable timelines or poor project planning." Poor planning, we're told, is not entirely uncommon, since consultants "often work on more than one project at a time", and are "never unstaffed for more than a day or two". According to one insider, "This is a much more efficient way of working, but it requires flawless project management." Project length "really varies, from three weeks to three months", and some can be "significantly longer".

Hourly requirements also vary, but "an average of 60 hours is quite realistic," despite the fact that "time lines are assigned accounting for 40 to 50 hours a week." Some sources even report working "an average of 70 hours a week with peaks of 100". Fortunately, "no meetings are set on weekends, and everybody respects others' time with the family." Office hours can be "intense", staffers say, but there is "always time to pursue hobbies and plan weekends away". One remarks, "I have only spent one weekend where I had a significant amount to do on both days." Overall, then, insiders feel that work/life balance is "very good".

Vacation could be perked up

ZS consultants get a "very competitive base salary, with annual increases of about 10 per cent". However, year-end bonuses, which come at Christmastime, are "slightly below the market average". Staffers receive additional perks such as cell phones, medical and life insurance, and "pension matching of up to 3 per cent". Some offices also get "weekly breakfast", and enjoy "a summer event and Christmas dinner". As another extra, since ZS has "much cross-office staffing, especially within Europe", the firm offers "easy transfers to another office if desired". Consultants are granted "extended unpaid leave for travel", and "vacation time is fairly flexible, although not generous." A source explains, "The vacation allowance is only 20 days for the first three years."

Respondents also share their thoughts on their surroundings. The Paris office has a "half-open plan", which is "good for sharing knowledge and working in teams". There is a "very nice office" in Milan, although it's "not in the very centre of the city". Londoners aren't too happy with their abode, explaining that things can feel a bit "dark and dingy". No matter, according to a consultant based there, because "we will be moving to new offices in the summer."

Lots of learning for newbies

ZS consultants receive "continuous on-the-job training", as well as "expert advice" from managers, who uphold an "open-door policy". There is also "formalised training and knowledge sharing throughout the year". In addition, ZS covers the cost of "one-on-one foreign language courses" for whomever needs them. Insiders report that, especially in the beginning, training opportunities abound: "Colleagues are always very keen in teaching new hires." One consultant notes, though, that "when you first start, there is a good amount of official technical training. As you move through the company, training becomes much less frequent." Overall, most agree there is a "fair balance between formal and informal training."

That early training comes in handy for new staffers, who enjoy "quick client exposure". And newbies need not be shy about asking questions—according to a source, "I can ask anyone any question any time and they will do their best to help." And it's a good thing: The firm's "focus on few industries requires a passion for the health care environment", and "some projects are a bit technical."

Perform and you shall succeed

Promotions in the junior ranks occur "every one-and-a-half to three years, depending on experience and performance". The analyst to associate to consultant progression is "typically two to two-and-a-half years". Faster advancement is "allowed, but is not very common". A source explains that promotions are "based on a competency model, by which you are doing the job before actually getting promoted to that level". There is "no up-or-out policy", but the firm pays "strong attention to only retaining valid people". One contact feels, "There is never a reason to leave ZS if you are performing adequately and progressing." Performance reviews happen "every six months", and are "based on feedback and structured evaluation from the other team members."

> ❝ Travel tends to be 'at the lower end, compared with other consulting firms'. ❞

Informal about diversity and pro bono work

ZS Associates has "no specific programmes" for hiring or promoting women or ethnic minorities. In Milan, there are "not too many women hired", but the few who are brought onboard are "treated exactly the same as the other employees, with the same duties and opportunities". A consultant in that office admits to being "the only woman out of 15 consultants". There are some "individual staff members who may be unprofessional" toward women, but this is "very rare", as ZS generally is "culturally sensitive". One consultant shares a theory: "ZS is ready for women, but not vice versa." With regard to ethnic diversity, insiders say the firm is "really multicultural" and "does not discriminate based on background".

Charity-wise, ZS holds an "annual summer charity event in London", and "individual offices conduct charity fund-raising efforts." But the firm does not have any official efforts to guide broad community or pro bono activities. A source says, "In Europe, such initiatives are truly appreciated, but there are no formal company programmes." ☐

AAM Management Information
& Marsal • Arup • Atkins • Can
Commercial Advantage Consu
Detica • Diamond Manageme
Droege & Comp. • Infosys
MacDonald Business & Tec
Proudfoot Consulting • PRTM
Simon-Kucher & Partners • Ta
Perrin • Value Partners • Wa
XLENT Consulting Group • ZS
ormation Consulting Ltd. • Ab
Atkins • Candesic Limited • Cel
antage Consulting • Corporat
nond Management & Technol
Comp. • Infosys Consulting

APPENDIX

INDEX OF FIRMS

Firms with 50+ offices

ABOUT THE EDITOR

Naomi Newman is the global consulting editor at Vault. She graduated with a BA in American Studies from Barnard College in New York City, with a concentration in Economics.

Appendix

As a responsible publishing company,
Vault works with printers who source materials
from well managed sustainable forests. This helps
protect our environment.

We aim to grow our business while minimising our impact
on the environment.

We encourage our readers to download and read electronic versions
of our guides available via our website www.vault.com.

We are also proud to have installed the Vault Online Library at over 1,000
universities worldwide. With the Online Career Library, students are
able to download electronic versions of our guides as part of their job
search. This helps reduce the printing and shipping of our guides.

By leveraging the latest technology, we aim to contribute
responsibly to the world around us.

The Vault Europe Team